Easy-to-book holidays

All categories checked by the Wales Tourist Board

We want you to relax. So there's no fuss in finding out all you wish to know about the accommodation that's available.

It's all here at a glance – details of prices, services and local entertainments.

There are maps to help you get to Wales and find your way around when you're with us. Whether you choose to stay in a

Tenby Harbour and north beach.

Snowdon Mountain Railway.

Index of Towns and Villages

Symbols used in these entries

Bei deisen Eintragungen verwendete Symbole

Symboles utilisés dans ces insertions

Establishment is member of appropriate Regional Tourism Council in North, Mid or South Wales.

Diese Unterkunftsstätte ist Mitglied des zuständigen regionalen Fremdenverkehrsvereins in Nord-, Mittel- oder Südwales.

Appartient à l'un des conseils gallois régionaux du tourisme (régions nord, centre ou sud)

Reduced terms offered for children.

Preisnachlaß für Kinder.

Tarif réduit pour enfants.

The number of bedrooms available.

Anzahl verfügbarer Schlafzimmer.

Nombre de chambres.

Commission paid to Travel Agents.

Reisebüros erhalten eine Provision.

Commission versée aux agences de voyage.

Farmhouse Award Winner.

Das in der rechten oberen Ecke erscheinende Symbol ist ein Gütezeichen und bedeutet, daß die Beherbergungsstätte erstklassige Unterkunft, Einrichtungen und ausgezeichneten Service bietet.

Cet emblème est décerné aux exploitations agricoles qui offrent des garanties précises de qualité. Sur les terrains ou figure cet emblème, vous êtes assurés de trouver une haute qualité de service.

Please confirm prices and facilities when making your reservations and always enclose a stamped, addressed envelope with your enquiry.

Categories of facilities in Serviced Accommodation

To help you find the accommodation of your choice, the Wales Tourist Board has visited each establishment and has indicated in a scale from 1 to 6 how it rates bedrooms, services and meals. Full details are given in the last section of this book. Here is a brief resumé.

Bedrooms

1 Bedrooms are of a reasonable size and meet the basic (minimum) Tourist Board standards for furnishing and equipment.

2 Bedrooms meet a higher standard of basic furnishing and equipment, including washbasins with hot and cold running water. There is at least one bath or shower for every 15 guests.

3 All bedrooms must have heating without extra charge and electric shaver point.

4 Extra required facilities include central heating. At least 35% of bedrooms have private bath/shower and wc en suite.

5 Extra required facilities include telephone, radio or TV. 75% of bedrooms must have private bath/shower and wc en suite.

6 Bedrooms are very comfortably furnished and all have private bath, shower attachment and wc en suite.

Services

1 Simple basic level of service.

2 Guests have access to a telephone; there should also be a lounge area.

3 Extra required facilities including early morning tea/coffee and assistance with baggage.

4 Extra required facilities including TV and central heating.

5 Extra required facilities including night porter and lounge service until at least 2300 hrs.

6 A very comfortable establishment with a wide range of services for guests, for example valet and quick laundry service.

Meals

1 Breakfast only.

2 Breakfast and evening meal.

3 Breakfast, lunch and evening meal.

4 Choice of main dishes at all meals.

5 Choice of English or Continental breakfast. A la Carte menu in restaurant.

6 Extensive choice of catering facilities, including a coffee shop/buttery/grill room or second restaurant. All meals served in bedrooms on request.

smart seaside hotel, a cosy country inn or a friendly farmhouse or guest house, you'll be within easy reach of a whole range of attractions.

There are romantic ruins of ancient castles – and country parks where you can stretch your legs and walk forest trails.

We'll tell you how to enjoy a real taste of Wales – one your palate will remember! And some of the major events, from music festivals to seaside regattas, are listed.

Llanrwst's 17th century bridge and Afon Conwy.

Wind surfing near Saundersfoot.

Background picture: Mountains of Snowdonia National Park from Snowdon peak, North Wales.

Contents

Inhalt

Table des Matieres

Caernarfon Castle.

Service with a smile at Beddgelert.

North Wales

Happy days at Llandudno.

The mountains have a magic and mystery that give us a hint of the remote past, yet they are within a short distance of resorts with the most up-to-date entertainments. There are lakes, secluded beaches, historic castles – and quaint old market towns that reveal unexpected delights.

Snowdonia still draws a host of admirers, and no wonder. The grandeur of this mountain range, with Snowdon itself rising to a height of 3,560 ft, has been celebrated by poets from time immemorial, and modern transport has made it more accessible without diminishing its appeal. You don't have to be a mountaineer to climb to the summit – though sensible precautions should always be taken – and the Snowdon Mountain Railway, a gem in itself, goes to the very top. The highlands, though, begin further east, just after crossing the border into Wales. The Clwydian Hills stride above Ruthin and Denbigh, and the road snakes dizzily around the famous Horseshoe Pass before descending to a town whose name is familiar the world over – Llangollen. Then come the moorland and forest of Hiraethog and Clocaenog, with waymarked walks and visitor

A corner of Bodnant Garden (National Trust) in the Conwy Valley.

Colwyn Bay Mountain Zoo's penguins.

Porthdinllaen near Nefyn.

centres giving you a variety of information, and the lovely Vale of Conwy linking Betws-y-Coed with Conwy and Llandudno on the coast.

SERENE LAKES

North Wales has serene lakes and narrow valleys or 'cwms' carved by glaciers in the Ice Age. The well-surfaced mountain roads take one to places where the breezes carry the very essence of heather, bracken and gorse. High in the hills, the farmer has an endurance which the more kindly acres of the lowlands do not require – and these rural communities enjoy a distinctive culture reaching back through the mists of time.

There are native Welsh castles, such as Dolwyddelan, between Betws-y-Coed and Blaenau Ffestiniog, and mighty fortresses like Caernarfon and Conwy, built seven centuries ago by Edward I to confirm his conquest of North Wales. And the quiet lanes of the Lleyn Peninsula lead to little stone churches which still seem to enshrine the simplicity and virtue of the saintly men who first brought Christianity to these islands. Spiritually, it's a far cry from these to the more worldly appeal of resorts such as Rhyl and Llandudno. Yet it's all part of the charm of North Wales – a place of contrasts, where the past scuffs the heels of the present.

The seaside resorts are themselves rich in variety. The pertness of Prestatyn and razzmatazz of Rhyl give them a different appeal from that of Colwyn Bay and Llandudno, and all four are within 20 miles of each other.

FANTASY

Portmeirion, famous the world over, is an Italianate dream created by Clough Williams-Ellis near Porthmadog. Its streets are pure fantasy. And there's romance of another kind in Anglesey, an island of whitewashed villages and exquisite bays reached by road or rail across the Menai Strait. For steam railway enthusiasts, however, perhaps the most romantic sight of all is that of the narrow-gauge trains bustling out of Porthmadog!

Mid Wales

This is the heartland of Wales, where the green hills roll north to the rugged perimeter of Snowdonia and south to the fringes of the Brecon Beacons. Plynlimon rises over 2,000 ft and five rivers have their source there, including the Severn and Wye. The largest town is Aberystwyth, which

Placid water sailing in the mountains of Wales.

Harlech Castle.

The sunsets over Cardigan Bay have enticed some of the greatest landscape artists to these parts. There are lovely estuaries, harbours bright with yachts, and spa towns where shades of Victorian opulence still linger. It's a wide-open country of hills flecked with sheep and sparkling salmon rivers.

combines the roles of seaside resort and university town. Machynlleth, 18 miles away, was the home of a Welsh parliament when Owain Glyndwr rebelled against the English throne early in the 15th century. And in the north-west stands Harlech Castle, dramatically set on a rocky bluff overlooking a broad sweep of sand-dunes.

From Harlech south to Aberaeron and New Quay, the coastline is one of striking beauty. It takes in the estuaries of the Mawddach and Dovey, where the mountains stand like guardians of the quiet waters, and elsewhere there are cliffs ablaze with gorse. Seven miles north of Aberystwyth is the nature reserve of Ynyslas, an expanse of rolling dunes, and the Aberystwyth-Aberaeron coast road has superb seascapes.

WOODED VALLEY

A trip along the narrow-gauge Vale of Rheidol Railway from Aberystwyth to Devil's Bridge is a memorable experience. The track hugs the

between Llanwrtyd Wells and Tregaron.

There is a softer landscape to the east, where the steep mountains give way to the gentle hills of the Welsh Marches. The place-names here sound more English than Welsh – Radnor, Painscastle, Hay-on-Wye – and the accents have

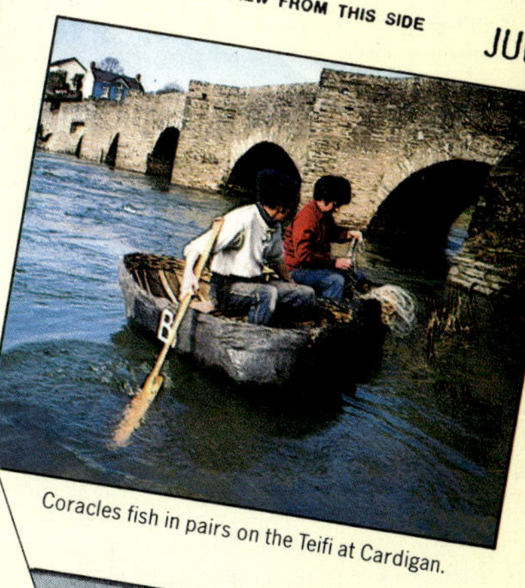

Coracles fish in pairs on the Teifi at Cardigan.

Typical farmhouse accommodation in Wales.

hillside high above the wooded valley, and near the terminus at Devil's Bridge are the famous Mynach Falls. There are other Great Little Trains in the region, too. They include the Talyllyn Railway, chuffing up into the hills from Tywyn, and the Welshpool and Llanfair, which follows a leafy route in the border country. Another line skirts Bala Lake, a fine stretch of water surrounded by hills. From here the spectacular Bwlch-y-Groes mountain road runs to Dinas Mawddwy, and if you have a taste for such things don't miss the road that climbs the dizzy heights of the Abergwesyn Pass

more than a hint of Herefordshire, but in fact you are in the county of Powys. Take your time exploring this serene countryside, and reflect that once it was the scene of bloodshed – for through it runs Offa's Dyke, the ancient boundary between Wales and England. (A long-distance footpath follows the line of the Dyke now). Clyro holds memories of the diarist Kilvert, and Hay-on-Wye has become a haven for those who love browsing through second-hand bookshops.

RIDING COUNTRY

A little further into Wales is the spa town of Llandrindod Wells, where there are hotels with a touch of Edwardian grandeur. The health-giving waters of the locality are still sought after, and this is a popular touring centre. The Elan Valley reservoirs, which supply Birmingham with its water, have great scenic beauty, and the hills near Llanidloes enclose another man-made lake, Llyn Clywedog.

There is fine riding country in Mid Wales, and even novices can enjoy the quiet delights of pony trekking. It's a paradise for golfers, too – as anyone who has swung a club on the famous Royal St David's at Harlech will know!

South Wales

Some of Britain's finest coastal scenery is to be found here. There are mountains and moorlands, prehistoric sites and Roman remains of outstanding interest. In fact, you'll be surprised by the variety of scenery you'll discover. For although the chief centres of population are in south-east Wales, the countryside is never far away.

When people of means started to embark on Grand Tours two centuries ago, South Wales was high on their list of destinations. They wrote awesome accounts of the torrents and falls in the Neath Valley, and praised the sylvan beauty of the Usk and the Wye.

We've had the Industrial Revolution since then, yet the greater part of South Wales is hardly touched by it. And even the so-called mining valleys reaching north of Cardiff and Newport like outstretched fingers have dramatically changed in appearance. They were never irredeemably urban, as the clustered terraces soon give way to mountains and moors where the scenery has scarcely changed since the days of the legions. Today most of the houses are brightly painted – a high proportion of them are owner-occupied – conifers grow

Quadrant Shopping Centre, Swansea.

Pentre Ifan burial chamber near Newport, Dyf

on reclaimed tips, and there are museums and interpretive centres which throw a fascinating light on the history of the area.

SPACIOUS PARKS

The variety of scenery in South Wales can be judged by the fact that within an hour's drive of Cardiff are the Brecon Beacons, sweeping to heights of 2,000 ft, the Heritage Coast near Porthcawl, the Roman settlements of Caerleon and Caerwent, and the grandeur of Tintern Abbey in the Wye Valley. Cardiff itself is a city of distinction with a superb civic centre, spacious parks and a bizarre castle with fantastically decorated rooms. Forty miles to the west along the M4 is Swansea, which is palpably Welsh and boasts a multi-million pound leisure centre and one of the finest fresh food markets in the British Isles. Between the two cities is the Vale of Glamorgan, an endearing stretch of countryside dotted with ruins of Norman castles and Elizabethan manor houses.

Just outside Swansea, the Gower Peninsula has picturesque villages and lovely sandy bays. Carmarthen, a busy market town which is the agricultural centre for miles around, is on the River Towy, which winds along a valley of serene beauty. This is Dylan Thomas Country and the 'heron-priested' shore of Laugharne, where the poet lived for many years in the Boat House – now open to the public – is a few miles to the south.

IMPOSING RUINS

Pembrokeshire, 'Little England Beyond Wales', has an atmosphere all its own. The mysterious Preseli Hills are said to have provided some of the stones for Stonehenge – though no-one knows for certain how they were taken all that way – and the Pembrokeshire Coast Path gives unforgettable views of its renowned coastline.

There are neolithic tombs in South Wales, architectural gems such as St David's Cathedral, and the imposing ruins of one of Europe's biggest castles – Caerphilly, which has a leaning tower and, supposedly, the ghost of a faithless lady eternally seeking her lover. We can't guarantee you'll see her – but even if you don't, the more tangible attractions of South Wales will ensure you'll have an eventful time!

Barafundle Bay near Pembroke.

St. David's Cathedral.

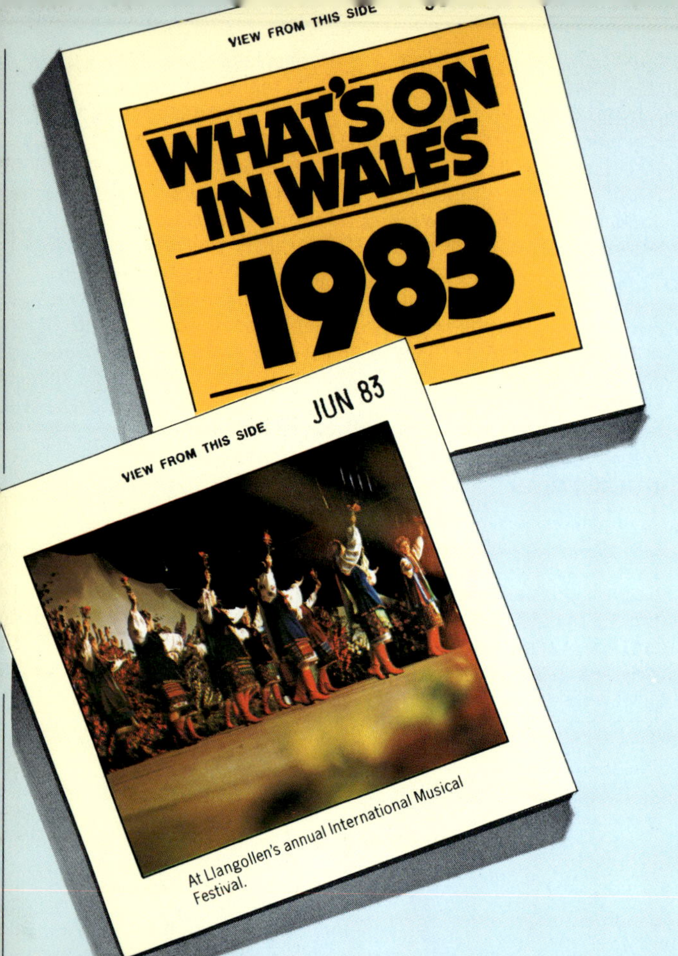

At Llangollen's annual International Musical Festival.

Wales has a musical tradition which is reflected in the major events that take place. The National Eisteddfod is a showpiece for poets and singers. And people of many nations meet in friendship at the colourful International Eisteddfod at Llangollen.

There are concerts and operas – and in different fields of endeavour, motorists compete in testing car rallies and yachtsmen in regattas.

Here are a few, month by month. The nearest Tourist Information Centre (list at back) will be able to give you the exact dates.

February – Mid March

Welsh National Opera Spring Season, New Theatre, Cardiff.

April – May

Aberystwyth Festival, Aberystwyth

May

International Welsh Rally, Cardiff

Welsh National Opera Early Summer Season, Cardiff

June

St David's Cathedral Bach Festival, St David's

Dunlop Masters Golf Tournament, St. Pierre Golf and Country Club, Chepstow, Gwent

Llandaff Festival of Music, Cardiff

Welsh National Opera Summer Season, Theatr Clwyd, Mold

July

International Musical Eisteddfod, Llangollen (for one week)

Royal Welsh Agricultural Show, Builth Wells (for three days)

Gower Festival, Swansea

Fishguard Music Festival, Fishguard

August

Festival of Cardiff 1983

Royal National Eisteddfod of Wales, Llangefni, Isle of Anglesey (for one week)

Menai Strait Regatta, Isle of Anglesey

September

Welsh International Four Days Walks, Llanwrtyd Wells, Powys

September – October

North Wales Music Festival, St. Asaph

October

Swansea Festival, Swansea

November – December

Cardiff Festival of Music, Cardiff

CESTYLL 83

In 1983 the castles of Wales will be the setting for many exciting encounters.

This is just a small selection of the events planned for 1983 in the historic castles of Wales.
Fill in the coupon at the bottom for full lists to be sent to you as they are issued.

BEAUMARIS CASTLE

March–December
"Storming the Castle" Weekends

Early July
"Round the Castles" Yacht Race, Beaumaris-Conwy-Caernarfon-Beaumaris.

CAERNARFON CASTLE

Throughout season
Audio-Visual Display.

CAERPHILLY CASTLE

March 1
Grand Banquet.

June 20-July 3
Festival Fortnight – mediaeval fair, choral competition, banquets, etc.

CALDICOT CASTLE

Early May
Spring Spectacular.

Throughout season
Mediaeval Banquets.

CARDIFF CASTLE

June 29-July 3
A week of varied events – international night, choirs, pageant of youth, ox-roast, cymanfa ganu (community singing night).

CARDIFF-TO-CAERNARFON ROAD RELAY

June
Involving seven Welsh Castles

CHEPSTOW CASTLE

Throughout season
Historical Display.
July 28, 29, 30
Pageant.

CHIRK CASTLE

June 25
Summer Ball.

CILGERRAN CASTLE

August 19
Ox Roast

August 20
Open-air music and dancing.

CRICCIETH CASTLE

Throughout
Permanent Exhibition.

CYFARTHFA CASTLE

Merthyr Tydfil
August 29-September 3
Festival of Castles Week. Concerts, Exhibitions, Lectures, Poetry Readings.

FLINT CASTLE

Early June
Professional Cycle Races.

HAVERFORDWEST CASTLE

August
Mediaeval Fair, Archaeological "dig".

LLANTRISANT CASTLE

May 2-7
Festival Week. Folk singing and music on castle plain. Exhibition on "The Black Army" (the bowmen of Llantrisant who fought at Crecy).

MONMOUTH CASTLE

(Parade Ground)
Late June and mid-September Drama and musical events.

MONTGOMERY CASTLE

Festival week including "Sealed Knot" muster.

NEWCASTLE

(Bridgend)
May 21
Mediaeval Fair and "battle" in armour.

OYSTERMOUTH CASTLE

August 1-7
Ostreme Festival – open-air concerts, music, dancing.

PENHOW CASTLE

June 22
Music of the later Middle Ages.

August 20
Castellan's Dinner – feast on venison and quaff mulled ale.

POWIS CASTLE

Throughout season
Clive of India Exhibition.

RAGLAN CASTLE

May
Mediaeval Fair.

RHUDDLAN

August
Mock battle. River Procession.

RUTHIN CASTLE

Every Wednesday
Mediaeval Fair.

ST. DONAT'S CASTLE

August
Son et Lumiere.
Vintage farm machinery display; barbecue.

TENBY CASTLE

May 27-29
Folk Festival on castle headland.

USK CASTLE

July 9
Victorian afternoon (opening event in Usk Festival Week).

Events Lists 1983

Please send me free your latest list of Events at Castles in Wales in 1983.

Name _______________________

Address _____________________

____

_____________ Post Code __________

Wales Tourist Board, Dept. C83 Events, PO Box 1, Cardiff CF1 2XN

Award-winning holidays

Sunday 'dry' area Summer 1982.

From the time when the mediaeval bards toasted their patrons in mead, Wales has had its own distinctive drinks and dishes. Welsh cuisine is more readily available to the visitor than ever. A taste of Wales is yours for the taking!

Eating out in Wales

You may have heard of Welsh cakes and the edible seaweed called laverbread – delicious with a bacon-and-egg breakfast – but there's far more to Welsh cuisine than that.

You'll find tastier ways than ever of enjoying Welsh lamb, and for starters there'll be cawl – that's distinctively Welsh soup – or something completely different.

In every part of Wales there are restaurateurs who have taken a delight in reviving traditional Welsh dishes, and like all creative artists, the chefs love to give them that little bit extra to tickle the modern palate!

The Wales Tourist Board takes pride in its 'Taste of Wales' scheme. This has encouraged more and more establishments to offer genuine Welsh cooking to tourists.

Look for a coloured bakestone symbol with the words 'Blas Ar Gymru – A Taste of Wales'. This means the establishment meets the high standards of the scheme and will have a choice of genuine Welsh dishes based, wherever possible, on fresh local produce and recipes passed down through many generations. You'll be in for a pleasant surprise. Even that tired old cheese-on-toast combination, Welsh Rarebit, becomes a rare delight!

Caldicot's Mediaeval Banquets.

Cawl, a traditional Welsh lamb dish.

The Farmhouse Award

We've come a long way since the time when farmers' wives hopefully stuck a 'B and B' sign on the gate to tell the world they offered overnight accommodation.

Farmhouse holidays are now an integral part of the tourist scene. But one thing hasn't changed – the warmth of the welcome.

The Wales Farmhouse Award – Gwobr Ffermdy Cymru – has been in existence since 1979. It goes only to places which meet the stringent demands of the Wales Tourist Board and is a recognised endorsement of high quality.

To qualify, the operator must have successfully completed a farm tourism course run by colleges all over Wales, and have accommodation and facilities of a particular standard, all checked out by the Wales Tourist Board.

A stay on a Welsh farm – for a week or longer – is an enriching holiday experience. It's especially popular with families – the children love it!

Look out for the 'Wales Farmhouse Award' symbol. Any farm displaying it has every reason to feel proud. The entries for award winners included in this guide have a special triangular flash across the corner.

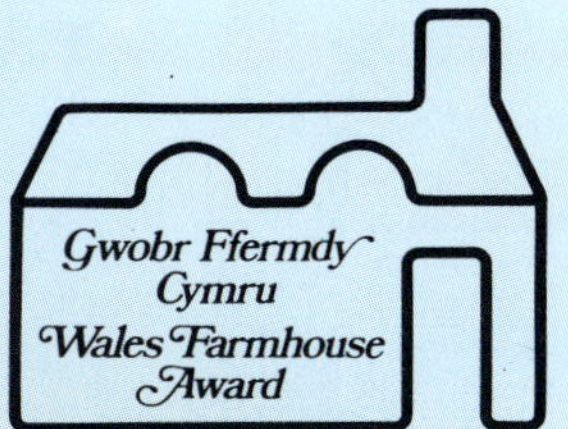

Drinks on Sunday

The traditional Welsh Sunday meant that until the early Sixties, pubs opened only six days a week. Now, however, you can get a drink in most parts of Wales on a Sunday.

The decision is entirely in the hands of local people. Every seven years, they have a right to call a poll on Sunday drinks – so each area settles this matter for itself. The visitor who finds it perplexing might reflect that it proves, at any rate, that Wales is different.

Generally speaking, the further west you go the less likely you are to find the pubs open – though the pattern was piecemeal even before the last referendum in the autumn of 1982.

If you're staying at a licensed restaurant or hotel, of course, it's less complicated – you're entitled to a drink with your meal even in a 'dry' area.

British Tourist Authority Schemes

There are a variety of places where you can eat in the country. And often it's hard to decide which will suit us best.

To help you choose, the British Tourist Authority has three commendation schemes. One is for country hotels with a restaurant, another for county guest houses, and a third for country restaurants.

The idea is to encourage smaller establishments which give a warm welcome as well as meeting high standards of food, wine, service and accommodation. Value for money comes into it, too. For details write to: BTA Commendation Schemes Officer, British Tourist Authority, 64 St. James's Street, London SW1.

A glass and a chat, 'on Sunday, too, in many places.'

Easy ways to Wales

By Road

Once upon a time it took 27 hours to go from London to Holyhead. But relax – that was in stage coach days!

If you're driving to your holiday spot, you'll find that road improvements in many parts of Wales have made your journey that much easier.

In the south, there's the M4 – which now takes you all the way from London to the very heart of West Wales, near Carmarthen, where the Pembrokeshire coast is only a short distance away along good roads.

The A40 – the old mail coach road from London to south-west Wales – goes via Oxford and Gloucester through Brecon and Llandovery to Haverfordwest and thence to Fishguard. It's a scenic and reasonably fast route.

The A458 from Shrewsbury takes one west through Welshpool towards the Cardigan Bay coast, while those making for Aberystwyth from Birmingham complete their journey on the A44.

Another former mail coach route, the A5 – which runs along a route brilliantly engineered by Telford – is the main road through Llangollen and Betws-y-Coed to Bangor. The coast road from Chester, the A55, is now an expressway for much of the route and is easily reached from the motorway network.

If you're not in a hurry, you can ease yourself into the holiday mood by stopping off for bed-and-breakfast en route. There's plenty of choice!

By Rail

The speed and comfort of British Rail's expresses would have astonished those who came to dip a brave toe into the brine just a few short years ago.

It's now only four hours from London (Euston) to Colwyn Bay and the Inter-City from London (Paddington) reaches Cardiff in less than two hours.

Aberystwyth is reached from Shrewsbury along a line with wooded valleys, and the Cambrian Coast line through Barmouth to Pwllheli runs through spectacular scenery.

The Heart of Wales line from Shrewsbury through Llandrindod Wells to Swansea and Llanelli is ingeniously engineered, with the Sugar Loaf tunnel and Cynghordy viaduct among its triumphs.

Fares and Tickets

With so many holiday centres in Wales served by British Rail's passenger services, take a look at their wide range of standard and reduced fares and other facilities. There may be one tailored to your needs.

Runabout Season Tickets

You get a week's unlimited travel (half price for children) by British Rail in a particular area after 9.00am on Mondays to Fridays, and any time on Saturdays and Sundays.

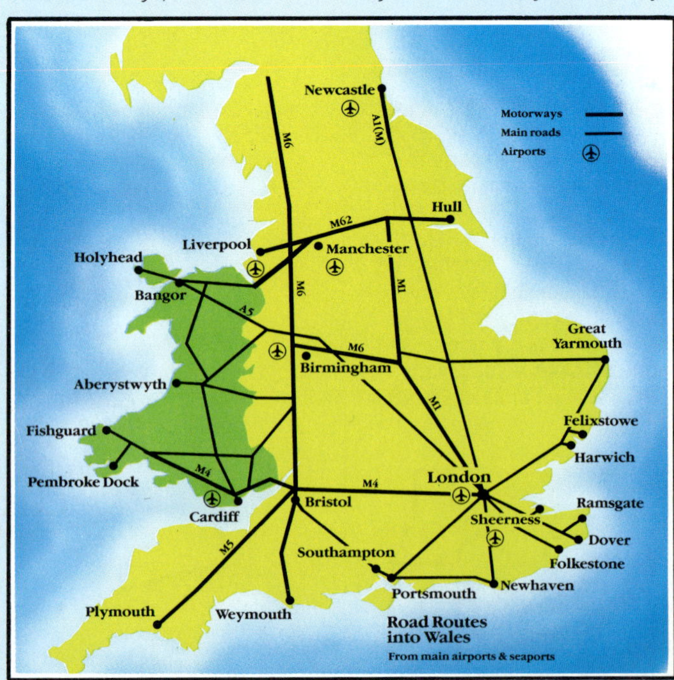

Buy your ticket in the area. You get 7 consecutive days, go as you please. Example of an area: All stations Chester – Holyhead – Llandudno – Blaenau Ffestiniog.

Tourist Tickets

These give unlimited travel for seven days on nine of the ten 'Great Little Trains' of Wales. The narrow-gauge line not included is the Snowdon Mountain Railway.
The nine are: Bala Lake; Fairbourne; Ffestiniog; Welsh Highland Railway; Llanberis Lake; Talyllyn; Vale of Rheidol; Welshpool & Llanfair; Brecon Mountain Railway.
Buy your tickets at the offices of these narrow-gauge railways and at the British Rail station at Aberystwyth, which is also the terminus of the Vale of Rheidol Railway.

Inclusive Holiday Tickets

You can book accommodation and other services at the same time as your rail ticket, and these packages are obtained either from British Rail or recognised travel agents. Ask for Golden Rail Holidays or Golden Rail Breathers.

Evening Rover Tickets

Fancy an evening tour along the coast and back – after 5.30pm? Ask your holiday station about these tickets.

> For the young, the old folk and the family

The Family Railcard

Either one or two adults buy a £10 Family Railcard. Then they, as well as one or two other adults going with them, can travel for half the normal fare each – so long as between one and four children also go with them for a flat fare of £1 each.

For these journeys, there must always be an adult Railcard holder and at least one child. Whatever size the group, it must stay together for the whole journey.
Railcards last a whole year so mean big savings.

Young Persons Railcard

If you're under 24, you're entitled to a Young Persons Railcard – even if you're not a student. It enables you to travel anywhere you like for half the standard fare for twelve months from the date of issue – with very few restrictions.
Ask for a Young Persons Railcard application form at your local station.

Senior Citizens Railcard

For one payment only, a man over 65 or a woman over 60 gets an identity card entitling them to half-price rail travel on Awayday and standard single and return tickets – and a reduction on Golden Rail holidays into the bargain.
A half payment secures Awayday ticket reductions only. Most stations sell Senior Citizen Railcards, but be sure to take your pension documents and birth certificate with you when you apply.

Disabled Persons Railcard

If your friend or relative is blind or severely disabled, they could qualify for a £10 Railcard which would allow them and an adult escort to travel at half fare. Cards are valid until 31st December. Leaflets with full details are available at Post Offices or British Rail Stations and Agents.

How to read the entries

Wie Man die Eintragungenliest
Comment lire les rubriques

Order of listing

The guide has been compiled to feature every resort, city, town and village in alphabetical order. Every establishment is also subsequently listed within its category and also in alphabetical order.

Rates

The B & B single rate per night refers to one person sharing a double room, VAT included.

The dinner, B & B single rate per week refers to one person sharing a double room for seven nights, VAT included, with table d'hôte menu, or set meal, unless stated otherwise in the text.

Period of opening

The period the establishment is open during the year is denoted by numbers, e.g.
1–12 means open all the year, January to December inclusive.
4–10 means open April to October inclusive.

Telephone numbers

Where the name of a town and its telephone exchange are identical only telephone numbers are given.

Anleitung zum Gebrauch der Broschüre.

Der Reiseführer enthält zunächst in alphabetischer Reihenfolge eine Zusammenstellung sämtlicher Urlaubsorte, Städte und Dörfer. Im Anschluß daran werden die einzelnen Unterkunftseinrichtungen, ebenfalls in alphabetischer Reihenfolge, innerhalb ihrer Kategorien aufgeführt.

Preise

Der Enzelpreis für eine Übernachtung mit Frühstück bezieht sich auf eine ein Doppelzimmer teilende Person und versteht sich enschließlich MwSt.

Der Einzelpreis pro Woche einschließlich Abendessen, Übernachtung und Frühstück bezieht sich auf eine ein Doppelzimmer teilende Person für sieben Nächte und schlißt MwSt und Tagesmenü ein, falls im Text nichts anderes angegeben ist.

Betriebssaison

Die Zeit, während der Unterkunftseinrichtungen im Laufe des Jahres geöffnet sind, ist durch Zahlen gekennzeichnet. Zum Beispiel:
1–12 bedeutet: das ganze Jahr hindurch geöffnet, d.h. Januar bis einschließlich Dezember.
4–10 bedeutet: von April bis einschließlich Oktober geöffnet.

Telefonnummern

In Fällen, in denen der Name einer Stadt und ihr Fernsprechamt miteinander übereinstimmen, sind lediglich die jeweiligen Telefonnummern aufgeführt.

Comment utiliser cet ouvrage.

Les présent guide donne la liste de toutes les villes, stations, villages dans l'ordre alphabétique. Les noms des établissements suivent, classés par catégorie, également dans l'ordre alphabétique.

Tarif

Le prix chambre-petit déjeuner s'entend par personne partageant une chambre deux personnes, TVA comprise.

Le prix demi-pension s'entend à la semaine par personne partageant une chambre de deux personnes pour sept nuits, TVA comprise, repas du soir au menu table d'hôte sauf indication contraire.

Dates d'ouverture

Les périodes d'ouverture des établissements durant l'année sont indiquées par des chiffres. Ainsi: 1–12: l'établissement est ouvert toute l'année de janvier à décembre.
4–10: l'établissement est ouvert d'avril à octobre inclus.

Numéros de téléphone

Lorsque l'indicatif d'une ville n'est autre que le nom de la ville, seul le numéro est donné.

List of Hotels, Motels, Inns, Guest Houses, Private Houses, Farm Guest Houses and Activity Holidays

Hotels, Motels, Gasthauser, Pensionen und Bauernhof – Pensionen.

Hotels, motels, auberges, Pensions de famille et logement a là ferme.

Aberaeron

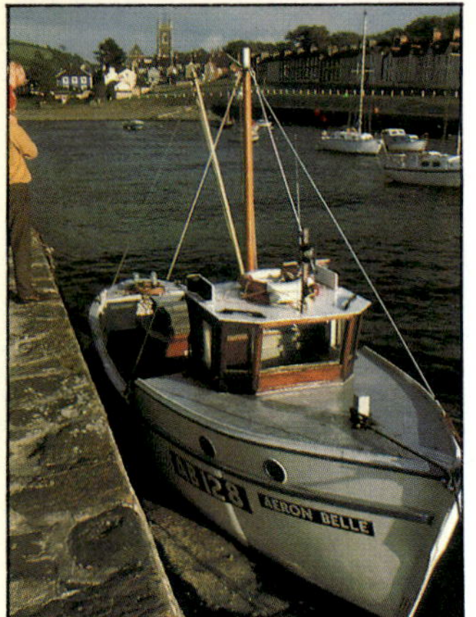

Map ref: Fc3
Coastal town on Cardigan Bay with pleasant harbour and a distinctive architecture. Sailing and fishing popular. Good centre for the coast between Cardigan and Aberystwyth.

Hotels

Feathers Royal Hotel

Aberaeron
SA46 0AQ
Tel: (0545) 570214

CATEGORIES

| 4 | 4 | 5 |

Family hotel once an old posting inn situated three hundred yards from beach and river. There are sixteen bedrooms with private bathrooms radio, room-call. Also apartments within the hotel complex facilities which include bars, restaurant and indoor swimming pool, baby listening service, pony trekking and sailing.

C	B & B PER PERSON PER NIGHT		DINNER B & B PER PERSON PER WEEK		16
	MIN £	MAX £	MIN £	MAX £	OPEN
	12				1—12

Monachty Arms Hotel*

Market Street, Aberaeron
Dyfed SA46 0AS
Tel: (0545) 570389

CATEGORIES

| 3 | 4 | 3 |

Situated in the middle of a small Georgian town with harbour, beaches and beautiful riverside walks and fishing, boating, tennis, bowls. Hotel has welcome bar, cellar bar and beer garden. Television lounge. Bedrooms have tea and coffee making facility and some with private bathrooms and centrally heated throughout.

T C	B & B PER PERSON PER NIGHT		DINNER B & B PER PERSON PER WEEK		7
	MIN £	MAX £	MIN £	MAX £	OPEN
	13	15			1—12

Guest Houses

Henllan*

Ffosyffin, Aberaeron
Dyfed SA46 0HD
Tel: (0545) 570806

CATEGORIES

| 1 | 3 | 2 |

Bed and breakfast, evening dinner optional. 50 yards off main coast road, 1 mile sea. Situated between New Quay and Aberaeron. Colour TV, homely personal service. Ample parking. Full central heating. New modern bungalow. SAE for enquiries.

C	B & B PER PERSON PER NIGHT		DINNER B & B PER PERSON PER WEEK		3
	MIN £	MAX £	MIN £	MAX £	OPEN
	7	8	70	77	1—12

Llys Aeron*

Lampeter Road, Aberaeron
Dyfed SA46 0ED
Tel: (0545) 570276

CATEGORIES

| 1 | 1 | 1 |

A lovely area to spend a relaxed holiday. Aberaeron sits around a small harbour, with friendly shops. Cheerful and comfortable bedrooms all with wash basins. Breakfast room overlooking garden. Parking on private forecourt. We welcome you and yours.

C	B & B PER PERSON PER NIGHT		DINNER B & B PER PERSON PER WEEK		4
	MIN £	MAX £	MIN £	MAX £	OPEN
	6	7.50			1—12

'Swn-y-Gwynt'*

Crossways, Ffosyffin, Aberaeron
Dyfed SA46 0HA
Tel: (0545) 570041

CATEGORIES

| 1 | 3 | 2 |

Three bed luxury bungalow set in beautiful gardens, large car park. Rural area just off Cardigan Coast road. Equidistance to Cardigan and Aberystwyth. 1 mile Aberaeron, home produce and preserves. Excellent cooking, every comfort, TV lounge. Highly recommended. Pets accommodation in garden chalet. Central heating and shower.

C	B & B PER PERSON PER NIGHT		DINNER B & B PER PERSON PER WEEK		3
	MIN £	MAX £	MIN £	MAX £	OPEN
		7		84	1—12

Farmhouses

Bikerehyd Farm*

Pennant, Llanon
Dyfed SY23 5PB
Tel: (09746) 365

CATEGORIES

| 4 | 3 | 4 |

FARMHOUSE AWARD

Beautiful modernised farmhouse with three bedrooms in the house and a further three bedrooms with shower and toilet en-suite in the 14th century stone cottages alongside, all with heating. Coffee and tea making facilities available at all times. Renowned for its superb, mainly home-produced food and peaceful surroundings.

T C	B & B PER PERSON PER NIGHT		DINNER B & B PER PERSON PER WEEK		5
	MIN £	MAX £	MIN £	MAX £	OPEN
	7	7.50	75	82	1—12

Brynog Mansion*

Felinfach, Lampeter
Dyfed
Tel: (0570) 470266

CATEGORIES

| 3 | 3 | 2 |

FARMHOUSE AWARD

Brynog is an old country mansion situated in the beautiful Vale of Aeron, 3/4 mile off the A482 road main road and a short drive to the sea. Ideally situated in the centre of Ceredigion. Private fishing and shooting. 200 acre working farm. Wholesome home cooking and a real Welsh welcome. Closed Christmas and New Year.

T C	B & B PER PERSON PER NIGHT		DINNER B & B PER PERSON PER WEEK		8
	MIN £	MAX £	MIN £	MAX £	OPEN
	7	7.50	70	77	1—12

C	**Children stay at reduced rates, wherever you see this symbol.**

Hotel

Aberafan Hotel*

Sea Front, Aberavon, Port Talbot
West Glamorgan, SA12 6QP
Tel: (0639) 884949

CATEGORIES

| 6 | 5 | 5 |

Modern hotel situated on the sea front with two miles of flat promenade and sandy beach. Facilities for the disabled. Children stay free when sharing parents room, only meals charged for; early suppers, junior menus. Baby listening service. Dinner dance every Saturday. Ideal touring base. An Eagle Hotel.

T C	B & B PER PERSON PER NIGHT		DINNER B & B PER PERSON PER WEEK		70
	MIN £	MAX £	MIN £	MAX £	OPEN
	15.50	15.50	119	119	1—12

Motel and Inn

Abercrave Inn*

Abercrave, Swansea
West Glamorgan, SA9 1XS
Tel: (0639 77) 460

CATEGORIES

| 3 | 3 | 1 |

200 yards off A4067, Brecon 22 miles, Swansea 18 miles, Dan-yr-Ogof Caves 3 miles. Situated at the southern gateway to the beautiful Brecon Beacons National Park. Amenities: Pony trekking, caving, fishing, interesting walks to mountain lakes and water falls and a short drive to the Gower Coast. All bedrooms have shower/bathroom and central heating. TV lounge. Double room £18.00.

T C	B & B PER PERSON PER NIGHT		DINNER B & B PER PERSON PER WEEK		8
	MIN £	MAX £	MIN £	MAX £	OPEN
	10.50	10.50	95	110	1—12

Dan-yr-Ogof Apartments*

Abercrave, Glyntawe
Powys
Tel: (0639) 730284/730693

CATEGORIES

| 3 | 3 | 1 |

These attractive new bungalow-style apartments are situated in an area containing some of the finest mountain scenery that the Brecon Beacons National Park offers. The apartments have won three Tourist Board awards. The complex includes a swimming pool, sauna, solarium, jacuzzi, adventure playground. Locally, trekking and fishing.

T	B & B PER PERSON PER NIGHT		DINNER B & B PER PERSON PER WEEK		18
	MIN £	MAX £	MIN £	MAX £	OPEN
	11	13			4—10

Dan-yr-Ogof Motel*

Abercrave, Glyntawe
Powys
Tel: (0639) 730284/730693

CATEGORIES

| 1 | 1 | 1 |

This small hotel is situated in an area containing some of the finest mountain scenery that the Brecon Beacons National Park offers. An ideal base to tour the Park, with trekking and fishing available nearby.

T	B & B PER PERSON PER NIGHT		DINNER B & B PER PERSON PER WEEK		5
	MIN £	MAX £	MIN £	MAX £	OPEN
	6	7			4—10

Farmhouse

Rhoswaun Farm*

Llwydcoed, Aberdare
Mid Glamorgan, CF44 0YF
Tel: (0685) 872818

CATEGORIES

| 3 | 2 | 2 |

Small farm at foot of Dyllas Mountain. Beef and poultry. Good home cooking, warm welcome. Ideal for touring Brecon Beacons, Dan-yr-Orgof caves etc. Very comfortable.

	B & B PER PERSON PER NIGHT		DINNER B & B PER PERSON PER WEEK		2
	MIN £	MAX £	MIN £	MAX £	OPEN
	6	6.50	59.50		1—12

Hotel

Ty Newydd Hotel*

Aberdaron, Pwllheli
Gwynedd, LL53 8BE
Tel: (0758-86) 207

CATEGORIES

| 4 | 4 | 4 |

Uniquely situated with direct access to the beach in the beautiful heritage coast village of Aberdaron. Enjoy local lobster in the restaurant with unrivalled view of sea and surf. Colour TV, room-call and central heating throughout. Nine private bath/shower. Free parking. No pets. Telephone for information. *AA. *RAC.

T C	B & B PER PERSON PER NIGHT		DINNER B & B PER PERSON PER WEEK		14
	MIN £	MAX £	MIN £	MAX £	OPEN
	11.75	13.75	115.75	130	1—12

Hotels

The Harbour Hotel*

Glandovey Terrace, Aberdovey
Gwynedd
Tel: (065472) 250

CATEGORIES

| 3 | 4 | 4 |

Harbour Hotel, Aberdovey—Tel. 250 Modernised centrally situated sea front position. AA*. All rooms have private bath/shower facilities, tea and coffee making facilities, licensed restaurant and lounge bar, reduced prices for children sharing. Golf parties speciality. Centrally heated.

C	B & B PER PERSON PER NIGHT		DINNER B & B PER PERSON PER WEEK		6
	MIN £	MAX £	MIN £	MAX £	OPEN
	9.50	12	55	75	1—12

Penhelig Arms Hotel

Aberdovey
Gwynedd LL35 OLT
Tel: (065472) 215 Telex 338751

CATEGORIES: 4 4 4

Completely refurbished to a very high standard. Facing the glorious Dovey Estuary, with its own slipway to the sheltered waters immensely rich in their variety of bird life. All rooms have bath/shower, teasmade, colour television. Full central heating. Fire Certificate granted. Children 10 years of age or over welcome. No pets please. Ideally situated for golf, fishing, pony trekking, walking. The glorious sandy beaches and generally touring Snowdonia, with the Talyllyn Railway. Cader Idris, Bird rock and the Dolgoch Falls within easy reach.

C	B & B PER PERSON PER NIGHT		DINNER B & B PER PERSON PER WEEK		12
	MIN £	MAX £	MIN £	MAX £	OPEN
	13	18	120	150	1—12

Guest House

Bryn-y-Mor*

6 Glandovey Terrace, Aberdovey
Gwynedd LL35 OEB
Tel: (065472) 515

CATEGORIES: 3 3 2

Bryn-y-Mor is a small Guest House offering a friendly atmosphere and home cooked meals. Comfortable furnished bedrooms with wash basin. Shaver points. Central Heating. Television lounge. Facing Dovey Estuary 50 yards from beach. Ideal sailing and fishing. Golf, tennis and bowling green nearby. Fire certificate granted.

C	B & B PER PERSON PER NIGHT		DINNER B & B PER PERSON PER WEEK		6
	MIN £	MAX £	MIN £	MAX £	OPEN
	10		112		3—10

Abergavenny
SOUTH WALES

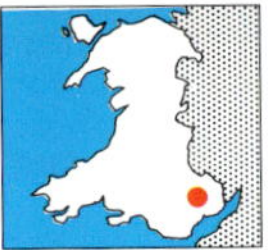

Map ref: Mc1 Gateway from the east to the highlands of Brecon Beacons National Park, the town is well placed for the enjoyment of touring the valleys of the Usk and Wye, walking the Beacons and Black Mountains, game fishing and canal cruising. Agriculture is its mainstay and the useful shopping streets are an attraction for the hill farming folk who throng to market. The town's castle houses an interesting museum.

Hotels

Angel*

Cross Street, Abergavenny
Gwent NP7 5EN
Tel: (0873) 7121

CATEGORIES: 5 4 5

A comfortable old posting house in the town centre with 29 bedrooms. All with private bath or shower, telephone, radio, colour TV and tea and coffee making facilities. Central heating and ample car parking. Weekend bargain breaks available. An excellent base for touring the Brecon Beacons and Black Mountains.

T	B & B PER PERSON PER NIGHT		DINNER B & B PER PERSON PER WEEK		20
C	MIN £	MAX £	MIN £	MAX £	OPEN
	23				1—12

Llanwenarth House*

Govilon, near Abergavenny
Gwent
Tel: (0873) 830289

CATEGORIES: 5 5 5

This historic Elizabethan Manor House stands in beautiful tranquil private gardens and parkland in the Brecon Beacons National Park, offering highest standards of comfort with 'cordon bleu' cooking and fine wines, making it the ideal centre for visiting the many beauty spots and historic sites in the area.

T	B & B PER PERSON PER NIGHT		DINNER B & B PER PERSON PER WEEK		4
C	MIN £	MAX £	MIN £	MAX £	OPEN
	14	16			1—12

The Swan Hotel

Cross Street, Abergavenny
Gwent NT7 5ER
Tel: (0873) 2829

CATEGORIES: 3 3 3

12 bedrooms, some with private shower. Centrally situated, adjacent to the bus station, close to the railway station, easy access to the M4. Licensed restaurant. Comfortable lounge bar serving excellent choice of bar meals. All rooms have radio, tea/coffee making facilities, central heating. Residents' lounge with colour TV. Car Park.
Telephone for reservation or write for colour brochure.

T	B & B PER PERSON PER NIGHT		DINNER B & B PER PERSON PER WEEK		12
C	MIN £	MAX £	MIN £	MAX £	OPEN
	8	11			1—12

Guest Houses

Belchamps Guest House*

1 Holywell Road, Abergavenny
Gwent NP7 5LP
Tel: (0873) 3204

CATEGORIES: 3 3 2

Pleasant outlook. Conveniently located town centre, bus and rail stations. Excellent centre for touring, walking, Brecon Beacons, Black Mountains, Usk and Wye Valleys. Tastefully furnished, carpeted throughout. All rooms with hot and cold water, power points. Bath and toilet or shower and toilet. TV lounge, pleasant dining room, 1 family room, 2 treble, 1 double, 1 single room. Bed and breakfast rates or bed and breakfast with evening meal. Full heating. Parking. Fire Certificate.

C	B & B PER PERSON PER NIGHT		DINNER B & B PER PERSON PER WEEK		5
	MIN £	MAX £	MIN £	MAX £	OPEN
	7	8	66	71	1—12

Belgrave Guest House

81 Brecon Road, Abergavenny
Gwent NP7 7RD
Tel: (0873) 2691

CATEGORIES: 3 2 1

Belgrave house, 81 Brecon Road, Abergavenny, Gwent. Easy reach Black Mountains, Brecon Beacons, Wye Valley, Offa's Dyke. Beautiful walking and hand gliding country. Guests welcome all year. Hot and cold water in all rooms. Double glazed. Large car park. Large lounge with TV. Sunbathing on lawn. Fire Certificate. No pets.

C	B & B PER PERSON PER NIGHT		DINNER B & B PER PERSON PER WEEK		🛏 5
	MIN £	MAX £	MIN £	MAX £	OPEN
	7	7			1—11

Plas Derwen

Monmouth Road, Abergavenny
Gwent NP7 9SP
Tel: (0873) 3144

CATEGORIES: 1 1 2

Large country house on A40 at entrance to town. Short walk from railway station and near bus station and town centre. Extensive grounds with farm animals and poultry. Farm produce and home cooking. Large double and family rooms. Central heating. Pony trekking arranged with transport.

C	B & B PER PERSON PER NIGHT		DINNER B & B PER PERSON PER WEEK		🛏 3
	MIN £	MAX £	MIN £	MAX £	OPEN
	6	7	60	75	2—11

South View*

Llangattock-Lingoed
Nr. Abergavenny, Gwent NP7 8RR
Tel: (087 386) 326

CATEGORIES: 1 3 2

A tranquil former rectory of some antiquity with idyllic surroundings. Views and own extensive acreage. Ideally situated for Black Mountains, Brecon Beacons, Wye Valley. Centrally heated. It offers year round a variety of rooms and all anticipated amenities including a table licence. Fire Authority approval. Car essential.

C	B & B PER PERSON PER NIGHT		DINNER B & B PER PERSON PER WEEK		🛏 6
	MIN £	MAX £	MIN £	MAX £	OPEN
	6.50	7.50	63	70	1—12

Farmhouses

Ar-Bryn

Maesyberan, Llanthony Valley
Near Abergavenny, Gwent
Tel: (0873 82) 621

CATEGORIES: 1 2 1

Ar-Bryn, Llanthony, near Abergavenny, Gwent. 9 miles Abergavenny, OS ref. 298 266. National Park. Enquiries to Mrs Esther Morgan. Bedrooms—1 single, 1 double, 1 public bathroom, 1 separate toilet. Bed and breakfast— Single £7, Double £14. Open 4-10. 150 acres sheep farm. Take Hereford Road from Abergavenny to Llanfihangel Crucorney, turn left at Skirrid Mountain Inn for Llanthony Road. Ar-Bryn sign posted on right.

C	B & B PER PERSON PER NIGHT		DINNER B & B PER PERSON PER WEEK		🛏 2
	MIN £	MAX £	MIN £	MAX £	OPEN
	7				4—10

Lower Cadvor Farm*

Govilon, Nr Abergavenny
Gwent NP7 9SG
Tel: (0873) 4186

CATEGORIES: 1 2 1

53 acres mixed stock farm situated 2 miles west of Abergavenny. On A465. Land on banks of river Usk. Modernised farmhouse. Central Heating.

C	B & B PER PERSON PER NIGHT		DINNER B & B PER PERSON PER WEEK		🛏 2
	MIN £	MAX £	MIN £	MAX £	OPEN
	5.50	6			4—10

Upper Goytre Farm*

Enquiries to: F I Whistance
Pandy, Abergavenny
Gwent NP7 8EE
Tel: (0873 82) 204

CATEGORIES: 1 2 2

Enjoy good home cooking in comfortable farmhouse on 224 acres. Family run cattle and sheep farm. Situated on the Grosmont, Llanvihangel Crucorney Road. Overlooking the Black Mountains with superb views. Ideal touring Brecon Beacons, Wye Valley, Forest of Dean and many castles and places of historical interest.

C	B & B PER PERSON PER NIGHT		DINNER B & B PER PERSON PER WEEK		🛏 2
	MIN £	MAX £	MIN £	MAX £	OPEN
	6.50	7.50	66.50	73.50	4—10

Hotels

Bee Hotel

Market Street, Abergele
Clwyd LL22 7AA
Tel: (0745) 822300

CATEGORIES: 3 3 2

Town centre close to beach and country. Hot and cold water and shaver points in all bedrooms. Special rate for children. Lounge with colour TV. Dining room with separate tables. Full central heating. Large garden and play area. Large car parks. Golf, fishing close by. Ideal for touring.

C	B & B PER PERSON PER NIGHT		DINNER B & B PER PERSON PER WEEK		🛏 11
	MIN £	MAX £	MIN £	MAX £	OPEN
	8	8			1—12

Kinmel Manor Hotel*

St George Road, Abergele
Clwyd LL22 9AS
Tel: (0745) 822014/825874

CATEGORIES: 5 4 5

A superb garden setting secluded and warm together with comfort and service in a building re-created as a modern hotel. 22 bedrooms, 21 en suite, well-equipped with colour television, radio, telephone, teasmaid and central heating. The hotel restaurant with its magnificent fireplace serves both A la carte and table d'hôte lunches and dinners. The hotel is an ideal centre for the tourist. The hotel has an out-door swimming pool open to both residents and non-residents. Resident proprietors: Mr & Mrs T C Morpeth.

T	B & B PER PERSON PER NIGHT		DINNER B & B PER PERSON PER WEEK		🛏 22
C	MIN £	MAX £	MIN £	MAX £	OPEN
	17.50	19.50	152.25	166.25	1—12

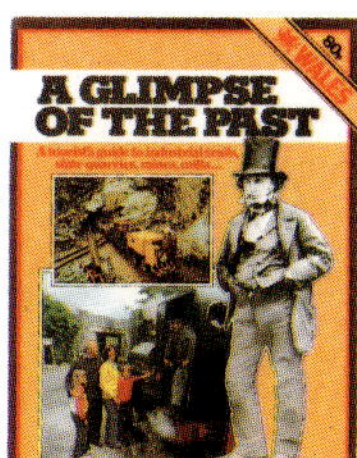

**Wales —
A Glimpse of the Past**

Many new and exciting attractions are springing up in the industrial areas of Wales — slate caverns, silver, lead mines, ironworks, canals and Wales' only coal mine open to visitors. A selection of industrial trails, plus museums, exhibitions and interpretive centres are featured.
Available from: Wales Tourist Board Department W.T.S. P.O. Box 1, CARDIFF CF1 2XN. Price: £1.00 including postage and packing.

Guest House

Garswood Guest House*

Llanfair Road
Abergele, Clwyd
Tel: (0745) 823638 or 823168

CATEGORIES

| 1 | 3 | 1 |

Delightful accommodation in a large detached house on the country fringe and standing in ¾ of an acre of landscaped gardens. Ample parking space for 8 cars. Residential lounge with colour TV. Fitted carpets throughout. The 5 letting bedrooms have wash basins, hot and cold water in every room. Guest bathroom and 2 separate toilets. The breakfasts have been complimented by guests. One mile from beaches, golf courses, horse riding, 5 miles from Rhyl's leisure facilities and Sun Centre. Relax in the restful atmosphere of the rural setting. Bed and Breakfast only.

T C	B & B PER PERSON PER NIGHT		DINNER B & B PER PERSON PER WEEK		4
	MIN £	MAX £	MIN £	MAX £	OPEN
	5.50	7			4—10

Abergynolwyn MID WALES

Farmhouse

Tynybryn Farm*

Llanfihangel-y-Pennant, Tywyn
Gwynedd LL36 9TN
Tel: (065477) 277

CATEGORIES

| 1 | 2 | 2 |

Tynbryn has 3 bedrooms with coloured TV. 2 bathrooms, one with shower, 1 bedroom with washbasin. All modern conveniences. Sitting and dining room. 2 double family bedrooms. Excellent condition. Snowdonia Park, 8 miles. Trout fishing. On land, cattle, ponies, sheep farm. 6 miles to the nearest beach, near Bere Castle and Bird Park. Talyllyn Lake. Golf at Aberdovey. Walking. Near terminus of Talyllyn Railway. Facilities in bedroom for snacks.

T C	B & B PER PERSON PER NIGHT		DINNER B & B PER PERSON PER WEEK		3
	MIN £	MAX £	MIN £	MAX £	OPEN
	6	7	60	70	1—12

For autumn to spring breaks send for our free Great Little Breaks booklet.

Aberporth MID WALES

Motel

Morlan Motel*

Aberporth, Cardigan
Dyfed SA43 2EN
Tel: (0239) 810611

CATEGORIES

| 4 | 4 | 5 |

Ideally located for touring the attractive coastline and countryside or for relaxing on the sandy beach three minutes walk away. From single to family suites available, all with private bathrooms, TV, and full facilities including central heating. Licensed restaurant renowned for its excellent wine and cuisine. Ashley Courtney recommended.

T C	B & B PER PERSON PER NIGHT		DINNER B & B PER PERSON PER WEEK		16
	MIN £	MAX £	MIN £	MAX £	OPEN
	11.25	11.75	110.25	115.50	3—10

Guest Houses

Ffynonwen Country Guest House

Aberporth, Cardigan
Dyfed SA43 2HT
Tel: (0239) 810312

CATEGORIES

| 3 | 3 | 2 |

This is a 300 year old farmhouse with a modern wing added. It retains its olde worlde charm and enjoys a country setting, one mile from the sea. Ideal for family holidays with home cooking, bar and friendly atmosphere. Recommended by BTA and AA.*

C	B & B PER PERSON PER NIGHT		DINNER B & B PER PERSON PER WEEK		12
	MIN £	MAX £	MIN £	MAX £	OPEN
	9		91		1—12

Neuadd Wen*

Aberporth, Cardigan
Dyfed SA43 2HA
Tel: (0239) 810719

CATEGORIES

| 1 | 3 | 2 |

Neuadd Wen is a small licensed Guest House offering a relaxed welcoming atmosphere, delicious food and comfortable accommodation (including wash basins in all bedrooms). Coast and countryside are very beautiful, the sandy beach is three minutes walk away and within easy reach there are opportunities for walking, golf, birdwatching, pony trekking, boating.

C	B & B PER PERSON PER NIGHT		DINNER B & B PER PERSON PER WEEK		4
	MIN £	MAX £	MIN £	MAX £	OPEN
	8	8.50	72	78	1—12

Seaview

Aberporth, Cardigan
Dyfed SA43 2EN
Tel: (0239 810) 358

CATEGORIES

| 1 | 2 | 2 |

Seaview. Wonderfully situated on sea front overlooking the two pretty bays of Aberporth. The nearest guest house to the beach, ½ minute. Safe for swimming, sailing, fishing, water ski-ing. A homely family atmosphere. Cot, high chair, baby-sitting, lounge, colour TV. Video. Parking. Sorry no pets.

C	B & B PER PERSON PER NIGHT		DINNER B & B PER PERSON PER WEEK		3
	MIN £	MAX £	MIN £	MAX £	OPEN
	6.50	7	60	70	3—10

Abersoch NORTH WALES

Map ref: Ac5
Popular, sheltered sailing centre on Lleyn Peninsula, with lovely walks along the coast. Though quiet, it has good facilities and restaurants, golf course, yacht and chandlery stores. Lleyn, its remote sandy beaches, with good fishing and walking, is an excellent family holiday centre.

The Carisbrooke Hotel*

Abersoch
Gwynedd LL53 7DY
Tel: (0758-81) 2526

CATEGORIES

| 3 | 3 | 3 |

Situated in the centre of Abersoch, convenient for shops, harbour, beaches, yacht/golf clubs. This small detached family hotel is known for its cleanliness, friendliness, good food and service, and informal happy atmosphere, comfortable TV lounge, well stocked bar, car park for guests. Family rooms available. Fire certificate granted.

C	B & B PER PERSON PER NIGHT		DINNER B & B PER PERSON PER WEEK		8
	MIN £	MAX £	MIN £	MAX £	OPEN
	8	10	84	101.50	3—10

Deucoch Hotel*

Abersoch, Pwllheli
Gwynedd LL53 7LD
Tel: (075881) 2680

CATEGORIES

| 4 | 4 | 5 |

Originally a nineteenth century farmhouse, situated in an elevated position overlooking Abersoch, with a panoramic view of Cardigan Bay. Well appointed lounge, bar and dining room. English/Welsh cuisine, noted for fresh vegetables. The personal involvement of the resident proprietors ensures a warm welcome and attentive service.

T C	B & B PER PERSON PER NIGHT		DINNER B & B PER PERSON PER WEEK		10
	MIN £	MAX £	MIN £	MAX £	OPEN
	11	13.50	98	115.50	1—12

Egryn Hotel

Lon Sarn Bach (Main Street)
Abersoch, Gwynedd LL53 7EE
Tel: (075 881) 2332

CATEGORIES

| 2 | 3 | 3 |

Ideally situated near to the village centre and within easy walking distance of the beach. Licensed bar, TV/Video lounge, Dining room. Full English breakfast and evening meals (optional) at competitive rates. Bar meals. Children and pets welcome. No petty restrictions. Ample car parking. Good value—friendly service.

C	B & B PER PERSON PER NIGHT		DINNER B & B PER PERSON PER WEEK		8
	MIN £	MAX £	MIN £	MAX £	OPEN
	7	8.50	70	84	2—10

The Islander Restaurant and Hotel*

Main Street, Abersoch, Pwllheli
Gwynedd, N. Wales LL53 7LB
Tel: (075-881) 2778

CATEGORIES

| 3 | 3 | 5 |

Situated 2 minutes walk from sea, shops and golf course, overlooking Cardigan Bay. Renowned for cleanliness and good cuisine. Full central heating, bar, lounge and TV lounge. Large secluded garden. Restaurant offering à la carte and table d'hote menu's. Flambé dishes our speciality. Children reduced rates. Large car park.

C	B & B PER PERSON PER NIGHT		DINNER B & B PER PERSON PER WEEK		3
	MIN £	MAX £	MIN £	MAX £	OPEN
	8.50	12.50	98	118	1—12

Riverside Hotel*

Abersoch, Gwynedd
North Wales LL5 7HW
Tel: (075881) 2419/2818

CATEGORIES

| 3 | 3 | 4 |

A superbly situated comfortable family run hotel with a fine reputation for its interesting and creative cuisine. Overlooking the harbour with its colourful boats, close to the beach and shops. Complete with the only indoor swimming pool in the area. Be sure of an enjoyable stay at the Riverside. Brochure available on request.

T C	B & B PER PERSON PER NIGHT		DINNER B & B PER PERSON PER WEEK		14
	MIN £	MAX £	MIN £	MAX £	OPEN
	15	18	150	170	4—10

St. Tudwal's Hotel

Abersoch, Gwynedd
LL53 7DS
Tel: (075 881) 2539

CATEGORIES

| 3 | 3 | 5 |

Extensively re-furbished, prominently situated on main street, adjacent to shops and all amenities. Three minutes to beach and picturesque harbour. TV in all rooms, public bars selling Robinsons real ales. Excellent value. Bar snacks. Full à la carte restaurant menu with varied wine list.

C	B & B PER PERSON PER NIGHT		DINNER B & B PER PERSON PER WEEK		9
	MIN £	MAX £	MIN £	MAX £	OPEN
	8.50	12.50	98	126	1—12

Wylfa Hotel

Golf Road, Abersoch
Gwynedd LL53 7DY
Tel: (075 881) 2333

CATEGORIES

| 3 | 3 | 3 |

Small friendly hotel, licensed. Near beach. Bed, breakfast and evening meal. (Bar snacks available lunch times and evenings.) Food high in quality and quantity. All home comforts provided for in warm pleasant atmosphere. Parking facilities. Competitive rates. Proprietors, Jenny and Barrie Steeley. Abersoch 2333 or 2522.

C	B & B PER PERSON PER NIGHT		DINNER B & B PER PERSON PER WEEK		8
	MIN £	MAX £	MIN £	MAX £	OPEN
	7	8.50	77	100	1—12

Guest Houses

Lluesta

Abersoch, Gwynedd
LL53 7EB
Tel: (075881) 2487

CATEGORIES

| 3 | 3 | 1 |

Large family house overlooking bay. Ideal bed and breakfast, minutes from village, restaurants, cafes, shops, sandy beaches, harbour and golf links. The area is noted for sailing, windsurfing, water ski-ing, fishing trips, safe bathing and a wealth of quaint villages and crafts. TV, lounge cotton bed linen, ample free parking, choice of full English breakfast.

C	B & B PER PERSON PER NIGHT		DINNER B & B PER PERSON PER WEEK		11
	MIN £	MAX £	MIN £	MAX £	OPEN
	6.50	8			1—12

Llysfor Guest House*

Abersoch, Near Pwllheli
Gwynedd LL53 7AL
Tel: (075 881) 2248

CATEGORIES

| 3 | 3 | 2 |

Llysfor is a small, family guest house. Our aim is to provide comfort and personal attention. 1 minute beach, overlooking river, harbour. Pleasant garden. 5 minutes village, shops. H&C, shaver points, kettles all bedrooms. Cosy lounge, colour TV, comfortable dining room. Dinner optional. Residential licence. Fire Certificate granted. Free parking. Colour brochure SAE Mrs F. Hiorns.

C	B & B PER PERSON PER NIGHT		DINNER B & B PER PERSON PER WEEK		8
	MIN £	MAX £	MIN £	MAX £	OPEN
	8	8	87	87	4—10

Ty Draw

Lôn Sarn Bach, Abersoch
Gwynedd LL53 7EL
Tel: (075 881) 2647

CATEGORIES

| 3 | 2 | 2 |

Jean and Peter Collins ex-Lancastrians, offer you a warm welcome to their beautiful family house. Ideally situated overlooking golf course and bay. Three minutes walk village, beach. Fresh home cooked food. Family rooms. Reductions for children. Baby minding. Comfortable lounge. Colour TV. Large gardens, car and boat park.

C	B & B PER PERSON PER NIGHT		DINNER B & B PER PERSON PER WEEK		4
	MIN £	MAX £	MIN £	MAX £	OPEN
	7	8.50	77	87.50	4—9

Children stay at reduced rates, wherever you see this symbol. C

Map ref: Da7 Queen of the Cardigan Bay resorts is Aberystwyth, holiday town of the conventional promenade, and University campus. Favoured with one of the most beautiful hinterlands in Britain, it is a touring centre that reaches out on the Vale of Rheidol Narrow Gauge Railway to wooded hills, roaring waterfalls and sun streaked uplands. Nearby are Nant y Moch dam and the heights of Plynlimon. A boat-filled harbour, fine fishing and golf, good shopping and a unique cliff railway are extra attractions.

Hotels

Ailsa Craig Hotel*

Bridge Street, Aberystwyth
Dyfed SY23 1QB
Tel: (0970) 612189

CATEGORIES

| 3 | 3 | 2 |

Family hotel under the personal supervision of the owners. Conveniently situated for shops, beach, station. Central heating, colour TV lounge, residential licence, separate bar. Single, double and family rooms, children welcome. Brochure available on request from Janet Smith.

C	B & B PER PERSON PER NIGHT		DINNER B & B PER PERSON PER WEEK		8
	MIN £	MAX £	MIN £	MAX £	OPEN
	5.50	7	57.50	65	1—12

Ashleys Hotel

Promenade, Aberystwyth
Dyfed
Tel: (0970) 617115

CATEGORIES

| 3 | 3 | 4 |

Superb seafront position. Full central heating throughout, sea view from bedrooms. Licensed restaurant and lounge bar. Showers in most rooms, TV lounge with sea view. Ample car parking. Coaching parties catered for. Highly recommended for good food and value for money. Colour brochure on request. Pets welcome.

T	B & B PER PERSON PER NIGHT		DINNER B & B PER PERSON PER WEEK		16
C	MIN £	MAX £	MIN £	MAX £	OPEN
	7	11	70	90	1—12

Bay Hotel*

The Promenade, Aberystwyth
Dyfed SY23 2BX
Tel: (0970) 617356

CATEGORIES

| 3 | 4 | 5 |

Finest position on promenade overlooking Cardigan Bay. Renowned for its good food. 40 Bedrooms, 6 en-suite, 15 with showers, most with colour TV and tea making facilities. Large car park. Free golf available, also other activity holidays available. Brochure on request. RAC.*

T	B & B PER PERSON PER NIGHT		DINNER B & B PER PERSON PER WEEK		40
C	MIN £	MAX £	MIN £	MAX £	OPEN
	13	15.50	112	125	1—12

Belle Vue Royal Hotel

Marine Terrace, Aberystwyth
Dyfed SY23 2BA
Tel: (0970) 617558

CATEGORIES

| 4 | 5 | 5 |

Situated in a premier position overlooking Cardigan Bay, the Belle Vue Royal is the ideal centre for tourists and family—conference, organisers, comfortable bedrooms. Superb food and friendly bars ensure a memorable stay. We look forward to welcoming you.

T	B & B PER PERSON PER NIGHT		DINNER B & B PER PERSON PER WEEK		42
C	MIN £	MAX £	MIN £	MAX £	OPEN
	12	15.50	125	147	1—12

Conrah Country Hotel*

Rhydgaled, Chancery
Aberystwyth, Dyfed SY23 4DF
Tel: (0970) 617941

CATEGORIES

| 5 | 4 | 4 |

An impressive country mansion standing in its own beautiful grounds, stylishly appointed to compliment the warmth of welcome and reputation of our chef. Heated indoor pool, sauna, cocktail bar, 2 lounges, most rooms en-suite with colour TV. Three miles south of Aberystwyth on the A487.

T	B & B PER PERSON PER NIGHT		DINNER B & B PER PERSON PER WEEK		22
C	MIN £	MAX £	MIN £	MAX £	OPEN
	14	23	135	210	1—12

Four Seasons Hotel*

50-54 Portland Street
Aberystwyth, Dyfed SY23 2DX
Tel: (0970) 612120

CATEGORIES

| 4 | 4 | 5 |

Situated in a quiet yet central part of town. Fully appointed bedrooms, some with private bathrooms, central heating throughout. Licensed restaurant with excellent cuisine, cocktail bar and separate TV lounge. Car parking on premises. Free golf Monday to Friday. Concessionary rate weekends. Ideal base for fishing and touring.

C	B & B PER PERSON PER NIGHT		DINNER B & B PER PERSON PER WEEK		17
	MIN £	MAX £	MIN £	MAX £	OPEN
	12	16	110	135	1—12

Glan Aber Hotel*

Union Street, Aberystwyth
Dyfed SY23 1NX
Tel: (0970) 617610

CATEGORIES

| 3 | 4 | 4 |

Glan Aber Hotel, Aberystwyth tel: 617610. A first class hotel noted for its comfort and excellent cuisine. Situated near main line rail and bus stations. Central heating, tea making facilities. All bedrooms fully appointed, comfortable, TV lounge, cocktail bar open all year. Resident proprietors RM and CJ Round. (No extra supplement for singles)

C	B & B PER PERSON PER NIGHT		DINNER B & B PER PERSON PER WEEK		14
	MIN £	MAX £	MIN £	MAX £	OPEN
	8.50	8.50	65	75	1—12

Groves Hotel*

North Parade, Aberystwyth
Dyfed SY23 2NF
Tel: (0970) 617623

CATEGORIES

| 4 | 4 | 4 |

The hotel has recently been refurbished throughout and now offers all bedrooms en-suite with colour TV, radio, and tea and coffee making facilities. Ideally located for shops, promenade and University with the countryside a few minutes away by car. Tapestry room restaurant open to non-residents, serving fresh produce with local trout dishes a speciality. A wide selection of bar snacks are served daily in the lounge bar. Car park, squash courts, available to residents and seafishing. Bargain breaks available.

T C	B & B PER PERSON PER NIGHT		DINNER B & B PER PERSON PER WEEK		12
	MIN £	MAX £	MIN £	MAX £	OPEN
	12	17	105	128	1—12

Llety Gwyn*

Llanbadarn Fawr, Aberystwyth
SY23 3SX
Tel: (0970) 3965

CATEGORIES

| 3 | 3 | 4 |

Country house on edge of town only 1½ miles to seafront and shopping centre. Some rooms en-suite. TV lounge, heating throughout hotel. Licensed, small dance floor available for functions/coach parties. Ample parking for all residents. All rooms on ground or first floor. Suitable for disabled. A warm Welsh welcome from the Jones family.

T C	B & B PER PERSON PER NIGHT		DINNER B & B PER PERSON PER WEEK		13
	MIN £	MAX £	MIN £	MAX £	OPEN
	7.50	9	82	89	1—12

Marine Hotel*

Promenade, Aberystwyth
Dyfed SY23 2DA
Tel: (0970) 2444

CATEGORIES

| 4 | 4 | 5 |

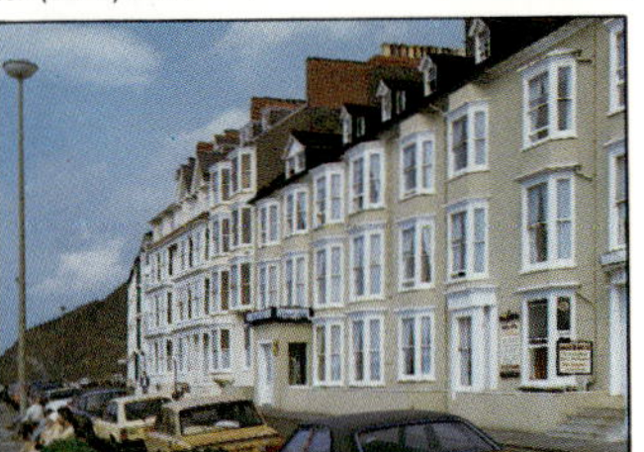

The hotel is situated in a central position on the promenade with superb views of Cardigan Bay. Well known for its excellent cuisine and service. Central heating, intercom and radios in all rooms, some en-suite. Welsh folk evening, ballroom dancing. Three bars, bar snacks, coaches catered for. Brochure on request.

T C	B & B PER PERSON PER NIGHT		DINNER B & B PER PERSON PER WEEK		25
	MIN £	MAX £	MIN £	MAX £	OPEN
	8	15	80	130	1—12

Manora Hotel*

North Parade, Aberystwyth
Dyfed
Tel: (0970) 615314

CATEGORIES

| 3 | 2 | 2 |

Good food and family-run hotel atmosphere, children very welcome. Full central heating, licensed, colour TV lounge. Centrally situated close to shops, beach pier, cinema, station. Personal attention and all the comforts of home from Don and Marion Lyon.

T C	B & B PER PERSON PER NIGHT		DINNER B & B PER PERSON PER WEEK		9
	MIN £	MAX £	MIN £	MAX £	OPEN
	7	8.50	70	80	1—12

Richmond Hotel*

44-45 Marine Terrace, Aberystwyth
Dyfed SY23 2BX
Tel: (0970) 612201

CATEGORIES

| 3 | 3 | 3 |

Central position on promenade, close to shops. This comfortable 25 bedroom hotel has a residential bar, full central heating, car park, two sea-front lounges, radio and tea-making facilities. Some en-suite. Choice of menu. Mini weekends and mid-week bookings also accepted.

T C	B & B PER PERSON PER NIGHT		DINNER B & B PER PERSON PER WEEK		25
	MIN £	MAX £	MIN £	MAX £	OPEN
	9	14	90	105	1—12

C	**Children stay at reduced rates, wherever you see this symbol.**

Bryn-y-Don*

36 Bridge Street, Aberystwyth
Dyfed SY23 1QB
Tel: (0970) 612011

CATEGORIES

| 2 | 2 | 2 |

A comfortable well situated guest house, central for shops, sea front only 3 minutes walk. Colour TV lounge. Full central heating in all rooms. Railway station close by. Pets and children welcome. A family-run guest house under the supervision of Mrs Evans.

T C	B & B PER PERSON PER NIGHT		DINNER B & B PER PERSON PER WEEK		5
	MIN £	MAX £	MIN £	MAX £	OPEN
	5.50	6.50	50	55	1—12

Garreg Lwyd

Penygarn, Bow Street
Nr Aberystwyth
Tel: (0970) 828 830

CATEGORIES

| 1 | 2 | 2 |

Central heating. Good and varied menu, separate tables in dining room, modern, convenient, 2 toilets, TV. 2 miles Borth and Clarach Bay, 3 miles Aberystwyth. Ample parking space, on main A487 road in the village of Bow Street. Closed Christmas. Quietly situated in its own grounds. Dinner, B&B per day rate £9.

C	B & B PER PERSON PER NIGHT		DINNER B & B PER PERSON PER WEEK		2
	MIN £	MAX £	MIN £	MAX £	OPEN
	6				1—12

Glyn-Garth Licensed Guest House*

South Road, Aberystywth
SY23 1JS
Tel: (0970) 615050

CATEGORIES

| 3 | 4 | 2 |

Glyn-Garth is situated adjacent to the South Promenade, near Harbour and Castle. All 12 bedrooms have hot and cold water, are centrally heated and have tea making facilities. Some have private toilet and shower. There is a large Dining Room, a comfortable TV Lounge, and a cosy Basement Bar. Ample toilets, shower and constant hot water. This family-run Guest House is noted for excellent food and service. Fire Certificate No. 27/R1. SAE for Terms and Brochure. Proprietor Mrs E. Evans. Not open Christmas period.

T C	B & B PER PERSON PER NIGHT		DINNER B & B PER PERSON PER WEEK		12
	MIN £	MAX £	MIN £	MAX £	OPEN
	7.50	8.50	76	82	1—12

Haulfryn Guest House

19 & 20 Thespian Street, Aberystwyth
Dyfed, Wales SY23 2JW
Tel: (0970) 615331

CATEGORIES: 2 2 1

Hot and cold water and shaving points in all bedrooms. Single, double, twin and family rooms with special rates for children. Lounge with colour television, central heating. Fire Certificate granted. Central to station, bus terminus, shops, sea and car park. Member of Aberystwyth and District Tourist Association. Open all year, except Christmas.

C	B & B PER PERSON PER NIGHT		DINNER B & B PER PERSON PER WEEK		8
	MIN £	MAX £	MIN £	MAX £	OPEN
	6	7			1—12

Hemstal Guest House*

69 North Parade, Aberystwyth
Dyfed SY23 2JN
Tel: (0970) 4398

CATEGORIES: 2 2 2

Family-run guest house. 3 minutes from seafront, located in town centre. Hot and cold water in all rooms. Central heating. Fire Precautions. TV lounge. Bed and breakfast rates with optional evening meal on very reasonable terms. Write or telephone for details. Guests personally cared for by proprietors, Jean and Elwyn Thomas.

C	B & B PER PERSON PER NIGHT		DINNER B & B PER PERSON PER WEEK		6
	MIN £	MAX £	MIN £	MAX £	OPEN
	6.50	8.50	69	75	1—12

Sunnymead Guest House*

34 Bridge Street, Aberystwyth
Dyfed SY23 1QB
Tel: (0970) 617273

CATEGORIES: 2 2 2

A family-run comfortable guest house with full central heating in all rooms. Colour TV lounge. Within minutes of all town amenities, shopping main street, one minute away. The pier, beach and amusements three minutes walk. A welcome awaits you from Jan and Windsor Morgan.

T / C	B & B PER PERSON PER NIGHT		DINNER B & B PER PERSON PER WEEK		8
	MIN £	MAX £	MIN £	MAX £	OPEN
	5.50	6	49	52.50	1—12

Swn-y-Don Residential Guest House

40-42 North Parade, Aberystwyth
Dyfed SY23 2NF
Tel: (0970) 612647

CATEGORIES: 3 2 3

Centrally situated in town. The emphasis is on good value, home comforts and good food. Large bar lounge. Colour TV lounge. Central heating throughout. Residents parking available. Seafront only three minutes walk away. Brochure on request from Mrs Ann Mary Owen-Evans.

T / C	B & B PER PERSON PER NIGHT		DINNER B & B PER PERSON PER WEEK		25
	MIN £	MAX £	MIN £	MAX £	OPEN
	9.20	10.35	96	120	1—12

Farmhouses

Brynarth Farm*

Lledrod, Near Aberystwyth
Dyfed, Wales SY23 4HX
Tel: (09743) 367

CATEGORIES: 4 3 3

This over 300 year old farm is set in picturesque countryside in the foothills of the Cambrian Mountains. Eight miles from Aberystwyth and the coast. Centrally heated bedrooms with private bath/shower. Sauna, games room, TV, snooker, table tennis. Swiss/French cuisine. Licensed. Pony-trekking 500 yards. Brochure on application.

T / C	B & B PER PERSON PER NIGHT		DINNER B & B PER PERSON PER WEEK		10
	MIN £	MAX £	MIN £	MAX £	OPEN
	10.50	10.50	94.50	94.50	4—10

Elgar Farm

Llandre, Bow Street, Aberystwyth
Dyfed SY24 5AS
Tel: (0970) 828384

CATEGORIES: 1 1 2

Elgar farm is situated in peaceful and pleasant surroundings 6 miles north of the town of Aberystwyth, 1½ miles off the main A487 road. Hot and cold water in double bedrooms. Guests are welcomed to roam around the 220 acres and enjoy the marvellous view of Cardigan Bay.

C	B & B PER PERSON PER NIGHT		DINNER B & B PER PERSON PER WEEK		3
	MIN £	MAX £	MIN £	MAX £	OPEN
	12	14	60	65	4—10

Neuadd Parc*

Capel Bangor, Aberystwyth
Dyfed SY23 3NA
Tel: (0970) 260

CATEGORIES: 1 2 2

Neuadd Parc is a 207 acre farm with pedigree Freisian cows and show ponies in the lovely Rheidiol Valley, 8 miles from Aberystwyth. It is a Victorian style farmhouse. Good farmhouse fare, salmon and trout fishing on the land. Sitting room, dining room, one bathroom, one toilet, one family room, one double room, one twin room. Ideal for bird watching.

C	B & B PER PERSON PER NIGHT		DINNER B & B PER PERSON PER WEEK		3
	MIN £	MAX £	MIN £	MAX £	OPEN
	6	6.50	52.50	56	4—9

Pantyperan Farm

Llandre, Bow Street
Abersystwyth SY24 5BS
Tel: (0970) 828321

CATEGORIES: 1 3 2

500 yards from the Rhyd-y-penau garage off the A487 road to Borth. Pantyperan is a 60 acre predominantly Dairy Farm, three miles from the golden sands of Borth, five miles from Aberystwyth. Bus stop outside farm gate. Good wholesome food, made from fresh produce. Children welcome. Welsh and English spoken. Contact Mrs Hughes for further details.

T / C	B & B PER PERSON PER NIGHT		DINNER B & B PER PERSON PER WEEK		2
	MIN £	MAX £	MIN £	MAX £	OPEN
	6.50	7.50	65	75	1—12

Rhosfawr Farm*

Blaenplwyf, Aberystwyth
Dyfed SY23 4DL
Tel: (0970) 617627

CATEGORIES: 1 2 2

180 acres mixed farm. Poultry, dogs and dairy, 4½ miles south of Aberystwyth. Take A487 to village of Blaenplwyf, turn first right after Post Office. Farm sign-posted. On bus route. Evening meal served 18.00 hours. Distance from nearest bus stop— 300 yards.

C	B & B PER PERSON PER NIGHT		DINNER B & B PER PERSON PER WEEK		3
	MIN £	MAX £	MIN £	MAX £	OPEN
	6.50	7	55	60	3—11

Wernddu*

Moriah, Capel Seion
Aberystwyth, Dyfed
Tel: (0970) 617855

CATEGORIES: 3 2 2

Wernddu has a modern farmhouse and 160 acres rearing sheep and cattle. Situated 3 miles from Aberystwyth, it is convenient to the beaches of Cardigan Bay and the lovely mountains and lakes of Mid Wales. Rough shooting on the farm with fishing and pony trekking nearby. Good farmhouse fare served.

T / C	B & B PER PERSON PER NIGHT		DINNER B & B PER PERSON PER WEEK		3
	MIN £	MAX £	MIN £	MAX £	OPEN
	7	7.50	75	82	4—10

Cestyll '83 – 1983 is the year of the castles.

Hotel and Inn

The Mill at Glynhir*

Llandybie, Ammanford
Dyfed SA18 2TE
Tel: (0269) 850672

CATEGORIES

| 4 | 3 | 3 |

A warm welcome awaits you at our quiet, secluded hotel—originally a XVIIc corn mill. Perched on valley side there are extensive views over Loughor river and towards Brecon Beacons National Park. Terms include: Free use of adjacent golf course, free use of indoor swimming pool and our own trout fishing.

T	B & B PER PERSON PER NIGHT		DINNER B & B PER PERSON PER WEEK		8
	MIN £	MAX £	MIN £	MAX £	OPEN
	18.60	18.60	120	155	2—11

Plough & Harrow Inn

Betws Road, Betws
Ammanford, Dyfed
Tel: (0269) 2189

CATEGORIES

| 1 | 1 | 2 |

Ideally situated for touring South West and Mid Wales. Small family run licensed village inn, just 6 miles M4 motorway. Fishing and golf nearby. Pony trekking. Weekends throughout the year. 1 mile town centre beer garden. Car park. Locally brewed beers, country parks and beaches short drive.

T C	B & B PER PERSON PER NIGHT		DINNER B & B PER PERSON PER WEEK		3
	MIN £	MAX £	MIN £	MAX £	OPEN
	5.50	6.75	56	64	1—12

Guest House

Herongate

Arthog, Gwynedd
LL39 1BJ
Tel: (0341) 250349

CATEGORIES

| 3 | 3 | 2 |

High class guest house situated at water's edge of beautiful Mawddach Estuary. Especially suitable for adults wanting a quiet holiday and good catering away from it all, in a lovely area. Hot and cold water and shaving point in every bedroom. Plenty of parking space.

C	B & B PER PERSON PER NIGHT		DINNER B & B PER PERSON PER WEEK		3
	MIN £	MAX £	MIN £	MAX £	OPEN
	6	7	70	77	5—9

Map ref: De2
As Welsh as the mountains that surround it, the town of Bala enjoys a beautiful setting beside its 4-mile loch, Llyn Tegid, or Bala Lake. Aran and Arenig mountains are mirrored in its waters, rippled by canoeists, dinghy sailors and occasional fishermen. The lake can be explored along its southern bank by the Bala Lake Narrow Gauge Railway.

Hotels and Inns

New Inn Hotel

Llangynog (Powys) near Bala
Mid Wales SY10 0EX
Tel: (069-174) 229

CATEGORIES

| 4 | 4 | 5 |

Ideal touring, walking, climbing, fishing and trekking holiday centre. Family-run hotel. Personal comfort and service. Open Christmas. Fire Certificate granted. Parking. Lounge TV, restaurant, bars, centrally heated. Situated foot of Berwyn Mountains, edge of Snowdonia, close to lakes Bala and Vyrnwy. River in grounds. Spectacular scenery.

T C	B & B PER PERSON PER NIGHT		DINNER B & B PER PERSON PER WEEK		7
	MIN £	MAX £	MIN £	MAX £	OPEN
	8.50	9.50	82.50	87.50	1—12

Plas Coch Hotel

Bala
Gwynedd
Tel: (0678) 520309

CATEGORIES

| 3 | 3 | 3 |

The hotel is privately owned, fully licensed and situated on the High Street of Bala. Resident lounge and full central heating. Natural touring centre for Snowdonia, seaside resorts, castles and narrow gauge railway. There is unbounded scope for fishermen, sailing and ramblers. Send for brochure and tariff.

C	B & B PER PERSON PER NIGHT		DINNER B & B PER PERSON PER WEEK		10
	MIN £	MAX £	MIN £	MAX £	OPEN
	15.08	17.25	103	110	1—12

White Lion Royal Hotel*

Bala, Gwynedd
LL23 7AE
Tel: (0678) 520314 Telex: 629462

CATEGORIES

| 2 | 3 | 5 |

The White Lion Royal Hotel is one of Wales' oldest inns. Enjoy good wholesome food and Welsh company in the fish bar with the locals. Close to Bala Lake, the largest natural lake in Wales. Ideal centre for walking, canoeing and sailing.

T C	B & B PER PERSON PER NIGHT		DINNER B & B PER PERSON PER WEEK		22
	MIN £	MAX £	MIN £	MAX £	OPEN
	18.50	20	87	90	1—12

Bryntirion Inn*

Llandderfel near Bala
Gwynedd
Tel: (06783) 205

CATEGORIES

| 3 | 3 | 5 |

Set in beautiful scenery overlooking the River Dee. This 17th century Inn has tastefully furnished accommodation with three licensed bars and first class restaurant. An ideal centre for walking, fishing, touring, pony trekking, golf etc. Write for brochure to resident proprietors, Harry and Pat Kelso. Open all year. Free house.

C	B & B PER PERSON PER NIGHT		DINNER B & B PER PERSON PER WEEK		3
	MIN £	MAX £	MIN £	MAX £	OPEN
	10	11			1—12

Guest Houses

Maes Awelon

Bala
Gwynedd
Tel: (06782) 520756

CATEGORIES

| 1 | 2 | 1 |

Bungalow in a beautiful position ¾ mile from Bala with views over the town. Bed and breakfast in a comfortable Welsh home. 4 bedrooms, including one double room, two single rooms (one with two beds) and one family room. No evening meals provided in June, July and August as there is excellent provision in Bala.

C	B & B PER PERSON PER NIGHT		DINNER B & B PER PERSON PER WEEK		4
	MIN £	MAX £	MIN £	MAX £	OPEN
	5	6			1—12

Plas Teg Guest House*

45 Tegid Street, Bala
Gwynedd LL23 7EN
Tel: (0678) 520268

CATEGORIES

| 3 | 3 | 2 |

Pleasantly situated on the outskirts of the charming little town of Bala and overlooking the lake. Ample parking facilities. Quiet and secluded position. Excellent food and service. AA* and RAC* listed. Licensed. Under the personal supervision of the proprietors, Mr and Mrs C. Reynolds.

C	B & B PER PERSON PER NIGHT		DINNER B & B PER PERSON PER WEEK		8
	MIN £	MAX £	MIN £	MAX £	OPEN
	8.75	8.75	86	86	1—12

Farmhouses

Bryn Melyn*

Enquiries: Mrs H. Edwards
Rhydychaf, Bala
Gwynedd LL23 79G
Tel: (0678) 520376

CATEGORIES

| 1 | 2 | 2 |

Bryn Melyn is situated in the beautiful county of Meirionnydd. Open all year. Home cooking and home-produced food make it home from home. Two double rooms, one twin bedroom, two with washbasin, two with private bathrooms. Sitting room. dining room. Central heating. No pets. Open log fire in winter.

C	B & B PER PERSON PER NIGHT		DINNER B & B PER PERSON PER WEEK		3
	MIN £	MAX £	MIN £	MAX £	OPEN
	5.50	6	54	56	1—12

Eirianfa*

Sarnau
Bala, Gwynedd
Tel: (06783) 389

CATEGORIES

| 1 | 2 | 2 |

Eirianfa is a mixed farm 4 miles from Bala on the A494. Good farmhouse food served. Ideal base for touring mountainous countryside. Also woollen mills, castles and other places of interest. 1 family, 1 double and 1 twin-bedded room, all with washbasins. Bathroom with shower. Sitting room, dining room. No dogs. SAE for terms of bed, breakfast and evening dinner.

C	B & B PER PERSON PER NIGHT		DINNER B & B PER PERSON PER WEEK		3
	MIN £	MAX £	MIN £	MAX £	OPEN
	6	7	60	62	3—11

Erw Feurig*

Cefnddwysarn
Bala, Gwynedd
Tel: (06783) 262

CATEGORIES

| 3 | 3 | 2 |

Facing the beautiful Berwyn Mountains, this hill farm guest house is ideally situated for touring mountains, lakes and seaside. Excellent home cooked food served and guests are assured of every comfort. Family, double and twin bedrooms with full central heating. Fire Certificate held. Private trout lake on farm.

C	B & B PER PERSON PER NIGHT		DINNER B & B PER PERSON PER WEEK		4
	MIN £	MAX £	MIN £	MAX £	OPEN
	6.50	7	60	62	3—11

Penybryn Sarnau*

Bala
Gwynedd LL23 7LH
Tel: (06783) 297

CATEGORIES

| 2 | 2 | 2 |

Excellent touring base, highly recommended for its food, on a farm overlooking the charming Dee Valley, ample parking. Free fishing on private lake. Recreational facilities in the vicinity. Within 3 miles of Bala and its famous lake. All modern facilities available.

C	B & B PER PERSON PER NIGHT		DINNER B & B PER PERSON PER WEEK		6
	MIN £	MAX £	MIN £	MAX £	OPEN
	6	7	59	63	3—10

Talybont Isa*

Rhyduchaf
Bala, Gwynedd
Tel: (0678) 520234

CATEGORIES

| 2 | 2 | 2 |

Modern farmhouse with wash basins in all bedrooms. Lounge with colour TV. Ground floor, bathroom and toilet, shower and toilet upstairs. All home cooking. Visitors welcome to see variety of animals in farmyard. Ideal centre for touring north Wales.

C	B & B PER PERSON PER NIGHT		DINNER B & B PER PERSON PER WEEK		3
	MIN £	MAX £	MIN £	MAX £	OPEN
	6.50	7.50	55	60	4—10

Tynyffordd*

Rhyd Uchaf, Bala
Gwynedd LL23 7SB
Tel: (0678) 520545

CATEGORIES

| 1 | 2 | 2 |

Recently modernised farmhouse enjoying panoramic views of the surrounding countryside. 36 acre farm, part of a unit. The other unit is a sheep farm situated on the slopes of Arenig Mountain, where guests may visit. 1¼ miles from Bala. Turn left for sign post Rhyd Uchaf, continue for 1 mile, farm on left 200 yards from road S/P.

C	B & B PER PERSON PER NIGHT		DINNER B & B PER PERSON PER WEEK		2
	MIN £	MAX £	MIN £	MAX £	OPEN
	6		58		4—10

Hotel

British Hotel

High Street, Bangor
Gwynedd LL57 1NP
Tel: (0248) 4911

CATEGORIES

| 5 | 5 | 5 |

Situated in centre of town, convenient to main railway station and buses. All bedrooms with private bath, telephone and radio. TV to order. Dining room. Open all year. Butter bar open for lunch and dinner. RAC.*** Fire Certificate granted.

C	B & B PER PERSON PER NIGHT		DINNER B & B PER PERSON PER WEEK		53
	MIN £	MAX £	MIN £	MAX £	OPEN
	14	15	126	140	1—12

Farmhouse

Tros y Waen Holiday Farm*

Pentir, Bangor
Gwynedd LL57 4EF
Tel: (0248) 4448

CATEGORIES

| 1 | 3 | 2 |

On entering the drive of our farm, the steam of the Little Train which climbs to the summit of Snowdon can be clearly seen at certain times of the day. The farm itself, has plenty to offer, especially to children, who can join in activities, depending on season. Within a radius of approximately 7 miles, many well-known places can be visited, either sea, mountain or town.

T C	B & B PER PERSON PER NIGHT		DINNER B & B PER PERSON PER WEEK		4
	MIN £	MAX £	MIN £	MAX £	OPEN
	7	7.50	75	82	1—12

Tourist Information Centres are listed at back of book.

Barmouth

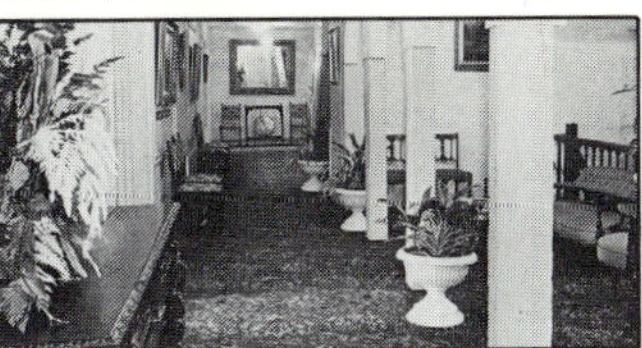

Map ref: Da4

If its rival is Queen, Barmouth must be Prince Charming of the Cardigan Coast resorts. Admired by artists for its glorious setting on Mawddach Estuary, the town is one of the liveliest for the young set along that part of the coast. Panoramas unfold from its hills—of estuary, mountains, sea and sky. Miles of golden sands extend north towards Harlech. Little wonder it has fine hotels and good eating places.

Hotels

Bryn Melyn Hotel*

Panorama Road, Barmouth
Gwynedd LL42 1DQ
Tel: (0341) 280556

CATEGORIES

| 3 | 3 | 3 |

Small family hotel with residential licence. Most rooms will have private facilities for 1983. Set in rural surroundings in the quietest area of Barmouth with views across the Mawddach Estuary to Cader Idris Mountain. Central heating, parking. Friendly personal service by the resident proprietors Carol and David Clay.

	B & B PER PERSON PER NIGHT		DINNER B & B PER PERSON PER WEEK		🛏 10
T **C**	MIN £	MAX £	MIN £	MAX £	OPEN
	9.50		89	99	4—11

Cors-y-Gedol Hotel*

High Street, Barmouth
Gwynedd, Wales LL42 1DP
Tel: (0341) 280402

CATEGORIES

| 4 | 4 | 5 |

Two star AA RAC Hotel. Originally a 17th century coaching inn, centrally situated, 300 m from beach. First class cuisine, comfort and personal service. Beautiful bedrooms, all with colour TV radio, tea/coffee facilities, central heating. Private coach/car park, lift, entertainment, sauna/solarium, three lounges, three bars. Superb beaches, sea views, magnificent mountains, marvellous Mawddach Estuary, delightful harbour. Hotel surroundings suitable for senior citizens and disabled. Excellent centre for touring. Out of season bargain breaks. Christmas programme, reduced terms for children. Free colour brochure on request.

	B & B PER PERSON PER NIGHT		DINNER B & B PER PERSON PER WEEK		🛏 25
T **C**	MIN £	MAX £	MIN £	MAX £	OPEN
	15	16.50	140	175	1—12

Marine Mansion Hotel*

Promenade, Barmouth
Gwynedd LL42 1NE
Tel: (0341) 280459

CATEGORIES

| 4 | 4 | 4 |

Beach front hotel situated next to the golden sands of Barmouth Beach. Many bedrooms with private bathrooms en-suite. 50% reductions for children sharing with parents in family rooms. Residential licence. Music and dancing to live entertainment during season. Games room. Centrally heated. Fire Certificate. Private car park.

	B & B PER PERSON PER NIGHT		DINNER B & B PER PERSON PER WEEK		🛏 30
T **C**	MIN £	MAX £	MIN £	MAX £	OPEN
	11.50	17.50	90	125	3—10

Min-y-Mor Hotel*

The Promenade, Barmouth
Gwynedd LL42 1HW
Tel: (0341) 280555

CATEGORIES

| 3 | 3 | 4 |

Situated in own grounds, an unrivalled position on sea front. We aim to offer cleanliness, comfortable beds and good food. Separate TV lounge. Bar is fully licensed with bar food served also children's room and play area. Ample parking space. Brochure from Mr and Mrs A. H. Williams.

	B & B PER PERSON PER NIGHT		DINNER B & B PER PERSON PER WEEK		🛏 55
C	MIN £	MAX £	MIN £	MAX £	OPEN
	8.50		101		1—12

Plas Mynach Castle Country House Hotel*

Llanaber Road, Barmouth
Gwynedd LL42 1YL
Tel: (0341) 280252

CATEGORIES

| 3 | 3 | 4 |

Standing in beautiful wooded grounds with superb views of sea and mountain in one of the finest positions on the Welsh Coast. It offers good food, fine wine and comfort. Restaurant, residential licence. Parking. Centre for climbing, walking, fishing and rough shooting. Beach path. Log fires. Brochure: Barmouth 280252.

	B & B PER PERSON PER NIGHT		DINNER B & B PER PERSON PER WEEK		🛏 15
T **C**	MIN £	MAX £	MIN £	MAX £	OPEN
	9.77	12.07	112.70	128.80	1—12

This symbol means you can book through your local travel agent.

Royal Hotel*

King Edward Street
Barmouth, Gwynedd
Tel: (0341) 280383

CATEGORIES

| 3 | 3 | 5 |

Situated a three minutes walk from glorious beaches. Central for golf, fishing, pony trekking, walking and touring Snowdonia. All rooms have private facilities. Colour television, lounge, games room, two licensed bars. Resident proprietor chef. Special rates for children. Adjacent car park. 10% reduction for three nights minimum stay.

C	B & B PER PERSON PER NIGHT		DINNER B & B PER PERSON PER WEEK		16
	MIN £	MAX £	MIN £	MAX £	OPEN
	12.50	15.50	120.40	133	4—10

Tyr Graig Castle Hotel*

Llanaber Road, Barmouth
Gwynedd LL42 1YN
Tel: (0341) 280470

CATEGORIES

| 3 | 4 | 4 |

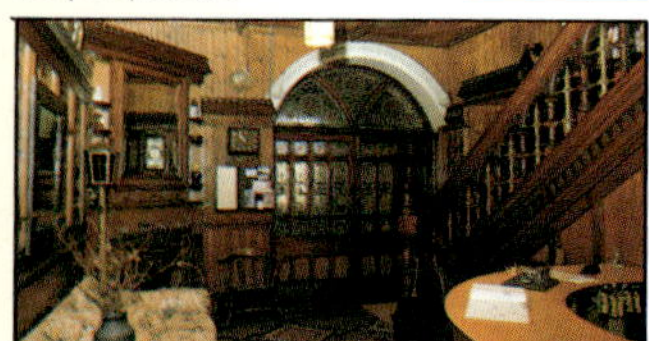

An hotel standing in its own grounds, overlooking Barmouth Bay. RAC* AA* noted for comfort and home cooking under the personal supervision of the owners. Restaurant and residential licence. Most bedrooms overlook the sea, some have showers. The Victorian Lounge and dining room afford magnificent views of the Bay as does the secluded terrace. Ample parking in grounds. Full central heating. Special terms for children. SAE or telephone for brochure. Mr & Mrs D. C. Wright.

C	B & B PER PERSON PER NIGHT		DINNER B & B PER PERSON PER WEEK		12
	MIN £	MAX £	MIN £	MAX £	OPEN
	8.50	10	84	101.50	2—10

Guest Houses

Cartrefle

Llanaber, Barmouth
Gwynedd LL42 1AJ
Tel: (0341) 280596

CATEGORIES

| 2 | 3 | 2 |

Overlooking Cardigan Bay, set in own grounds. One and a half miles from Barmouth. homely atmosphere with excellent home cooking. Car parking on forecourt. Fire Certificate held. 1982 rates B & B per person per night £6; Dinner, B & B £8.50 per person per night.

C	B & B PER PERSON PER NIGHT		DINNER B & B PER PERSON PER WEEK		6
	MIN £	MAX £	MIN £	MAX £	OPEN
					3—10

Lawrenny Lodge*

Barmouth
Gwynedd LL42 1SU
Tel: (0341) 280466

CATEGORIES

| 2 | 3 | 2 |

An attractive guest house overlooking the harbour and mouth of the beautiful Mawddach Estuary. Ample parking. Residential licence. Fire Certificate held. We offer you a standard of comfort and service and a quality of food which we are confident will please you.

T	B & B PER PERSON PER NIGHT		DINNER B & B PER PERSON PER WEEK		10
C	MIN £	MAX £	MIN £	MAX £	OPEN
		8.05		82.80	4—10

Wavecrest

8 Marine Parade, Barmouth
Gwynedd LL42 1NA
Tel: (0341) 280330

CATEGORIES

| 3 | 3 | 2 |

A family-run guest house, with a friendly, comfortable and relaxed atmosphere. Situated on the promenade with magnificent views of sea and mountains. Single, double and family rooms; some with private shower. Central heating, large colour television lounge. Package Little Trains, golf and "Castles '83" holidays catered for.

C	B & B PER PERSON PER NIGHT		DINNER B & B PER PERSON PER WEEK		10
	MIN £	MAX £	MIN £	MAX £	OPEN
	7	7.50	65		3—12

Barry

SOUTH WALES

Hotels, Motels and Inns

Aberthaw House*

Porthkerry Road, Barry
South Glamorgan CF6 8AX
Tel: (0446) 737314

CATEGORIES

| 3 | 4 | 5 |

Aberthaw House is a small licensed hotel providing good accommodation with excellent food. All rooms have hot and cold water, tea and coffee facilities and clock radios. Family rooms have TV. Lounge with colour television available all day. Whispers Restaurant with à la carte menu is also available for guests and now residents.

T	B & B PER PERSON PER NIGHT		DINNER B & B PER PERSON PER WEEK		5
C	MIN £	MAX £	MIN £	MAX £	OPEN
	10	13	85	105	1—12

Mount Sorrel Hotel

Porthkerry Road, Barry
South Glamorgan CF6 8AY
Tel: (0446) 740069

CATEGORIES

| 5 | 5 | 5 |

Situated close to beaches, Cardiff. 8 miles Cardiff Airport, 3 miles close to Porthkerry Country Park. Fully licensed with reputation for good food, regular Dinner/Dances every Saturday. Rooms with colour TV. Children welcome. The ideal holiday touring centre for the whole of South Wales. Egon Ronay recommended.

T	B & B PER PERSON PER NIGHT		DINNER B & B PER PERSON PER WEEK		37
C	MIN £	MAX £	MIN £	MAX £	OPEN
	20	22	150	200	1—12

Guest Houses

Maytree*

9 The Parade, Barry
South Glamorgan
Tel: (0446) 734075

CATEGORIES

| 2 | 2 | 1 |

Overlooking park and old harbour, and within easy walking distance of all beaches and restaurants. AA and RAC listed.

T	B & B PER PERSON PER NIGHT		DINNER B & B PER PERSON PER WEEK		5
C	MIN £	MAX £	MIN £	MAX £	OPEN
	6	10			1—12

Parkstone Guest House*

Park Avenue
Barry 6F6 8RL
Tel: 734812

CATEGORIES

| 3 | 3 | 1 |

Parkstone Guest House, Park Avenue, Barry. Large detached house overlooking sea. Large garden, central heating in all rooms. Full Fire Certificate. Colour television in lounge. Car parking space. Ideal for beaches, buses, trains and touring the Vale of Glamorgan.

C	B & B PER PERSON PER NIGHT		DINNER B & B PER PERSON PER WEEK		8
	MIN £	MAX £	MIN £	MAX £	OPEN
	6	7			1—12

Hotels

Henllys Hall*

Beaumaris, Isle of Anglesey
LL58 8AR
Tel: (0248) 810412

CATEGORIES

6	4	6

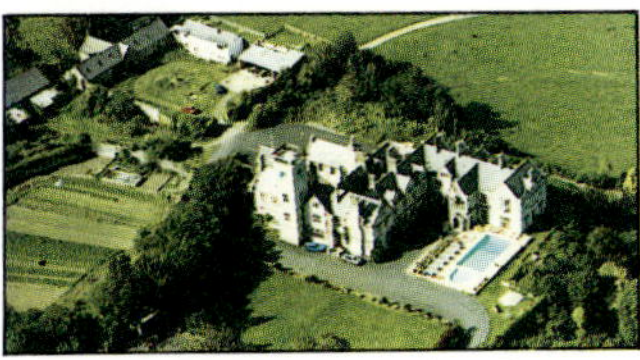

Country Manor House set in 50 acres. Excellent views of Snowdonia, near yachting centre. Golf and fishing nearby. Special Sunday to Friday, Dinner, bed and breakfast rate of £75 complete. Childrens reductions. 4 poster beds. Honeymoon weekends with champagne. Castle Storming and Fawlty Towers weekends. Health place with sauna, Jacuzzi, sun beds, heated outdoor pool and tennis court.

	B & B PER PERSON PER NIGHT		DINNER B & B PER PERSON PER WEEK		22
T **C**	MIN £	MAX £	MIN £	MAX £	OPEN
	14	16	112	130	1—12

White Lion Hotel

Castle Square, Beaumaris
Anglesey, Gwynedd LL58 8DA
Tel: (0248) 810589

CATEGORIES

3	4	4

Family hotel with two bars and restaurant adjacent to Beaumaris Castle on the shores of the Menai Strait. A friendly atmosphere with a nautical flavour—ideal for places of interest, sporting facilities or just relaxing on the numerous secluded sandy beaches. Parking available close by. Fire Certificate granted.

	B & B PER PERSON PER NIGHT		DINNER B & B PER PERSON PER WEEK		8
C	MIN £	MAX £	MIN £	MAX £	OPEN
	9.80	9.80	93.10	96.60	1—12

Guest House

Seaview Guest House

West End, Beaumaris, Anglesey
North Wales LL58 8BG
Tel: (0248) 810384

CATEGORIES

3	2	2

Within walking distance of the historic town of Beaumaris. Golf course and fishing. Ideal centre for touring North Wales and Snowdonia. Panoramic views overlooking Menai Strait and Snowdonia. Hot water and shaver points all rooms. Fire Certificate granted. Under personal supervision of proprietor.

	B & B PER PERSON PER NIGHT		DINNER B & B PER PERSON PER WEEK		6
	MIN £	MAX £	MIN £	MAX £	OPEN
	6	7	70	70	1—12

Farmhouse

Dinmor

Penmon, Beaumaris
Anglesey LL58 8SN
Tel: (0248) 78395

CATEGORIES

2	2	1

Dinmor is a smallholding with panoramic views over Snowdonia, 3½ miles from Beaumaris. 2 family rooms with hot and cold water. Open fire in sitting room, full central heating, colour TV available. Free range eggs. Home baked bread. Fishing, walking, bird watching.

	B & B PER PERSON PER NIGHT		DINNER B & B PER PERSON PER WEEK		2
C	MIN £	MAX £	MIN £	MAX £	OPEN
	6.50	6.50			1—12

Map ref: Ae5
Nestling deep beside the Glaslyn river, surrounded by towering mountains, the village of Beddgelert is picture-postcard attractive. Nearby are forest and hill walks and attractive, still lakes that reflect the colours of the seasons.

Hotels

Bryn Eglwys Country House Hotel*

Beddgelert
Gwynedd LL55 4NB
Tel: (076 686) 210

CATEGORIES

3	4	5

In the heart of Snowdonia in own grounds, overlooking River Glaslyn. Ideally situated for walking, climbing, fishing, canoeing, pony trekking, golf, touring of coast. Hot and cold water, central heating. Lounge, attractive bar, TV room. Open all year. Excellent cuisine under the personal supervision of the resident proprietor, Mrs C. E. Barton

	B & B PER PERSON PER NIGHT		DINNER B & B PER PERSON PER WEEK		10
T **C**	MIN £	MAX £	MIN £	MAX £	OPEN
	10	12	95	105	1—12

Prince Llewelyn Hotel

Beddgelert
Gwynedd
Tel: (076 686) 242

CATEGORIES

3	3	4

This hotel bears the name of the famous Welsh Prince, who according to legend, killed his faithful hound, Gelert, believing the dog to have killed his son, when in fact it had slain a wolf to protect his child. (The dogs reputed grave is just a short walk away). Residents bar and dining room, Bar-Dine. Packed lunches. Ideal base for walking, fishing, climbing, pony trekking or just motor touring around the scenic Snowdonia National Park. For just relaxing, the hotel has a lovely Alpine garden and patio area. No dogs accommodated, no television.

	B & B PER PERSON PER NIGHT		DINNER B & B PER PERSON PER WEEK		10
C	MIN £	MAX £	MIN £	MAX £	OPEN
	10	12			1—12

> # Cestyll '83 – 1983 is the year of the castles.

The Royal Goat Hotel*

Beddgelert
Gwynedd, North Wales LL55 4YE
Tel: (076 686) 224

CATEGORIES: 4 4 5

Ideally situated for golf, fishing, climbing, walking and touring Snowdonia. The hotel has full central heating, large newly decorated bedrooms (most of which have private bathrooms). Colour TV, lounge, two bars and restaurants offering extensive table d'hôte and à la carte menus. Large car park.

T C	B & B PER PERSON PER NIGHT		DINNER B & B PER PERSON PER WEEK		29
	MIN £	MAX £	MIN £	MAX £	OPEN
	14.50	16	137	147.50	1—12

The Saracen's Head Hotel

Beddgelert
Gwynedd
Tel: (076 686) 223

CATEGORIES: 3 3 4

An attractive hotel situated near the Snowdonia village Famous for its legend of 'Gelert', the Dog. Conveniently placed for a variety of outdoor activities—fishing on lake Dinas and the river Glaslyn, walking and mountaineering in the Snowdonia national park, motor touring, canoeing and wind-surfing on nearby lakes. The hotel itself offers excellent cuisine in its licensed restaurant. Licensed bars. Car parking. An excellent base for a quiet relaxing holiday. Open all year.

C	B & B PER PERSON PER NIGHT		DINNER B & B PER PERSON PER WEEK		18
	MIN £	MAX £	MIN £	MAX £	OPEN
	12	14			1—12

Sygun Fawr Country House Hotel*

Beddgelert, Gwynedd
North Wales LL55 4NE
Tel: (076 686) 258

CATEGORIES: 4 3 2

A 17th century Welsh Manor house situated within 22 acres of private land, commanding magnificent views of the Gwynant Valley and Snowdon range. 7 bedrooms, tariff for bed and breakfast from £11.50 per person. Resident proprietors, Norman and Peggy Wilson.

C	B & B PER PERSON PER NIGHT		DINNER B & B PER PERSON PER WEEK		7
	MIN £	MAX £	MIN £	MAX £	OPEN
	11.50	12.50	108	117	1—12

Tanronen Hotel

Beddgelert
Gwynedd LL55 4YB
Tel: (076 686) 347

CATEGORIES: 3 3 4

Situated at the head of the magnificent Glaslyn Pass amidst grandeur. Mountains, rushing streams, placid lakes, deep forests, all are here in abundance. The hotel is fully centrally heated. Excellent cuisine. TV lounge, coffee lounge, two intimate little bars make it the ideal place for an enjoyable holiday.

C	B & B PER PERSON PER NIGHT		DINNER B & B PER PERSON PER WEEK		10
	MIN £	MAX £	MIN £	MAX £	OPEN
	11	12.50	102	112	1—12

This symbol means you can book through your local travel agent.

T

Guest Houses

"Colwyn"*

Beddgelert
Gwynedd
Tel: (076 686) 276

CATEGORIES: 3 3 4

Miniature licenced hotel with a log fire in our 18th century beamed lounge. Super food (so we're told). In the Snowdon mountains but only 8m from lovely beaches. Mountain views and a river outside the door. Reduced rates over 3 days. Walk, tour, bathe, or just laze. Open all year. Central heating. New owners: Joan and John Lester.

C	B & B PER PERSON PER NIGHT		DINNER B & B PER PERSON PER WEEK		5
	MIN £	MAX £	MIN £	MAX £	OPEN
	7	9	84	105	1—12

Llety Plas Gwyn Guest House

Beddgelert, Caernarfon
Gwynedd LL55 4UY
Tel: (076 686) 413

CATEGORIES: 3 2 2

In the heart of Snowdonia yet within 20 minutes of a glorious sandy beach. Heating, hot and cold water. Shaver points and small television in all bedrooms. Plenty of food and a real Welsh welcome. Dining room with separate tables. Special children's rates. Own keys. Fire Certificate granted.

C	B & B PER PERSON PER NIGHT		DINNER B & B PER PERSON PER WEEK		4
	MIN £	MAX £	MIN £	MAX £	OPEN
	6	7	60	70	3—10

Plas Colwyn Guest House*

Plas Colwyn
Beddgelert Gwynedd
Tel: (076 686) 458

CATEGORIES: 3 3 3

Hot and cold water, shaver points and small TV in all bedrooms. Single, double and family rooms. Special rates for children. Fire Certificate granted. Full central heating. Snacks served until 10.30 pm; dinner served at 7 pm. Special rates for parties. Ideally suited for walking, pony trekking and touring Snowdonia.

T C	B & B PER PERSON PER NIGHT		DINNER B & B PER PERSON PER WEEK		5
	MIN £	MAX £	MIN £	MAX £	OPEN
	6	7	60	68	1—12

Plas Tan-y-Graig

Beddgelert
Gwynedd LL55 4LT
Tel: (076 686) 329

CATEGORIES: 3 2 1

Very well appointed and comfortable guest house in a magnificent position, overlooking the river in probably the prettiest village in Snowdonia. Residents lounge with TV. Fire Certificate, full central heating, drying facilities, two shower rooms in addition to bathroom. Full English breakfast.

C	B & B PER PERSON PER NIGHT		DINNER B & B PER PERSON PER WEEK		6
	MIN £	MAX £	MIN £	MAX £	OPEN
	8	10			4—10

Farmhouse

Cae Ddafydd Farm Wild Life Sanctuary

Llanfrothen, Penrhyndeudraeth
Gwynedd LL48 6SN
Tel: (076 686) 213

CATEGORIES: 2 3 3

Sheep farm, wildlife sanctuary, with pottery, woodturning and goats, pheasants, peafowl. Also donkeys, Jack Russel Terrier stud. We like guests to become integrated and part of the family, while they are here. Riding arranged and fishing possible. Glorious walks and private quiet places. Ideal for painting.

C	B & B PER PERSON PER NIGHT		DINNER B & B PER PERSON PER WEEK		3
	MIN £	MAX £	MIN £	MAX £	OPEN
	5.50	6	60.50		1—12

Hotel

Manian Lodge*

Begelly, Kilgetty
Dyfed SA68 0XE
Tel: (0834) 813273

CATEGORIES: 3 3 3

Family hotel ideally placed for enjoying Pembrokeshire's glorious coastline. Six miles to Tenby, 2½ miles from Saundersfoot and within easy reach of numerous sandy beaches. All rooms with shower and toilet. Three with separate childrens bedroom. Excellent cuisine. Residential licence, TV lounge. Extensive grounds. Pet donkey to ride, pool table.

C	B & B PER PERSON PER NIGHT		DINNER B & B PER PERSON PER WEEK		7
	MIN £	MAX £	MIN £	MAX £	OPEN
	7	10	65	80	5—9

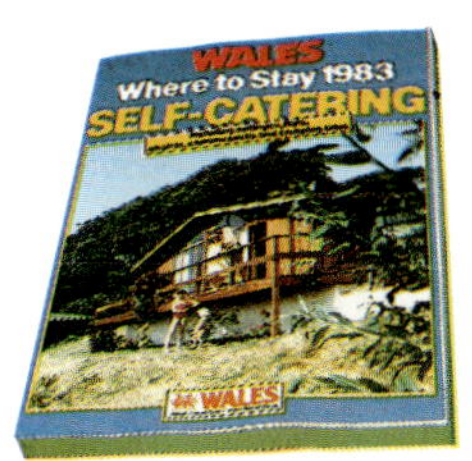

Pamper yourself on your main Wales holiday this year. But when you come back for that second, short break later in the year, remember we have a sister publication to this one. It's called "Where to Stay 1983 – Self Catering". Let us send you a copy. Details at back of book.

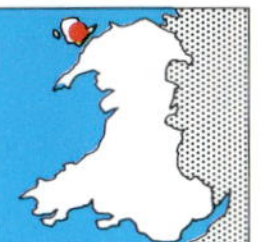

Map ref: Ad2
Sandy beaches, rural countryside, the eastern side of the Isle of Anglesey is pure holiday country. Benllech Bay is ideal for the family holidaymaker, for the fisherman and sailor, and for those who want the novelty of island life—albeit connected by two hefty bridges to mainland Snowdonia.

Hotels

Bay Court Hotel*

Beach Road, Benllech Bay
Isle of Anglesey, Gwynedd LL74
Tel: (0248) 852573/852606

CATEGORIES: 4 4 5

Modern centrally heated hotel. Delightfully situated 200 yards from Benllech's sandy beach. The informal friendly atmosphere is one of its key notes. With two comfortable fully licensed bars, coloured TV lounge. Well appointed bedrooms and dining room overlooking the Bay. The hotel is ideal for all the family.

C	B & B PER PERSON PER NIGHT		DINNER B & B PER PERSON PER WEEK		23
	MIN £	MAX £	MIN £	MAX £	OPEN
	12	16	110	120	1—12

The Hafodwyn*

Tynygongl, Benllech Bay
Isle of Anglesey LL74 8SD
Tel: (0248) 852357

CATEGORIES: 3 3 5

Open all year. All rooms en-suite. Children welcome. All rooms equipped with teasmades. Large air conditioned bar restaurant with dance floor. Residents lounge with colour TV. Larger separate lounge with ample comfortable seating. Elderly relatives welcome any time unaccompanied. Under the personal supervision of Stella and David French.

C	B & B PER PERSON PER NIGHT		DINNER B & B PER PERSON PER WEEK		8
	MIN £	MAX £	MIN £	MAX £	OPEN
	12		16		1—12

Rhostrefor Hotel

Benllech Bay, Isle of Anglesey
North Wales LL74 8SR
Tel: (0248) 852347

CATEGORIES: 3 4 5

Set in one acre of gardens overlooking the beautiful Benllech Bay, only minutes away from the activities of the beach. Fully modernised, offering many en-suite bedrooms where children are welcome. Family suites available. One of the finest à la carte restaurants on the Island. Easy parking. Golf, sailing, riding available. Disabled guests welcomed. Dinner rate reflects table d'hote menu.

T C	B & B PER PERSON PER NIGHT		DINNER B & B PER PERSON PER WEEK		12
	MIN £	MAX £	MIN £	MAX £	OPEN
	11	12.50	96.50	101.50	1—12

Wilma Lodge Private Hotel*

Bay View Road, Benllech
Isle of Anglesey, Gwynedd LL74 7TW
Tel: (0248) 852367

CATEGORIES: 3 3 4

Family run private hotel, five minutes from beach. Ideally located for touring the island and Snowdonia. Bar, TV, and quiet lounges. All rooms with hot and cold water. Some private bathrooms or showers. Children welcome and reduced rates available. Car parking. No service charge. Access and Visa facilities.

C	B & B PER PERSON PER NIGHT		DINNER B & B PER PERSON PER WEEK		12
	MIN £	MAX £	MIN £	MAX £	OPEN
	9.20	10.50	95	105.50	1—12

For autumn to spring breaks send for our free Great Little Breaks booklet.

Guest Houses

Traeth Arian*

Fern Hill, Benllech Bay
Isle of Anglesey, Gwynedd LL74 8UE
Tel: (024874) 2635
(To be altered to (024885)

CATEGORIES: 3 3 5

Traeth Arian was built during the reign of the Prince Regent (about 1830). Overlooking Benllech Bay secluded but close to the village. It is adapted to a high standard of comfort. We offer our guests consideration and courtesy, together with good quality food at reasonable prices. Licensed. B & B £8.50.

C	B & B PER PERSON PER NIGHT		DINNER B & B PER PERSON PER WEEK		5
	MIN £	MAX £	MIN £	MAX £	OPEN
	8.50	12.75			5—9

The Woodlands Guest House

Bangor Road, Benllech, Anglesey
Gwynedd LL74 8PU
Tel: (0248) 852735

CATEGORIES: 3 3 3

Situated between Benllech and Red Wharf bays. Recently refurbished and centrally heated throughout. Large car park and garden with magnificent sea-views. Residents bar, TV lounge, dining room with separate tables, games room. Single, double and family rooms with children's reductions. Special early/late season breaks.

C	B & B PER PERSON PER NIGHT		DINNER B & B PER PERSON PER WEEK		6
	MIN £	MAX £	MIN £	MAX £	OPEN
	7	8	70	77	12—10

Berriew

MID WALES

Farmhouse

Upper Pandy Farm*

Berriew, Welshpool
Powys SY21 8PW
Tel: (068685) 338

FARMHOUSE AWARD

CATEGORIES: 1 1 2

Upper Pandy Farm welcomes guests from Easter to October. One family unit, one double or twin bedded room. Children welcome. Good home produced food is served. Colour TV. Guests are free to come and go as they wish. Washbasins in bedrooms and shaving points. Heating in bedrooms.

C	B & B PER PERSON PER NIGHT		DINNER B & B PER PERSON PER WEEK		2
	MIN £	MAX £	MIN £	MAX £	OPEN
	6.50	7	63	66.50	4—10

Bethesda

NORTH WALES

Farmhouse

Maes Caradog Farm*

Nant Ffrancon, Bethesda,
Gwynedd LL57 3DQ
Tel: (0248) 600266

CATEGORIES: 2 2 2

Farmhouse, with all modern amenities, ideally situated for touring the Isle of Anglesey, Snowdonia and the North Wales coast. Bedrooms with hot and cold water. Good home cooking. Reduced rates for children. Full central heating, fitted carpets throughout. Car parking on forecourt.

C	B & B PER PERSON PER NIGHT		DINNER B & B PER PERSON PER WEEK		2
	MIN £	MAX £	MIN £	MAX £	OPEN
	5	5.50	51.80	54	1—12

Bethlehem

SOUTH WALES

Farmhouse

Rhuadymon*

Bethlehem, Llandeilo
Dyfed SA19 6YW
Tel: (0558) 823465

CATEGORIES: 3 3 2

Good home cooking our speciality in this lovely old farmhouse. Superb position Brecon Beacons National Park, unspoilt countryside, mountains, lakes, castles. Twin or single rooms, private bathrooms available. Comfortable sitting room with TV, dining room with separate tables. Central heating, log fires, games room, garden. Car essential.

C	B & B PER PERSON PER NIGHT		DINNER B & B PER PERSON PER WEEK		4
	MIN £	MAX £	MIN £	MAX £	OPEN
	6	6	65	65	1—12

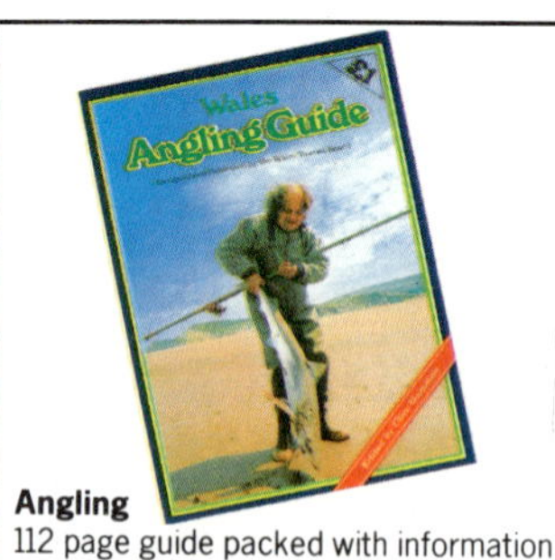

Angling

112 page guide packed with information and advice for visiting sea, game and coarse fishermen.
Available from: Wales Tourist Board Department W.T.S. P.O. Box 1, CARDIFF CF1 2XN. Price: £1.25p including postage and packing.

Betws Garmon

NORTH WALES

Hotel

Castell Cidwm Hotel*

Betws Garmon, Caernarfon
Gwynedd LL54 7YT
Tel: (028685) 243

CATEGORIES: 3 4 4

Family-run lakeside hotel, beautifully situated at the foot of Snowdon. On the banks of Llyn Cwellyn. Licensed bar, excellent cuisine. Sun lounge, hot and cold water throughout. Central heating in all rooms. Boating, windsurfing, fishing at hotel. Pony trekking arranged locally. Open all year. Ideal touring centre for all.

C	B & B PER PERSON PER NIGHT		DINNER B & B PER PERSON PER WEEK		7
	MIN £	MAX £	MIN £	MAX £	OPEN
	10	11	110	120	1—12

Betws y Coed

NORTH WALES

Map ref: Bb6
'Bead house in the wood'—the church in the wood—is said to be the derivation of the name of Betws. It is everyone's idea of a perfect Snowdonia village—tumbling rivers

and waterfalls and mountains that emerge from a tangle of treetops. Stone-built houses and hotels cling to rocky outcrops and woodland paths lead away to secret places. Trout fishing abounds. There is a theatre and Railway Museum, for Betws is served still by rail and road.

Hotels, Motels and Inns

Craig-y-Dderwen Country House Hotel*

Betws-y-Coed
Gwynedd LL24 0AS
Tel: (06902) 293

CATEGORIES

| 4 | 4 | 5 |

Luxurious country house overlooking river in its own gardens. Beautifully situated, has 2 day breaks. Dinner, bed and breakfast from £31 inclusive. Rooms with private bath. Colour TV, radio, room call, tea/coffee making. Central heating. Exceptional licensed restaurant. Ideally situated for fishing, pony trekking, shooting, free golf or touring Snowdonia. Brochure from Mr. W. G. Palmer.

	B & B PER PERSON PER NIGHT		DINNER B & B PER PERSON PER WEEK		🛏 23
T					
C	MIN £	MAX £	MIN £	MAX £	OPEN
	11.50		102		1—12

Fairy Glen Hotel*

Dolgellau Road, Betws-y-Coed
Gwynedd LL24 0SH
Tel: (06902) 269

CATEGORIES

| 4 | 4 | 4 |

Overlooking Beaver Pool and River. A delightful and peaceful location, surrounded by the most varied and magnificent Welsh scenery. Well equipped bedrooms, half with bathrooms. Private bar, lounge, car park. Excellent restaurant. Enjoy comfort, excellent food, pleasant helpful service at our 17th century hotel. Ideal for touring, walking in Snowdonia and relaxing.

	B & B PER PERSON PER NIGHT		DINNER B & B PER PERSON PER WEEK		🛏 10
T					
C	MIN £	MAX £	MIN £	MAX £	OPEN
	9.90		91		1—12

Henllys (Old Courthouse) Hotel*

Betws-y-Coed
Gwynedd LL24 0AL
Tel: (06902) 534

CATEGORIES

| 3 | 4 | 4 |

Charming small hotel in class of its own. Originally old Courthouse. Dine where magistrates once presided. Delightfully different bedrooms with river, mountain views. Heating, colour TV. Excellent food. Warm, friendly atmosphere. Residential restaurant, licensed. Large car park. Adjacent golf course. Colour brochure. Resident proprietors, Pete and Joan Smart.

	B & B PER PERSON PER NIGHT		DINNER B & B PER PERSON PER WEEK		🛏 10
T					
C	MIN £	MAX £	MIN £	MAX £	OPEN
	8.25	11.50	86	108	2—12

Mount Garmon Hotel*

Betws-y-Coed
Gwynedd LL24 0AN
Tel: (06902) 335

CATEGORIES

| 4 | 3 | 2 |

Small hotel, residential, licence, central heating in all bedrooms and bathrooms. Some bedrooms have bathroom en-suite. Lounge with colour TV, bar lounge, cheerful dining room. Full English breakfast, table d'hôte five course dinner, snack meals available, 11am to 11pm. Private car park. Public telephone. Fire Certificate.

	B & B PER PERSON PER NIGHT		DINNER B & B PER PERSON PER WEEK		🛏 5
C	PER NIGHT		PER PERSON PER WEEK		
	MIN £	MAX £	MIN £	MAX £	OPEN
	8		90		2—10

Park Hill Hotel*

Llanrwst Road, Betws-y-Coed
Gwynedd LL24 0HD
Tel: (06902) 540

CATEGORIES

| 4 | 4 | 4 |

An AA** RAC** Ashley Courtenay recommended, centrally heated licensed hotel. Quiet, friendly renowned for high standard of cuisine, accommodation and personal service set in over an acre of garden, overlooking Conwy Valley. Ten bedrooms mostly with private bathrooms. Children over six welcome. British Tourist Authority commended.

	B & B PER PERSON PER NIGHT		DINNER B & B PER PERSON PER WEEK		🛏 10
T					
C	MIN £	MAX £	MIN £	MAX £	OPEN
	11	13.50	92.50	115	1—12

Plas Hall Hotel & Restaurant*

Pont-y-Pant, near Betws-y-Coed
Gwynedd LL25 0PJ
Tel: (06906) 206

CATEGORIES

| 5 | 4 | 5 |

Old stone hall converted into luxurious 3 star hotel beautifully situated, overlooking River Lledr. All rooms with private bathroom, shower, colour TV. Clock-radio tea and coffee making facilities, telephone. Central heating, games room. Licensed. Four poster suite, exceptional restaurant. Fishing, pony trekking, shooting, free golf. Bargain breaks. Brochure from Mr. G. Palmer.

	B & B PER PERSON PER NIGHT		DINNER B & B PER PERSON PER WEEK		🛏 17
T					
C	MIN £	MAX £	MIN £	MAX £	OPEN
	12	16.50	103.50	130.50	1—12

Summer Hill*

Betws-y-Coed
Gwynedd LL24 0BL
Tel: (069 02) 306

CATEGORIES

| 3 | 3 | 2 |

Summer Hill, Betws-y-Coed, Gwynedd. Tel. 069-02 306. Delightfully situated in peaceful surroundings, overlooking the river. Nine attractive bedrooms with hot and cold water, tea-making facilities. Comfortable residents lounge, colour TV, large airy dining room, excellent food, residential licence. Golf, fishing, riding, guided mountain walks available, numerous forest trails start from our gate.

	B & B PER PERSON PER NIGHT		DINNER B & B PER PERSON PER WEEK		🛏 9
T					
C	MIN £	MAX £	MIN £	MAX £	OPEN
	7.50	9	80	89	4—10

Ty Gwyn Hotel*

Betws-y-Coed, North Wales
LL24 0SG
Tel: (06902) 383

CATEGORIES

| 3 | 3 | 6 |

Our door is always open. Small hotel—big welcome. Olde Worlde, part 17th century. Overlooking River Conwy. Licenced. Good food, warm rooms, no restrictions, no extras, no TV (no reception). Be prepared to enjoy yourselves. Dine, wine in candlelight, à la carte. All inclusive and bar menus. Very central. Golf, fishing, pony trekking 10 minutes. Snowdon and 100 walks, 15 minutes by car. Fishing ports, coves, beaches, 10 castles, little over ½ an hour. Guided hill-walking and mountaineering. Enquire information, brochure. Short break packages, or phone booking with credit card. Geoff Tyson. Non-residents welcome.

	B & B PER PERSON PER NIGHT		DINNER B & B PER PERSON PER WEEK		🛏 9
T					
C	MIN £	MAX £	MIN £	MAX £	OPEN
	8.50	10	90	112	1—12

Waterloo Hotel and Motel

Betws-y-Coed
Gwynedd LL24 0AR
Tel: (06902) 411

CATEGORIES: 5 4 5

RAC** Michelin. AA** Modern hotel, all rooms en-suite. TV lounge, superb restaurant with finest food and wine. Ideal base for touring Snowdonia and North Wales. Close to all outdoor pursuits. Local friendly efficient staff. Brochure from Mr. D. R. Nesbitt.

T	B & B PER PERSON PER NIGHT		DINNER B & B PER PERSON PER WEEK		28
C	MIN £	MAX £	.MIN £	MAX £	OPEN
	13.50	18.50			1—12

Guest Houses

Bryn Afon

Mill Street, Betws-y-Coed
Gwynedd LL24 0BB
Tel: (06902) 403

CATEGORIES: 2 2 1

Unique situation beside the river, newly decorated and offering every comfort. Central heating, hot and cold water in all bedrooms, drying and ironing facilities. Good car parking, golf, fishing, riding and walks in superb scenery. Guests are made really welcome in this large family home.

C	B & B PER PERSON PER NIGHT		DINNER B & B PER PERSON PER WEEK		4
	MIN £	MAX £	MIN £	MAX £	OPEN
	7	7.50			4—10

Glenwood*

Betws-y-Coed
Gwynedd LL24 0BN
Tel: (06902) 508

CATEGORIES: 3 4 3

Charming spacious house in own grounds. (Private parking) Scenic views all rooms. Owners personally ensure your every comfort. Idyllic Snowdonia Park situation for that relaxing holiday by forest lakes and mountains. Welsh cream teas served in the gardens. Our honeymoon couples still return—you'll want to come again. Closed Christmas.

T	B & B PER PERSON PER NIGHT		DINNER B & B PER PERSON PER WEEK		6
C	MIN £	MAX £	MIN £	MAX £	OPEN
	8	9.50	78	92	1—12

Hafan Guest House*

Hafan, Betws-y-Coed
Gwynedd. North Wales
Tel: (06902) 233

CATEGORIES: 3 3 3

First class cuisine. 3 rooms have shower. All home cooking. Toilet en-suite. Fresh farm dairy products, fires in rooms. Sun terrace, central heating. Beautiful gardens. Residents lounge, colour TV. Tea and coffee maker in all rooms. Licensed bar.

C	B & B PER PERSON PER NIGHT		DINNER B & B PER PERSON PER WEEK		6
	MIN £	MAX £	MIN £	MAX £	OPEN
	8.50	9.50	108		1—12

Llwyn Onn Cottage Guest House

Pentrefoelas, near Betws-y-Coed
Gwynedd LL24 0TW
Tel: (069 05) 678

CATEGORIES: 3 3 3

Small 17th century Guest House set in three acres. Quiet and secluded, overlooking Snowdonia. Electric blankets, hot and cold water and shaver points in all bedrooms. Tea making facilities, home cooking, using fresh local produce. Lounge with TV. Individual comfort and friendly welcome assured by resident proprietors. Access at all times.

T	B & B PER PERSON PER NIGHT		DINNER B & B PER PERSON PER WEEK		3
C	MIN £	MAX £	MIN £	MAX £	OPEN
	8	9	98	98	1—12

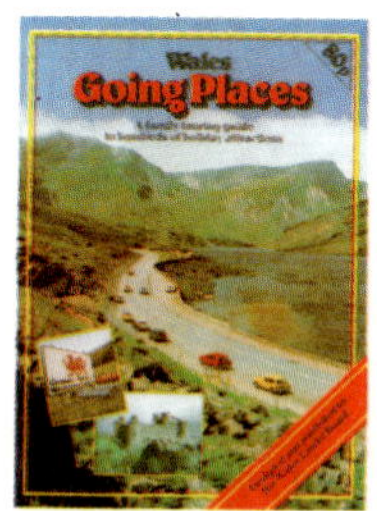

Going Places
Full of carefully-planned motor tours and information on places to visit. A must for family touring around Wales. Available from: Wales Tourist Board Department W.T.S. P.O. Box 1, CARDIFF CF1 2XN. Price: £1.05p including postage and packing.

Farmhouses

Cilcennus Farm*

Llanrwst
Gwynedd
Tel: (06902) 332

CATEGORIES: 1 3 2

Just off the A470 between Betws-y-Coed and Llanrwst, therefore ideally placed for walking. 25 minutes to the beaches. Set in the National Park, Cilcennus offers a peaceful and comfortable country holiday on this working farm. Central heating, log fires, home cooking, TV lounge. Send SAE please to Mrs. Williams.

T	B & B PER PERSON PER NIGHT		DINNER B & B PER PERSON PER WEEK		3
C	MIN £	MAX £	MIN £	MAX £	OPEN
	6	7	60	70	4—10

Cwmanog Uchaf*

Dinas Hill, Betws-y-Coed
Gwynedd LL24 0HH
Tel: (06902) 376

CATEGORIES: 1 2 2

Stone-built farmhouse with superb views looking over the Lledr and Conwy Valleys towards the mountains, in the Snowdonia National Park near Fairy Glen. Smallholding with ducks, hens, geese. Comfortable and cosy with woodburning stove. Heating in the bedrooms. Many local walks, fishing, pony trekking nearby. Ideal touring centre.

T	B & B PER PERSON PER NIGHT		DINNER B & B PER PERSON PER WEEK		3
C	MIN £	MAX £	MIN £	MAX £	OPEN
	6.50	7.50	70	80	1—12

This symbol means you can book through your local travel agent.

Maes Gwyn

Pentrefoelas, Betws-y-Coed
Gwynedd LL24 0LR
Tel: (06905) 668

CATEGORIES
| 1 | 2 | 2 |

Maes Gwyn is a 17th century farmhouse now modernised to today's standard. Good touring centre for North Wales. Only six miles from famous Betws-y-Coed and many other places of interest. One double and one family room available, bathroom with shower. Good home cooking.

C	B & B PER PERSON PER NIGHT		DINNER B & B PER PERSON PER WEEK		2
	MIN £	MAX £	MIN £	MAX £	OPEN
	5.50	6	63	70	4—11

Maes y Garnedd

Capel Garmon, Llanrwst
Betws-y-Coed, Gwynedd
Tel: (06902) 428

CATEGORIES
| 1 | 3 | 2 |

140-acre mixed farm superbly situated in Capel Garmon (2 miles off A5 road). Beautiful country scenery and excellent walks. Beaches at Llandudno and Colwyn Bay. Salmon and trout fishing (permit required). Excellent home-produced meals served including Welsh lamb and roast beef. Packed lunches available. One double and one family bedroom. Children welcome, cot, high chair and babysitting. Regret no pets. Car essential. Ample parking. SAE for brochure. Bala Lakes, Bodnant Garden, Ffestiniog Railway, Slate Quarries nearby.

C	B & B PER PERSON PER NIGHT		DINNER B & B PER PERSON PER WEEK		2
	MIN £	MAX £	MIN £	MAX £	OPEN
	6.50	7	59.50	68.45	4—10

Ty-Coch Farm*

Penmachno, near Betws-y-Coed
Gwynedd LL25 0HJ
Tel: (06903) 248

CATEGORIES
| 3 | 3 | 3 |

Hill farm with sheep and poultry. Pony trekking, centre attached. The picturesque village of Penmachno is two miles away and the attractive holiday resort of Betws-y-Coed is only a short drive. The farm is situated in a very quiet area in the heart of the Gwydyr Forest.

T C	B & B PER PERSON PER NIGHT		DINNER B & B PER PERSON PER WEEK		4
	MIN £	MAX £	MIN £	MAX £	OPEN
	7	7.50	75	82	3—10

Blackwood
SOUTH WALES

Hotel

Maes Manor Hotel*

Maesrudded, Blackwood
Gwent NP2 0AG
Tel: (0495) 224551

CATEGORIES
| 5 | 5 | 5 |

Maes Manor Hotel is situated in nine acres of unspoilt secluded woodland. All bedrooms are well furnished and incorporate baby listening, radio and colour TV. Dining here is a rewarding experience; one may choose from an extensive à la carte menu of Welsh, English and French dishes.

T C	B & B PER PERSON PER NIGHT		DINNER B & B PER PERSON PER WEEK		27
	MIN £	MAX £	MIN £	MAX £	OPEN
	22	24	154	168	1—12

Blaenannerch
MID WALES

Guest House

Rhyd Guest House and Restaurant*

Blaenannerch, near Cardigan
Dyfed SA43 4AB
Tel: (0239) 810062

CATEGORIES
| 3 | 3 | 3 |

A residence set in two acres of grounds on the A487 road, only two miles away from the beaches at Aberporth. Licensed restaurant, children's games room, tennis court, miniature golf. Single, double and family rooms. TV lounge. A highly recommended situation with an international clientele. Happiness at moderate prices!

C	B & B PER PERSON PER NIGHT		DINNER B & B PER PERSON PER WEEK		6
	MIN £	MAX £	MIN £	MAX £	OPEN
	5.50	8.50	63	91	1—12

Blaenau Ffestiniog
NORTH WALES

Hotel

Queens Hotel*

Blaenau Ffestiniog, Gwynedd
Tel: (076681) 338 Reservations
Tel: (076681) 203 Guests

CATEGORIES
| 2 | 3 | 4 |

Warm friendly hotel in Snowdonia under personal supervision of resident proprietors. Hotel next to Ffestiniog Railway and British Rail terminus. Near to fishing and golfing facilities. Local attractions include slate quarries, panoramic views from local dam. Children very welcome. If fact everything from family to 'single' holidays.

T C	B & B PER PERSON PER NIGHT		DINNER B & B PER PERSON PER WEEK		12
	MIN £	MAX £	MIN £	MAX £	OPEN
		8.70			1—12

Guest House

The Don Guest House*

147 High Street, Blaenau Ffestiniog
Gwynedd
Tel: (076681) 403

CATEGORIES
| 1 | 2 | 2 |

Friendly guest house set amongst some of the finest Snowdonia scenery. An ideal touring centre. Hot and cold water and shaver points in all bedrooms. Central heating, licensed bar. Colour TV. Fire Certificate. Horse riding, fishing, golf, mountain walks. Tourist attractions. All available in this area. Full restaurant facilities available.

C	B & B PER PERSON PER NIGHT		DINNER B & B PER PERSON PER WEEK		6
	MIN £	MAX £	MIN £	MAX £	OPEN
	11	12.50	112	122.50	1—12

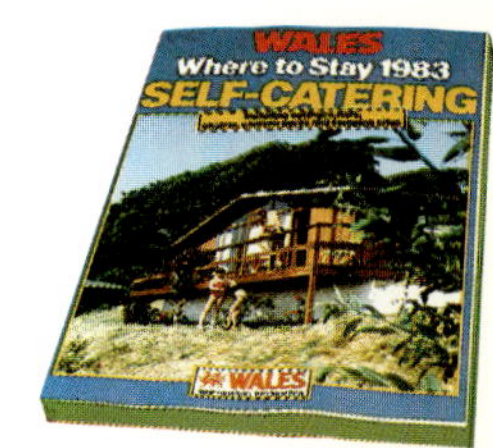

Bodedern

Hotel

Crown Hotel*

Bodedern, Anglesey
Gwynedd
Tel: (0407) 740734

CATEGORIES: 3 3 3

A village Inn with warm friendly atmosphere and popular bars. Hot and cold water and shaver points in all bedrooms. Central heating throughout. Listed by AA* and Camra.

C	B & B PER PERSON PER NIGHT		DINNER B & B PER PERSON PER WEEK		5
	MIN £	MAX £	MIN £	MAX £	OPEN
	7	7			1—12

Boncath

Guest Houses

Pant-y-Deri Farm Guest House

Boncath, Pembrokeshire
Dyfed SA37 0JB
Tel: (023974) 227 or 377

CATEGORIES: 3 3 2

Fully licensed farm guest house in beautiful setting. Private swimming pool and trout lake with boat, one mile of private fishing on the stream. Full size billiard table. Hot and cold water in all bedrooms. Ponies for hire. Bed and breakfast and evening meal, also self-catering cottages to let (BTA commended) for full particulars, send large SAE to Mrs. E. W. Jones.

C	B & B PER PERSON PER NIGHT		DINNER B & B PER PERSON PER WEEK		8
	MIN £	MAX £	MIN £	MAX £	OPEN
	9.75		96	98.90	3—10

Sunnyside

Newchapel, Boncath
Dyfed
Tel: (023974) 428

CATEGORIES: 1 1 2

Modern bungalow, quiet countryside on B4332 road, six miles from Cardigan and three miles from Cenarth Falls. Good centre for touring West Wales, Preseli Hills and Cardigan Bay's sandy beaches. TV and heating in bedrooms. We offer comfort, service and good food. Open all year. Reductions for children.

C	B & B PER PERSON PER NIGHT		DINNER B & B PER PERSON PER WEEK		2
	MIN £	MAX £	MIN £	MAX £	OPEN
	6	6	56	56	1—12

Borth

Hotel

Glanmor Hotel*

Borth, Dyfed
West Wales, SY24 5JP
Tel: (097 081) 385/689

CATEGORIES: 2 3 3

Overlooking the beautiful Cardigan Bay. Single, double and family rooms. Special rates for children. Hot and cold water and shaver points in all bedrooms. Residential licence, colour TV, lounge, private parking facilities. Childrens play-area, golf course 200 yards. Pony trekking arranged. Safe sandy beach. Pets accepted, children most welcome.

C	B & B PER PERSON PER NIGHT		DINNER B & B PER PERSON PER WEEK		7
	MIN £	MAX £	MIN £	MAX £	OPEN
	7	8	75	80	4—10

Guest House

6 Cambrian Terrace

Borth
Dyfed SY24 5HU
Tel: (097 081) 613

CATEGORIES: 2 2 2

Beach, shops and railway station within easy reach. Many places of interest easily reached by car. Ynyslas national nature reserve, Meirion weaving mill and shop. Llywernog lead and silver mine, Rheidol power station, Centre for Alternative Technology, Nanteos stately home, Narrow gauge steam railway from Aberystwyth to Devils Bridge. Also pony trekking available locally.

C	B & B PER PERSON PER NIGHT		DINNER B & B PER PERSON PER WEEK		4
	MIN £	MAX £	MIN £	MAX £	OPEN
	4.25	4.50	47	48	3—10

Borth y Gest

Guest Houses

Morannedd*

Borth-y-Gest, Porthmadog
Gwynedd LL49 9UA
Tel: (0766) 2587

CATEGORIES: 1 3 1

Select guest house in beautiful Borth-y-Gest on Glaslyn Estuary. Glorious panoramic views of mountains. Two minutes walk to sheltered coves with golden sands. Near famous Blackrock Sands and Ffestiniog Railway, Porthmadog. Ideal centre for North Wales, bathing, boating, climbing. Washbasins, hot and cold water, comfortable beds. Good food. Parking. Warm Welcome.

C	B & B PER PERSON PER NIGHT		DINNER B & B PER PERSON PER WEEK		4
	MIN £	MAX £	MIN £	MAX £	OPEN
	6	6.50			4—10

Brechfa

Hotel

Ty Mawr Country House Hotel & Restaurant*

Brechfa, near Carmarthen
Dyfed SA32 7RA
Tel: (026 789) 332

CATEGORIES: 4 4 5

British Tourist Authority commended hotel. Enjoy a taste of Wales in our comfortable 16th century country house hotel where cordon bleu cooking in our fully licensed restaurant is a feature. 5 centrally heated bedrooms, each with private bathroom. Beautiful countryside where you can enjoy salmon fishing, riding, shooting, golf and walking. Coast ½ hour drive. For details write to Cliff and Jill Ross. Egon Ronay, Good Hotel Guide, AA recommended. Mini Breaks from £22.

T C	B & B PER PERSON PER NIGHT		DINNER B & B PER PERSON PER WEEK		5
	MIN £	MAX £	MIN £	MAX £	OPEN
		19.50		180.50	1—12

For autumn to spring breaks send for our free Great Little Breaks booklet.

Brecon

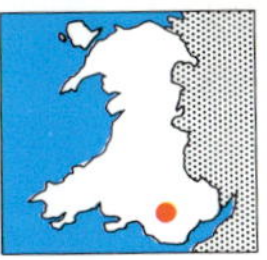

Map ref: Ge6
Capital town for an agricultural and tourism area that encompasses the Brecon Beacons National Park, the town is yet in itself an attraction. Set above the crystal Usk—with its salmon and trout—on Monmouthshire and Brecon Canal, now pleasure only, the old town gazes admiringly across at 2907ft. Pen y Fan and her sisters. The cathedral, remnants of a castle and Roman Fort, and narrow streets hark back to ancient days when the town was garrisoned by spur and lance. Golf, walking, fishing, canal cruising and pony trekking are all available.

Hotels, Motel and Inn

Bishop's Meadow Motel

Hay Road, Brecon
Powys
Tel: (0874) 2051

CATEGORIES: 4 1 5

Ideally situated, with magnificent views of Brecon Beacons. All rooms with private bathrooms and balconies. Pony trekking, fishing, water ski-ing, yachting, mountain climbing, within 4 miles. Lunches, teas, grills. Also lounge bar, cafeteria and filling station. Private swimming pool for residents.

	B & B PER PERSON PER NIGHT		DINNER B & B PER PERSON PER WEEK		26
C	MIN £	MAX £	MIN £	MAX £	OPEN
	15	15			1—12

Camden Arms

Pwllgloyw, Brecon
Powys LD3 9PY
Tel: (087489) 282

CATEGORIES: 1 3 5

Country inn offering a friendly local atmosphere only four miles from Brecon, situated in beautiful unspoilt country within easy reach of the Brecon beacons, fishing and golf nearby. Rooms are warm and comfortable with hot and cold, shaver points and are newly furnished and carpeted.

	B & B PER PERSON PER NIGHT		DINNER B & B PER PERSON PER WEEK		2
	MIN £	MAX £	MIN £	MAX £	OPEN
	7.50	8.50	80	100	1—12

The George Hotel*

George Street, Brecon
Powys LD3 7LD
Tel: (0874) 3422

CATEGORIES: 3 3 4

Close to town centre and shops. Single, double and family rooms. Special rates for children. Dining room with separate tables. Childrens menu, colour TV lounge Excellent centre for walking, riding, fishing, golf and touring. Two bars with real ale. Full central heating. Fire Certificate granted.

		B & B PER PERSON PER NIGHT		DINNER B & B PER PERSON PER WEEK		8
T		MIN £	MAX £	MIN £	MAX £	OPEN
C		11	.13	79	85	1—12

The Griffin Inn

Llyswen, near Brecon
Powys LD3 0UR
Tel: (087485) 241

CATEGORIES: 3 3 4

Olde Worlde Village Inn situated in the beautiful Wye Valley. Ideal centre for salmon fishing, golfing and touring the majestic Mid and South Wales countryside. Modern, centrally heated bedrooms with private bathrooms and excellent à la carte menu. Bar snacks in separate dining room. Egan Ronay recommended. Fire Certificate granted.

	B & B PER PERSON PER NIGHT		DINNER B & B PER PERSON PER WEEK		6
C	MIN £	MAX £	MIN £	MAX £	OPEN
	12	15	112	128	1—12

Lansdowne Hotel*

The Watton, Brecon
Powys
Tel: (0874) 3321

CATEGORIES: 3 4 4

Ideally situated for touring, walking, pony trekking and golf. AA* Georgian hotel with 12 comfortable bedrooms. One with four poster bed. Family suite with private bathroom, sleep 4. Residents lounge with colour TV. Licensed restaurant is open to non-residents for lunch and dinner. Special parties catered for, 2 day inclusive package offered. Please send for brochure. Access and Barclaycard. Under the personal supervision of Mr. & Mrs. R. L. Withey M.H.C.I.M.A.

		B & B PER PERSON PER NIGHT		DINNER B & B PER PERSON PER WEEK		12
T		MIN £	MAX £	MIN £	MAX £	OPEN
C		8	10.50	83.70	95	3—11

Nythfa House Hotel*

Brecon
Powys LD3 7NG
Tel: (0874) 4287

CATEGORIES: 4 4 3

RAC** Quietly situated in 4 acres of mature gardens and woodland in sight of Beacons. Ideal for country pursuits. Squash courts and sauna. Indoor pool and tennis courts nearby. All bedrooms with bathrooms, including family rooms. Some annexe accommodation. Licensed. October/May reduced rate. 2/3/4 night breaks.

		B & B PER PERSON PER NIGHT		DINNER B & B PER PERSON PER WEEK		13
T		MIN £	MAX £	MIN £	MAX £	OPEN
C		12.50	14	117	126	1—12

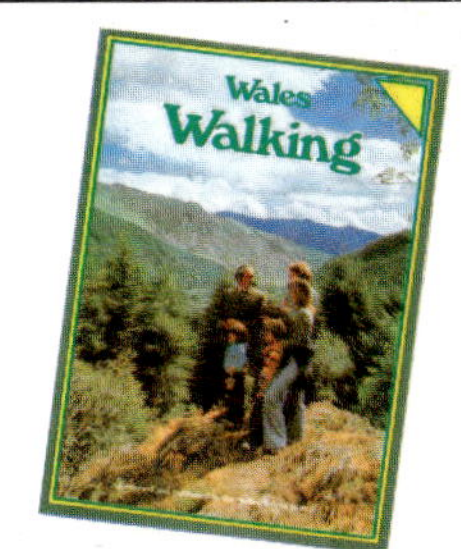

Walking
For 1983, a completely revised edition of this best-selling guide to Walking in Wales. Describes hundreds of way-marked and unway-marked walks designed for families and the more enthusiastic rambler.
Available from: Wales Tourist Board Department W.T.S. P.O. Box 1, CARDIFF CF1 2XN. Price: £1.35p including postage and packing.

The Three Cocks Hotel & Restaurant*

Three Cocks, near Brecon
Powys LD3 0SL
Tel: (04974) 215

CATEGORIES: 3 3 5

Come and stay in our 15th century hostelry. Log fires in winter . . . tea on the lawn in summer. Eat in our restaurant from our fixed price gourmet menu, commended by the BTA and awarded a Rosette by the AA. Let us send you our very special brochure.

T C	B & B PER PERSON PER NIGHT		DINNER B & B PER PERSON PER WEEK		🛏 7
	MIN £	MAX £	MIN £	MAX £	OPEN
	13	15	135	155	3—12

Guest Houses

Flag & Castle Guest House

11 Orchard Street, Llanfaes
Brecon, Powys LD3 8AN
Tel: (0874) 5860

CATEGORIES: 2 2 2

Facing Christ College and near riverside walks, boating, fishing, cinema, library and museum. On arrival our guests relax with free refreshments to herald the start of a comfortable stay. English and continental breakfasts, vegetarian dishes a speciality. Colour television. Separate tables. Ample parking. Many guests come back repeatedly.

T C	B & B PER PERSON PER NIGHT		DINNER B & B PER PERSON PER WEEK		🛏 6
	MIN £	MAX £	MIN £	MAX £	OPEN
	5.50	6.50	56	63	1—12

The Gables

Libanus, near Brecon
Powys LD3 8EN
Tel: (0874) 2033

CATEGORIES: 3 2 1

Brecon Beacons National park. Ranch type bungalow. All modern conveniences. Golfing, trekking, climbing. Good rambling area. Good restaurant in village. Brecon 3 miles. Mountain centre and Beacons close by. Set in beautiful surroundings.

C	B & B PER PERSON PER NIGHT		DINNER B & B PER PERSON PER WEEK		🛏 3
	MIN £	MAX £	MIN £	MAX £	OPEN
	6				4—9

Old Castle Farm Guest House*

18 Penpentre, Llanfaes
Brecon, Powys
Tel: (0874) 2120

CATEGORIES: 3 3 3

A 17th century Farmhouse with all modern facilities west of the old market town of Brecon, half mile from town centre and in easy reach of mountain centre. Golf, pony-trekking, swimming. The house caters for 26 persons. All rooms have hot and cold water, tea making facilities. Central heating, some with private shower, toilet and TV. Licensed TC lounge, bar lounge. Fire Certificate held. Private car park. Access to guest house at all times.

C	B & B PER PERSON PER NIGHT		DINNER B & B PER PERSON PER WEEK		🛏 12
	MIN £	MAX £	MIN £	MAX £	OPEN
	7	8	73.50	80.50	1—11

The Old Greyhound Guest House*

47 The Struet, Brecon
Powys LD3 7LW
Tel: (0874) 4818

CATEGORIES: 1 3 2

Small family concern situated in the town 3 minutes walk from Brecon Cathedral. Closed for one week over Christmas. Guest lounge with colour TV, central heating, tea or coffee on arrival included in B & B price. More details and sample menu sent on request. Special rates for children. Dogs accepted.

C	B & B PER PERSON PER NIGHT		DINNER B & B PER PERSON PER WEEK		🛏 6
	MIN £	MAX £	MIN £	MAX £	OPEN
	6	6.50	56	63	1—12

Peterstone Court*

Llanhamlach, Brecon
Powys LD3 7YB
Tel: (087486) 666

CATEGORIES: 3 3 2

Charming 18th century country house in the beautiful Usk Valley in secluded setting. 3 miles from Brecon. Comfortable accommodation. Hot and cold and shaver points in bedrooms. Central heating. Log fires. Separate lounge and dining room with separate tables. Swimming pool. Beautiful views. Ample parking. Sorry no pets.

C	B & B PER PERSON PER NIGHT		DINNER B & B PER PERSON PER WEEK		🛏 3
	MIN £	MAX £	MIN £	MAX £	OPEN
	7	8	70	77	3—11

Farmhouses

Cefncoedbach Farm*

Llandefaelogfach, Brecon
Powys LD3 9PT
Tel: (0874) 3548

CATEGORIES: 1 3 1

A mixed farm of 130 acres four miles from cathedral town of Brecon. Excellent base to tour Brecon Beacons, caves, dams or to go walking, pony trekking. 1 double room, 1 twin-bedded room, washbasins, hot and cold water. Central heating, TV lounge. Children welcome. Car essential. Babysitting.

C	B & B PER PERSON PER NIGHT		DINNER B & B PER PERSON PER WEEK		🛏 2
	MIN £	MAX £	MIN £	MAX £	OPEN
	6	7	40	46	1—12

Llwynfedwen Farm*

Libanus, Brecon
Powys LD3 8NN
Tel: (982) 626

CATEGORIES: 1 1 1

54 acre dairy and sheep farm, situated peacefully in Brecon Beacons National Park with superb views. One family room and one double room. Reduced rate for children. Bus one mile. Local interests include, Dan-yr-Ogof Caves, Ystradfellte Waterfalls, Penscynor Wildlife Park, Brecon Mountain Railway, golf, fishing, walking, pony trekking.

C	B & B PER PERSON PER NIGHT		DINNER B & B PER PERSON PER WEEK		🛏 2
	MIN £	MAX £	MIN £	MAX £	OPEN
	5.50	6			4—10

Llwynhir Farm*

Cray, Brecon
Powys LD3 8YW
Tel: (087 482) 563

CATEGORIES: 1 2 2

500 acre mixed farm in Brecon Beacons National Park with access to guests of 10,000 acres of private mountains 900ft rising to 2,500ft. Five miles to Dan-yr-Ogof Caves, Craig-y-Nos Country Park. Pony trekking and fishing nearby. Swansea 26 miles. Lounge and colour TV for guests.

C	B & B PER PERSON PER NIGHT		DINNER B & B PER PERSON PER WEEK		🛏 3
	MIN £	MAX £	MIN £	MAX £	OPEN
	6	7	65	80	3—10

Tregoyd Trekking Centre

Tregoyd, Three Cocks
Brecon, Powys
Tel: (04974) 351

CATEGORIES: 1 3 2

Call at Tregoyd Trekking Centre and enjoy a day or half-day pony trek in the Black Mountains. All ages welcome, whether beginners or experienced riders. Special terms for groups. If you want to stay awhile accommodation is available in farmhouse or guest house. If you have camping gear we have a picturesque campsite. Ideal for Scouts, Guides, or similar groups. Call or send for details and colour brochure, we are easy to find: just turn off the A438 at Three Cocks and follow the Tregoyd signs.

T C	B & B PER PERSON PER NIGHT		DINNER B & B PER PERSON PER WEEK		🛏 2
	MIN £	MAX £	MIN £	MAX £	OPEN
	6.50		66.70		4—9

Wernyfed Farm*

Trallong, Brecon
LD3 8HF
Tel: (087482) 442

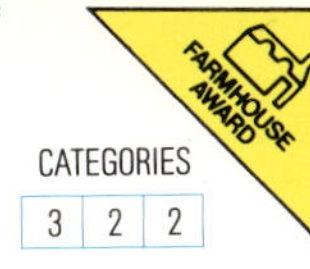

CATEGORIES: 3 2 2

A friendly welcome in this modern bungalow. Set in the heart of the Welsh countryside. Easily accessible from A40. Offering a double and family room overlooking the Usk Valley, where the charm is of absolute peace. Ideal centre for walking fishing, trekking, golf, bird-watching and sight-seeing.

	B & B PER PERSON PER NIGHT		DINNER B & B PER PERSON PER WEEK		2
T					
C	MIN £	MAX £	MIN £	MAX £	OPEN
	6.50	7.50	73	80	1—11

Bridgend
SOUTH WALES

Hotel

Heronston Hotel

Ewenny, Bridgend
Mid Glamorgan CF35 5AW
Tel: (0656) 68811 Telex: 498232

CATEGORIES: 6 5 5

Twenty modern bedrooms include telephone, television, hair-dryer, fully fitted wardrobes, bathroom, shower and w.c. Single, double and twin rooms available. Swimming pool, sauna, jacuzzi and solarium facilities. A la carte restaurant and bar. Open all year round.

	B & B PER PERSON PER NIGHT		DINNER B & B PER PERSON PER WEEK		20
T					
C	MIN £	MAX £	MIN £	MAX £	OPEN
	25	25			1—12

Farmhouse

Castle-Upon-Alun Farm

St. Bride's Major, Bridgend
Mid-Glamorgan CF32 0TN
Tel: (0656) 880200

CATEGORIES: 3 3 2

This farm is in the heart of the countryside. Two miles from the nearest beach. Golf, surfing and pony riding nearby. Good position for visiting Cardiff, Swansea, Gower, Brecon Beacons etc. Reductions for Senior Citizens. One double, one twin-bedded room. Free range eggs, home grown produce as available.

	B & B PER PERSON PER NIGHT		DINNER B & B PER PERSON PER WEEK		2
	MIN £	MAX £	MIN £	MAX £	OPEN
	6.50	6.75	64	68	1—11

Broad Haven
SOUTH WALES

Map ref: Jb5
6 miles west of Haverfordwest by B4341 road, in the middle of Pembrokeshire Coast National Park at one of its most beautiful stretches lies Broad Haven and little sister, Little Haven. Sand and velvet green hills cradle the village, much of it holiday accommodation. On the odd wet day—it enjoys a high sunshine record—tour up the coast to St. David's Cathedral, east to Haverfordwest's castle, shops and museum or south to the Milford Haven.

Hotels

Broad Haven Hotel*

near Haverfordwest
SA62 3JN
Tel: (043 783) 366

CATEGORIES: 3 4 3

Opposite beautiful beach. All 38 bedrooms have TV, radios, intercom, baby listening, tea and coffee making facilities, nearly all have bathroom en-suite. Heated swimming pool and sun-bathing terraces, solarium. Games rooms. Two bars. Ample parking. Fire Certificate. Children all ages half-price when sharing parents suite.

	B & B PER PERSON PER NIGHT		DINNER B & B PER PERSON PER WEEK		38
T					
C	MIN £	MAX £	MIN £	MAX £	OPEN
	7.50	9.50	85	118	2—10

Haven Fort Hotel

Settlands Hill, Little Haven
Near Haverfordwest,
Pembrokeshire, Dyfed SA62 3LA
Tel: (043 783) 401

CATEGORIES: 4 4 4

Commanding a stupendous view of St. Bride's Bay, the fortress offers an atmosphere of medieval charm and peaceful tranquility. Modern bedrooms with private bathrooms. Our restaurant serves good fresh food of a high standard. Continental dishes our speciality. The hotel is recommended in a well-known continental guide book. AA.*

	B & B PER PERSON PER NIGHT		DINNER B & B PER PERSON PER WEEK		15
C	MIN £	MAX £	MIN £	MAX £	OPEN
	14.50		133	.	3—10

The Private Hotel*

Broad Haven, Haverfordwest
Pembrokeshire SA62 3JW
Tel: (0437) 286

CATEGORIES: 2 2 2

Small family hotel on sea front, non-licensed. Large airy lounge overlooking Bay, 50 yards from beach with safe bathing. Separate dining tables in large pleasant dining room. Cordon Bleu cooking. Miles of beautiful cliff walks. Children welcomed.

	B & B PER PERSON PER NIGHT		DINNER B & B PER PERSON PER WEEK		6
C	MIN £	MAX £	MIN £	MAX £	OPEN
	6	6	52	52	4—9

Guest Houses

Anchor House*

Broad Haven, Haverfordwest
Dyfed SA62 3JW
Tel: (043783) 542

CATEGORIES: 2 2 2

Standing alongside a magnificent sandy beach, Anchor House is ideally situated for a holiday in the Pembrokeshire Coast National Park. Three double and three family rooms command superb views of St. Bride's Bay. Car parking. Residential licence. Early morning tea service. Reduced rates for children. Fire Certificate held.

	B & B PER PERSON PER NIGHT		DINNER B & B PER PERSON PER WEEK		6
C	MIN £	MAX £	MIN £	MAX £	OPEN
	6.50	7.50	70	77	4—9

T

This symbol means you can book through your local travel agent.

Glenfield,*

5 Atlantic Drive, Broad Haven
Haverfordwest, Dyfed SA62 3JA
Tel: (043 783) 502

CATEGORIES

1	2	2

A friendly welcome awaits you at this small Guest House. First class breakfast and optional evening meal. Quietly situated off main road. Five minutes walk to beach and coastal path. Colour television. Own keys and access to rooms at all times. "Home from home but no washing up."

C	B & B PER PERSON PER NIGHT		DINNER B & B PER PERSON PER WEEK		4
	MIN £	MAX £	MIN £	MAX £	OPEN
	6	6.50	66.50	70	1—12

Farmhouse

Moor Farm*

Walwyns Castle, Haverfordwest
Pembrokeshire, Dyfed SA62 3EE
Tel: (0437) 890288

CATEGORIES

1	2	1

One family room, one double, two single and cot with private sitting/dining room. One double room with wash basin. Bed rooms look out on ½ acre lawn. Three miles from Broad Haven, Five miles Haverfordwest. Pony riding near. Away from farm yard. Baby sitting arranged.

C	B & B PER PERSON PER NIGHT		DINNER B & B PER PERSON PER WEEK		2
	MIN £	MAX £	MIN £	MAX £	OPEN
	5	6	35		3—11

Broughton SOUTH WALES

Farmhouse

Broughton House

Broughton, Near Cowbridge
South Glamorgan CF7 7QR
Tel: (065 679) 237

CATEGORIES

1	2	1

Non-working farmhouse in farming area. One mile from sea. Several country pubs serving lunch and evening meals in village.

C	B & B PER PERSON PER NIGHT		DINNER B & B PER PERSON PER WEEK		3
	MIN £	MAX £	MIN £	MAX £	OPEN
	7	7.50			1—12

Tourist Information Centres are listed at back of book.

Builth Wells MID WALES

Map ref: Ge4
The agricultural centre if not the geographical centre of Wales, when in July each year the Royal Welsh Agricultural Society puts on its 3-day mammoth show. Cradled in a ring of hills, watered by the Wye—at its best, in this area, just below the town—Builth, whose Wells are no more, is a busy little crossroads town very interested in the business of cattle and sheep which throng to the local mart.

Guest Houses

Llanfair Guest House*

Llanfair, No. 1 The Strand
Builth Wells, Powys LD2 3BG
Tel: (0982) 553253

CATEGORIES

3	3	5

Overlooking river and park. Friendly atmosphere. All bedrooms have wash basins and TV. Family rooms available with reductions for children. Lounge bar, dining room, à la carte menu. Free parking. Lawns for lounging. Ideal for touring, walking, fishing, golf. Restaurant and bar meals available.

C	B & B PER PERSON PER NIGHT		DINNER B & B PER PERSON PER WEEK		10
	MIN £	MAX £	MIN £	MAX £	OPEN
	5.75	6.50	68	78	1—12

Querida*

43 Garth Road, Builth Wells
Powys LD2 3AR
Tel: (0982) 553642

CATEGORIES

3	3	2

Querida is in easy reach of town centre with its golf, fishing facilities, sports hall etc., nearby. Excellent walks beside the Wye. Also easy reach of Brecon Beacons, Black Mountain, Elan Valley. Pony trekking in area, also Welsh craft shops.

T	B & B PER PERSON PER NIGHT		DINNER B & B PER PERSON PER WEEK		3
C	MIN £	MAX £	MIN £	MAX £	OPEN
	5.50	6	56		1—12

Rhydfelin Farm Guest House*

Cwmbach, near Builth Wells
Powys LD2 3RT
Tel: (0982) 553678

CATEGORIES

3	3	4

Rhydfelin is ideally situated close to the old market town of Builth Wells and to many local leisure and sporting activities. The house contains licensed bar, TV lounge, full central heating, hot and cold water and shaving points in all bedrooms. Separate dining tables, parking. Fire Certificate granted.

C	B & B PER PERSON PER NIGHT		DINNER B & B PER PERSON PER WEEK		5
	MIN £	MAX £	MIN £	MAX £	OPEN
	6	7	65	70	1—12

Farmhouses

Caepandy Farm*

Builth Wells
Powys LD2 3NS
Tel: (0982) 553793

CATEGORIES

3	2	2

Caepandy farm is 1 mile out of Builth Wells on A483 Llandovery Road, in an excellent position for touring Mid Wales. There are magnificent views of the Irfon and Wye valleys. Mixed farming, farm house is modernised all with wash-basins, bathroom and shower, toilet, sitting room with TV, central heating, ample parking. Adjoining golf club.

T	B & B PER PERSON PER NIGHT		DINNER B & B PER PERSON PER WEEK		3
C	MIN £	MAX £	MIN £	MAX £	OPEN
	5.50	6	56	59	1—12

Don't forget that 1983 is Festival of Castles Year in Wales with events planned for all the major historic sites.

Carneddau Farm

Llanelwedd
Builth Wells, Powys LD2 3TF
Tel: (0982) 553368

CATEGORIES

| 1 | 3 | 2 |

An 18th century farmhouse with all modern amenities situated on hill with beautiful views ideally placed for touring mid Wales, dining room with separate tables, lounge with TV, children welcomed, cot and baby sitting available. 1½ miles from Royal Welsh Showground. Sorry no pets.

C	B & B PER PERSON PER NIGHT		DINNER B & B PER PERSON PER WEEK		3
	MIN £	MAX £	MIN £	MAX £	OPEN
	5	7	50	70	5—10

Disserth Mill*

Builth Wells
Powys LD2 3TN
Tel: (0982) 553217

CATEGORIES

| 1 | 2 | 3 |

Disserth Mill is on A483, 3 miles north of Builth with 3 letting rooms. Hot water, comfortable beds, children, pets welcome. Ideally situated for walking, climbing, sight-seeing, relaxing in beautiful country. Pony trekking, golfing, swimming within easy reach. Personal attention with good home cooking. Railway station 2 miles. National Coaches, 2 miles.

C	B & B PER PERSON PER NIGHT		DINNER B & B PER PERSON PER WEEK		3
	MIN £	MAX £	MIN £	MAX £	OPEN
	6.50	8	59.50	70	3—10

Bwlch

SOUTH WALES

Farmhouse

Middlewood Farm*

Bwlch, Brecon
Powys LD3 7HQ
Tel: (0874) 730246

CATEGORIES

| 1 | 2 | 1 |

Situated in the Brecon Beacons National Park on the outskirts of Bwlch, commanding panoramic views of the surrounding countryside. Personal service and a warm welcome assured. There is an abundance of outdoor pursuits including, hiking, fishing, golf, sailing and pony trekking within easy reach.

C	B & B PER PERSON PER NIGHT		DINNER B & B PER PERSON PER WEEK		3
	MIN £	MAX £	MIN £	MAX £	OPEN
	6	7			5—9

Caernarfon

NORTH WALES

Map ref: Ad4
King Edward I in 1284 chose this spot beside Menai Strait to build his most powerful castle in an effort to contain the Welsh in their mountain fastness just 5 miles down the road. Strong town walls and tight-packed streets show little has altered—at least on the ground—down the centuries. The market square doubles as bus terminal. Up the street is a Roman Fort and Museum. Along the quay are yachting folk and old steamer doing duty as a museum. With boat trips along the Strait and coach trips into Snowdonia, Caernarfon makes a versatile holiday centre.

Hotels

Alexandra Hotel*

North Road, Caernarfon
Gwynedd LL55 1BA
Tel: (0286) 2871

CATEGORIES

| 2 | 2 | 1 |

Small friendly hotel situated approximately 400 metres from the centre of Caernarfon town and castle. Ideal centre for touring Snowdonia also boating, fishing, golf, swimming, walking. Hot and cold water in all rooms. Fire Certificate.

C	B & B PER PERSON PER NIGHT		DINNER B & B PER PERSON PER WEEK		3
	MIN £	MAX £	MIN £	MAX £	OPEN
	6.50	8.50			1—12

Menai View*

North Road, Caernarfon Gwynedd
North Wales LL55 1BD
Tel: (0286) 4602

CATEGORIES

| 3 | 4 | 5 |

Menai View hotel overlooks the Menai Strait and Anglesey, standing in the ideal position for exploring Caernarfon, Snowdonia National Park etc. Many facilities near at hand, boating, fishing, swimming, water-skiing, pony trekking, climbing and hiking. Food served up to midnight, good food and good service our speciality. Hotel open until midnight each night.

C	B & B PER PERSON PER NIGHT		DINNER B & B PER PERSON PER WEEK		5
	MIN £	MAX £	MIN £	MAX £	OPEN
	8.05	8.05	104.65	104.65	3—10

Prince of Wales*

Bangor Street
Caernarfon LL55 1AR
Tel: (0286) 3367

CATEGORIES

| 3 | 3 | 4 |

Located on the north approach road to this historic town. The hotel has 20 comfortable bedrooms including 3 family rooms. A choice of two attractive bars and a luxurious restaurant serving fine food and wines. Residents lounge with colour TV and car parking available.

T C	B & B PER PERSON PER NIGHT		DINNER B & B PER PERSON PER WEEK		20
	MIN £	MAX £	MIN £	MAX £	OPEN
	11	12.50	102	110	1—12

The Stables Hotel*

Llanwnda, Caernarfon
LL54 5SD
Tel: (0286) 830711 & 830413

CATEGORIES

| 6 | 3 | 5 |

Luxury accommodation in a secluded rural setting. Renowned restaurant, offering consistently good Welsh and international cuisine. Outdoor swimming pool. Excellent touring base for Snowdonia and Lleyn Peninsula. Personal service in a relaxed atmosphere. BTA commended country hotel/restaurant. Egon Ronay. Les Routiers. Brochure on request.

T C	B & B PER PERSON PER NIGHT		DINNER B & B PER PERSON PER WEEK		12
	MIN £	MAX £	MIN £	MAX £	OPEN
	19.50	23.50	145	175	1—12

For autumn to spring breaks send for our free Great Little Breaks booklet.

Guest Houses

'Bron Eifion'*

South Road, Caernarfon
Gwynedd LL55 2HP
Tel: (0286) 2565

CATEGORIES

| 3 | 3 | 2 |

A Georgian style house with this beautiful view. 10 minutes from castle and shops. 10 miles Snowdon. Central heating. 3 bedrooms, single, double and family. (Lloyd George slept here.) Cot hire, separate guest lounge. Colour TV, dining room, laundry facilities. Optional evening meals.

C	B & B PER PERSON PER NIGHT		DINNER B & B PER PERSON PER WEEK		3
	MIN £	MAX £	MIN £	MAX £	OPEN
	6	6	70	70	3—9

Bron-y-Maen*

North Road, Caernarfon
Gwynedd LL55 1BA
Tel: (0286) 2683

CATEGORIES

| 2 | 3 | 4 |

This guest house overlooks the Menai Strait near Caernarfon Castle. It is an ideal base for exploring the Snowdonia National Park, the Lleyn Peninsula and Anglesey. Eileen and John Taylor offer good home cooking and personal services. Cot, high chair, baby sitting available. Dogs welcome. SAE for brochure.

C	B & B PER PERSON PER NIGHT		DINNER B & B PER PERSON PER WEEK		6
	MIN £	MAX £	MIN £	MAX £	OPEN
	8	8	91	91	1—12

Glan Aber*

Constantine Road, Caernarfon
Gwynedd LL55 2LF
Tel: (0286) 3535

CATEGORIES

| 2 | 2 | 2 |

A family-run guest house. Five minutes walk to shops, buses and castle. Hot and cold water in double rooms. Special rates for children. Cot and high chair available. Lounge with TV dining room with separate tables. Evening meals. Snacks and packed lunches on request. Special winter rates.

C	B & B PER PERSON PER NIGHT		DINNER B & B PER PERSON PER WEEK		3
	MIN £	MAX £	MIN £	MAX £	OPEN
	5	7	56	70	1—12

Llys Olwen*

Morfa Netyn
Gwynedd LL53 6BT
Tel: (0758) 720493

CATEGORIES

| 2 | 3 | 2 |

Llys Olwen is located in a village of quiet beauty on the Lleyn Peninsula famous for its sandy beaches and safe bathing. Bed, Breakfast and Evening Dinner and packed lunches available. Children of all ages welcome (cots provided). Large lounge with colour television and stereo. Ample parking space. Brochure, tariff and further details from proprietors. Mr and Mrs D. A. Middleton.

C	B & B PER PERSON PER NIGHT		DINNER B & B PER PERSON PER WEEK		8
	MIN £	MAX £	MIN £	MAX £	OPEN
					4—10

Tal Menai*

Bangor Road, Caernarfon
Gwynedd LL55 1TP
Tel: (0286) 2160

CATEGORIES

| 3 | 3 | 2 |

Unobstructed view of Menai Strait and Anglesey. Private parking. Stands in its own grounds, one mile from town centre. Television lounge, hot and cold water, and shaver points in bedrooms. Fire certificate. RAC listed. Reductions for children and weekly bookings. Sorry no pets. Closed Easter.

C	B & B PER PERSON PER NIGHT		DINNER B & B PER PERSON PER WEEK		5
	MIN £	MAX £	MIN £	MAX £	OPEN
	6.50	7	60	62	3—10

Wallasea Guest House*

21 Segontium Terrace, Caernarfon
Gwynedd LL55 2PH
Tel: (0286) 3564

CATEGORIES

| 3 | 4 | 1 |

Quiet guest house overlooking castle, river and Menai Strait. Hot and cold water and shaver points all bedrooms. Double and family rooms. Full central heating. Lounge with colour television. Fire Certificated. Showers. Tea and coffee making facilities in bedrooms. No nylon sheets used. Three minutes to shops and buses.

T	B & B PER PERSON PER NIGHT		DINNER B & B PER PERSON PER WEEK		4
C	MIN £	MAX £	MIN £	MAX £	OPEN
	6	6.50			1—12

Farmhouses

Bronant Farm*

Bontnewydd, Caernarfon
Gwynedd LL54 7YF
Tel: (0286) 451

CATEGORIES

| 3 | 3 | 3 |

Bronant is architect designed stone house of character, over 100 years old. Mixed farm of 60 acres situated on a lovely spot overlooking Caernarfon Bay and Menai Strait, 500 yards from main road. Lounge with colour TV, dining room with separate tables. Good farmhouse food a speciality.

C	B & B PER PERSON PER NIGHT		DINNER B & B PER PERSON PER WEEK		4
	MIN £	MAX £	MIN £	MAX £	OPEN
	6	7.50	60	66	1—12

Bryn Gloch Farm

Betws Garmon, Caernarfon
Gwynedd LL54 7YY
Tel: (028 685) 216

CATEGORIES

| 2 | 2 | 2 |

Pleasantly situated on the fringe of the Snowdonia National Park. The converted farmhouse lies in the valley of the river Gwyrfai of which a ½ mile stretch is reserved for our guests to fish. Bryn Gloch is run under the personal supervision of the resident proprietors.

C	B & B PER PERSON PER NIGHT		DINNER B & B PER PERSON PER WEEK		5
	MIN £	MAX £	MIN £	MAX £	OPEN
	6	6.50	70	77	1—12

Ty'n Rhos Farm*

Seion, Llanddeiniolen
Caernarfon, Gwynedd LL55 3AE
Tel: (0248) 670489

CATEGORIES

| 3 | 3 | 2 |

A 72 acres dairy farm. Ideally situated close to Snowdonia and Anglesey. All bedrooms have wash basins, central heating and tea-making facilities. Cream is made on the farm from the herd of Pedigree Jersey cattle. Excellent cuisine offered using only fresh local or home produce. Ample parking.

T	B & B PER PERSON PER NIGHT		DINNER B & B PER PERSON PER WEEK		4
C	MIN £	MAX £	MIN £	MAX £	OPEN
	6		70		3—11

ℹ Tourist Information Centres are listed at back of book.

Caerphilly SOUTH WALES

Guesthouse

Watford Fach Farmhouse*

Watford Road, Caerphilly
Mid Glamorgan
Tel: (0222) 868949

CATEGORIES: 3 3 2

16th century listed farmhouse, countryside setting. Modern amenities. All rooms with hot and cold water. Central heating, TV lounge, separate dining room. Evening meal optional. Access to rooms any time. Large gardens. Private car park. Ideally placed Cardiff, Valleys and coast. 5 minutes Caerphilly Castle, town centre, municipal golf course and M4 motorway.

C	B & B PER PERSON PER NIGHT		DINNER B & B PER PERSON PER WEEK		6
	MIN £	MAX £	MIN £	MAX £	OPEN
	6	8	50	70	1—12

Caldicot SOUTH WALES

Motel

Deepweir Motel*

Deepweir, Caldicot
Newport, Gwent NP64 JD
Tel: (0291) 420271

CATEGORIES: 5 4 3

Situated in beautiful grounds near castle. Approximately ¾ mile to Severn Estuary. Three miles to St. Pierre golf club. Individual decor. All bedrooms colour TV. Restaurant. Extensive menu open to everyone. Dining during summer on the Patio. Plenty of parking space for cars. Honeymoon suite with four poster bed.

C	B & B PER PERSON PER NIGHT		DINNER B & B PER PERSON PER WEEK		10
	MIN £	MAX £	MIN £	MAX £	OPEN
	13	16.50			1—12

Capel Bangor MID WALES

Farmhouse

Fron Farm

Capel Bangor, Aberystwyth
Dyfed SY23 3LT
Tel: (097 084) 221

CATEGORIES: 1 2 2

Standing on a hillside overlooking the Rheidol Valley and beautiful scenery. A delightful place for a country holiday, yet only five miles from Aberystwyth and the sea. Excellent food served. Facilities for varied sports in the area, shooting on the farm. A warm welcome is guaranteed.

C	B & B PER PERSON PER NIGHT		DINNER B & B PER PERSON PER WEEK		2
	MIN £	MAX £	MIN £	MAX £	OPEN
	5.50	6.50	55	60	1—12

Capel Curig NORTH WALES

Hotels

Bryn Tyrch Hotel

Capel Curig
Gwynedd LL24 0EL
Tel: (06904) 223

CATEGORIES: 3 4 4

Spectacular views around Snowdonia from this comfortable attractive 2 star hotel. The ideal centre for climbing, walking or family holidays. 350 yards of own trout fishing plus golf and pony trekking and choice of sandy beaches nearby. Restaurant with excellent table d'hôte menu. Bar snacks, 3 bars, 2 lounges, colour TV, large garden.

T C	B & B PER PERSON PER NIGHT		DINNER B & B PER PERSON PER WEEK		16
	MIN £	MAX £	MIN £	MAX £	OPEN
	9.75	10.75	103.50	117.50	1—12

Cobden's Hotel*

Capel Curig
near Betws-y-Coed, Gwynedd
Tel: (06904) 243

CATEGORIES: 3 4 5

Extensively refurbished, situated on the A5 in the heart of Snowdonia Park. The ideal homely base for exploring North Wales. Full licence, full central heating, restaurant, bar meals, children and dogs welcome. TV lounge, pony trekking, fishing, walking, climbing, castles and slates.

T C	B & B PER PERSON PER NIGHT		DINNER B & B PER PERSON PER WEEK		19
	MIN £	MAX £	MIN £	MAX £	OPEN
	9.50	15.50	102.50	185.50	1—12

Capel Garmon NORTH WALES

Inn

White Horse Inn*

Capel Garmon, Llanrwst
Gwynedd LL26 0RW
Tel: (06902) 271

CATEGORIES: 4 3 4

Situated in the village of Capel Garmon, 1½ miles from Betws-y-Coed. Within easy reach of Conwy, Snowdonia and coastal resorts. The Inn affords all modern comforts, whilst retaining the old world charm. All bedrooms having private bathrooms and toilet en suite. Tea and coffee making facilities. Centrally heated.

	B & B PER PERSON PER NIGHT		DINNER B & B PER PERSON PER WEEK		6
	MIN £	MAX £	MIN £	MAX £	OPEN
	10	12			1—12

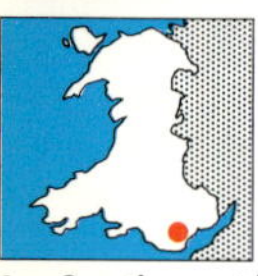

Map ref: Mb5
Capital of Wales, Cardiff is a coal port turned commercial centre for South-east Wales and seat of much of the administration of Wales. Many of the buildings reflect this: National Museum, Welsh office, University and Castle. Shopping draws visitors from 50 miles around to the precincts and St. David's shopping centre. As gateway to the valleys, served by rail and road, tourists find a convenient centre to explore coast and country in a region crammed with interest.

Hotels, Motels and Inns

Auden Hotel*

Romilly Road, Cardiff
South Glamorgan, CF5 1FL
Tel: (0222) 31999

CATEGORIES: 3 4 4

Easy access to City Centre and M4 motorway. Large car park. Modern hotel accommodation. All rooms centrally heated, TV, and tea-making facilities. Licensed bar. Fine cuisine. RAC listed. Ideal touring base. On bus routes. Let us welcome you to the friendly and well run Auden Hotel.

	B & B PER PERSON PER NIGHT		DINNER B & B PER PERSON PER WEEK		8
	MIN £	MAX £	MIN £	MAX £	OPEN
	9	10.50	91	101.50	1—12

Balkan Hotel

144 Newport Road
Cardiff
Tel: (0222) 491790

CATEGORIES: 3 3 2

The hotel is a small family hotel run by proprietors. Residents lounge with coloured television, car park, some bedrooms with private shower and coloured televisons. Two minutes from Cardiff city centre with all its many attractions. Travelling distance of Castell Coch, Brecon Beacons, Caerphilly castle. Full fire certificate.

C	B & B PER PERSON PER NIGHT		DINNER B & B PER PERSON PER WEEK		14
	MIN £	MAX £	MIN £	MAX £	OPEN
	9.20	11.50	96.60	112.70	1—12

Beverley Hotel

Cathedral Road
Cardiff CF1 9PG
Tel: (0222) 43443

CATEGORIES: 5 4 5

Recently completely refurbished and conveniently located north-west of the city centre near to Bute Park. An ideal location for the motorist. All 18 bedrooms are most comfortably furnished and have private bathroom, colour television and tea and coffee making facilities etc. Pleasant restaurant and bar. Free parking.

T	B & B PER PERSON PER NIGHT		DINNER B & B PER PERSON PER WEEK		18
C	MIN £	MAX £	MIN £	MAX £	OPEN
	31				1—12

Bristol Hotel*

9 Penarth Road, Cardiff
CF1 5DH
Tel: (0222) 373488/27084

CATEGORIES: 3 3 4

A privately owned city centre hotel close to Cardiff Castle, National Stadium and Train/Bus Stations. 21 bedrooms, all with en suite facilities, colour TV, radio/intercom. Weekend £29 includes room and English breakfast for 2 nights, Fri/Sat or Sat/Sun. 2 dinners and VAT. Offer available all year except Christmas and Rugby International weekends.

T	B & B PER PERSON PER NIGHT		DINNER B & B PER PERSON PER WEEK		21
C	MIN £	MAX £	MIN £	MAX £	OPEN
		14.38		110	1—12

Bronte Hotel

160-162 Newport Road, Cardiff
Glamorgan CF2 1DL
Tel: (0222) 499167

CATEGORIES: 3 4 4

Welcome to Cardiff and The Bronte, 160-162 Newport Road, Cardiff. Close to city centre. TV, telephone, coffee facilities to all rooms. Sauna, solarium, gymnasium. Access, Barclaycard accepted. Cardiff (0222) 499167 4 lines.

C	B & B PER PERSON PER NIGHT		DINNER B & B PER PERSON PER WEEK		23
	MIN £	MAX £	MIN £	MAX £	OPEN
	12.50	15	108.50		1—12

Central Hotel

St Mary Street, Cardiff
CF1 5RH
Tel: (0222) 396455

CATEGORIES: 3 4 4

For a visit to Wales capital city, the Central Hotel provides an ideal budget-price basis, convenient for Cardiff Castle, main shopping areas, city centre and adjacent to the main railway station. Various brochure available all year.

T	B & B PER PERSON PER NIGHT		DINNER B & B PER PERSON PER WEEK		78
C	MIN £	MAX £	MIN £	MAX £	OPEN
	13.75				1—12

Cheriton Hotel

98 Fidlas Road, Llanishen, Cardiff
South Glamorgan, CF4 5NE
Tel: (0222) 759730

CATEGORIES: 3 3 2

This family-run licensed hotel is on the northern end of the city and 3½ miles from the centre. All meals are prepared on the premises by the proprietress who is well known amongst her clients for the excellent cuisine. Ample car park. Bus and train service nearby.

C	B & B PER PERSON PER NIGHT		DINNER B & B PER PERSON PER WEEK		11
	MIN £	MAX £	MIN £	MAX £	OPEN
	9.20	9.20	98.63	98.63	1—12

Clayton Hotel

65 Stacey Road, Roath, Cardiff
South Glamorgan
Tel: (0222) 492345/491592

CATEGORIES: 3 3 2

This long established, well recommended hotel provides personal ownership, service and excellent five course home-cooked evening meal. A comfortable TV lounge is provided with separate bar and full residential licence. Ideally situated for city centre and castle and to junction 29 of M4 for convenient weekend break.

T	B & B PER PERSON PER NIGHT		DINNER B & B PER PERSON PER WEEK		10
C	MIN £	MAX £	MIN £	MAX £	OPEN
	10	14	105	133	1—12

Colum House Hotel*

1 Colum Road, Cathays, Cardiff
South Glamorgan
Tel: (0222) 394204

CATEGORIES

3	3	1

Well appointed small family-run hotel. Ten minutes walk through Cathays park to city centre, castle and museum. On main bus route to and from bus/railway stations. Dining lounge separate from colour TV lounge. Single beds 3'6", double beds 4'6". Many rooms sound-proofed. Full Fire Certificate.

	B & B PER PERSON PER NIGHT		DINNER B & B PER PERSON PER WEEK		6
	MIN £	MAX £	MIN £	MAX £	OPEN
	9	10			1—12

Crest Hotel

Westgate Street, Cardiff, CF1 1JB
Tel: (0222) 388681
Telex: 497258

CATEGORIES

6	5	6

Situated on the banks of the Taff, overlooking Cardiff Castle in the city centre. Within walking distance of shopping centre, next to the Arms Park. All bedrooms have private bathroom, plus colour television, radio, tea and coffee making facilities etc. Two bars and restaurant. Free car parking.

T C	B & B PER PERSON PER NIGHT		DINNER B & B PER PERSON PER WEEK		160
	MIN £	MAX £	MIN £	MAX £	OPEN
	35				1—12

Four Firs Motel & Restaurant*

Coedcae Lane, Pontyclun
near Cardiff
Tel: (0443) 222012/225285

CATEGORIES

4	4	4

Modern motel complex, all rooms en-suite. Colour television, tea-making facilities, radio, intercom, fully licensed. 5 minutes from M4 exit 34. Ideal centre for major industrial concerns. Royal Mint, L'Oreal, Fram, BSC, Ford, etc. Conference facilities available. Send for full colour brochure.

T C	B & B PER PERSON PER NIGHT		DINNER B & B PER PERSON PER WEEK		20
	MIN £	MAX £	MIN £	MAX £	OPEN
	18	18			1—12

Gwesty Caerdydd Cardiff Hotel

55/59 Despencer Street, Riverside
Canton, Cardiff
Tel: (0222) 395601

CATEGORIES

4	5	6

A privately owned modern hotel with artistic character, situated close to town centre. Full central heating. Most bedrooms with own toilet and TV and tea/coffee making facilities. Fully licensed. Three bars, conference room, hair salon. Contact the Manageress for further details. Brochure available.

T C	B & B PER PERSON PER NIGHT		DINNER B & B PER PERSON PER WEEK		38
	MIN £	MAX £	MIN £	MAX £	OPEN
	19	29	170	240	1—12

Imperial Hotel

132 Newport Road, Cardiff
South Wales, CF2 1DJ
Tel: (0222) 490032/491548

CATEGORIES

3	3	2

The Imperial is situated on the main through road, five minutes from the city centre. 32 comfortable bedrooms with shaver points and radios, some with showers. A relaxing comfortable television lounge and a fully stocked lounge bar. A la carte or table d'hote menus are available. Car park.

C	B & B PER PERSON PER NIGHT		DINNER B & B PER PERSON PER WEEK		32
	MIN £	MAX £	MIN £	MAX £	OPEN
	10.50	12.50	98.50	100.50	1—12

Inn on the Avenue*

Circle Way East, Cardiff, CF3 7XF
Tel: (0222) 732520
Telex: 497582

CATEGORIES

6	6	6

When in Cardiff, stay at Wales's premier hotel. AA**** RAC**** with impressive character and quiet dignity. Dominating Eastern Avenue, just off M4. Central to Cardiff's industrial, cultural and sports complexes. Ideal touring base for historic valleys and Brecon Beacons National Park. Spacious car parking. A hotel with style.

T C	B & B PER PERSON PER NIGHT		DINNER B & B PER PERSON PER WEEK		152
	MIN £	MAX £	MIN £	MAX £	OPEN
	33	33	158	158	1—12

Olympos Hotel

104 Penylan Road, Cardiff
South Glamorgan, CF2 5HY
Tel: (0222) 491940

CATEGORIES

3	3	3

A city hotel with the advantage of a large garden and car park. Adjacent to Roath Park Lake and convenient to city centre and M4. Hot and cold water in all bedrooms, Lounge with colour TV. Dining room and residents bar. Central heating. Fire Certificate granted.

C	B & B PER PERSON PER NIGHT		DINNER B & B PER PERSON PER WEEK		13
	MIN £	MAX £	MIN £	MAX £	OPEN
	9.20	9.20	98	98	1—12

Park Hotel

Park Place, Cardiff, South Glamorgan
CF1 3UD
Tel: (0222) 23471 & Telex: 497195

CATEGORIES

6	6	6

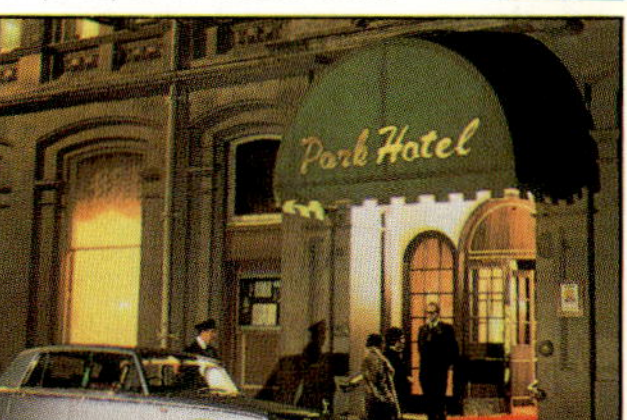

City centre luxury hotel close to castle and shopping precinct. All bedrooms with private bath and shower, colour TV. In-house movies. Two restaurants offering both traditional and French cuisine. The Theatre Garden Restaurant and bar is open until 2.00am. Large car park adjacent to hotel. Special weekend rates available.

T C	B & B PER PERSON PER NIGHT		DINNER B & B PER PERSON PER WEEK		108
	MIN £	MAX £	MIN £	MAX £	OPEN
	21.50	24.50	196	217	1—12

Phoenix Hotel Ltd*

199/201 Fidlas Road, Llanishen
Cardiff
Tel: (0222) 764615

CATEGORIES

3	5	5

A warm and friendly hotel personally run and supervised by the proprietor. 26 letting rooms (most with bath). Charming à la carte restaurant. Fully licensed.

T C	B & B PER PERSON PER NIGHT		DINNER B & B PER PERSON PER WEEK		25
	MIN £	MAX £	MIN £	MAX £	OPEN
	13	17			1—12

Children stay at reduced rates, wherever you see this symbol.

C

Post House Hotel*

Pentwyn Road, Pentwyn, Cardiff
South Glamorgan CF2 7XA
Tel: (0222) 731212 & Telex: 497633

CATEGORIES: 6 | 5 | 6

A modern hotel 4 miles from the city centre, close to the M4 motorway extension. All 150 bedrooms have private bath, telephone, radio, colour TV and tea/coffee making facilities. Central heating and ample car parking. Restaurant and coffee shop. Bargain break weekends available. Ideal base for touring.

T	B & B PER PERSON PER NIGHT		DINNER B & B PER PERSON PER WEEK		🛏 150
C	MIN £	MAX £	MIN £	MAX £	OPEN
	23.45				1—12

Royal Hotel

St Mary's Street, Cardiff
South Glamorgan CF1 1LL
Tel: (0222) 23321

CATEGORIES: 4 | 6 | 5

Well known city centre hotel close to railway station and main shopping area. Convenient for St. David's shopping centre and Concert Hall. New Royal Carving Room offers value for money food. Choice of comfortable bars. All rooms with colour TV many with bath. Special weekend rates available. An Embassy Hotel.

T	B & B PER PERSON PER NIGHT		DINNER B & B PER PERSON PER WEEK		🛏 68
C	MIN £	MAX £	MIN £	MAX £	OPEN
	15	18			1—12

St Mellons Hotel & Country Club*

St. Mellons, Cardiff
South Glamorgan CF3 8XR
Tel: (0633) 680355

CATEGORIES: 6 | 4 | 6

Situated half-way between Cardiff and Newport, just off the M4. Set in private gardens. St. Mellons offers excellent food and accommodation facilities. Include pleasant public rooms, French cuisine, bars. Conference rooms. Ample parking. Leisure centre which residents may use on the same basis as members.

T	B & B PER PERSON PER NIGHT		DINNER B & B PER PERSON PER WEEK		🛏 27
C	MIN £	MAX £	MIN £	MAX £	OPEN
	21	29			1—12

Sandringham Hotel

St. Mary Street, Cardiff
CF1 29L
Tel: (0222) 32161

CATEGORIES: 3 | 3 | 5

A friendly commercial hotel situated in the centre of Cardiff. Perfectly situated for shopping, sightseeing and the National Stadium. Busby's restaurant is pleasant, relaxing and offers excellent food. Doogals the ultimate new fun experience in eating and drinking. An unforgettable fun experience with exciting food, cocktails and ice creams.

T	B & B PER PERSON PER NIGHT		DINNER B & B PER PERSON PER WEEK		🛏 29
C	MIN £	MAX £	MIN £	MAX £	OPEN
	16.50	17.60	150.50	158.20	1—12

Tane's Hotel*

148 Newport Road, Cardiff
CF2 1DJ
Tel: (0222) 491755

CATEGORIES: 3 | 3 | 2

A warm welcome awaits you at this small family hotel run under the personal supervision of proprietors. Residents lounge with colour television. Car Park. Convenient to M4. On main bus route. Ideally situated for easy access to city centre, Cardiff Castle and all local amenities. Full fire certificate.

C	B & B PER PERSON PER NIGHT		DINNER B & B PER PERSON PER WEEK		🛏 9
	MIN £	MAX £	MIN £	MAX £	OPEN
	9.20	11.50	96.60	112.70	1—12

Wentloog Castle Hotel

Castleton, near Cardiff
CF3 8UQ
Tel: (0633) 680591

CATEGORIES: 6 | 6 | 5

55 bedrooms with bath, shower, colour TV, telephone, tea/coffee making facilities. Situated off main Cardiff-Newport Road, for business visitors requiring a central base and tourists bound for beauty spots of Chepstow, Severn Valley, new shopping mall, St. David's Centre, Cardiff. Weekend packages and full conference facilities.

T	B & B PER PERSON PER NIGHT		DINNER B & B PER PERSON PER WEEK		🛏 55
C	MIN £	MAX £	MIN £	MAX £	OPEN
	17.90	20.90	162.50	183.80	1—12

Wenvoe Hotel

477 Cowbridge Road West, Ely
Cardiff, South Glamorgan
Tel: (0222) 591050

CATEGORIES: 3 | 3 | 2

An attractive, licensed, family-run hotel, ideal for both commercial business and tourist alike. Situated on A48, west side of Cardiff. An easy to find hotel with large car park. Close to famous Welsh Folk Museum and coastal resorts. Cardiff-Wales Airport 15 minutes drive away.

C	B & B PER PERSON PER NIGHT		DINNER B & B PER PERSON PER WEEK		🛏 10
	MIN £	MAX £	MIN £	MAX £	OPEN
	8.50		14		1—12

Wynford Hotel

Clare Street, Riverside
Cardiff, CF1 8SD
Tel: (0222) 371983

CATEGORIES: 4 | 5 | 6

Very close to the city centre, train and bus stations, the Wynford is a privately owned hotel, personally supervised by the proprietor and priding itself on a warm welcome, attentive service and excellent facilities. These include a comfortable lounge, 2 cosy bars, music and dancing and our 2 restaurants. All rooms have colour TV and telephone and several offer private shower and toilet. Car park. French, German and Spanish spoken.

C	B & B PER PERSON PER NIGHT		DINNER B & B PER PERSON PER WEEK		🛏 20
	MIN £	MAX £	MIN £	MAX £	OPEN
	10.50	16	97.30	131.95	1—12

Guest Houses

Acorn Lodge*

182 Cathedral Road, Cardiff
South Glamorgan, CF1 9JE
Tel: (0222) 21373

CATEGORIES: 3 | 3 | 1

Near parkland on bus route and within a few minutes walk from city centre. Full English breakfast, full central heating. All rooms with hot and cold water and shaving sockets. Car park. Guest lounge with colour television. Bathrooms with showers. Evening tea and coffee included in price.

	B & B PER PERSON PER NIGHT		DINNER B & B PER PERSON PER WEEK		🛏 6
	MIN £	MAX £	MIN £	MAX £	OPEN
	6.50	7.50			1—12

Ace House*

154 The Philog, Whitchurch, Cardiff
South Wales, CF4 1ED
Tel: (0222) 67850

CATEGORIES: 2 | 2 | 2

We offer clean and comfortable accommodation, with a good breakfast at our privately run, small guest house. Hot and cold water, shaver points and tea-making facilities in each room. Colour TV in sitting room. Ideally situated 2 miles from city centre on A470 with easy parking. Alternatively, taxi available on premises.

C	B & B PER PERSON PER NIGHT		DINNER B & B PER PERSON PER WEEK		🛏 3
	MIN £	MAX £	MIN £	MAX £	OPEN
	7	8	75	85	1—12

Alvely Guest House*

42 Plasturton Gardens
(off Cathedral Road), Canton, Cardiff
South Glamorgan, CF1 9HF
Tel: (0222) 30432

CATEGORIES: 3 | 3 | 1

Cardiff. Alvely guest house 42 Plasturton Gardens, off Cathedral Road, Canton, Cardiff is a three storey Victorian residence, centrally located for most tourist attractions. Cardiff Castle, Civic Centre, town centre. Happy family atmosphere. Bed and breakfast £6.50 per person per night. Street parking, central heating, TV lounge. Telephone 0222/30432.

C	B & B PER PERSON PER NIGHT		DINNER B & B PER PERSON PER WEEK		4
	MIN £	MAX £	MIN £	MAX £	OPEN
	6.50	6.50			1—12

Anthony House

7 Teilo Street, off Cathedral Road
Cardiff, South Glamorgan
Tel: (0222) 24597

CATEGORIES: 3 | 2 | 2

Situated in beautiful Victorian setting surrounded by quiet parklands, castle, river, walks. 1 mile city centre, sports facilities, horse riding, mini-golf, shops. Good restaurant, hot and cold water. Shaving points in all bedrooms, single, double, family rooms. Special rates children, lounge with colour TV. Full central heating.

T C	B & B PER PERSON PER NIGHT		DINNER B & B PER PERSON PER WEEK		5
	MIN £	MAX £	MIN £	MAX £	OPEN
	8	10	75		1—12

"Bon Maison"*

39 Plasturton Gardens
(off Cathedral Road), Pontcanna
Cardiff, CF1 9HG
Tel: (0222) 23660

CATEGORIES: 3 | 2 | 2

Bon Maison, family-run guest house. Situated in beautiful and quiet area. 10 minutes walk city and civic centre, castle, cathedral, parks. Reduced rates for children sharing with parents, cots available. All diets catered for. Pets by arrangement. 2 mins walk bus stop for train and bus station.

C	B & B PER PERSON PER NIGHT		DINNER B & B PER PERSON PER WEEK		3
	MIN £	MAX £	MIN £	MAX £	OPEN
	7	7.50	56.50		1—12

Coniston House*

11 Dyfrig Street, off Cathedral Road
Cardiff, South Glamorgan CF1 9LR
Tel: (0222) 32249

CATEGORIES: 2 | 2 | 1

Homely friendly atmosphere. Colour TV in lounge. Full breakfast. Within walking distance of city centre and shops. Central for all tourist attractions, castle and museums. Also situated on main bus route. Close to railway station. For weekly terms and further details contact Mrs. Freda Heron.

	B & B PER PERSON PER NIGHT		DINNER B & B PER PERSON PER WEEK		4
	MIN £	MAX £	MIN £	MAX £	OPEN
	6.50	7.50			1—12

Domus Guest House

201 Newport Road, Roath, Cardiff
South Glamorgan, CF2 1AJ
Tel: (0222) 495785

CATEGORIES: 3 | 2 | 2

Situated one mile from city centre with frequent bus services to coach, bus and railway stations and central area. The guest house is AA and RAC listed and is run under the personal supervision of the proprietors. There is a licensed bar, secure car park and fire Certificate granted.

T C	B & B PER PERSON PER NIGHT		DINNER B & B PER PERSON PER WEEK		8
	MIN £	MAX £	MIN £	MAX £	OPEN
	7.75	10	85.75	101.50	1—12

Glan-y-Dwr

157 Lake Road West, Roath
Cardiff
Tel: (0222) 758126

CATEGORIES: 2 | 1 | 1

Glan-y-Dwr means "Water's Edge". Large and pretty family room in a family house. Gets morning sun. Room overlooks Roath Park Lake and can sleep five (two in bunk-beds). Special rates for children. Gas fire. Wash basin with shaver points. Very convenient bus. No parking problems.

C	B & B PER PERSON PER NIGHT		DINNER B & B PER PERSON PER WEEK		1
	MIN £	MAX £	MIN £	MAX £	OPEN
	6	8			1—12

Hillside Guest House*

42 Ty Gwyn Road, Penylan, Cardiff
CF2 5JG
Tel: Priv. 485577 Guests 491665

CATEGORIES: 1 | 3 | 2

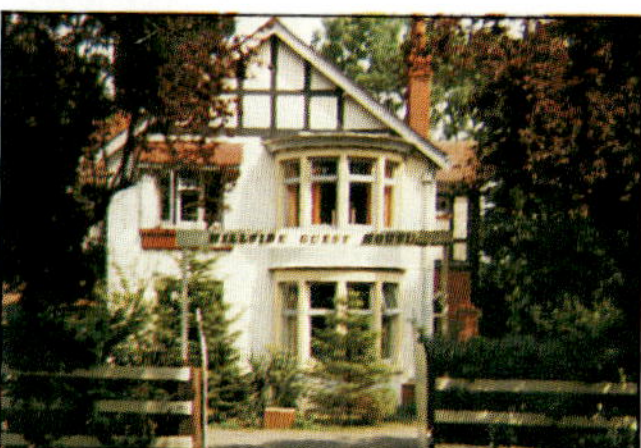

Under new management. The guest house is situated in quiet, secluded surroundings and offers a friendly welcome with comfortable homely accommodation. Snacks, beverages and meals available. 2 miles from city centre, 10 minutes away from shops, cinema, buses and beautiful Roath Park Lake. Fully centrally heated. Car park facilities.

	B & B PER PERSON PER NIGHT		DINNER B & B PER PERSON PER WEEK		9
	MIN £	MAX £	MIN £	MAX £	OPEN
	8.50	10	80.15	90.65	1—12

Novatel*

7 Plasturton Place, Pontcanna
Cardiff, South Glamorgan, CF1 9HP
Tel: (0222) 387677

CATEGORIES: 3 | 4 | 2

Novatel is situated in the Victorian area of Cardiff, overlooking gardens. Full central heating, hot and cold water in rooms, colour TV lounge, close to the city centre, Cardiff Castle and all local amenities. Guests assured of friendly personal service. Access and Barclay Card credit facilities available.

C	B & B PER PERSON PER NIGHT		DINNER B & B PER PERSON PER WEEK		7
	MIN £	MAX £	MIN £	MAX £	OPEN
	8.25	8.25		75.50	1—12

Rosanna House*

175 Cathedral Road, Pontcanna
Cardiff, CF1 9PL
Tel: (0222) 29780

CATEGORIES: 3 | 3 | 2

Recently re-modernised and re-furbished, Rosanna House is close to city centre, Cardiff Castle, Sophia Gardens and Llandaff Cathedral. Each of the nine rooms has handbasin with hot and cold water. Tea/coffee making facilities. A comfortable lounge with colour television.

C	B & B PER PERSON PER NIGHT		DINNER B & B PER PERSON PER WEEK		9
	MIN £	MAX £	MIN £	MAX £	OPEN
	8	10	70	80	1—12

Tyla'r Eos*

Heol-y-Parc, Pentyrch, near Cardiff
South Glamorgan, CF4 8NB
Tel: (0222) 890266

CATEGORIES: 1 | 2 | 2

Unusually attractive house, spacious garden, quiet country area. 15 minutes drive from city centre. Ideal touring, walking. Private lounge, colour television, every consideration. Excellent food. Bed and breakfast, evening meal optional, home cooking. Good parking space.

	B & B PER PERSON PER NIGHT		DINNER B & B PER PERSON PER WEEK		3
	MIN £	MAX £	MIN £	MAX £	OPEN
	8	10	78	90	1—12

Map ref: Fa5
A truly agricultural town, Cardigan sits astride the Teifi river, 3 miles from its mouth at Gwbert. St. Dogmael's Abbey and Cardigan Castle testify to a lengthy history but the area's chief charm lies in a sylvan river and sandy coast near at hand.

Hotels and Inn

Bell Hotel*

4 Pendre, Cardigan
Dyfed
Tel: (0239) 612629

CATEGORIES

| 3 | 2 | 4 |

For those who enjoy staying at inns, small and friendly with lots of character. The Bell has 8 bedrooms and a moderately priced restaurant within a short car ride of beaches, golf course, salmon river and delightful countryside. Proprietors Jenny and Malcolm Wood. Telephone or write for terms.

T	B & B PER PERSON PER NIGHT		DINNER B & B PER PERSON PER WEEK		8
C	MIN £	MAX £	MIN £	MAX £	OPEN
	8.50	9.50	86	92	1—12

The Glanteifi Private Hotel*

St. Dogmaels, Cardigan
Dyfed SA43 3LL
Tel: (0239) 612353

CATEGORIES

| 3 | 3 | 3 |

Comfortable, well appointed family-run hotel. Picturesque position overlooking Teifi estuary. Cardigan market town 1½ miles. Near beaches. Bedrooms with private bathrooms. Family suites. Full central heating. Residential license. Colour television. Choice of menu. Special childrens dinner. Easy parking. Seven acres of grounds. Riding, sailing, canoeing, tennis on premises. Colour brochure.

T	B & B PER PERSON PER NIGHT		DINNER B & B PER PERSON PER WEEK		12
C	MIN £	MAX £	MIN £	MAX £	OPEN
	9.50	13.75	101	128.50	1—12

Gwesty Castell Malgwyn Hotel

Llechryd, Cardigan
Dyfed SA43 2QA
Tel: (023 987) 382

CATEGORIES

| 4 | 4 | 5 |

Elegant country mansion set in 50 acres of meadow and woodland alongside the River Teifi. Famous for its salmon and coracle fishermen. Recent improvements have provided superb guest rooms, restaurant offering traditional Welsh and chef's specialities, heated swimming pool (open May to September). Numerous sandy beaches and tourist attractions within easy reach. Golf at Cardigan and Newport. Salmon and sewin fishing available to residents on 5 mile stretch of Teifi. Ideal for touring holiday. Bargain breaks available—details from resident proprietors.

T	B & B PER PERSON PER NIGHT		DINNER B & B PER PERSON PER WEEK		24
C	MIN £	MAX £	MIN £	MAX £	OPEN
	14	21	117	165	1—12

Llwyndyrys Mansion Hotel

Llechryd, Cardigan
Dyfed SA43 2QP
Tel: (023987) 263

CATEGORIES

| 3 | 3 | 4 |

Homely hotel renowned for food, entertainment, friendliness. Magnificent views of own stretch of Teifi (Salmon, Trout, Sewin). Parkland walks, pitch and putt. "Welsh" nights etc. midweek in ballroom. Central for beaches. National Park and mountains. Tea-making facilities. Central heating. Mini weekends with dinner dances—early and late season.

T	B & B PER PERSON PER NIGHT		DINNER B & B PER PERSON PER WEEK		12
C	MIN £	MAX £	MIN £	MAX £	OPEN
	8	8	70	70	1—12

Rhydgarnwen Mansion

Rhydgarnwen, Llantood, Cardigan
Dyfed SA43 3NW
Tel: (0239) 612742

CATEGORIES

| 3 | 3 | 5 |

A small country house hotel under the personal supervision of the owners, Susan and Huw Jones. Cordon Bleu food, selected wines. Pretty bedrooms overlooking gardens. A lovely setting in its own grounds. Excellent local facilities for golf, riding, fishing, hill and coastal walking. Historical interests. Sea 1 mile.

T	B & B PER PERSON PER NIGHT		DINNER B & B PER PERSON PER WEEK		3
	MIN £	MAX £	MIN £	MAX £	OPEN
	14.50	15.50	120	135	1—12

Tourist Information Centres are listed at back of book.

This symbol means you can book through your local travel agent.

Webley Hotel

Poppit Sands, St. Dogmael's
Cardigan, Dyfed SA43 3LN
Tel: (0239) 612085

CATEGORIES

| 3 | 3 | 4 |

Detached riverside, fully licensed hotel. Sandy beach and National Trust park 400 yards. Rooms with sea/river views, showers, TV, tea-making facilities. Choose from our varied menu and enjoy real ale. Games room. Fishing trips, trekking or lessons arranged from hotel. Car park.

	B & B PER PERSON PER NIGHT		DINNER B & B PER PERSON PER WEEK		10
T C	MIN £	MAX £	MIN £	MAX £	OPEN
	9	10.75	85.50	96	1—12

Guest Houses

Brynhyfryd Guest House*

Gwbert Road, Cardigan
Dyfed
Tel: (0239) 612861

CATEGORIES

| 3 | 3 | 4 |

Situated on the pleasant outskirts of the town, two miles from the coast. An ideal centre for touring West Wales or relaxing on the many sandy beaches. All bedrooms have heating and hot and cold water, comfortable television lounge. Homely atmosphere, good food, offering real value for money. Parking readily available.

	B & B PER PERSON PER NIGHT		DINNER B & B PER PERSON PER WEEK		5
C	MIN £	MAX £	MIN £	MAX £	OPEN
	6	7	60	66	1—12

The Old Vicarage

Llandygwydd, Cardigan
West Wales, Dyfed
Tel: (023987) 587

CATEGORIES

| 1 | 2 | 2 |

Take a get away from it all break at the old Vicarage in the lovely village of Llandygwydd. Great centre for walking, fishing, beaches. All home cooking and produce. Few mins. drive from famous Cenarth Falls and the River Teifi.

	B & B PER PERSON PER NIGHT		DINNER B & B PER PERSON PER WEEK		4
C	MIN £	MAX £	MIN £	MAX £	OPEN
	5	6.50	60	65	3—10

Children stay at reduced rates, wherever you see this symbol.

C

Carmarthen

SOUTH WALES

Map ref: Kc2
Hub of west Wales' agricultural life and communications, Carmarthen, astride the Towy river, is central for a diverse touring mixture. South lie sand beaches and old castles— Kidwelly and Laugharne—and the wonderful world of Dylan Thomas country. To the north lie wooded valleys and wool weaving mills nestling on the riverbanks.

Hotels

The Cothi Bridge Hotel*

Pontarcothi, Carmarthen
Dyfed SA32 7NG
Tel: (026 788) 251

CATEGORIES

| 4 | 4 | 5 |

A country hotel delightfully situated on the banks of the Cothi and personally run by the owners. Our restaurant has an excellent reputation and our bar a warm and friendly atmosphere. Close to the end of the M4 and central for exploring Mid and West Wales. Salmon fishing.

	B & B PER PERSON PER NIGHT		DINNER B & B PER PERSON PER WEEK		16
T C	MIN £	MAX £	MIN £	MAX £	OPEN
	12	14	99	123	1—12

Derlwyn Mansion Hotel*

Alltwalis Road, Carmarthen
Dyfed SA32 7DZ
Tel: (055 934) 636

CATEGORIES

| 3 | 3 | 5 |

Small friendly hotel with relaxed informal atmosphere. A la carte menu accompanied by free glass of wine. TV, lounge, bar, modern bedrooms, some en suite. Attractive gardens. Full Fire Certificate. Indoor swimming pool planned for 1983. Well situated for fishing, riding, golf, beaches. Let us make your holiday happy.

	B & B PER PERSON PER NIGHT		DINNER B & B PER PERSON PER WEEK		7
C	MIN £	MAX £	MIN £	MAX £	OPEN
	9.50	11.50	90	110	1—12

Ivy Bush Royal Hotel*

Spilman Street, Carmarthen
Dyfed SA31 1LG
Tel: (0267) 5111 Telex: 48520

CATEGORIES

| 5 | 5 | 6 |

Historic hotel in town centre with 88 bedrooms, mostly with private bath and all with telephone, radio, colour TV and tea/coffee making facilities. Central heating, car park. Weekend bargain breaks available. Ideal base for touring West Wales and visiting the many fine castles in the vicinity.

	B & B PER PERSON PER NIGHT		DINNER B & B PER PERSON PER WEEK		80
T C	MIN £	MAX £	MIN £	MAX £	OPEN
	20.25				1—12

Werndale Hotel*

Bancyfelin, Carmarthen
Dyfed SA33 5NE
Tel: (026782) 204

CATEGORIES

| 3 | 3 | 2 |

Situated 6 miles west of Carmarthen on main A40. Hot and cold water and shaver points in all bedrooms. Single, double and family rooms available, lounge with colour television, dining room with separate tables. Full central heating. Fire Certificate granted. Car parking facilities. Fishing can be arranged.

	B & B PER PERSON PER NIGHT		DINNER B & B PER PERSON PER WEEK		9
C	MIN £	MAX £	MIN £	MAX £	OPEN
	18	20	100	110	1—12

Guest Houses

The Laurels*

Johnstown, Carmarthen
Dyfed, South Wales, SA31 3HH
Tel: (0267) 7066

CATEGORIES: 3 2 1

Ten minutes walk from town centre. Hot and cold water in all rooms. Lounge with TV. Dining room with separate tables. Full central heating. Double and family rooms with special rates for children. Within half hour run by car to all beaches. Good touring area. Free car park.

C	B & B PER PERSON PER NIGHT		DINNER B & B PER PERSON PER WEEK		3
	MIN £	MAX £	MIN £	MAX £	OPEN
	6	7			4—9

Magnolia Guest House*

20 Wellfield Road, Carmarthen
Dyfed SA31 1DS
Tel: (0267) 7562

CATEGORIES: 1 3 2

Five minutes walk to town centre, near bus and rail transport. Riding, trekking, swimming, golf, fishing locally. Single, double, family rooms. Reduced rates for children. Lounge with colour TV. Situated in quiet residential area, homely atmosphere.

C	B & B PER PERSON PER NIGHT		DINNER B & B PER PERSON PER WEEK		3
	MIN £	MAX £	MIN £	MAX £	OPEN
	6.50	7.50			1—12

Spilman Guest House

Spilman Street, Carmarthen
Dyfed SA31 1LQ
Tel: (0267) 7037

CATEGORIES: 3 3 1

Ten bedroom guest house in centre of market town with private car park, Fire Certificate, colour TV lounge, full size snooker table, spacious family rooms and all bedrooms have hot and cold water, tea and coffee-making facilities and full central heating. Moderate tariff and special rates for children.

C	B & B PER PERSON PER NIGHT		DINNER B & B PER PERSON PER WEEK		10
	MIN £	MAX £	MIN £	MAX £	OPEN
	8	9			1—12

Tyn-y-Grug*

7 Francis Terrace, Carmarthen
Dyfed SA31 1EY
Tel: (0267) 6893

CATEGORIES: 1 1 1

A small guest house situated in the town centre of Carmarthen. Family-run by Mrs. Rees who offers a warm Welsh welcome to her visitors. Television lounge. Near to shops and town facilities and many good pubs and eating places. Ideally situated for touring South-West Wales

C	B & B PER PERSON PER NIGHT		DINNER B & B PER PERSON PER WEEK		3
	MIN £	MAX £	MIN £	MAX £	OPEN
	5.50	6			1—12

Farmhouses

Beilibedw Farm

Llanllwni, Pencader
Dyfed
Tel: (095935) 289

CATEGORIES: 1 2 2

A large 130 acre dairy farm 12 miles north of Carmarthen and 11 miles from the beaches. Shooting, fishing, riding available. Guests welcome to feed the animals. Pony rides free for children. Baby sitting. Carmarthen Market on Wednesdays. Largest horse market in Wales. Contact Heulwen Jones for further details.

T C	B & B PER PERSON PER NIGHT		DINNER B & B PER PERSON PER WEEK		9
	MIN £	MAX £	MIN £	MAX £	OPEN
	6.50	7.50	65	75	1—12

Blaen-Nant-y-Mab

Dryslwyn, Carmarthen
Dyfed SA32 8S
Tel: (05584) 348

CATEGORIES: 1 2 2

Guests assured of a warm Welsh welcome and personal service on our 140 acre family farm, overlooking Dryslwyn Castle and the beautiful Towy Valley. Ideally situated as a base for touring south and west coast or the Cambrian Mountains. One family room, one twin room, one single room. Lounge with colour TV. Reduced rates for children. Cot provided.

C	B & B PER PERSON PER NIGHT		DINNER B & B PER PERSON PER WEEK		3
	MIN £	MAX £	MIN £	MAX £	OPEN
	5.50	6	56	60	5—10

Cwmtwrch Farm*

Nantgaredig, Carmarthen
Dyfed SA32 7NY
Tel: (026788) 238

FARMHOUSE AWARD

CATEGORIES: 3 3 2

Enjoy comfort, relaxation and excellent meals with home baking and fresh farm products, in our carefully restored 18th century stone farmhouse. Set in lovely countryside, the farm is 5 miles from Carmarthen market town, and within easy distance of the coast. AA*. Restaurant license.

T C	B & B PER PERSON PER NIGHT		DINNER B & B PER PERSON PER WEEK		3
	MIN £	MAX £	MIN £	MAX £	OPEN
	7	8.50	84	90	1—12

Fferm Tyllwyd

Felingwm Uchaf, Carmarthen
Dyfed SA32 7QE
Tel: (026 788) 537

CATEGORIES: 1 3 2

Why not spend your holiday on a Welsh family farm with milking cows, calves, hens, lambs and Meg the sheep dog. Farm overlooks the Towy Valley with lovely views of Black Mountains and Brechfa Forest 3 miles. 90 acres to walk around. Small stream, meandering through farmland.

T C	B & B PER PERSON PER NIGHT		DINNER B & B PER PERSON PER WEEK		2
	MIN £	MAX £	MIN £	MAX £	OPEN
	5	7	56	70	6—10

Glog Farm*

Llangain, Carmarthen
Dyfed SA33 5AY
Tel: (026783) 271

CATEGORIES: 3 2 2

We are a 40 acre dairy farm situated 5 miles from a quiet sandy beach at Llanstephan and 5 miles from the market town of Carmarthen. Within easy reach of Saundersfoot, Tenby and the West Wales coast. Ironing facilities, washing machine, cot available. Packed lunches. Choice of menu, riding, golf, fishing locally.

C	B & B PER PERSON PER NIGHT		DINNER B & B PER PERSON PER WEEK		4
	MIN £	MAX £	MIN £	MAX £	OPEN
	7	7.50	75	82	1—12

Grove Grand Stand*

Llysonnen Road, Carmarthen
Dyfed
Tel: (026 782) 369

CATEGORIES: 1 2 1

Grove Farm Guest House, a delightful 12-acre small-holding, ideally situated for touring Pembroke, Cardigan and Gower coasts. 1 single, 2 double, 1 family room and public bathroom. Bed and breakfast—£6.50. Personal attention assured. Open throughout the year. Fresh local produce used. Discount for children. Weekly prices on application. Enquiries: Mrs. Harries.

C	B & B PER PERSON PER NIGHT		DINNER B & B PER PERSON PER WEEK		4
	MIN £	MAX £	MIN £	MAX £	OPEN
	6.50	7			1—12

For autumn to spring breaks send for our free Great Little Breaks booklet.

Penrheol*

Meidrim, Carmarthen
Dyfed SA33 5NX
Tel: (0994) 230477

CATEGORIES: 1 | 3 | 2

Penrheol, a Georgian Mansion surrounded by lawns and trees welcomes you. Comfortably furnished dining room with separate tables. Lounge with colour TV. Children welcome at reduced rates. Toys, books, games available. Good home cooking with own produce when possible. Ideally situated for all West Wales attractions.

C	B & B PER PERSON PER NIGHT		DINNER B & B PER PERSON PER WEEK		🛏 2
	MIN £	MAX £	MIN £	MAX £	OPEN
	6	7	75	82	5—10

Trefynys*

Peniel Road, Carmarthen
Dyfed SA32 7HU
Tel: (0267) 7093

CATEGORIES: 1 | 2 | 2

Situated four miles north on A485 from Carmarthen. A 200 acre dairy farm, fully centrally heated, with good home cooking from foods mainly produced on the farm. Garden, swimming pool. Trout and sewin fishing available on farm. For further details write or phone Mrs. Enid Evans.

T C	B & B PER PERSON PER NIGHT		DINNER B & B PER PERSON PER WEEK		🛏 3
	MIN £	MAX £	MIN £	MAX £	OPEN
	6.50	7.50	65	75	1—12

Carrog — NORTH WALES

Guest House

The Dell

Llidiart-y-Parc, Carrog
Corwen, Clwyd
Tel: (0490-83) 630

CATEGORIES: 1 | 3 | 1

We have peace and quiet and beautiful views from every window. There is a pleasant drawing room and each bedroom has its own spacious bathroom. We give undivided attention and complete comfort and we are only 300 yards from the A5.

T C	B & B PER PERSON PER NIGHT		DINNER B & B PER PERSON PER WEEK		🛏 2
	MIN £	MAX £	MIN £	MAX £	OPEN
	7.50				3—12

Castlemartin — SOUTH WALES

Farmhouse

Gupton Farm*

Castlemartin, Pembroke
Dyfed SA71 5HW
Tel: (064 681) 268

CATEGORIES: 1 | 1 | 2

Family dairy farm situated near Freshwater-West beach on Pembrokeshire coastal path. 5 miles west of Pembroke, surrounded by beautiful beaches.

C	B & B PER PERSON PER NIGHT		DINNER B & B PER PERSON PER WEEK		🛏 3
	MIN £	MAX £	MIN £	MAX £	OPEN
	5	6	49	56	1—12

Cemaes Bay — NORTH WALES

Guest House

Treddolphin Guest House*

Cemaes Bay, Isle of Anglesey
Gwynedd LL67 0ET
Tel: (0407) 710388

CATEGORIES: 3 | 3 | 2

Standing in its own grounds and commanding a panoramic coastal view. All bedrooms have H & C and showers. Two family rooms, three twins, one double. Visitors lounge, colour TV, central heating and Fire Certificate. Ample parking. The beach is only yards away. Children welcome at half price up to 14 years, sharing parents room. Free evening tea and biscuits in lounge. Free babysitting service. For a welcoming service ring Harold and Roberta Williams.

	B & B PER PERSON PER NIGHT		DINNER B & B PER PERSON PER WEEK		🛏 6
	MIN £	MAX £	MIN £	MAX £	OPEN
	6		42	45.50	1—12

Farmhouse

Mynydd Ithel*

Cemlyn, Cemaes Bay, Anglesey
LL68 0UB
Tel: (0407) 710263
Enquiries to: Mrs. J. Cadman

CATEGORIES: 2 | 3 | 2

Modern farmhouse, hot and cold water all bedrooms. TV lounge, dining room, parking. Children welcome. SAE. Mixed livestock. From Menai Bridge take A5025 to Cemaes Bay. Turn right 1 mile after village, sign-posted Cemlyn, at phone box turn left. Second farm on left.

C	B & B PER PERSON PER NIGHT		DINNER B & B PER PERSON PER WEEK		🛏 4
	MIN £	MAX £	MIN £	MAX £	OPEN
	5.50	6.50	52.50	63	3—10

Cenarth — SOUTH WALES

Farmhouse

Yet Farm*

Cenarth, Newcastle Emlyn
Dyfed SA38 9JL
Tel: (0239) 710069

CATEGORIES: 1 | 1 | 2

Comfortable Welsh 18th century farmhouse just 300 yds from Cenarth Falls. Ideal centre for touring; beaches 9 miles, pubs, shops and cafes nearby. Spacious rooms, comfortably furnished, colour TV in guests' lounge, separate tables in dining room. Plenty of free parking. A warm welcome accompanies a substantial breakfast.

C	B & B PER PERSON PER NIGHT		DINNER B & B PER PERSON PER WEEK		🛏 3
	MIN £	MAX £	MIN £	MAX £	OPEN
	7.50	7.50		84.00	4—9

Chepstow — SOUTH WALES

Map ref: Me4
Striguil, the ancient name for the still all-powerful castle of Strongbow at Chepstow, recalls Norman knights and chivalrous acts. The town, still with fortified gate and walls mainly intact, has an historic atmosphere to add to its excellent shopping, fine racecourse and the Wye Valley at its backdoor.

Hotels

Castle View Hotel*

16, Bridge Street, Chepstow,
Gwent NP6 5EZ
Tel: (02912) 70349

CATEGORIES: 5 | 4 | 5

Small luxury hotel. All bedrooms with bathroom, colour TV tea and coffee making facilities. Relais Routier/ Egon Ronay commended food. Located close to town centre, opposite Chepstow Castle and car park. Short holiday and weekend break terms available. "We aim to offer comfort, good food and personal attention."

T C	B & B PER PERSON PER NIGHT		DINNER B & B PER PERSON PER WEEK		🛏 8
	MIN £	MAX £	MIN £	MAX £	OPEN
	15	18	133	161	1—12

The First Hurdle*

9 Upper Church Street
Chepstow, Gwent
Tel: (02912) 2189

CATEGORIES | 3 | 3 | 5

A family run hotel. Edwardian mahogany furniture in all bedrooms with blending pretty decor. Own restaurant, popular with locals. Hot and cold water in all rooms. TV lounge. Central heating. Fire Certificate. Many guests come again.

C	B & B PER PERSON PER NIGHT		DINNER B & B PER PERSON PER WEEK		6
	MIN £	MAX £	MIN £	MAX £	OPEN
	10	12	80	100	1—12

George*

Moor Street, Chepstow
Gwent NP6 5DB
Tel: (02912) 2365

CATEGORIES | 3 | 4 | 5

Standing next to the 16th century gate in the medieval town walls, this comfortable hotel has 20 bedrooms. Some with private bath, and all with telephone, radio, colour TV and tea/coffee making facilities. Central heating. Car park. Weekend and mid-week bargain breaks available. Wye Valley touring base.

T C	B & B PER PERSON PER NIGHT		DINNER B & B PER PERSON PER WEEK		20
	MIN £	MAX £	MIN £	MAX £	OPEN
	18.75	21.50			1—12

Two Rivers Hotel*

Newport Road, Chepstow
Gwent NP6 5PR
Tel: (029 12) 5151

CATEGORIES | 5 | 5 | 5

Well equipped, privately owned, modern hotel. Five minutes from Severn Bridge. Golf, race course and aviaries ten minutes. Edwardian dining room and five bars. Entertainment—Fridays and Saturdays. Children and dogs welcome. Bargain breaks and mini weekends. Large car park, ideal for touring Wye Valley, Wales and West.

T C	B & B PER PERSON PER NIGHT		DINNER B & B PER PERSON PER WEEK		31
	MIN £	MAX £	MIN £	MAX £	OPEN
	22.50	22.50			1—12

Guest Houses

The Firs*

Devauden, Chepstow
Gwent NP6 6PL
Tel: (02915) 543

CATEGORIES | 1 | 2 | 1

Welcome to a country home in the Welsh Borders. More for your money, real comfort and freedom to come and go as you please. Ideal touring area packed with historic and scenic interest. Eat at local inns in beautiful Usk and Wye Valleys. A personal welcome awaits you. Weekly bed and breakfast rate (exclusive) £42-£48.

T C	B & B PER PERSON PER NIGHT		DINNER B & B PER PERSON PER WEEK		2
	MIN £	MAX £	MIN £	MAX £	OPEN
	6.50	7.50			4—11

Tara Guest House*

Mynydd Bach, Chepstow
Gwent NP6 6RN
Tel: (02917) 277

CATEGORIES | 2 | 3 | 2

We offer you a warm friendly atmosphere, a place to relax. Delicious home cooking, farm produce. Cosy lounge, log fires, TV. Full central heating, beautiful countryside. Ideal centre for walks or tours, riding, golf, historic towns and cities.

T C	B & B PER PERSON PER NIGHT		DINNER B & B PER PERSON PER WEEK		6
	MIN £	MAX £	MIN £	MAX £	OPEN
	6.50	8.50	65	85	1—12

Chirk
NORTH WALES

Guest Houses

Berwyn House

Holyhead Road, Chirk
Wrexham, Clwyd LL14 5HG
Tel: (0691) 772698

CATEGORIES | 3 | 3 | 2

18th century house with all modern amenities set in two acres of lawns and gardens. Full central heating. Family room available with reductions for children. Ideally situated for touring and walking in the Ceiriog and Dee Valleys. Riding, fishing and golf available locally. Close to historic Chirk Castle.

C	B & B PER PERSON PER NIGHT		DINNER B & B PER PERSON PER WEEK		3
	MIN £	MAX £	MIN £	MAX £	OPEN
	7	8	70		1—12

Plas Celyn*

Pentre, Chirk, Nr Wrexham
Clwyd LL14 5AW
Tel: (0691) 772103

CATEGORIES | 1 | 2 | 2

Plas Celyn, Pentre, Chirk small personally-run guest house ½ mile A5. Overlooking River Dee. Offers warm welcome. Home cooking, garden produce (in season). Full central heating. Winter breaks available. Offa's Dyke ¼ mile. All facilities walkers. SAE for leaflet from Mrs J Valentine. Charming old house. Every comfort.

C	B & B PER PERSON PER NIGHT		DINNER B & B PER PERSON PER WEEK		5
	MIN £	MAX £	MIN £	MAX £	OPEN
	6	8	65	80	1—12

Clynnog Fawr
NORTH WALES

Hotel

Clynnog Hotel

Clynnog Fawr, Caernarvon
North Wales
Tel: (028 686) 305

CATEGORIES | 3 | 3 | 4

Between Caernarvon and Pwllheli. Ideal centre for Lleyn Peninsula, Anglesey, Snowdonia. Every comfort, excellent menu, ample car parking. Fully licensed free house owner management. All bedrooms hot and cold water. Shaver points. Full central heating, colour television, games room, dining room with separate tables. Single, double and family rooms.

C	B & B PER PERSON PER NIGHT		DINNER B & B PER PERSON PER WEEK		8
	MIN £	MAX £	MIN £	MAX £	OPEN
	8.80	8.80	89.60	89.60	1—12

 **Tourist Information Centres are listed at back of book.**

C **Children stay at reduced rates, wherever you see this symbol.**

Map ref: Bc4
Attractive seaside Colwyn Bay is one of the top three North Wales resorts. As middle of the group it acts as a convenient touring centre, sending out its guests, when they wish, to explore the Vale of Clwyd and Conwy, Snowdonia and Isle of Anglesey. Its pier, promenade, mountain zoo and shopping keep busy those who don't want to roam, that is if they tire of the multitude of attractions in the town's Eirias Park. Theatre and cinema, as well as a novel Harlequin Puppet Theatre, add to the holiday richness, supported by an excellent range of hotels and guest houses.

Hotels

Ashmount Hotel*

College Avenue, Rhos-on-Sea
Colwyn Bay, Clwyd
North Wales LL28 4NT
Tel: (0492) 45479

CATEGORIES

| 4 | 4 | 4 |

AA* RAC* Ashmount is a detached luxury one star licensed hotel where quality, elegance and service really matter. All bedrooms en-suite with central heating, colour television and radio and tea-making facilities. 125 yards from the beach and ideal for touring North Wales. Parking on premises. Children welcome.

T	B & B PER PERSON PER NIGHT		DINNER B & B PER PERSON PER WEEK		14
C	MIN £	MAX £	MIN £	MAX £	OPEN
	11.55	11.55	99	99	1—12

Clevedon Hotel*

Hawarden Hotel, Colwyn Bay
Clwyd
Tel: (0492) 2368

CATEGORIES

| 3 | 3 | 3 |

Central situation close to promenade, town centre and station. Family run with modern bedrooms, cosy TV lounge and bar. Superbly appointed restaurant with menu choice. Private parking. Relais Routiers welcome assured. Brochure and tariff SAE to Dept. TB Clevedon Hotel, Hawarden Road, Colwyn Bay or phone 0492-2368.

T	B & B PER PERSON PER NIGHT		DINNER B & B PER PERSON PER WEEK		14
C	MIN £	MAX £	MIN £	MAX £	OPEN
	7	8	70	85	1—12

Commodore Hotel

Conway Road, Colwyn Bay, Clwyd
LL29 7AW
Tel: (0492) 2720

CATEGORIES

| 3 | 3 | 3 |

Under new ownership. Minutes to shops and sea front. Hot and cold water and shaver points in all bedrooms. Single, double and family rooms with special rates for children. Lounge and television room. Dining room with separate tables. Fire Certificate. Golf, fishing and horse riding. Lovely beaches.

C	B & B PER PERSON PER NIGHT		DINNER B & B PER PERSON PER WEEK		23
	MIN £	MAX £	MIN £	MAX £	OPEN
	7.48	8.63	75.50	80.50	1—12

Edelweiss Hotel*

Off Lawson Road, Colwyn Bay
Clwyd, North Wales LL29 8HD
Tel: (0492) 2314

CATEGORIES

| 3 | 4 | 4 |

Peacefully situated away from traffic in own gardens adjoining Colwyn's famous Eirias Park and Leisure Centre. Central for shops, entertainments and zoo. Ideal for touring. Large car park. TV room, lounge, bar, games room. Some ground floor bedrooms. Reductions for OAP's and children. Some rooms en-suite 1983.

T	B & B PER PERSON PER NIGHT		DINNER B & B PER PERSON PER WEEK		27
C	MIN £	MAX £	MIN £	MAX £	OPEN
	11.90		106.60		1—12

Fairways

12 Ellesmere Road, Colwyn Bay
Clwyd
Tel: (0492) 30528

CATEGORIES

| 3 | 3 | 2 |

Ann and Graham welcome you to Fairways. We have everything to make your stay pleasurable. Our guests say it all. "No words can express our thanks for such a marvellous time. Wonderful stay. Fab food, charming hosts. Thank you both for Fairways. Such comfort; the garden, such a memorable show."

C	B & B PER PERSON PER NIGHT		DINNER B & B PER PERSON PER WEEK		9
	MIN £	MAX £	MIN £	MAX £	OPEN
	7	8	63	70	4—9

Family Holidays Association Limited*

Meadowcroft, Llannerch Road East
Rhos-on-Sea, Colwyn Bay LL28 4DF
Tel: (0492) 48375

CATEGORIES

| 3 | 3 | 3 |

Family Holidays Association Ltd., Cae Mor, Llandudno, Meadowcroft, Rhos-on-Sea. Where children are welcome. Both specially equipped for families. Large lounge, games room, separate TV lounge, mother's kitchen, washing, drying, airing, ironing facilities. Hot and cold water in all bedrooms, razor points, baby-listening, bar, residents only. Free car parking. Free colour brochure: FWT Phillips, General Manager, Family Holidays Association Ltd., Meadowcroft Hotel, Llannerch Road East, Rhos-on-Sea, Colwyn Bay, Clwyd LL28 4DF.

C	B & B PER PERSON PER NIGHT		DINNER B & B PER PERSON PER WEEK		30
	MIN £	MAX £	MIN £	MAX £	OPEN
			82.48	86.23	4—9

Grosvenor Hotel

Abergele Road, Colwyn Bay
Clwyd LL29 7PS
Tel: (0492) 30798

CATEGORIES

| 3 | 4 | 4 |

A comfortable private hotel, occupying a commanding position in the centre of Colwyn Bay and is ideally situated for the beach and the shopping centre. Central heating in public rooms. And a cellar bar to enjoy drinks and bar snacks. A large car park for guests use. All meals prepared and served under the personal supervision of the proprietor.

T	B & B PER PERSON PER NIGHT		DINNER B & B PER PERSON PER WEEK		18
C	MIN £	MAX £	MIN £	MAX £	OPEN
	8	10	79.50	90	1—12

Don't forget that 1983 is Festival of Castles Year in Wales with events planned for all the major historic sites.

Hotel 70°*

Penmaenhead, Colwyn Bay, Clwyd
North Wales LL29 9LD
Tel: (0492) 56555 Telex: 61362

CATEGORIES

6	5	5

Unique hotel on clifftops overlooking bay of Colwyn. Privately owned. Open all year. Situated on A55. All bedrooms have telephone, radio, colour TV. Two bars. French restaurant. Weekend breaks. Golf. Midweek breaks available. Ring or write for brochure. Resident Proprietor, Mr ML Sexton. Telephone 0492-56555 Telex 61362.

T C	B & B PER PERSON PER NIGHT		DINNER B & B PER PERSON PER WEEK		44
	MIN £	MAX £	MIN £	MAX £	OPEN
	24	29.50	206	226	1—12

Lyndale Hotel*

Abergele Road, Colwyn Bay
Clwyd LL29 9AB
Tel: (0492) 55429

CATEGORIES

4	4	4

Modern detached hotel overlooking the beautiful bay of Colwyn. Family managed and offering guests every facility. Modern bedrooms, all containing colour television, radio, intercom. Tea and coffee making facilities. Baby listening units and full central heating. Many rooms en-suite. Reductions, plus limited free accommodation for children. Private car park.

T C	B & B PER PERSON PER NIGHT		DINNER B & B PER PERSON PER WEEK		16
	MIN £	MAX £	MIN £	MAX £	OPEN
	10.50	12.00	79	101.50	1—12

Norfolk House Hotel*

Prince's Drive, Colwyn Bay
Clwyd, North Wales LL29 8PF
Tel: (0492) 31757 Telex 61254

CATEGORIES

5	5	5

All bedrooms with private bath or shower and toilet, colour television, radio and telephone. Excellent cuisine, service and appointments. Lift. Recently extended and modernised. In grounds of over one acre, within 200 yards of the sea and central position for all amenities. Ample parking. Excellent touring base. BTA commended.

T C	B & B PER PERSON PER NIGHT		DINNER B & B PER PERSON PER WEEK		33
	MIN £	MAX £	MIN £	MAX £	OPEN
	19		169.75		1—12

Kennack Private Hotel*

Cayley Promenade, Rhos on Sea
Clwyd LL28 4EP
Tel: (0492) 48340

CATEGORIES

4	3	4

Sea-front hotel. High standard of comfort and hospitality, home cooking with choice of menu. Perfect base for exploring Snowdonia and coast. Golfing, sailing, squash and leisure centre close by. 1982 prices for weekly bookings for May, June, September, October. En suite facilities inclusive where applicable. No service charge.

C	B & B PER PERSON PER NIGHT		DINNER B & B PER PERSON PER WEEK		9
	MIN £	MAX £	MIN £	MAX £	OPEN
	8	9	79	85	4—10

Monksweir Hotel

66 Colwyn Avenue, Rhos-on-Sea
Colwyn Bay, Clwyd LL28 4NN
Tel: (0492) 49420

CATEGORIES

3	3	2

Family run ten bedroomed hotel situated at Rhos Point. 300 yards to beach and shops. Modern spring interior divan beds. Comfortable lounge with colour TV. Parking in own grounds. Bed and breakfast, (optional) evening meal. Terms on request, SAE for brochure.

C	B & B PER PERSON PER NIGHT		DINNER B & B PER PERSON PER WEEK		10
	MIN £	MAX £	MIN £	MAX £	OPEN
	6.50	6.95	65	70	3—10

Penrhyn Private Hotel*

2 Mostyn Road
Colwyn Bay LL29 8PB
Tel: (0492) 2227

CATEGORIES

3	3	2

Small comfortable licensed hotel offering bed and breakfast, dinner optional. Reduction for children sharing parents bedrooms. Central for parks, beach, entertainments and shops. Ideal base for touring North Wales. All bedrooms have radios, hot and cold water and shaver points. Colour TV, lounge. Access at all times. Parking.

T C	B & B PER PERSON PER NIGHT		DINNER B & B PER PERSON PER WEEK		7
	MIN £	MAX £	MIN £	MAX £	OPEN
	8	9	77	85	1—12

Raynham Hotel

Ellesmere Road, Colwyn Bay
Clwyd LL29 8RP
Tel: (0492) 30738

CATEGORIES

3	3	3

Family run hotel under new ownership. 250 yards from sandy beaches. Well situated for all other amenities. Open all year and Christmas. Lounge with colour television. Lounge, bar. Full central heating and Fire Certificate. Hot and cold water. Shaving points. Radio/intercom. Tea-making facilities in all rooms.

C	B & B PER PERSON PER NIGHT		DINNER B & B PER PERSON PER WEEK		9
	MIN £	MAX £	MIN £	MAX £	OPEN
	8.20		83		1—12

Rhos Abbey Hotel*

Rhos Promenade, Colwyn Bay
Clwyd LL28 4NG
Tel: (0492) 46601 Telex 61254

CATEGORIES

| 5 | 5 | 5 |

This famous 3 star hotel on the promenade has 32 rooms, all with private facilities: colour TV, telephone and central heating. There is a first class restaurant and choice of three attractive bars. Lift, night porter. Large car park. Entertainment during season. Golf and fishing locally. Special weekend terms.

	B & B PER PERSON PER NIGHT		DINNER B & B PER PERSON PER WEEK		32
T	MIN £	MAX £	MIN £	MAX £	OPEN
C	23	25	148	156	1—12

Silver Howe Hotel*

Llanerch Road East, Rhos-On-Sea
Colwyn Bay, Clwyd LL28 4DE
Tel: (0492) 44593

CATEGORIES

| 3 | 3 | 4 |

Situated on the upper promenade, we offer our guests the best in homely cooking with excellent friendly service. Ideal base for touring Snowdonia and the castles of North Wales. Sea views from most bedrooms. Your comfort is our main concern and most of our guests make yearly visits.

	B & B PER PERSON PER NIGHT		DINNER B & B PER PERSON PER WEEK		18
T	MIN £	MAX £	MIN £	MAX £	OPEN
C	9.50		105		3—10

Southlea Private Hotel*

4 Upper Promenade
Colwyn Bay, Clwyd
Tel: (0492) 2004

CATEGORIES

| 3 | 3 | 4 |

AA RAC listed. One minute to beach. 5 minutes to shops etc. We offer a high standard of home cooking and service. Lounge bar. Separate TV lounge. Radio and baby listening in all rooms. Pets welcome. Reductions for children. Children 2 and under no charge, one free out of main season.

	B & B PER PERSON PER NIGHT		DINNER B & B PER PERSON PER WEEK		9
T	MIN £	MAX £	MIN £	MAX £	OPEN
C	7.50	8.50	56	63	1—12

St. Enoch's Hotel*

Promenade, Colwyn Bay
LL28 4BL
Tel: (0492) 2031

CATEGORIES

| 3 | 3 | 4 |

Delightfully situated on the sea front with every amenity. Some rooms en-suite with colour TV. TV lounge, cocktail lounge and dining rooms overlooking the bay. Children most welcome. Holders of Wales in Bloom trophy 1977 to 1981. Contact P & G Owen for colour brochure and further information. Members BH & RA.

	B & B PER PERSON PER NIGHT		DINNER B & B PER PERSON PER WEEK		22
T	MIN £	MAX £	MIN £	MAX £	OPEN
C	11	14	80	95	1—12

Stanton House Hotel*

33 Whitehall Road, Rhos-On-Sea
Colwyn Bay, Clwyd LL28 4ET
Tel: (0492) 44363

CATEGORIES

| 4 | 4 | 4 |

Centrally situated within minutes walk of beach, and all amenities. Ideal centre for touring North Wales. Central heating. Licensed. Comfort and excellent cuisine are our main considerations. Choice of menu and special diets catered for. Write for brochure and tariff to resident proprietors, Mr & Mrs CA Harris. Open all year.

	B & B PER PERSON PER NIGHT		DINNER B & B PER PERSON PER WEEK		10
T	MIN £	MAX £	MIN £	MAX £	OPEN
C	8.50	10.90	72.50	79.50	1—12

Sunny Downs Hotel*

66 Abbey Road, Rhos-On-Sea
Colwyn Bay, Clwyd LL28 4NU
Tel: (0492) 44256

CATEGORIES

| 3 | 3 | 3 |

Detached, licensed, centrally heated, we offer comfort service and good food. Some rooms en-suite. Private car park. Situated between Colwyn Bay and Llandudno. Ideal touring base. Special rates for off-peak party bookings and short breaks. Send for brochure to S Hanson, Proprietor. AA RAC listed.

	B & B PER PERSON PER NIGHT		DINNER B & B PER PERSON PER WEEK		17
T	MIN £	MAX £	MIN £	MAX £	OPEN
C	8.45	9.95	90.50	94.15	1—12

Whitehall Hotel*

Cayley Promenade, Rhos-On-Sea
Colwyn Bay, Clwyd LL28 4EP
Tel: (0492) 47296

CATEGORIES

| 3 | 3 | 3 |

The very best of both worlds at the Whitehall. Touring or relaxing. Excellent food to suit all tastes. All bedrooms have tea/coffee making facilities and heating, some en-suite. Cocktail bar. Residents TV lounge. AA* RAC* Special weekend breaks from £22. Near golf course. Windsurf lessons from hotel.

	B & B PER PERSON PER NIGHT		DINNER B & B PER PERSON PER WEEK		14
T	MIN £	MAX £	MIN £	MAX £	OPEN
C	9.50	12	75	100	4—10

Guest Houses

Crossroads*

Coed Pella Road, Colwyn Bay
Clwyd LL29 7AT
Tel: (0492) 30736

CATEGORIES

| 2 | 3 | 2 |

Town centre, close to the station and bus, shops. Parking facilities opposite. Minutes walk from the beach, within short walks or drives to the most beautiful and historic places of interest. Family-run house, excellent food, comes highly recommended. Our bedrooms are up to modern standards and we can offer singles, twins, doubles, comfortable lounge with colour television. Charming dining room with separate tables. Access to rooms at all times. Please SAE for our brochure. Closed Christmas.

	B & B PER PERSON PER NIGHT		DINNER B & B PER PERSON PER WEEK		6
C	MIN £	MAX £	MIN £	MAX £	OPEN
	5	6	48	52	1—12

Haven Villa Guest House*

Hillside Road
Colwyn Bay, Clwyd
Tel: (0492) 31931

CATEGORIES

| 2 | 3 | 4 |

Why pay more? Bed and breakfast, evening meal (continental breakfast) from £38 per week. 14 choice English breakfast menu—supplementary prices. Evening meal menu at no extra cost. Small homely guest house with a warm welcome. For further details send SAE to Haven Villa Guest House, Hillside Road, Colwyn Bay or phone Colwyn Bay 0492-31931.

C	B & B PER PERSON PER NIGHT		DINNER B & B PER PERSON PER WEEK		5
	MIN £	MAX £	MIN £	MAX £	OPEN
	4.50	6	38	48	—

"Oakley"

35 Woodhill Road, Colwyn Bay
Clwyd, North Wales
Tel: (0492) 30438

CATEGORIES

| 3 | 2 | 1 |

"Oakley" is a select private guest house in a quiet residential area, close to shops, station, bus routes, sea and entertainments. Beautiful countryside within easy reach. Hot and cold water in modern bedrooms, centrally heated, shower room, bathroom, separate tables. Colour TV. Access at all times.

C	B & B PER PERSON PER NIGHT		DINNER B & B PER PERSON PER WEEK		3
	MIN £	MAX £	MIN £	MAX £	OPEN
	6	7			1—12

Ridgeway

Hawarden Road, Colwyn Bay
Clwyd, North Wales
Tel: (0492) 33828

CATEGORIES

| 2 | 3 | 2 |

Ridgeway is a pleasant guest house with a high standard of cooking and cleanliness, in a friendly atmosphere. Newly decorated with full central heating. Hot and cold water in all bedrooms. Lounge with colour TV, dining room has separate tables. Within 4 minutes walk of beach and town centre. You won't be disappointed.

T C	B & B PER PERSON PER NIGHT		DINNER B & B PER PERSON PER WEEK		5
	MIN £	MAX £	MIN £	MAX £	OPEN
	5	5	49	52.50	3—10

Tara

33 Hillside Road, Colwyn Bay
Clwyd LL29 7EP
Tel: (0492) 30960

CATEGORIES

| 1 | 3 | 2 |

Comfortable detached residence, hot and cold water, shaver points in all bedrooms, plus tea making facilities, central heating, lounge with colour television, convenient for town centre and touring Snowdonia. Ample parking. Full breakfast, excellent evening meal, prepared by chef proprietor.

C	B & B PER PERSON PER NIGHT		DINNER B & B PER PERSON PER WEEK		3
	MIN £	MAX £	MIN £	MAX £	OPEN
	5	5.75	48	55	4—9

Farmhouse

Tyn-y-Coed Farm*

Llanelian, Colwyn Bay
Clwyd LL29 8YR
Tel: (0492) 56142

CATEGORIES

| 1 | 2 | 2 |

Large modern bungalow overlooking bay of Colwyn and Clwydian Hills. Shops and beach 3 miles. Lounge for guests. Black and white television. Evening tea and biscuits. Sorry no pets. Enquiries: Eirwen Davies.

C	B & B PER PERSON PER NIGHT		DINNER B & B PER PERSON PER WEEK		2
	MIN £	MAX £	MIN £	MAX £	OPEN
	5.50	6	50	56	4—10

Conwy

Map ref: Bb4
Mediaeval town at the mouth of the Conwy river, with a magnificent 13th century castle, complete town walls and interesting old buildings along its narrow streets. Fishing boats line the quay beneath the castle walls and the town is overlooked by the foothills of the Snowdonia ranges with many ancient remains of pre-history and paths that are followed by pony trekkers and walkers. It is centrally placed for the coastal resorts, for Snowdonia and Isle of Anglesey.

Hotels and Motel

Castle

High Street, Conwy
Gwynedd LL32 8DB
Tel: (049263) 2324

CATEGORIES

| 5 | 4 | 4 |

Standing in the old town, this former coaching house contains fine murals and collection of Welsh antiques and china. All 25 bedrooms have private bath, telephone, radio, colour TV and tea/coffee making facilities. Weekend and mid-week bargain breaks and nightime holidays available. Car park.

T C	B & B PER PERSON PER NIGHT		DINNER B & B PER PERSON PER WEEK		25
	MIN £	MAX £	MIN £	MAX £	OPEN
	23				1—12

Castle Bank Hotel*

Mount Pleasant, Conwy
Gwynedd LL32 8NY
Tel: (0492-63) 3888

CATEGORIES

| 3 | 3 | 4 |

Delightfully situated in its own grounds with magnificent views over Conwy and surrounding countryside. The hotel has a TV lounge, bar lounge and is furnished to a high standard. Noted for our excellent menus and high standard of cooking. Ample parking within the hotel grounds. AA* RAC.

C	B & B PER PERSON PER NIGHT		DINNER B & B PER PERSON PER WEEK		9
	MIN £	MAX £	MIN £	MAX £	OPEN
	9	11	95	110	1—12

Cyfnant Private Hotel*

Henryd Road, Conwy
Gwynedd LL32 8HW
Tel: (049 263) 2442

CATEGORIES

| 3 | 3 | 3 |

A relaxed, friendly, small licensed hotel. The food is delicious and personal attention is given to your comfort by the owners. Bedrooms have TV, washbasins, shaverpoints, heating and most have a shower en suite. The comfortable lounge has colour TV. Car park. AA and RAC listed. Brochure on request.

C	B & B PER PERSON PER NIGHT		DINNER B & B PER PERSON PER WEEK		6
	MIN £	MAX £	MIN £	MAX £	OPEN
	7.25	8.50	75.25	85.75	2—12

The Erskine Hotel*

Rose Hill Street, Conwy
Gwynedd LL32 8LD
Tel: (049 263) 3415

CATEGORIES

| 3 | 3 | 3 |

Fully licensed hotel situated within the ancient town walls of this historic castled, fishing town, close to Snowdonia National Park. 10 bedrooms with radio/intercom, teasmade and heating. Antique furnished dining room, colour TV lounge and two licensed bars.

C	B & B PER PERSON PER NIGHT		DINNER B & B PER PERSON PER WEEK		10
	MIN £	MAX £	MIN £	MAX £	OPEN
	8.50	11	80	94	1—12

Llys Llewelyn Hotel*

Mount Pleasant
Conwy, Gwynedd
Tel: (049263) 3257

CATEGORIES

| 3 | 3 | 4 |

Imposing Victorian house now a small and friendly hotel run by resident proprietors. Panoramic views of Conwy Castle and town. We offer clean and well furnished accommodation. Excellent food and service at a reasonable price. Car park. Very attractive dining room with bar, colour TV lounge. Close to town centre.

T	B & B PER PERSON PER NIGHT		DINNER B & B PER PERSON PER WEEK		9
C	MIN £	MAX £	MIN £	MAX £	OPEN
	8.50	9	85	90	1—12

The Lodge*

Tal y Bont
Conwy LL32 8YX
Tel: (0492 69) 534

CATEGORIES

| 4 | 4 | 5 |

A British Tourist Authority commended country restaurant serving local and own grown produce prepared by the resident proprietors. Ten comfortable bedrooms with bathrooms. Colour TV radio and hot drink facilities. Ideal for touring Snowdonia and coastal areas. Bargain breaks throughout year. Ashley Courtney recommended. An Inter Hotel.

T	B & B PER PERSON PER NIGHT		DINNER B & B PER PERSON PER WEEK		10
C	MIN £	MAX £	MIN £	MAX £	OPEN
	12.50	15	117.50	140	1—12

The Park Hall Hotel*

Bangor Road, Conwy
Gwynedd LL32 8DP
Tel: (049 263) 2279

CATEGORIES

| 3 | 3 | 4 |

The Park Hall Hotel has rapidly established a top reputation for hospitality and comfort. This fully licensed hotel is situated in three acres of private grounds. Television lounge. Most bedrooms with showers. Sandy beaches only minutes from the door and the ancient town of Conwy just 1/2 mile away.

C	B & B PER PERSON PER NIGHT		DINNER B & B PER PERSON PER WEEK		9
	MIN £	MAX £	MIN £	MAX £	OPEN
	10	12	95	120	2—11

Sychnant Pass Hotel*

Sychnant Pass Road, Conwy
Gwynedd LL32 8BJ
Tel: (0492 63) 6868/9

CATEGORIES

| 5 | 4 | 4 |

Situated in area of outstanding natural beauty. Close to resorts and all activities. All bedrooms with private facilities. Colour television. Telephone and tea/coffee tray. Special attention given to quality of food which features fresh local produce. Value for money wines. Families very welcome. Facilities for disabled.

T	B & B PER PERSON PER NIGHT		DINNER B & B PER PERSON PER WEEK		10
C	MIN £	MAX £	MIN £	MAX £	OPEN
	12	18	120	164	1—12

Tir-y-Coed Country House Hotel*

Rowen, Nr Conwy
Gwynedd LL32 8TP
Tel: (0492) 67.219

CATEGORIES

| 4 | 4 | 4 |

Nestled in landscaped gardens amidst Snowdonia's beauty the Tir-y-Coed combines home from home atmosphere with high standard of comfort and cuisine. All double bedrooms have private bathroom, heating, colour TV, tea-making. Ideal centre for touring, golfing, walking or simply eating, drinking and relaxing. AA* RAC.* Ashley Courtenay recommended.

C	B & B PER PERSON PER NIGHT		DINNER B & B PER PERSON PER WEEK		8
	MIN £	MAX £	MIN £	MAX £	OPEN
	12	15	110	130	3—11

Guest Houses

Angorfa Guest House*

25 Cadnant Park
Conwy LL32 8PR
Tel: (0492 63) 3280

CATEGORIES

| 3 | 3 | 2 |

Semi detached guest house within level walking distance to the town. Ideal touring centre. Double family rooms with hot and cold water. TV lounge. Separate tables in dining room. Centrally heated. Parking on premises. Fire Certificate. Open all year except Christmas. Small pets accepted. Golf, riding, fishing close by. SAE for replies.

C	B & B PER PERSON PER NIGHT		DINNER B & B PER PERSON PER WEEK		5
	MIN £	MAX £	MIN £	MAX £	OPEN
	5.50	6	56	60	1—12

Bryn Guest House*

Sychnant Pass Road, Conwy
Gwynedd LL32 8NS
Tel: (0492 63) 2449

CATEGORIES

| 3 | 2 | 2 |

Bryn is situated in its own grounds, bounded by the ancient town walls of the picturesque castled town of Conwy. Attractive bedrooms with hot and cold water, shaver points and central heating. Bed and breakfast, evening meal optional. Lounge, colour television. Parking. Town centre four minutes walk.

C	B & B PER PERSON PER NIGHT		DINNER B & B PER PERSON PER WEEK		3
	MIN £	MAX £	MIN £	MAX £	OPEN
	13	15	77	87.50	1—12

Children stay at reduced rates, wherever you see this symbol.

Fishermore

Llanrwst Road, Gyffin
Conwy, Gwynedd
Tel: (049 263) 2891

CATEGORIES
| 3 | 2 | 2 |

Small, friendly guest house set in its own grounds with all amenities, yet only one mile from Conwy and ideally placed for touring Snowdonia. All bedrooms are centrally heated with coffee and tea-making facilities. TV lounge, ample car parking, children and well-behaved pets welcome.

C	B & B PER PERSON PER NIGHT		DINNER B & B PER PERSON PER WEEK		3
	MIN £	MAX £	MIN £	MAX £	OPEN
	5.50	7	52.50	63	4—10

Glen Maye

1 Warren Drive, Deganwy
Conwy, North Wales LL31 9ST
Tel: (0492) 83726

CATEGORIES
| 1 | 1 | 1 |

Open all year. Ideally situated with beautiful views over Conwy Estuary, castle and mountains. Hot and cold water and shaver points in all bedrooms. Very comfortable and cleanliness assured. Car park. Superb base for golf, fishing and touring Snowdonia.

C	B & B PER PERSON PER NIGHT		DINNER B & B PER PERSON PER WEEK		3
	MIN £	MAX £	MIN £	MAX £	OPEN
	6	7.50			1—12

Llys Gwilym Guest House*

3 Mountain Road, Cadnant Park
Conwy, Gwynedd LL32 8PU
Tel: (049 263) 2351

CATEGORIES
| 3 | 3 | 2 |

Bed and breakfast, evening meal, dinner. All food chef prepared in comfortable surroundings. AA listed. Licensed. Ideal for walking, touring, golf, horse riding, fishing. Sea and river situated at foot of Conwy mountain. Mid-week booking and weekends accepted. On the edge of beautiful Snowdonia.

C	B & B PER PERSON PER NIGHT		DINNER B & B PER PERSON PER WEEK		6
	MIN £	MAX £	MIN £	MAX £	OPEN
	6	7	57	63	1—9

Meifod Guest House*

13 Cadnant Park
Conwy LL32 8PR
Tel: (0492 63) 3782

CATEGORIES
| 3 | 3 | 1 |

Completely refurbished just outside town walls close to shops buses and quay. Quiet and secluded. Hot and cold water and shaver points all bedrooms, single, double and family rooms. Special rates for children, dining room with separate tables, colour television—full central heating. Parking readily available. Fire Certificate.

T C	B & B PER PERSON PER NIGHT		DINNER B & B PER PERSON PER WEEK		7
	MIN £	MAX £	MIN £	MAX £	OPEN
	5.50				1—12

The Old Ship*

28 High Street, Lancaster Square
Conwy
Tel: (0492 63) 6445

CATEGORIES
| 3 | 3 | 2 |

Newly opened guest house within Conwy's historic walls. Close to all amenities. The Old Ship is a listed building offering all modern comforts, whilst maintaining a cosy old world charm. All bedrooms have central heating, hot and cold water, shaver points. Tea and coffee making facilities. TV lounge. Dining room. Separate tables.

C	B & B PER PERSON PER NIGHT		DINNER B & B PER PERSON PER WEEK		5
	MIN £	MAX £	MIN £	MAX £	OPEN
	7	10	70	90	1—12

Sunnybanks Guest House*

Woodlands, Conwy, Gwynedd
North Wales LL32 8LT
Tel: (049 263) 3845

CATEGORIES
| 3 | 3 | 2 |

Attractive residence, secluded from the road, flanked by Canadian pine trees in a pleasant coastal resort near River Conwy. Few minutes walk from the pretty village of Conwy with its picturesque harbour. Adjacent to Conwy Castle and bus and railway stations. Ideal for touring North Wales and family holidays, convenient for Snowdonia, sailing, mountaineering, fishing, riding, golf. 7 Double bedrooms (2 family size). Excellent home-cooking. Personal attention. Thoroughly recommended. AA* and RAC.* Car park. Continental terrace. SAE for details.

C	B & B PER PERSON PER NIGHT		DINNER B & B PER PERSON PER WEEK		7
	MIN £	MAX £	MIN £	MAX £	OPEN
	5.50	6	56	60	3—10

Farmhouse

Henllys Farm*

Llechwedd, Conwy
Gwynedd LL32 8DJ
Tel: (049 263) 3269

CATEGORIES
| 1 | 2 | 2 |

Ideally placed for touring Snowdonia and the North Wales coast. 1½ miles from the historic town of Conwy. TV lounge, separate dining room, bathroom with shaver point, bath and shower, one double, one family room. Magnificent views of the surrounding countryside. Fitted carpets throughout. 140 acres mixed farm. Parking space.

C	B & B PER PERSON PER NIGHT		DINNER B & B PER PERSON PER WEEK		2
	MIN £	MAX £	MIN £	MAX £	OPEN
	5	6	56	63	4—10

Hotel

Braich Goch Hotel & Restaurant*

Corris near Machynlleth
Powys SY20 9RD
Tel: (065473) 229

CATEGORIES
| 3 | 3 | 5 |

RAC* "Guestaccom". We ensure the wellbeing of our guests by providing first class food, comfortable congenial surroundings and personal attention. Low season breaks at reduced rates. Special Christmas package. Open fires in winter. Ideal location for outdoor pursuits. Fully licensed. Brochure with pleasure: Write or telephone Elizabeth Skeen.

C	B & B PER PERSON PER NIGHT		DINNER B & B PER PERSON PER WEEK		6
	MIN £	MAX £	MIN £	MAX £	OPEN
	8.50	10	84	98	1—12

Farmhouse

The Goedwig*

Corris near Machynlleth
Gwynedd
Tel: (065473) 203

CATEGORIES
| 1 | 2 | 2 |

Accommodation in farmhouse overlooking Dulas Valley, set in the Dyfi forest within the Snowdonia National Park. Easy access for mountain and forest trails. Fishing and pony trekking available by arrangement. Tal y llyn railway and Corris Rail Museum nearby. Beaches, golf, sea fishing and sailing. Within easy reach of Aberdyfi.

C	B & B PER PERSON PER NIGHT		DINNER B & B PER PERSON PER WEEK		3
	MIN £	MAX £	MIN £	MAX £	OPEN
	6	7	63	77	1—12

This symbol means you can book through your local travel agent.

Hotel

Owain Glyndwr

The Square
Corwen, Clwyd
Tel: (0490) 2115

CATEGORIES

3	3	4

Situated in the small attractive country town of Corwen in the lovely Dee Valley. The emphasis is on good food, recommended by Egon Ronay. A choice of restaurant or bar food. Three bars and a function room catering for 100 guests. The location makes for easy touring to the coast or trips to the Snowdonia National Park.

	B & B PER PERSON PER NIGHT		DINNER B & B PER PERSON PER WEEK		14
T					
C	MIN £	MAX £	MIN £	MAX £	OPEN
	12	15	120	140	1—12

Farmhouse

Llawr-Betws Farm*

Corwen
Clwyd LL21 0HD
Tel: (0490 81) 224

CATEGORIES

2	1	2

Llawr-Betws, situated on a quiet road between the market towns of Corwen and Bala, is a 62 acre farm with sheep and store cattle. The meals are excellent and prepared by Mrs Jones's son David who is a trainee chef. Children welcome. Welsh and English spoken.

	B & B PER PERSON PER NIGHT		DINNER B & B PER PERSON PER WEEK		5
T					
C	MIN £	MAX £	MIN £	MAX £	OPEN
	6	6	65	65	1—12

Cestyll '83 – 1983 is the year of the castles.

Map ref: Ad6
A family's ideal resort: Safe, sandy beach about a tumbledown castle, a little town with all facilities and close to some of Britain's finest touring country—Lleyn Peninsula and the Snowdonia National Park. Hotels line the seafront and climb the hills behind. Just west is Llanystumdwy, boyhood home of Lloyd George, where there is a museum of his mementoes.

Hotels

Abereistedd Hotel*

West Parade, Criccieth
Gwynedd LL52 0EN
Tel: (076 671) 2710

CATEGORIES

3	3	3

AA* and RAC* appointed. Detached 14 bedroom licensed hotel on the sea front overlooking Cardigan Bay, at the quiet west side of the beach. Superb views. Comfortable family-run with all tastes catered for. Parking. Central heating. SAE please.

	B & B PER PERSON PER NIGHT		DINNER B & B PER PERSON PER WEEK		14
T					
C	MIN £	MAX £	MIN £	MAX £	OPEN
	9	11.50	74	96	3—10

Bodlondeb Hotel

Porthmadog Road
Criccieth, Gwynedd
Tel: (076 671) 2249

CATEGORIES

3	3	3

Restaurant and residential license. Magnificent view of Cardigan Bay. Friendly atmosphere, home cooking. Cocktail bar. TV lounge. Large car park in hotel grounds. Coach parties welcome, phone or write.

	B & B PER PERSON PER NIGHT		DINNER B & B PER PERSON PER WEEK		12
T					
C	MIN £	MAX £	MIN £	MAX £	OPEN
	8.50	11	77	77	4—9

Caerwylan Hotel*

Beach Bank, Criccieth
Gwynedd LL52 0HW
Tel: (076 671) 2547

CATEGORIES

3	3	4

AA* RAC* appointed. Comfortable family run hotel superbly situated 30 yards from beach. Radio/intercom in all bedrooms. Some bedrooms with private bathrooms. Lift to all floors. Residential and restaurant licence. Garages and parking. Fire Certificate granted. for full details write to the proprietors D. C & P. Davies.

	B & B PER PERSON PER NIGHT		DINNER B & B PER PERSON PER WEEK		32
T					
C	MIN £	MAX £	MIN £	MAX £	OPEN
	8		80.50		3—10

George IV Hotel*

Criccieth, Gwynedd
North Wales
Tel: (076 671) 2168

CATEGORIES

3	4	5

AA/RAC**. A fine hotel overlooking Cardigan Bay and ideally situated for wonderful scenery and beaches, excellent food, attractive restaurant. Bars and lounges radio/intercom and tea-makers in all bedrooms. Lift, gardens and car park. Special prices for holidays and weekend breaks. Reduced rates for children details write—phone.

	B & B PER PERSON PER NIGHT		DINNER B & B PER PERSON PER WEEK		40
T					
C	MIN £	MAX £	MIN £	MAX £	OPEN
	11.25	14.75	99.75	129.75	1—12

Glyn-y-Coed Hotel*

Portmadoc Road, Criccieth
Gwynedd LL52 0HL
Tel: (076 671) 2870

CATEGORIES 3 3 3

Family hotel overlooking Esplanade facing due South. Licensed. Separate dining tables. Home cooking. Moderate terms. Reduction for children sharing with parents. Hot and cold, shaver points all bedrooms. AA RAC listed. Private parking, fishing, golf, riding locally. Brochure with pleasure. SAE please. Fire Certificate issued. Member Tourism Council.

C	B & B PER PERSON PER NIGHT		DINNER B & B PER PERSON PER WEEK		10
	MIN £	MAX £	MIN £	MAX £	OPEN
	7.60	8.10	65	80	1—11

Lion Hotel

Criccieth, Gwynedd
North Wales LL52 0AA
Tel: (076 671) 2460

CATEGORIES 4 4 4

Renowned for its homely atmosphere service and good food. The Lion is situated in the centre of the town overlooking the village green and beyond that, Cardigan Bay. Free golf available to hotel guests.

T C	B & B PER PERSON PER NIGHT		DINNER B & B PER PERSON PER WEEK		40
	MIN £	MAX £	MIN £	MAX £	OPEN
	13.20	13.20	83.16	83.16	1—12

Min-y-Gaer*

Portmadoc Road, Criccieth
Gwynedd LL52 0HP
Tel: (076 671) 2151

CATEGORIES 3 3 3

Ten bedroomed, licensed private hotel. Conveniently situated near beach and shops. Overlooking esplanade with delightful views of the Cardigan Bay coastline, ideal base for touring or relaxing, children welcome, colour TV lounge, tea coffee facilities in bedrooms. Free parking. AA and RAC listed. SAE for brochure.

T C	B & B PER PERSON PER NIGHT		DINNER B & B PER PERSON PER WEEK		10
	MIN £	MAX £	MIN £	MAX £	OPEN
	6.50	8	66	77	3—10

Mynydd Ednyfed Country House Hotel*

Caernarfon Road
Criccieth, North Wales
Tel: (076 671) 2200

CATEGORIES 3 3 3

For real comfort and excellent meals relax at any time in the peaceful surroundings of this friendly Country House Hotel. Ten, quiet, individually furnished bedrooms overlook the gardens and countryside while amenities include easy parking in extensive grounds. Full central heating, residents bar, colour television, beautiful public room. Tea-making facilities in garden lounge. Fire Certificate. Special rates available for group bookings.

T C	B & B PER PERSON PER NIGHT		DINNER B & B PER PERSON PER WEEK		10
	MIN £	MAX £	MIN £	MAX £	OPEN
	12.50	15	115	135	1—12

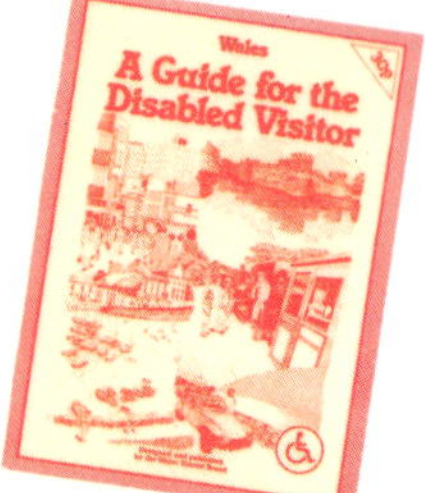

Wales — A Guide for the Disabled Visitor

A most useful guide, includes detailed information about accommodation, tourist attractions and amenities, such as theatres and sports centres, with facilities for the disabled visitor. Available from: Wales Tourist Board Department W.T.S. P.O. Box 1, CARDIFF CF1 2XN. Price: 50p including postage and packing.

Neptune & Mor Heli Hotels*

Min y Mor, Criccieth
Gwynedd LL52 0EF
Tel: (076 671) 2794/2878

CATEGORIES 3 3 3

Well established family-run hotels situated on sea front. Noted for good food and friendly atmosphere. Comfortably furnished throughout with an attractive licensed bar for guests and diners. For brochure and terms contact Mrs C. Williams. Coach parties catered for out of season. Licensed. Car Park. Fire Certificate.

T C	B & B PER PERSON PER NIGHT		DINNER B & B PER PERSON PER WEEK		26
	MIN £	MAX £	MIN £	MAX £	OPEN
	7.50		66.50		3—10

Parciau Mawr Hotel

Criccieth
Gwynedd LL52 0RP
Tel: (076 671) 2368

CATEGORIES 4 3 2

A two-star hotel in own 4 acre grounds overlooking the bay. All rooms are fully centrally heated with colour TV and tea making facilities. Many rooms with private bath or shower. Large family rooms and suites. Some ground floor rooms. Easy access to town and beach. Early season bargains. Fire Certificate. Licensed restaurant with table d'hote and à la carte menus. Comprehensive wine list.

T C	B & B PER PERSON PER NIGHT		DINNER B & B PER PERSON PER WEEK		13
	MIN £	MAX £	MIN £	MAX £	OPEN
	14	16	138	158	3—10

Rymont Private Hotel

29 Marine Terrace, Criccieth
Gwynedd LL52 0EF
Tel: (076 671) 2086

CATEGORIES 1 3 3

Rymont is ideally situated 30 yards from the beach. 13 bedrooms with hot and cold water and shaving points. Comfortable lounge with colour TV. Separate bar lounge. An ideal base for touring Snowdonia and the Lleyn Peninsula. Family-run hotel offering good food and friendly atmosphere. Enquiries, write or phone Criccieth 2086.

C	B & B PER PERSON PER NIGHT		DINNER B & B PER PERSON PER WEEK		13
	MIN £	MAX £	MIN £	MAX £	OPEN
	7.50		75		1—12

Seabank Hotel

Marine Parade, Criccieth
Gwynedd LL52 0EL
Tel: (076 671) 2255

CATEGORIES

| 2 | 3 | 2 |

Situated on the seafront with unsurpassed views of sea and mountains. 17 bedrooms, all with H & C, shaver points, electric fires; some with private showers. Table d'hote menu. Open throughout the year. For brochure write or telephone Michael and Jean Maloney. School parties catered for.

C	B & B PER PERSON PER NIGHT		DINNER B & B PER PERSON PER WEEK		17
	MIN £	MAX £	MIN £	MAX £	OPEN
	6		59.50	63	1—12

Guesthouses

Cardigan Guest House*

28 Marine Terrace
Criccieth LL52 0EL
Tel: (076 671) 2866

CATEGORIES

| 2 | 2 | 3 |

Family-run, on seafront overlooks Cardigan Bay. Ideal for family/group holidays. School parties etc., welcome. All bedrooms with hot and cold water and shaver points. Fire Certificate. Lounge with colour TV. Central heating in public areas. Pets welcome by arrangement. Good centre for touring Snowdonia. Access/Barclaycard accepted.

C	B & B PER PERSON PER NIGHT		DINNER B & B PER PERSON PER WEEK		10
	MIN £	MAX £	MIN £	MAX £	OPEN
	6.50	8	70	85	1—12

Meirionfa

Criccieth
Gwynedd LL52 0DB
Tel: (076 671) 2437

CATEGORIES

| 2 | 1 | 2 |

Small guest house with all amenities. Separate tables, lounge with TV, hot and cold. Good food and friendly atmosphere assured. Short walk from beach. Parking. Fire Certificate granted.

C	B & B PER PERSON PER NIGHT		DINNER B & B PER PERSON PER WEEK		4
	MIN £	MAX £	MIN £	MAX £	OPEN
	6	7.50	56	70	4—10

Meirion View Guest House*

Marine Terrace, Criccieth
Gwynedd LL52 0EF
Tel: (076 671) 2201

CATEGORIES

| 3 | 2 | 2 |

Situated on promenade overlooking the beach. Colour TV. Residential table licence. Within easy reach of the Snowdonia National Park, the Lleyn Peninsula and numerous golden beaches with safe bathing. Open all the year round. Early morning tea, late snacks available on request. Please write or phone for brochure and tariff to Mrs B. Cope.

C	B & B PER PERSON PER NIGHT		DINNER B & B PER PERSON PER WEEK		6
	MIN £	MAX £	MIN £	MAX £	OPEN
	6.25	7	57.75	70	1—12

The Moorings*

20 Marine Terrace, Criccieth
Gwynedd LL52 0EF
Tel: (076 671) 2802

CATEGORIES

| 3 | 2 | 4 |

A family guest house delightfully situated on the seafront with magnificent views over Cardigan Bay to the surrounding mountains. Personal service and comfortable bedrooms with tea and coffee making facilities. Choice of English or Continental breakfast. Packed lunched and childrens terms available. Open from March to October.

C	B & B PER PERSON PER NIGHT		DINNER B & B PER PERSON PER WEEK		7
	MIN £	MAX £	MIN £	MAX £	OPEN
	6.50	8	70	80	3—10

Preswylfa Guest House

Criccieth
Gwynedd LL52 0DY
Tel: (076 671) 2829

CATEGORIES

| 2 | 3 | 2 |

Near both beaches, shops, buses. Hot and cold water, shaver points all rooms, family double, single twin bed. Dining room with separate tables. Lounge with colour TV. Partial central heating, Fire Certificate, special rates children sharing family room. Pets welcome by arrangement. Good home cooking and service.

C	B & B PER PERSON PER NIGHT		DINNER B & B PER PERSON PER WEEK		4
	MIN £	MAX £	MIN £	MAX £	OPEN
	6	7	56	63	1—12

The Rhoslyn Guest House

8 Marine Terrace
Criccieth, Gwynedd
Tel: (076 671) 2685

CATEGORIES

| 3 | 3 | 3 |

A warm welcome awaits you at our comfortable family guest house, with ample home cooked meals and friendly service. Tea and coffee making facilities in all bedrooms, packed lunches available, babysitting. Guest lounge, colour TV. Ideal centre for touring Snowdonia and Lleyn Peninsula. Entertainments include fishing, boating, safe beaches, golf, tennis and pony trekking. Brochure and terms available on request.
Pam & Ken Rose.

C	B & B PER PERSON PER NIGHT		DINNER B & B PER PERSON PER WEEK		7
	MIN £	MAX £	MIN £	MAX £	OPEN
	6.50	7.50	70	80	3—10

"Wayside"*

Pentre-Felin, Criccieth, Gwynedd
North Wales LL52 0PU
Tel: (076 671) 2468

CATEGORIES

| 1 | 2 | 2 |

Situated centrally for guests to enjoy walking in National Park, exploring slate caverns and castles, or sunny beaches. We extend a welcome and offer comfortably unsophisticated cottage atmosphere. Easily reached by rail and car. Lounge with television. Full attention given to guests with special dietary requirements. House photograph available.

C	B & B PER PERSON PER NIGHT		DINNER B & B PER PERSON PER WEEK		4
	MIN £	MAX £	MIN £	MAX £	OPEN
	5.50	6	59	63	4—9

Farmhouse

Trem-yr-Eifl Farm*

Enquiries: Mrs E. Roberts
Rhoslan Criccieth
Tel: (076 671) 2320

CATEGORIES

| 2 | 2 | 2 |

Trem-yr-Eifl is 2½ miles from Criccieth. Ideally placed for touring Snowdonia and North Wales. All bedrooms have hot and cold water. Bathroom with shower, toilet. Separate tables in dining room. Lounge with colour TV. Children welcome. No pets.

C	B & B PER PERSON PER NIGHT		DINNER B & B PER PERSON PER WEEK		3
	MIN £	MAX £	MIN £	MAX £	OPEN
	7	8	63	65	4—9

Crickhowell
SOUTH WALES

Map ref: Mb1
Nestling between Black Mountains and Brecon Beacons in the National Park is Crickhowell. Pony trekking and riding in the hills about, and salmon fishing in the mature Usk, are its chief delights.

Hotels

The Bear Hotel

Crickhowell
Powys NP8 1BW
Tel: (0873) 810408

CATEGORIES

| 4 | 4 | 5 |

An award winning 16th century coaching inn. Delightful atmosphere with all modern amenities in centre of small market town. Ideally situated for touring Black Mountains/Brecon Beacons area. Many recreational activities. Charming restaurant. Home cooking. Extensive imaginative menu. Personal and friendly service. Open fires. Secluded garden.

T C	B & B PER PERSON PER NIGHT		DINNER B & B PER PERSON PER WEEK		12
	MIN £	MAX £	MIN £	MAX £	OPEN
	14.50	20.50			1—12

Dragon House Hotel*

High Street
Crickhowell NP8 1BE
Tel: (0873) 810362

CATEGORIES

3	3	3

Enjoy the cosy surroundings of this early 18th century hotel set in the picturesque market town of Crickhowell within the National Park. Ideal for walking, pony-trekking, boating, fishing, hang-gliding etc., residents lounge with colour TV and log fire. Cellar bar, restaurant, tea-room, offering conventional and vegetarian menu. Children welcome, play area available. Ample car parking.

	B & B PER PERSON PER NIGHT		DINNER B & B PER PERSON PER WEEK		11
T	MIN £	MAX £	MIN £	MAX £	OPEN
C	8.50	13.50	82.50	122.50	1—12

Gliffaes Country House Hotel*

Crickhowell
Powys NP8 1RH
Tel: (0874) 730371

CATEGORIES

4	4	4

2½ miles west of Crickhowell off the A40. Gliffaes lies between the Brecon Beacons and the Black Mountains overlooking the River Usk. It offers a peaceful holiday in beautiful surroundings. Private fishing, hard tennis court, wonderful walks, billiards, and golf courses nearby.

	B & B PER PERSON PER NIGHT		DINNER B & B PER PERSON PER WEEK		20
C	MIN £	MAX £	MIN £	MAX £	OPEN
	13.50	21	140	210	2—12

Guest House

Glan-y-Dwr Gourmet Restaurant*

Brecon Road,
Crickhowell, Powys
Tel: (0873) 810756

CATEGORIES

4	2	5

Superb cooking by proprietor Jean-Pierre Vermeire in relaxed and luxurious surroundings. Interesting menus changed frequently. Lunch served Wednesday to Sunday 3 courses £6.00 also a la carte. Dinner Wednesday to Saturday 7 course £14.50 also a la carte. Advance reservations advisable. Bedrooms beautifully appointed with private bathrooms.

	B & B PER PERSON PER NIGHT		DINNER B & B PER PERSON PER WEEK		2
	MIN £	MAX £	MIN £	MAX £	OPEN
	10	15			1—12

Farmhouses

Crickhowell Riding Stables, Neuadd Farm & Restaurant

Llangattock, Crickhowell
Powys NP8 1LE
Tel: (0873) 810244

CATEGORIES

2	3	5

Crickhowell Riding Stables and Neuadd Restaurant. Residential—bar-restaurant. Telephone (0873) 810244 for reservations. Superb position overlooking the mountains with an acre of gardens and own stables. Instruction to all levels, children and adults. Mountain rides, full day and half day. Self catering holiday apartments. Colour brochure—from Mrs P. Davies.

	B & B PER PERSON PER NIGHT		DINNER B & B PER PERSON PER WEEK		3
C	MIN £	MAX £	MIN £	MAX £	OPEN
	10	12	110	126	1—12

Dolfawr Farm*

Cwmdu, Crickhowell
Powys NP8 1RT
Tel: (0874) 730684

CATEGORIES

2	2	2

Situated in the beautiful Brecon Beacons National Park, Dolfawr is a 170 acre mixed farm. It is a good base for exploring the Elan Valley, Black Mountains, Brecon Beacons or just walking, pony trekking, swimming or sailing nearby. Children are always welcome. Home produce is served when available.

	B & B PER PERSON PER NIGHT		DINNER B & B PER PERSON PER WEEK		3
C	MIN £	MAX £	MIN £	MAX £	OPEN
	5.50		59		4—10

Croesgoch SOUTH WALES

Farmhouse

Torbant Farm Guest House*

Croesgoch, Haverfordwest
Pembrokeshire, Dyfed SA62 5JN
Tel: (03483) 276

CATEGORIES

5	3	2

Torbant Farm Guest House. Croesgoch, Haverfordwest, Pembrokeshire SA62 5JN. Tel: Croesgoch (03483) 276. Comfortable farmhouse with good home cooking. All rooms centrally heated and hot and cold water. TV lounge. Bar. Utility room. No dogs. 110 acres mixed farm near St. David's. 1½ miles to sea. Also private family suite. AA* RAC* SAE please.

	B & B PER PERSON PER NIGHT		DINNER B & B PER PERSON PER WEEK		13
T	MIN £	MAX £	MIN £	MAX £	OPEN
C	6.50	7.50	75	85	4—10

For autumn to spring breaks send for our free Great Little Breaks booklet.

Trearched Farm Guest House*

Trearched Farm, Croes Goch
Haverfordwest, Dyfed SA62 5JP
Tel: (034 83) 310

CATEGORIES

3	3	2

Comfortable centrally heated farmhouse down farm lane. Unlicensed. Warm welcome. Outside games room. Lawns. Children's play area. Overlooks 2 miles St. George's Channel between Strumble and St. David's head. Ideally situated for coastal path walks. Variety of beaches.

	B & B PER PERSON PER NIGHT		DINNER B & B PER PERSON PER WEEK		🛏 8
C	MIN £	MAX £	MIN £	MAX £	OPEN
	7	10	70	84	1—12

Crugybar
MID WALES

Hotel

Glanrannell Park Hotel

Crugybar, Llanwrda
Dyfed SA19 8SA
Tel: (05583) 230

CATEGORIES

3	4	4

AA* RAC* BTA commended country house hotel in the lovely Cothi valley. An ideal centre for a restful or active holiday in West Wales. Super hill walking, game fishing and birdwatching. Our aim is service and friendliness. Please send or phone for our colour brochure.

	B & B PER PERSON PER NIGHT		DINNER B & B PER PERSON PER WEEK		🛏 8
T C	MIN £	MAX £	MIN £	MAX £	OPEN
	12.50		120		4—10

Children stay at reduced rates, wherever you see this symbol.

Crymych
SOUTH WALES

Guest House

Preseli Farm Stud*

Crymych, near Whitland
Dyfed
Tel: (099 47) 425

CATEGORIES

3	4	5

This must be one of the most beautifully situated guest houses in the Pembrokeshire Coast National Park. 60 acres of grounds used as a stud to breed race horses. Intimate licensed restaurant offers French/English cuisine of highest standard. All cooked by resident proprietor. Only fresh ingredients used. Extremely well furnished bedrooms, all with superb views. Few minutes drive off Cardigan/Tenby road (A478), 4 miles south of Crymych. Coast 20 minutes drive. All sporting amenities available within easy reach. Bargain Breaks. Colour brochure available.

	B & B PER PERSON PER NIGHT		DINNER B & B PER PERSON PER WEEK		🛏 6
T C	MIN £	MAX £	MIN £	MAX £	OPEN
	14	19	125	145	1—12

Cwmbran
SOUTH WALES

Hotel

Somerton House Hotel

379 Llantarnam Road, Cwmbran
Gwent
Tel: (06333) 5588

CATEGORIES

3	3	5

Small licensed family hotel within easy access of M4 and Newport. 16 bedrooms. TV lounge and restaurant. Families welcome. The hotel provides an ideal base for touring the whole of Gwent, the Brecon Beacons National Park and the South Wales Valleys. Fishing and boating at nearby Llandegfedd Lake.

	B & B PER PERSON PER NIGHT		DINNER B & B PER PERSON PER WEEK		🛏 16
T C	MIN £	MAX £	MIN £	MAX £	OPEN
	9.20	11.50	64.40	80.50	1—12

Guest House

Springfields Guest House*

371 Llantarnam Road
Cwmbran
Tel: (06333) 2509

CATEGORIES

3	4	3

We are situated in a pleasant area, within 1 mile of town centre, Stadium. Close to M4 on 4042 to Abergavenny and Wye Valley. Children and pets welcome. Private car park. We think this area is lovely and feel sure you will not regret coming to stay here. Joan Graham.

	B & B PER PERSON PER NIGHT		DINNER B & B PER PERSON PER WEEK		🛏 8
T C	MIN £	MAX £	MIN £	MAX £	OPEN
	8		65		1—12

Cwmystwyth
MID WALES

Farmhouse

Bwlch-y-Gwynt Farm

Cwmystwyth, Aberystwyth
Dyfed SY23 4AG
Tel: (097 422) 620

CATEGORIES

1	2	3

A quiet location in the Ystwyth valley surrounded by beautiful scenery. Follow A4120 from Aberystwyth to Devil's Bridge. 4 miles on A4674 to Cwmystwyth. 1 mile from shop, by cattle grid. Farm sign posted.

	B & B PER PERSON PER NIGHT		DINNER B & B PER PERSON PER WEEK		🛏 3
C	MIN £	MAX £	MIN £	MAX £	OPEN
	6	8	60	70	1—12

Dale
SOUTH WALES

Guest Houses

Monk Haven Manor Guest House*

St. Ishmaels, Haverfordwest
Pembrokeshire, Dyfed SA62 3TH
Tel: (06465) 216

CATEGORIES

3	3	2

Quiet guest house set in 8 acres of Pembrokeshire Coast National Park. We offer modern comforts with traditional old fashion qualities of wholesome home cooking, personal service and hospitality. TV lounge, cosy lounge bar. Safe beaches, sailing, pony trekking. Coastal footpaths in vicinity. Children welcome. Ideal for touring Pembrokeshire.

	B & B PER PERSON PER NIGHT		DINNER B & B PER PERSON PER WEEK		🛏 5
C	MIN £	MAX £	MIN £	MAX £	OPEN
	9	10	80	85	3—11

Officers House*

Coastguard Cottages, St. Anns Head
Dale, Haverfordwest, Dyfed SA62 3RT
Tel: (06465) 407

CATEGORIES | 1 | 2 | 2

Set in the Pembrokeshire Coast National Park with the Pembrokeshire Coastal Path close by. We offer a small, friendly, family guest house, with home cooking, overlooking the sea. Carpeted throughout, TV, and parking. The sailing village of Dale is nearby. Ideally situated for touring, walking, sunbathing, fishing and sailing.

C	B & B PER PERSON PER NIGHT		DINNER B & B PER PERSON PER WEEK		3
	MIN £	MAX £	MIN £	MAX £	OPEN
	6	7	66	77	1—12

The Post House*

Dale, near Haverfordwest
Pembrokeshire, Dyfed SA62 3RE
Tel: (06465) 201

CATEGORIES | 3 | 3 | 4

Friendly family guest house and renowned licensed restaurant in delightful coastal village in the Pembrokeshire National Park. Comfortable bedrooms. Lounge with colour television. Fire certificate. Superb food from fresh local produce. Children and pets welcome. Ideal base for touring, walking, swimming, sailing and boat trips to the islands.

C	B & B PER PERSON PER NIGHT		DINNER B & B PER PERSON PER WEEK		5
	MIN £	MAX £	MIN £	MAX £	OPEN
	8.50		90		1—12

Farmhouse

Slate Mill Bridge*

Dale Road, Haverfordwest
Pembrokeshire, Dyfed SA62 3QR
Tel: (064 65) 258

CATEGORIES | 1 | 2 | 2

Slate Mill is located within Pembrokeshire coast national park. The area abounds in wildlife and wild flowers. Close to sandy beach, and boat trips to Skomer Island. Pony Trekking nearby. Children and dogs always welcome.

C	B & B PER PERSON PER NIGHT		DINNER B & B PER PERSON PER WEEK		2
	MIN £	MAX £	MIN £	MAX £	OPEN
	6.50	8	73.50	84	3—10

Guest House

Cayo Guest House*

74 Vale Street, Denbigh
Clwyd LL16 2BW
Tel: (074 571) 2686

CATEGORIES | 2 | 3 | 2

Excellent position for Snowdonia, beaches and general touring. Golf, fishing, pony trekking, good walks, all in reasonable distance. Fresh local food bought daily. Home made jams, marmalade, farm butter and cheese etc. Full central heating family rooms.

T C	B & B PER PERSON PER NIGHT		DINNER B & B PER PERSON PER WEEK		6
	MIN £	MAX £	MIN £	MAX £	OPEN
	7.50	8	75	85	1—12

Devil's Bridge — MID WALES

Hotel

The Woodlands Hotel and Licensed Restaurant*

Devil's Bridge
Aberystwyth SY23 3JW
Tel: (097085) 666

CATEGORIES | 3 | 2 | 2

A family hotel, situated amongst beautiful scenery. Close to Devil's Bridge Gorge, and ideal centre for the tourist walker and naturalist, where your comfort is our prime concern. We pride ourselves on the high standard of our cuisine and cater for all special diets. Fire certificate granted.

C	B & B PER PERSON PER NIGHT		DINNER B & B PER PERSON PER WEEK		8
	MIN £	MAX £	MIN £	MAX £	OPEN
	8.10	8.60	81.90		1—12

Dinas Cross — SOUTH WALES

Farmhouse

Cilwenen Hill

Dinas Cross, Pembrokeshire
Dyfed SA42 0XH
Tel: (034 86) 239

CATEGORIES | 1 | 3 | 2

Beautiful views overlooking woodland and beach. Guests welcome all year in two double-bedded rooms, hot and cold water, and 1 twin room. Shaver points in all rooms. We produce our own beef and vegetables. Footpath to beach to link up with Pembrokeshire National Park coastal path. Lounge with colour television.

C	B & B PER PERSON PER NIGHT		DINNER B & B PER PERSON PER WEEK		3
	MIN £	MAX £	MIN £	MAX £	OPEN
	6	7	75	80	1—12

Dolgellau — MID WALES

Map ref: Dc4
As a town, its setting in wooded mountains is probably unrivalled in southern Britain. Its stone buildings are the flower of their type, particularly the smaller cottages. Welsh in ways and speech, it dominates routes along both shores of the lovely Mawddach Estuary to Cader Idris mountain and Coed-y-Brenin forest and is a fine touring centre.

Hotels and Inns

Cross Foxes Inn*

Cross Foxes, Brithdir, Dolgellau
Gwynedd
Tel: (0341) 422487

CATEGORIES | 3 | 2 | 4

An attractive, small country hotel, full of character and under the personal supervision of the owners. Situated at the foot of Cader Idris, 3 miles from Dolgellau and 10 miles from the coast. Trout fishing in own grounds, other activities arranged. Walking, climbing, pony trekking. For details contact Mr. & Mrs. Watts.

T C	B & B PER PERSON PER NIGHT		DINNER B & B PER PERSON PER WEEK		4
	MIN £	MAX £	MIN £	MAX £	OPEN
	8	12	84	100	1—12

George III

Penmaenpool, Dogellau
Gwynedd LL40 1YD
Tel: (0341) 422525

CATEGORIES: 4 4 5

This 17th century Inn situated at the head of the beautiful Mawddach estuary offers old world atmosphere with modern comforts. Full central heating, TV and tea/coffee making facilities in all bedrooms, most en suite. Enjoy the excellent cuisine in the Riverside restaurant. The George is delightfully placed in the Snowdonia National Park.

T	B & B PER PERSON PER NIGHT		DINNER B & B PER PERSON PER WEEK		14
C	MIN £	MAX £	MIN £	MAX £	OPEN
	14	23			1—12

Royal Ship Hotel

Queens Square, Dolgellau
Gwynedd LL40 1AR
Tel: (0341422) 209

CATEGORIES: 3 4 4

This extensively modernised hotel stands in the centre of Dolgellau with a fine view of the Cader Idris. Residents lounge with colour TV. Some bedrooms with bathroom en-suite. Large car park. Many beautiful walks within easy reach and a choice of river, lake and sea fishing.

C	B & B PER PERSON PER NIGHT		DINNER B & B PER PERSON PER WEEK		23
	MIN £	MAX £	MIN £	MAX £	OPEN
	12	15.50	108	135	1—12

Guest Houses

Dwy Olwyn*

Coed Y Fronallt, Dolgellau
Gwynedd LL40 2YG
Tel: (0341) 422822

CATEGORIES: 1 2 2

Dwy Olwyn is pleasantly situated in a country setting with outstanding views of the Cader Idris mountain range. An ideal centre for touring within easy reach to sandy beaches. Pony trekking, trout and salmon fishing. Narrow gauge railways and picturesque walks. Ample parking. Lounge with colour TV.

C	B & B PER PERSON PER NIGHT		DINNER B & B PER PERSON PER WEEK		3
	MIN £	MAX £	MIN £	MAX £	OPEN
	5	5.50	56	59.50	4—11

Penbryn Croft*

Cader Road, Dolgellau
LL40 1RN
Tel: (0341) 422 815

CATEGORIES: 2 3 3

Penbryn Croft is almost 200 years old, situated within two minutes walk of the centre of Dolgellau, with pony trekking, old gold mines, narrow gauge railways, salmon and trout fishing, all within easy reach. Sitting room with TV, dining room with separate tables. Excellent cuisine; diets catered for. SAE please.

T	B & B PER PERSON PER NIGHT		DINNER B & B PER PERSON PER WEEK		5
C	MIN £	MAX £	MIN £	MAX £	OPEN
	6.75		63		1—10

Troed-y-Rhiw

Rhydymain, Dolgellau
Gwynedd LL40 2AR
Tel: (0341) 643

CATEGORIES: 3 3 2

Attractive Georgian Guest House. Family and double bedrooms. Hot and cold. Basins in all, shower room. Bathroom, central heating. Comfortable furnished old world charm. Excellent full breakfast and 4 course dinner. Good food is always served and our aim is to please our guests. Ideal for touring. SAE for brochure.

C	B & B PER PERSON PER NIGHT		DINNER B & B PER PERSON PER WEEK		3
	MIN £	MAX £	MIN £	MAX £	OPEN
	6	8	54	70	1—12

Y Goedlan*

Brithdir, Dolgellau
Gwynedd LL40 2RN
Tel: (0341) 423131

CATEGORIES: 1 2 1

This old vicarage offers peaceful accommodation in pleasant rural surrounding. Ideally placed (on B4416 road) for pleasant walks, sea, and mountains. Spacious bedrooms with H & C. Double, twin bedded and family rooms. Reduced rates for children under 10. Colour TV. Lounge. Separate tables in dining room. Ample parking space. Comfort.

C	B & B PER PERSON PER NIGHT		DINNER B & B PER PERSON PER WEEK		3
	MIN £	MAX £	MIN £	MAX £	OPEN
	6	7			2—10

Farmhouses

Glyn Farm

Dolgellau, Gwynedd
LL40 1YR
Tel: (0341) 422286

CATEGORIES: 1 3 2

Working farm 750 acres, Welsh black cattle, mountain sheep. Free range chickens, plus nanny goat. 300 year old house situated on hill overlooking picturesque Mawddach Estuary, one mile Dolgellau on A493 road. Hot cuppa served 10 pm. Fire Certificate held. Private trout fishing, ample parking area. Children welcome. Dogs by arrangment.

C	B & B PER PERSON PER NIGHT		DINNER B & B PER PERSON PER WEEK		5
	MIN £	MAX £	MIN £	MAX £	OPEN
	5.50	6	50	60	3—11

Gwanas*

Cross Foxes, Dolgellau
Gwynedd, North Wales, LL40 2SH
Tel: (0341) 422624

CATEGORIES: 1 2 1

Peace and comfort assured on 1,100 acre sheep farm. Also two riding ponies, cattle, ducks, chickens. Spacious farmhouse offers homely atmosphere and hearty breakfast. Single, double family rooms with basins, two bathrooms, TV, central heating. Reductions for children. 700 yards from Cross Foxes Hotel off A470 road. Dolgellau 3 miles.

C	B & B PER PERSON PER NIGHT		DINNER B & B PER PERSON PER WEEK		3
	MIN £	MAX £	MIN £	MAX £	OPEN
	6	7			3—11

Hengwrt Farm

Rhydymain, Dolgellau
Gwynedd LL40 2AR
Tel: (034141) 252

CATEGORIES: 1 2 2

This working farm is in a quiet spot above the A494 Dolgellau to Bala road. Ideal centre from which to explore castles, forest trails, lakes, miniature railways and beaches. Good home cooking. Children over six welcomed at reduced prices.

C	B & B PER PERSON PER NIGHT		DINNER B & B PER PERSON PER WEEK		3
	MIN £	MAX £	MIN £	MAX £	OPEN
	7	7.50	66.50	70	5—9

Tyddyngarreg Farm

Tabor, Dogellau, Gwynedd
North Wales
Tel: (0341) 422 361

CATEGORIES: 1 2 2

Old Quaker farm house with history. Beautiful views. Ideal for walking holidays. 800 acres. Sheep, cows, horses, hens, working farm. Pony trekking 1 mile. Sea 8 miles. 2 miles shops. Ample parking. No pets. Children welcome. Separate tables for guests in dining room. Home cooking, farm produce used. Lounge and dining room. Baby sitting.

C	B & B PER PERSON PER NIGHT		DINNER B & B PER PERSON PER WEEK		3
	MIN £	MAX £	MIN £	MAX £	OPEN
	6	8.50	65	70	3—11

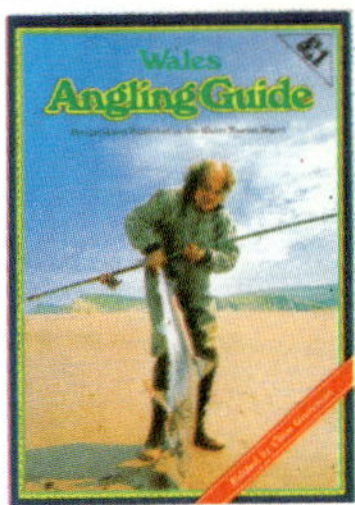

Angling
112 page guide packed with information and advice for visiting sea, game and coarse fishermen.
Available from: Wales Tourist Board Department W.T.S. P.O. Box 1, CARDIFF CF1 2XN. Price: £1.25p including postage and packing.

Dolwyddelan

Hotel

Elen's Castle Hotel*

Dolwyddelan, Gwynedd
LL25 0EJ
Tel: (06906) 207

CATEGORIES		
4	4	4

Elaine and John invite new guests to a warm welcome at Elen's Castle in a relaxed atmosphere and surroundings of the beautiful Lledr Valley. Slate floored residential bar. 4 poster and other en-suite bedrooms. Centrally heated. Car parking in 2½ acre grounds. Fishing and canoeing from hotel. Excellent touring area. AA* RAC*

C	B & B PER PERSON PER NIGHT		DINNER B & B PER PERSON PER WEEK		10
	MIN £	MAX £	MIN £	MAX £	OPEN
	9.80	10.90	86.90	95.70	4—9

Dyffryn Ardudwy

Farmhouses

Byrdir Farm

Dyffryn Ardudwy, Meirionnydd
Gwynedd LL44 2EA
Tel: (03417) 200

CATEGORIES		
2	3	2

Byrdir is a 40 acre Welsh beef and sheep farm. It is set in the heart of the Snowdonia National Park, with beautiful views of Cardigan Bay and the Rhinog Mountains. Golf, fishing, swimming, pony trekking and mountain walks all available nearby. Children are most welcome. Welsh spoken.

T C	B & B PER PERSON PER NIGHT		DINNER B & B PER PERSON PER WEEK		4
	MIN £	MAX £	MIN £	MAX £	OPEN
	7	7.50	75	82	3—10

Cors-y-Gedol Hall Farm

Dyffryn-Ardudwy
Gwynedd
Tel: (03417) 231

CATEGORIES		
3	2	2

The 18th century farmhouse in the grounds of a 14th century Manor House and unique Gatehouse, forms part of a large working farm (approximately 4,000 acres). The house is comfortably furnished with antiques and contains two bathrooms. Food is served to a high standard. One mile to the sea and many tourist attractions nearby, e.g., slate mines, railways, craft villages etc.

C	B & B PER PERSON PER NIGHT		DINNER B & B PER PERSON PER WEEK		3
	MIN £	MAX £	MIN £	MAX £	OPEN
	6	7	71.25	77.90	1—12

Dolgau

Dyffryn Ardudwy, Gwynedd LL44 2RQ
Tel: (03417) 617
Enquiries: Mrs. E. M. Evans "Dolgau"

CATEGORIES		
1	2	2

A delightful 14th century farmhouse, listed ancient monument of Wales, offering 5 super bedrooms with character. Situated in an unspoilt area between Harlech and Barmouth, it offers miles of golden sands, countryside with mountains, lakes and rivers, golf, riding, fishing and sailing.

C	B & B PER PERSON PER NIGHT		DINNER B & B PER PERSON PER WEEK		5
	MIN £	MAX £	MIN £	MAX £	OPEN
	5.25	7	59.50	70	5—10

Meadow Farm

Llwyngwian Fawr, Dyffryn Ardudwy
near Barmouth, Gwynedd LL42 2DY
Tel: (03417) 655

CATEGORIES		
3	2	2

William and Margaret Roberts invite you to visit their farmhouse/Guest house. Modernised with hot and cold water. All bedrooms, some with showers managed professionally by the proprietors. Free ample parking. Evening dinners, English breakfasts. 5 miles Barmouth, 5 miles Harlech, 2½ miles beach. Ideal centre for Snowdonia, touring, walking. Quiet peaceful setting. Beautiful views. Central heating. Fire certificate.

T C	B & B PER PERSON PER NIGHT		DINNER B & B PER PERSON PER WEEK		6
	MIN £	MAX £	MIN £	MAX £	OPEN
	7	8	10.50	12	1—12

Eglwys-Fach

Hotel

Ynyshirhall Country House Hotel*

Eglwysfach, Machynlleth
Powys SY20 8TA
Tel: (065474) 209

CATEGORIES		
4	4	5

Luxurious drawing rooms with log fires and central heating. Eleven comfortable bedrooms most have bathrooms en-suite and glorious views. The cuisine is superb and this together with the personal attention of your hosts will make your visit truly memorable. Winter breaks available. AA* One rosette Egon Ronay.

T C	B & B PER PERSON PER NIGHT		DINNER B & B PER PERSON PER WEEK		11
	MIN £	MAX £	MIN £	MAX £	OPEN
	21.50	24	238	255.50	2—12

Eglwyswrw

Inn

Serjeants Inn*

Eglwyswrw, Crymych
Dyfed SA41 2UJ
Tel: (023979) 271

CATEGORIES		
3	3	5

12th century inn in centre of village. All rooms are centrally heated with hot and cold water and shaving points. Tea making facilities included. Lunches and evening meals available from bar and dining room menus. Home made food a speciality. Large car park. Easy access to beaches and Preseli mountains.

C	B & B PER PERSON PER NIGHT		DINNER B & B PER PERSON PER WEEK		4
	MIN £	MAX £	MIN £	MAX £	OPEN
	7.50				1—12

This symbol means you can book through your local travel agent.

Farmhouse

Ty Isaf Farm*

Erwood, Builth Wells, Powys LD2 3SZ
Tel: (09823) 607
Enquiries: N. M. Jones

FARMHOUSE AWARD

CATEGORIES

3	3	2

Ty Isaf farm is just off the A470 south of Erwood village 340 acres mixed farm overlooking Wye valley, excellent spot from which to tour Mid Wales, Black Mountains, Hay on Wye. Visitors are welcome to walk round the farm. Erwood just a short walk away has two handy country inns.

	B & B PER PERSON PER NIGHT		DINNER B & B PER PERSON PER WEEK		4
T C	MIN £	MAX £	MIN £	MAX £	OPEN
	5.50	6.50	63	70	1—12

Fairbourne — MID WALES

Hotels

Brackenhurst Hotel*

Fairbourne, Gwynedd
Wales, LL38 2HX
Tel: (0341) 250226

CATEGORIES

3	4	4

Small country house hotel with extensive views over mountains and sea. Well appointed, offering every comfort. Ideal centre for exploring beautiful Merioneth and Snowdonia. Good food, friendly atmosphere. Residents bar. Nearby facilities for pony trekking, fishing, boating, sailing, golf, tennis, climbing, walking. Safe sandy beach. Bargain breaks available.

	B & B PER PERSON PER NIGHT		DINNER B & B PER PERSON PER WEEK		10
T C	MIN £	MAX £	MIN £	MAX £	OPEN
	8.50	11.50	75	90	4—10

Children stay at reduced rates, wherever you see this symbol.

Springfield Hotel

Beach Road, Fairbourne
Gwynedd LL38 2PX
Tel: (0341) 250414/250378

CATEGORIES

3	4	4

Well appointed AA** and RAC** hotel, in centre of seaside village overlooking sea and mountain ranges. Ideal centre for touring west coast of Wales. Coach parties welcome for meal. Friendly staff, ideal for conferences, weddings, parties in our Dining Room/ Ballroom. Children and pets welcome. Tariff on application.

	B & B PER PERSON PER NIGHT		DINNER B & B PER PERSON PER WEEK		15
C	MIN £	MAX £	MIN £	MAX £	OPEN
					1—12

Guest Houses

Einion Guest House*

Friog, Fairbourne
Gwynedd LL38 2NX
Tel: (0341) 250644

CATEGORIES

3	3	3

Excellent quiet, licensed family accommodation on three floors situated on coast, south of Barmouth. Four double, two family, one single bedroom. TV lounge and dining room. Area fulfills exceptional holiday interests. Good touring centre, Snowdonia National Park and miniature railways. Group reductions. Choice menu. Fire certificate. Parking. Pets welcome.

	B & B PER PERSON PER NIGHT		DINNER B & B PER PERSON PER WEEK		7
C	MIN £	MAX £	MIN £	MAX £	OPEN
	6.25	7	58	65	1—11

Sea View Guest House

Friog, near Fairbourne
Gwynedd LL38 2NX
Tel: (0341) 250388

CATEGORIES

3	3	4

Family-run business with good home cooking. Adjacent to Snowdonia National Park, close to safe beach. Ideally placed for outdoor activites and touring. Fully heated accommodation. Lounge with colour television. easy parking close by.

	B & B PER PERSON PER NIGHT		DINNER B & B PER PERSON PER WEEK		6
C	MIN £	MAX £	MIN £	MAX £	OPEN
	7.10	8	70.60	70.60	1—12

Tourist Information Centres are listed at back of book.

Ferryside — SOUTH WALES

Inns

The Ferry Hotel*

Ferryside, near Carmarthen
Dyfed, S. W. Wales, SA17 5SL
Tel: (026 785) 553

CATEGORIES

1	1	3

Freehouse situated with our back to the river Towy. Opposite side of estuary to Llanstephan Castle. Centre for fishing, sailing, walking, hang gliding. Beautiful beaches nearby. Selection of local real ales. Full central heating, shaver point, hot and cold water. Tea and coffee in all rooms. Home cooking. Taste the local sewin (sea trout) and salmon.

	B & B PER PERSON PER NIGHT		DINNER B & B PER PERSON PER WEEK		3
C	MIN £	MAX £	MIN £	MAX £	OPEN
	8.50		75		1—12

Red Lion Inn

Llandyfaelog, near Ferryside
Dyfed, West Wales, SA17 5PR
Tel: (026785) 530/267

CATEGORIES

2	2	3

Once a farmhouse, converted into an inn 70 years ago in the heart of beautiful countryside. Llandyfaelog is situated on the main A484 road between Llanelli and Carmarthen. Excellent home cooking. Ferryside beach and sailing club some 3 miles away.

	B & B PER PERSON PER NIGHT		DINNER B & B PER PERSON PER WEEK		5
C	MIN £	MAX £	MIN £	MAX £	OPEN
	6.50	7.50			1—12

Ffestiniog — NORTH WALES

Guest House

Newborough House Hotel

Church Square, Ffestiniog
Gwynedd, North Wales, LL41 4LL
Tel: (076 676) 2682

CATEGORIES

3	3	3

This beautiful 17th century character house is situated in the heart of Snowdonia in the old village of Ffestiniog. Ideally located for mountains, sea. Ffestiniog railway, slate mines. Fishing, walking, riding ect. The excellent accommodation includes a beamed lounge, with inglenook fireplace and colour TV, a cosy olde worlde bar. All bedrooms have heating and washbasins. Excellent food. Open all year (Winter breaks at reasonable rates). Full fire certificate.

	B & B PER PERSON PER NIGHT		DINNER B & B PER PERSON PER WEEK		6
C	MIN £	MAX £	MIN £	MAX £	OPEN
	7.50		78		1—12

Map ref: Jc2
Sea port and resort on the attractive north Pembrokeshire coast. The town, scene of surrender of French invasion in 1798, is small but has all facilities. Lower Fishguard, the town's original harbour, was the attractive setting for the film version of Dylan Thomas 'Under Milk Wood'. Irish Ferry terminal. Rail served.

Hotels, Motel and Inn

Fishguard Bay Hotel Ltd.*

Quay Road, Goodwick
Fishguard, Dyfed
Tel: (0348) 873571

CATEGORIES | 4 | 5 | 5

The largest hotel in north Pembrokeshire having a unique setting in 10 acres of woodland with terraced paths leading to the magnificent cliff scenery around Strumble Head. Ideal touring base for South West Wales and the Pembrokeshire Coast National Park. Perfect for overnight stops en-route or returning from Ireland. Within yards of the ferry terminal. Centrally heated. Lift, colour TV, lounge, residents lounge. Heated swimming pool. A la carte restaurant open to non residents. Midweek breaks available from October to March. Colour brochure available.

	B & B PER PERSON PER NIGHT		DINNER B & B PER PERSON PER WEEK		62
T C	MIN £	MAX £	MIN £	MAX £	OPEN
	15	17.50	130	160	1—12

Frenchman Motel

St. Davids Road, Goodwick
Fishguard Harbour, Dyfed
Tel: (0348) 873555

CATEGORIES | 3 | 2 | 2

Simple, comfortable, reasonably priced accommodation, conveniently situated for visiting Pembrokeshire. Every room has own private facilities. Car parking adjacent to room. Special family rooms, can take six persons. Large bar and lounge. Reasonable food. Specially open late for the Irish ferry. Family run, so we do care.

	B & B PER PERSON PER NIGHT		DINNER B & B PER PERSON PER WEEK		70
T C	MIN £	MAX £	MIN £	MAX £	OPEN
	6	12	60	80	1—12

Glanmoy Country House*

Goodwick, Pembrokeshire
Dyfed SA64 0JX
Tel: (0348) 872844

CATEGORIES | 4 | 4 | 5

Charming country house standing in mature grounds of 3 acres with delightful views of the countryside and the sea beyond. Peace and tranquility with every comfort and superb cooking. Centrally heated throughout. All rooms with bath. Colour TV and tea/coffee making facilities. Restaurant and residential licence.

	B & B PER PERSON PER NIGHT		DINNER B & B PER PERSON PER WEEK		3
	MIN £	MAX £	MIN £	MAX £	OPEN
	13	15	112	126	1—12

Hope & Anchor Inn*

Goodwick, Fishguard
Dyfed
Tel: (0348) 872314

CATEGORIES | 3 | 3 | 5

Small family inn on the Pembrokeshire Coast mid-way between Cardigan and St. David's. Close to coastal path and many popular beaches. A short distance from the Sealink ferry. Famous for our fresh crab, lobster and salmon during season à la carte or table d'hôte meals. Reduced terms for children.

	B & B PER PERSON PER NIGHT		DINNER B & B PER PERSON PER WEEK		3
C	MIN £	MAX £	MIN £	MAX £	OPEN
	8	8.50	63	71.50	1—12

Penlan Oleu*

Llanychaer, Fishguard
Dyfed SA65 9TL
Tel: (034882) 314

CATEGORIES | 4 | 4 | 2

Set in the Preseli Hills above Fishguard Bay, Penlan Oleu is a small secluded private licensed country hotel and gourmet restaurant. With magnificent views, the converted farmhouse makes good centre for holidays or quiet weekends. Please apply to the resident proprietor, Mrs. A. Stuart-Lyon for brochure and tariff.

	B & B PER PERSON PER NIGHT		DINNER B & B PER PERSON PER WEEK		4
T	MIN £	MAX £	MIN £	MAX £	OPEN
	8.50	9.50	102	115	1—12

Plas Glyn y Mel*

Lower Fishguard
Dyfed SA65 9LY
Tel: (0348) 872803

CATEGORIES | 3 | 3 | 3

Historic Georgean house near unspoilt old fishing harbour. The river Gwaun runs through peaceful secluded grounds of 50 acres. Bird Sanctuary. ½ mile to Fishguard. Also a self-contained flat. Beaches, sailing, golf nearby. Car park. Licensed. German spoken. Personally supervised by Lt. Col. and Mrs. F. H. Blofield.

	B & B PER PERSON PER NIGHT		DINNER B & B PER PERSON PER WEEK		7
C	MIN £	MAX £	MIN £	MAX £	OPEN
	8	9	82	90	4—9

Guest Houses

3 Parc-y-Shwt*

Fishguard
Dyfed SA65 9AP
Tel: (0348) 872597

CATEGORIES | 1 | 3 | 2

Two minutes from the centre of town in a quiet little street, open all year. Hot and cold water, shaver points in bedrooms. Full central heating, lounge with colour TV. Separate dining room. Children welcome.

	B & B PER PERSON PER NIGHT		DINNER B & B PER PERSON PER WEEK		4
T C	MIN £	MAX £	MIN £	MAX £	OPEN
	5.50	6.50	64.75	71.75	1—12

"Siriole"*

Quay Road, Goodwick
Dyfed SA64 0BS
Tel: (0348) 873203

CATEGORIES: 3 3 1

On the edge of Fishguard Bay. About ¼ mile from Irish ferry port—open for late boats. Panoramic views of Preseli hills. On the Pembrokeshire coastal path. Open all the year. Central heating, hot and cold water in all bedrooms. Showers at any time. No pets.

C	B & B PER PERSON PER NIGHT		DINNER B & B PER PERSON PER WEEK		6
	MIN £	MAX £	MIN £	MAX £	OPEN
	6	6	38	38	1—12

Farmhouse

Gilfach Goch Farmhouse*

Fishguard, Dyfed
Wales SA65 9SR
Tel: (0348) 873871

CATEGORIES: 1 3 3

Smallholding in superb position overlooking sea, town and hills, 2 miles Fishguard. Well equipped and comfortable family, double and single bedrooms. Central heating, guest lounge with coloured TV, dining room of character with inglenook fireplace and open beams. Excellent cooking using home produce when possible.

C	B & B PER PERSON PER NIGHT		DINNER B & B PER PERSON PER WEEK		3
	MIN £	MAX £	MIN £	MAX £	OPEN
	6	8	63	77	1—12

Flint
NORTH WALES

Guest House

"Cân-y-Gwynt"

Northop Road, Flint Mountain
Flint, Clwyd CH6 5QG
Tel: (03526) 61871

CATEGORIES: 3 3 3

Modern well-furnished house, with pleasant garden in open country. Single, double and family rooms. With hot and cold water and shaver points. Lounge with colour television. Centrally heated throughout. Cot and high chair available. Car parking. Situated on A5119 road off A55. Convenient for touring North Wales and Cheshire.

C	B & B PER PERSON PER NIGHT		DINNER B & B PER PERSON PER WEEK		3
	MIN £	MAX £	MIN £	MAX £	OPEN
	8	11	66	75	1—12

For autumn to spring breaks send for our free Great Little Breaks booklet.

Freshwater East
SOUTH WALES

Guest House

Seahorses

Freshwater East, Pembroke
Pembrokeshire, SA71 5LA
Tel: (0646) 672405

CATEGORIES: 1 2 2

Ideal touring centre, beaches and castles. Overlooking Freshwater East Bay. Excellent food. Friendly service, car park.

C	B & B PER PERSON PER NIGHT		DINNER B & B PER PERSON PER WEEK		2
	MIN £	MAX £	MIN £	MAX £	OPEN
	6	8	50	60	4—9

Gaerwen
NORTH WALES

Motel

Star Motel*

Ace Motels Limited, Gaerwen
Isle of Anglesey, Gwynedd
Tel: (0248) 714698

CATEGORIES: 3 1 4

Situated on main A5 trunk road. Ideal as touring base for all North Wales. All rooms have colour TV. Two-day package available throughout year. Pets welcome at £1.50 nightly. Fully licensed.

C	B & B PER PERSON PER NIGHT		DINNER B & B PER PERSON PER WEEK		12
	MIN £	MAX £	MIN £	MAX £	OPEN
	13	13			1—12

Garndolbenmaen
NORTH WALES

Guest House

Auron

Garn Dolbenmaen, Gwynedd
LL51 9TQ
Tel: (076 675) 358

CATEGORIES: 3 3 2

Mrs. Aurwen Jones, Auron, Garn Dolbenmaen, attractive new bungalow in open ground in the Snowdonia National Park near the village of Garn Dolbenmaen.

C	B & B PER PERSON PER NIGHT		DINNER B & B PER PERSON PER WEEK		2
	MIN £	MAX £	MIN £	MAX £	OPEN
	5.50	7	60	70	4—10

Farmhouse

Hendre Cennin Farm

Garndolbenmaen
Gwynedd LL51 9EX
Tel: (076675) 253

CATEGORIES: 1 2 2

A 17th century farmhouse with modern amenities. Ideal for touring the Snowdonia mountain range and a breathtaking view over the Cardigan Bay. Six miles from nearest beach at Criccieth. Ample car park.

C	B & B PER PERSON PER NIGHT		DINNER B & B PER PERSON PER WEEK		3
	MIN £	MAX £	MIN £	MAX £	OPEN
			60	65	5—9

Glynceiriog
NORTH WALES

Hotels, Motels and Inns

Golden Pheasant Hotel*

Glynceiriog, near Chirk
Llangollen, LL20 7BB
Tel: (069172) 281

CATEGORIES: 3 5 5

Unique! Charming! Rural Bliss! Finest views from every window. Gorgeous bedrooms. Original old bar. Best country cooking. Gardens and terraces for alfresco dining. Award winning riding stables. Organised walking and shooting holidays. 5 miles to A5 main road at Chirk. Please write for colour brochures. Proprietor Jenny Turner.

T / C	B & B PER PERSON PER NIGHT		DINNER B & B PER PERSON PER WEEK		19
	MIN £	MAX £	MIN £	MAX £	OPEN
	18	20	159	175	1—12

Don't forget that 1983 is Festival of Castles Year in Wales with events planned for all the major historic sites.

The Glyn Valley Hotel*

Glyn Ceiriog, Llangollen, Clwyd
Wales, LL20 7EU
Tel: (069 172) 210 or 254

CATEGORIES

| 3 | 4 | 5 |

One star country hotel with AA hospitality award. Exceptional food quality and variety breakfast any time. Relaxed informal atmosphere with frequent Welsh singing. Real ale. Three bars restaurant/functions room for 100. Colour TV. Lounge. Pony trekking, fishing, hiking, squash, tennis, golf, swimming, climbing, excursions. All arranged from hotel.

	B & B PER PERSON PER NIGHT		DINNER B & B PER PERSON PER WEEK		9
T	MIN £	MAX £	MIN £	MAX £	OPEN
C	12	13	114	132	1—12

Plas Owen Hotel

Glyn Ceiriog, Llangollen
Clwyd LL20 7DA
Tel: (0691) 707

CATEGORIES

| 5 | 4 | 5 |

Newly built, in 3 acres and under personal management of the owners. Beautiful views of the Ceiriog Valley. Olde worlde atmosphere. 13 bedrooms, all en-suite with tea/coffee facilities. Central heating. Traditional and à la carte menus, in the Tudor Restaurant. Residents' lounge. Ideal trekking, walking and touring. Brochure on request, Dept. WTS. Ample parking.

	B & B PER PERSON PER NIGHT		DINNER B & B PER PERSON PER WEEK		13
T	MIN £	MAX £	MIN £	MAX £	OPEN
C	14	16	130	140	1—12

This symbol means you can book through your local travel agent.

Glyn Neath
SOUTH WALES

Hotel

Dinas Hotel

Pont-Nedd Fechan, near Glyn Neath
West Glamorgan, SA11 5NH
Tel: (0639) 720378

CATEGORIES

| 3 | 3 | 4 |

Walks, Waterfalls, Fishing and Golf.

	B & B PER PERSON PER NIGHT		DINNER B & B PER PERSON PER WEEK		5
C	MIN £	MAX £	MIN £	MAX £	OPEN
	12.50				1—12

Farmhouse

Werfa Cottages

Rhigos Road, Rhigos, near Aberdare
Mid. Glamorgan
Tel: (0685) 811 633

CATEGORIES

| 1 | 3 | 2 |

A comfortable nicely situated farmhouse on the edge of the Brecon Beacons National Park. Midway between Swansea and Merthyr Tydfil. Cardiff only 23 miles away. Ideal for walking, fishing. Own gliding club, lessons available or bring your own glider. Full central heating. Home grown produce. For further details of accommodation or gliding please write to Jean Penney.

	B & B PER PERSON PER NIGHT		DINNER B & B PER PERSON PER WEEK		3
T	MIN £	MAX £	MIN £	MAX £	OPEN
C	6	7	65	75	1—12

Gwaun Valley
SOUTH WALES

Farmhouse

Tregynon Farmhouse*

Pontfaen, near Fishguard
Dyfed SA65 9TU
Tel: (0239) 820531
Enquiries: Mrs. S. D. Heard

CATEGORIES

| 1 | 2 | 2 |

Located in Pembrokeshire Coast National Park comfortable, beamed, 17th century family-run farmhouse in foothills of Preseli Mountains with magnificent views over Gwaun Valley. Stroll through our ancient oaken forest and study the abundance of wildlife or simply sunbathe on the nearby sweep of Newport sands. Pony trekking, fishing, sailing and golf available locally. Excellent cuisine—trout from our own ponds—vegetarian speciality, licensed. Babysitting services. Open all year. Centrally heated and glowing log fires in inglenook. AA listed.

	B & B PER PERSON PER NIGHT		DINNER B & B PER PERSON PER WEEK		4
C	MIN £	MAX £	MIN £	MAX £	OPEN
	6.90	6.90	78.20	78.20	1—12

Gwbert
MID WALES

Guest House

Brynteifi Guest House*

Gwbert-on-Sea
Cardigan
Tel: (0239) 612171

CATEGORIES

| 3 | 3 | 2 |

Brynteifi is set in its own grounds with lovely views of Cardigan Bay with its sunsets. There is an 18 and 9 hole golf course also squash courts within a few minutes walk. Also tennis, bowls, riding, swimming pool at nearby Cardigan (3 miles).

	B & B PER PERSON PER NIGHT		DINNER B & B PER PERSON PER WEEK		5
T	MIN £	MAX £	MIN £	MAX £	OPEN
C	5.50	6	63	66.50	4—11

Harlech
MID WALES

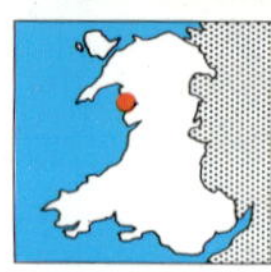

Map ref: Da2
Castle, immortalised in song 'March of the men of Harlech', built 1283.

Glorious views of mountains of Snowdonia from the town on its high hill position, overlooking miles of sand beach and Royal St. David's Golf Course. Heated swimming pool, miles of hill walking and good touring spot in Snowdonia National Park. Llanfair slate show caverns, 1 mile south.

Castle Cottage Hotel and Resturant*

Harlech, Gwynedd
LL46 2YL
Tel: (0766) 780 479

CATEGORIES

| 3 | 4 | 5 |

A small hotel and restaurant in one of the oldest houses in Harlech. Close to the castle with rooms comfortably furnished in the style of the house. The menu includes dishes from home and abroad and vegetarians are welcome. The wine list is unusually extensive and modestly priced.

C	B & B PER PERSON PER NIGHT		DINNER B & B PER PERSON PER WEEK		4
	MIN £	MAX £	MIN £	MAX £	OPEN
	8.75		87.50		1—12

Estuary Motel

Talsarnau, near Harlech
Gwynedd
Tel: (0766) 770639

CATEGORIES

| 4 | 3 | 2 |

Ten unit purpose-built motel within the National Park. Perfect base for visiting the many wonderful attractions, this part of Wales has to offer. Licensed restaurant serving breakfast and à la carte dinner. Colour TV in all units. Cars parked at the door.

C	B & B PER PERSON PER NIGHT		DINNER B & B PER PERSON PER WEEK		10
	MIN £	MAX £	MIN £	MAX £	OPEN
	11.50	13			1—12

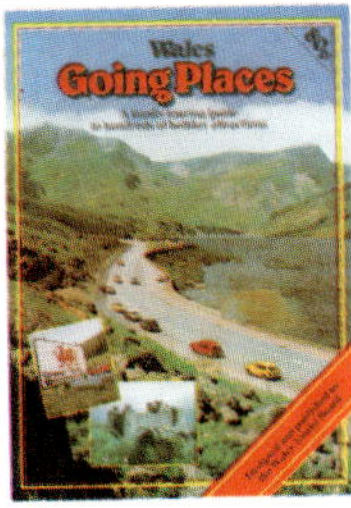

Going Places

Full of carefully-planned motor tours and information on places to visit. A must for family touring around Wales. Available from: Wales Tourist Board Department W.T.S. P.O. Box 1, CARDIFF CF1 2XN. Price: £1.05p including postage and packing.

Hotel Maes-y-Neuadd*

Talsarnau, near Harlech
Gwynedd LL47 6YA
Tel: (0766) 780200

CATEGORIES

| 4 | 4 | 5 |

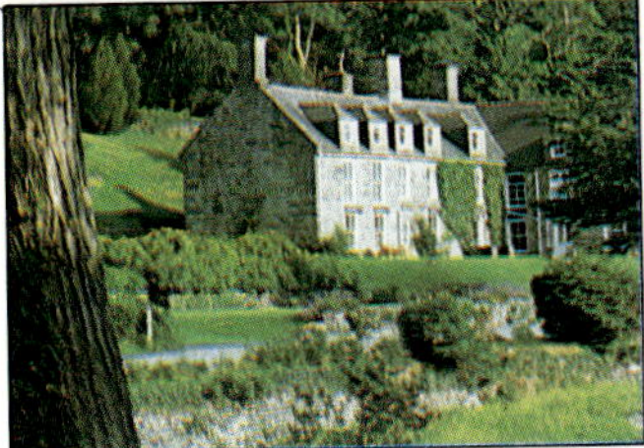

14th century manor house in beautiful secluded setting. Breathtaking view of Snowdonia. Elegant dining room, excellent food. Beamed bar with log fires. Personally run by resident owners. Comfortable bedrooms with private bathrooms, colour television and central heating. Golf (Royal St. David's). Walking, riding, beaches 'Great Little Trains'. 'Winter Breaks' and Christmas.

T	B & B PER PERSON PER NIGHT		DINNER B & B PER PERSON PER WEEK		14
	MIN £	MAX £	MIN £	MAX £	OPEN
	12.25	20	135	186	1—12

Noddfa Hotel*

Lower Road, Harlech
Gwynedd LL46 2UB
Tel: (0766) 780043

CATEGORIES

| 3 | 4 | 3 |

The hotel is situated in an elevated position opposite the Royal St. David's golf course and commands magnificent views of mountains and sea. Bedrooms have hot and cold water, central heating, some with bathroom or shower en-suite. Tea and coffee making facilities in rooms. Licensed bar lounge. TV lounge.

C	B & B PER PERSON PER NIGHT		DINNER B & B PER PERSON PER WEEK		7
	MIN £	MAX £	MIN £	MAX £	OPEN
	6.90	12.50	68.50	106	1—12

Pensarn Hall

Llanbedr, via Barmouth
Gwynedd LL45 2HS
Tel: (034 123) 236

CATEGORIES

| 4 | 4 | 2 |

We offer our guests dinner and Bed and Breakfast with excellent accommodation in this restored Victorian hall. High class cuisine. Interesting and inexpensive wine list. Own grounds. Games facilities. Two miles south of Harlech. Relaxed and happy atmosphere and the proprietors particular care and attention. Brochure on request.

C	B & B PER PERSON PER NIGHT		DINNER B & B PER PERSON PER WEEK		8
	MIN £	MAX £	MIN £	MAX £	OPEN
	11	12.50	110	120	1—12

Rum Hole Hotel

Harlech, Gwynedd
North Wales, LL46 2UB
Tel: (0766) 780477

CATEGORIES

| 3 | 2 | 4 |

Nestling under the castle walls, facing beach and golf club, only 200 yards from town centre, superbly furnished rooms with baby-listening service, huge discounts for children. All rooms heated. Local sailing, golf, riding, fishing, climbing. Breathtaking views. Family run, we assure your comfort and a good holiday.

T / C	B & B PER PERSON PER NIGHT		DINNER B & B PER PERSON PER WEEK		8
	MIN £	MAX £	MIN £	MAX £	OPEN
	7.50	9.50	80	96	1—12

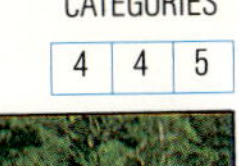

| C |

Children stay at reduced rates, wherever you see this symbol.

Guest Houses

"Aris"*

Pen-y-Bryn, Harlech
Gwynedd LL46 2SL
Tel: (0766) 780409

CATEGORIES: 1 3 3

Quiet situation, two minutes above Harlech village, overlooking golf course, beach, Snowdonia, sea. Ideal golfing, touring, walking, climbing or just resting. Safe, sandy beach ten minutes' walk. Parking, reduction children. Open Christmas. Central heating, log fire, electric blankets, tea-making facilities all rooms. Dinners, salads, toasted snacks any time.

C	B & B PER PERSON PER NIGHT		DINNER B & B PER PERSON PER WEEK		4
	MIN £	MAX £	MIN £	MAX £	OPEN
	7	8.50	70	80	1—12

Ty Mawr*

Llanfair, Harlech
Gwyneed LL46 2SA
Tel: (0766) 780 446

CATEGORIES: 1 3 1

A lovely old stone house with interesting history, standing in 1½ acres of garden, with views of sea and hills. Hot and cold water in all rooms, lounge with colour TV, log fire. Dining room with separate tables. Central heating. An ideal centre for sandy beaches, walking and touring Snowdonia.

C	B & B PER PERSON PER NIGHT		DINNER B & B PER PERSON PER WEEK		4
	MIN £	MAX £	MIN £	MAX £	OPEN
	6	7			1—12

Farmhouses

Mrs. G. Evans

Maesyraelfor, Harlech
Gwynedd
Tel: (0766) 780571

CATEGORIES: 1 2 2

Sheep and cattle farm situated approximately 1½ miles inland from Harlech. There are beautiful views of sea and mountains to be seen from the house. It is situated in the Snowdonia National Park area. Two double bedrooms.

C	B & B PER PERSON PER NIGHT		DINNER B & B PER PERSON PER WEEK		3
	MIN £	MAX £	MIN £	MAX £	OPEN
	5		48		1—12

Tyddyn Gwynt*

Harlech, Gwynedd
LL46 2TH
Tel: (0766) 780 298

CATEGORIES: 2 2 2

Tyddyn-Gwynt is beautifully situated within the Snowdonia National Park. Visitors are warmly welcome all the year. Children and pets welcome. A car is essential to make the most of your holiday. Many tourist attractions within reach e.g. Harlech Castle, Caernarfon, Royal St. David's golf course, narrow gauge railways, show quarries, Portmeirion and many others, sandy beach at Harlech and Shell Island. Fire certificate held.

C	B & B PER PERSON PER NIGHT		DINNER B & B PER PERSON PER WEEK		4
	MIN £	MAX £	MIN £	MAX £	OPEN
	5.50		50		1—12

Map ref: Jc5
Population about 10,000, central to and centre for all Pembrokeshire Coast and ideal touring base for far west of Wales. Good shopping, castle—now museum—medieval churches and old narrow streets, heated swimming pool and indoor market with local produce. Graham Sutherland Gallery of paintings in Picton Castle, few miles east.

Hotels and Inns

County Hotel

Salutation Square, Haverfordwest
Pembrokeshire
Tel: (0437) 3542

CATEGORIES: 3 3 4

Well-established family hotel, centrally situated in the county town of Pembrokeshire. Ideally placed for touring the Pembrokeshire Coast National Park within easy reach of bus and rail stations. Free house, serving various types of real ale, Good Beer Guide. Horse riding, fishing, gliding, golf, all within easy reach.

C	B & B PER PERSON PER NIGHT		DINNER B & B PER PERSON PER WEEK		19
	MIN £	MAX £	MIN £	MAX £	OPEN
	11	15	105	125	1—12

Denant Mill Hotel*

Dreenhill, Haverfordwest
Dyfed
Tel: (0437) 66569

CATEGORIES: 3 3 4

Small licensed country hotel set in 6 acres with trout stream, situated in secluded valley only 3 miles from coast. Internal mill wheel and workings have been carefully restored, presenting an interesting feature. Pony trekking, hunting and shooting available locally. Also river, reservoir, sea and game fishing.

T	B & B PER PERSON PER NIGHT		DINNER B & B PER PERSON PER WEEK		8
C	MIN £	MAX £	MIN £	MAX £	OPEN
	7	10.50	83	105	1—12

Elliotts Hill Hotel

Crow Hill, Haverfordwest
Dyfed SA62 6HT
Tel: (0437) 2383

CATEGORIES: 3 4 4

Under new ownership and partly refurnished, standing in 3 acres one mile from town. Open Christmas. Hot and cold water and shaver points in all bedrooms, single, double and family rooms with special rates for children. Full central heating. Fire certificate. Ideally situated for golf, fishing, horse riding, walking beaches and touring Dyfed. Private parking. Pets by arrangement. Lovely gardens.

C	B & B PER PERSON PER NIGHT		DINNER B & B PER PERSON PER WEEK		20
	MIN £	MAX £	MIN £	MAX £	OPEN
	10.35	12	65	75	1—12

Mariners Inn*

Nolton Haven, Haverfordwest
Dyfed SA62 3NH
Tel: (043 784) 469

CATEGORIES: 3 3 5

Licensed residential coastal inn. Open all year. Beachside setting, 10 modern bedrooms in new extension, many with showers. Hot and cold water. Situated in beautiful Pembrokeshire Coast National Park. Good food, 2 feature bars with panoramic views. Local activities include pony trekking, fishing, boating, walking the Coastal Path, diving and golfing. Real ale house, enjoy a sing-song with our organist at weekends! Warm welcome assured. Ring Margaret and Peter Skudder now on (043 784) 469. Brochure with pleasure.

T	B & B PER PERSON PER NIGHT		DINNER B & B PER PERSON PER WEEK		12
C	MIN £	MAX £	MIN £	MAX £	OPEN
	8	10.10	80.10	100.10	1—12

Hotel Mariners*

Mariners Square, Haverfordwest
Dyfed SA61 2DU
Tel: (0437) 3353

CATEGORIES: 4 5 5

Comfortable market town hotel RAC** AA** rating. Ideal centre for touring beautiful coastline and countryside. Easy access to shops, golf, sailing, surfing etc. All rooms have colour TV, radio, telephone, tea/coffee facilities. Popular bars and restaurant. Fire Certificate. Special weekend tariff.

T	B & B PER PERSON PER NIGHT		DINNER B & B PER PERSON PER WEEK		29
C	MIN £	MAX £	MIN £	MAX £	OPEN
	17.50	24.50	119	129.50	1—12

Masons Arms*

Cartlett, Haverfordwest
Dyfed
Tel: (0437) 66190

CATEGORIES: 1 1 3

Free house situated on outskirts of Haverfordwest on A40 and Cartlett Brook. Attractive bar, lounge and restaurant. Live entertainment 4 nights per week. Railway station adjacent, bus station and shops close by. Single, double and family rooms all with hot and cold, TV, and tea-making facilities. Ample parking space.

C	B & B PER PERSON PER NIGHT		DINNER B & B PER PERSON PER WEEK		9
	MIN £	MAX £	MIN £	MAX £	OPEN
	7.50	8.50	66.50	73.50	1—12

New House Hotel

Hill Street, Haverfordwest
Dyfed
Tel: (0437) 2721/3281

CATEGORIES: 3 3 5

Comfortable rooms with bath and toilet en-suite ('max price' price) or without ('min' price). Popular Tudor Cellar Restaurant with fresh food traditionally cooked in front of you. Full à la carte menu, wine list and chefs specials. Lounge bar, sauna and solarium. Friendly atmosphere with efficient service.

	B & B PER PERSON PER NIGHT		DINNER B & B PER PERSON PER WEEK		25
	MIN £	MAX £	MIN £	MAX £	OPEN
	8.75	11.50	85	108	1—12

Portfield Hotel & Restaurant*

Hawthorn Rise, Haverfordwest
Pembrokeshire, Dyfed SA61 2BA
Tel: (0437) 3257

CATEGORIES: 2 3 3

Central for touring the county, near many seaside villages namely Broad Haven, Newgale, Nolton and Little Haven. We offer a warm welcome and a clean and spacious licensed establishment with beautiful scenery. Parking available and Fire Certificate granted. A fully descriptive colour brochure on request to Mrs. Gwenda Griffiths, telephone Haverfordwest 3257.

C	B & B PER PERSON PER NIGHT		DINNER B & B PER PERSON PER WEEK		15
	MIN £	MAX £	MIN £	MAX £	OPEN
	6.50	6.50	63	63	1—12

Rosehill Country Hotel

Portfield Gate, Nr Broad Haven
Haverfordwest, Pembrokeshire
SA62 3LX
Tel: (043 783) 304

CATEGORIES: 3 3 3

Standing in secluded position. Rosehill offers restful and relaxing holidays. Under personal supervision of the Proprietors. A varied selection of food and wine are offered. Residents lounge with colour TV, lounge bar, pool room and evening dancing, provide comfort and entertainment. Weekends and short breaks out of season.

C	B & B PER PERSON PER NIGHT		DINNER B & B PER PERSON PER WEEK		10
	MIN £	MAX £	MIN £	MAX £	OPEN
	9.20	11.50	80.50	97.75	1—12

Guest Houses

Barch Farm*

Roch, Haverfordwest
Pembrokeshire SA62 6HE
Tel: (043 784) 515

CATEGORIES: 3 3 2

A newly converted stone barn set in 12 acres in a peaceful country position with sea views over St. Bride's Bay. Tastefully furnished rooms. Beamed dining and sitting-room. Colour television. Single, double and family bedrooms with hot and cold water and heating. Ideal touring centre for Pembrokeshire. Children welcome.

C	B & B PER PERSON PER NIGHT		DINNER B & B PER PERSON PER WEEK		4
	MIN £	MAX £	MIN £	MAX £	OPEN
	7	8	82	88	1—12

College Guest House*

St Thomas Green,
Haverfordwest, Pembs
Tel: (0437) 3710

CATEGORIES: 3 2 1

Pat and Mike Gerson, College Guest House, St Thomas' Green, Haverfordwest. Georgian, family run guest house, 3 mins town. TV Lounge. Snacks available, licensed. Large car park opposite. Ideally situated for touring national parks coastal paths, sailing, riding, fishing, golf etc. Tel: (0437) 3710 (Closed Christmas).

C	B & B PER PERSON PER NIGHT		DINNER B & B PER PERSON PER WEEK		8
	MIN £	MAX £	MIN £	MAX £	OPEN
	6.50	7	70		1—12

Cornerways

Simpson Cross, Haverfordwest
Pembrokeshire, Dyfed SA62 6EP
Tel: (043784) 465

CATEGORIES: 1 3 2

Small homely modernised farmhouse in heart of National Park area. 4 miles from a selection of beautiful safe beaches and coves. Enjoy breathtaking coast, path walks, horse-riding and sailing. Separate dining room. Lounge with TV. Private car park. Evening meal entirely optional, but homemade cream teas available every afternoon.

C	B & B PER PERSON PER NIGHT		DINNER B & B PER PERSON PER WEEK		4
	MIN £	MAX £	MIN £	MAX £	OPEN
	5.50	6.50	56	63	1—12

Greenacre Guest House*

Spittal, Haverfordwest
Pembrokeshire, Dyfed SA62 5RE
Tel: (043782) 201

CATEGORIES: 3 3 3

Quiet country guest house, ideally situated for all beaches. Fishing and riding nearby. Children's pony on premises available at no extra charge. Baby-sitting. Ample lawns and grounds for children to play safely. Suitable disabled. Car essential. Warm welcome. Pets allowed. Open all year.

C	B & B PER PERSON PER NIGHT		DINNER B & B PER PERSON PER WEEK		3
	MIN £	MAX £	MIN £	MAX £	OPEN
	5	8	50	60	1—12

Haroldston House*

Clay Lanes, Haverfordwest
Pembrokeshire, Dyfed SA61 1UH
Tel: (0437) 2611

CATEGORIES: 1 3 1

Lovely old house beside river, fishing and boating. Comfortable, centrally heated accommodation. Good home cooking. Lounge with colour television. Centrally Placed for beaches and mountains. Nearby facilities for riding, golf, swimming, walking, sailing. Weekend courses for painting—qualified instruction and studio. Children welcome. Pets by arrangement—stable available.

C	B & B PER PERSON PER NIGHT		DINNER B & B PER PERSON PER WEEK		3
	MIN £	MAX £	MIN £	MAX £	OPEN
	6.50	7.50	65	80	1—12

Normandie House Hotel

1 Merlins Hill, Haverfordwest
Dyfed, South Wales
Tel: (0437) 2337

CATEGORIES

3	3	3

Family-run licensed hotel close to town centre with full central heating and fire certificate. Comfortable residents lounge with colour television. Pool room and private bar. Baby sitter available on request. Children welcome. Pets by arrangement only.

	B & B PER PERSON PER NIGHT		DINNER B & B PER PERSON PER WEEK		4
C	MIN £	MAX £	MIN £	MAX £	OPEN
	7	7.50	75	80	1—12

"Stainton"*

200 Haven Road, Haverfordwest
SA61 1DG
Tel: (0437) 3702

CATEGORIES

1	2	1

Modern house with ideal spot touring and beaches, indoor swimming pool, pony trekking, fishing near by, one double two family rooms with wash basins, separate tables, free car park, lounge with TV reductions for children evening meal. Optional with the finest country view.

	B & B PER PERSON PER NIGHT		DINNER B & B PER PERSON PER WEEK		3
C	MIN £	MAX £	MIN £	MAX £	OPEN
	5	6.50	35	45.50	1—12

Farmhouses

Cuckoo Grove Farm*

Broad Haven Road, Haverfordwest
Dyfed SA61 2UY
Tel: (0437) 2429

CATEGORIES

3	3	2

Comfortable accommodation, for non-smokers only. Recently refurbished farmhouse close to Haverfordwest. Swimming pool in grounds. Wash basins, shaver points in all bedrooms. Oak beamed dining room. Cosy lounge with colour TV. Full central heating. Log fires in winter. Sorry no pets. AA RAC listed.

	B & B PER PERSON PER NIGHT		DINNER B & B PER PERSON PER WEEK		5
C	MIN £	MAX £	MIN £	MAX £	OPEN
		6.50	73	80	1—12

Cestyll '83 – 1983 is the year of the castles.

Spittal Cross Farm*

Haverfordwest
Dyfed SA62 5DB
Tel: (0437 87) 253

CATEGORIES

3	2	2

Modern farmhouse situated in the centre of Pembrokeshire offering comfortable accommodation in double, twin or family bedrooms. All with hot and cold water. Ideal for family holidays at school holiday time and peaceful relaxing holidays during May, June and September. Reputation for good food. Farmhouse on road side.

	B & B PER PERSON PER NIGHT		DINNER B & B PER PERSON PER WEEK		3
T					
C	MIN £	MAX £	MIN £	MAX £	OPEN
	6	7	65	70	5—10

Hay on Wye
SOUTH WALES

Hotels

Baskerville Arms Hotel

Clyro, Powys
(via Hereford)
Tel: (0497) 820670

CATEGORIES

3	4	5

Early Georgian, open Christmas. Dancing Friday, Saturday. Hot and cold water and shaver points in all bedrooms, single and double and family rooms, many with bathrooms. Special rates for children. Lounge with colour television. Pony trekking, caving, canoeing, climbing, fishing can be arranged by hotel. Fire certificate granted.

	B & B PER PERSON PER NIGHT		DINNER B & B PER PERSON PER WEEK		16
C	MIN £	MAX £	MIN £	MAX £	OPEN
	7.50	10	85	95	1—12

Crown Hotel*

Broad Street, Hay-on-Wye
via Hereford (Postal) HR3 5DB
Tel: (0497) 820435

CATEGORIES

3	3	4

Border town housing the world's largest second-hand bookshop. Noted for good food and comfortable accommodation at reasonable prices. Centrally situated. Touring centre for Brecon Beacons and Black Mountains areas. Fishing, shooting, pony trekking by arrangement. Close to Offa's Dyke and Golden Valley. Personal attention by resident owners.

	B & B PER PERSON PER NIGHT		DINNER B & B PER PERSON PER WEEK		14
T					
C	MIN £	MAX £	MIN £	MAX £	OPEN
	11	11.50	105	110	1—12

The Old Black Lion Hotel

Hay-on-Wye
Hereford HR3 5AD
Tel: (0497) 820841

CATEGORIES

4	3	4

Enjoy a well deserved break at this charming old Welsh coaching inn offering really comfortable accommodation. 8 rooms, 6 with private shower and toilet. Hay is the second-hand bookshop centre of Great Britain and is set in picturesque countryside, Wye Valley, Black Mountains and Brecon Beacons. Dine on the best of mid-European and Welsh food in our oak-beamed dining room or treat yourself to snacks with a difference in our friendly bar.

	B & B PER PERSON PER NIGHT		DINNER B & B PER PERSON PER WEEK		8
	MIN £	MAX £	MIN £	MAX £	OPEN
	10.60	15.80			1—12

Guest House

Clifton House

1 Belmont Road, Hay-on-Wye
Hereford HR3 5DA
Tel: (0497) 820659

CATEGORIES

1	1	2

On Offa's Dyke footpath, near centre of Hay-on-Wye. Home of world's largest second-hand bookshop. Ideal centre for walking, canoeing, fishing and touring Welsh border country. Pony trekking arranged. Packed lunches, hot drinks. Full central heating, colour television in guests lounge-dining room. Private car park.

	B & B PER PERSON PER NIGHT		DINNER B & B PER PERSON PER WEEK		2
C	MIN £	MAX £	MIN £	MAX £	OPEN
	6	7	70	77	3—10

Holyhead
NORTH WALES

Hotel

Scimitar Hotel & Water Sports Centre*

Porth-y-Felin
Holyhead LL65 1YF
Tel: (0407) 3178 or 2094

CATEGORIES

1	2	6

The hotel which is situated on the seafront has all central heating. Private bathrooms, bar snacks, steak bar, spacious restaurant, games and pool room. Fully licensed. Large car park. Private beach with slipway and full facilities for diving, sailing and angling. Local pony trekking and mountain climbing.

	B & B PER PERSON PER NIGHT		DINNER B & B PER PERSON PER WEEK		10
T					
C	MIN £	MAX £	MIN £	MAX £	OPEN
	6.90	11	72.80	101.78	1—12

Guest House

Garreg Wen*

Mrs. M. Humphrey
17 Seabourne Road, Holyhead
Gwynedd LL64 1AL
Tel: (0407) 4687

CATEGORIES

3	3	2

Near beach and car ferry terminal, station, recreation park. 5 minutes from town. Parking in drive. Climbing and fishing locally. Cot facilities.

C	B & B PER PERSON PER NIGHT		DINNER B & B PER PERSON PER WEEK		🛏 3
	MIN £	MAX £	MIN £	MAX £	OPEN
	5	5.25	60	66	1—12

Farmhouse

Ty-Mawr Farm

Llanrhyddlad
Holyhead, Anglesey
Tel: (040 788) 408

CATEGORIES

3	3	1

The farm house is a modern semi-bungalow situated on the main coastal road (A5025) approximately 10 miles from Holyhead, making easy access to the Irish Ferry and within close proximity to the beautiful coastline and sandy beaches. The farm is mixed having dairy beef and sheep.

C	B & B PER PERSON PER NIGHT		DINNER B & B PER PERSON PER WEEK		🛏 3
	MIN £	MAX £	MIN £	MAX £	OPEN
	6	7			3—12

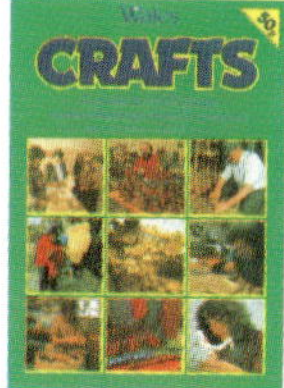

Crafts

Attractive, completely revised guide to craft workshops in Wales – including woollen mills, potteries, slate, stone and woodcarvers, jewellery, metal and leatherworkers. Available from: Wales Tourist Board Department W.T.S. P.O. Box 1, CARDIFF CF1 2XN. Price: 65p including postage and packing.

Farmhouses

Bryn Glas*

Babell, nr. Holywell
Clwyd, North Wales
Tel: (035 282) 493

CATEGORIES

1	3	2

A comfortable modern farmhouse situated in a rural area. Near to Mold with Theatr Clwyd, Chester Great Tourist Centre. Twenty minutes ride from Rhyl. Forty acre farm rearing sheep, cattle and breeding riding ponies. Fresh farm-produce used in cooking. Small pony kept for children's use.

T C	B & B PER PERSON PER N'GHT		DINNER B & B PER PERSON PER WEEK		🛏 2
	MIN £	MAX £	MIN £	MAX £	OPEN
	5.50		9.50		2—11

Greenhill Farm*

Bryn Celyn, Holywell
Clwyd CH8 7QF
Tel: (0352) 713270

CATEGORIES

3	2	2

A 16th century working farm overlooking the Dee Estuary. With an oak panelled dining room and coal fire in the lounge. Bedrooms are modernised with fitted carpets, washbasins, shaver points and one bedroom with shower. We serve typical farmhouse food, using local produce and we especially welcome children.

T C	B & B PER PERSON PER NIGHT		DINNER B & B PER PERSON PER WEEK		🛏 4
	MIN £	MAX £	MIN £	MAX £	OPEN
	6	7	66	77	2—11

For autumn to spring breaks send for our free Great Little Breaks booklet.

Guest House

The Hollies*

Horton, Gower
Swansea
Tel: (044 120) 423

CATEGORIES

1	3	3

Family-run licensed guest house, and restaurant. Home cooking and personal service. Vegetables from large garden with lawn tennis court adjacent to beach. Packed or bar lunches, children's supper available. Lounge with colour television. Ideal for boat owners. Children's play area. Reasonable terms.

C	B & B PER PERSON PER NIGHT		DINNER B & B PER PERSON PER WEEK		🛏 8
	MIN £	MAX £	MIN £	MAX £	OPEN
	7.50	8.50	10.50	12.50	4—10

Motel

Silverdale Motel*

Johnston near Haverfordwest
Dyfed West Wales
Tel: (0437) 0890407 or 890624

CATEGORIES

3	2	4

Single, double family rooms, intercom radio, tele, private bathroom, tea/coffee facilities, swimming pool, bar, restaurant. Fire certificated. Ideal situation for exploring National Park area, places of interest, beaches, boating, riding, fishing, walking, gliding.

C	B & B PER PERSON PER NIGHT		DINNER B & B PER PERSON PER WEEK		🛏 24
	MIN £	MAX £	MIN £	MAX £	OPEN
	10.93	14.48	108	109	1—12

Motel

Crossroads Motel and Steakhouse*

Begelly, Kilgetty
South Pembrokeshire
Dyfed SA68 0YF
Tel: (0834) 813285

CATEGORIES

| 3 | 3 | 4 |

Modern motel chalets with private bathrooms, colour TV, radio, baby-listening service etc. The motel is ideally situated for direct access to the Pembrokeshire Coast National Park and the coastal resorts of Tenby and Saundersfoot are close at hand. Value for money accommodation and dining in our Steakhouse restaurant.

	B & B PER PERSON PER NIGHT		DINNER B & B PER PERSON PER WEEK		🛏 16
T C	MIN £	MAX £	MIN £	MAX £	OPEN
	15	17	110	130	1—12

Guest House

Pleasant View Guest House*

25 Ryelands Road, Kilgetty
Dyfed SA68 0UY
Tel: (0834) 812759

CATEGORIES

| 3 | 3 | 3 |

Award-winning family-run guest house. Beautifully situated near Tenby and Saundersfoot. Good food, every comfort, pleasant bedrooms with hot and cold water, shaver points. Large dining room, separate tables. Colour TV, lounge, games room, residential licence, full central heating. Ample parking in grounds. Fire certificate granted. Reductions for pensioners.

	B & B PER PERSON PER NIGHT		DINNER B & B PER PERSON PER WEEK		🛏 8
C	MIN £	MAX £	MIN £	MAX £	OPEN
	6	6.50	56	70	5—9

Farmhouse

Heartsease*

Knighton
Powys, Wales
Tel: (05474) 220

CATEGORIES

| 1 | 3 | 2 |

Georgian farmhouse overlooking beautiful hills and valleys. Home produced meats good cooking, colour TV. Single, double, family rooms.

	B & B PER PERSON PER NIGHT		DINNER B & B PER PERSON PER WEEK		🛏 3
C	MIN £	MAX £	MIN £	MAX £	OPEN
	8	10	84		4—10

Hotels

Falcondale Hotel*

Lampeter, Dyfed
SA48 7RX
Tel: (0570) 422910

CATEGORIES

| 4 | 4 | 5 |

At the head of forested valley 1 mile from Lampeter, in 12 acres parkland. 17 bedrooms—double and family with private bath/shower rooms. Colour TV, radio, tea/coffee-makers. Central and independent heating. 10 acre lake, coarse fishing, tennis court, clay pigeon range, 2 bars, lift, log fires. 2 conference rooms.

	B & B PER PERSON PER NIGHT		DINNER B & B PER PERSON PER WEEK		🛏 17
T C	MIN £	MAX £	MIN £	MAX £	OPEN
	14.95	14.95	120	120	1—12

Tourist Information Centres are listed at back of book.

The Red Lion Inn

Pencarreg, near Llanybyther
Dyfed SA40 9XP
Tel: (0570) 480018

CATEGORIES

| 1 | 3 | 4 |

Lampeter 3 miles, coast 15 miles. Ideally placed for touring, in fact a very pleasant part of Wales. Open all year. A warm friendly welcome. Good food—set evening meals or à la carte menu. Children very welcome. Single, double and family rooms. Tea and coffee facilities. Pleasant garden. Ample car space.

	B & B PER PERSON PER NIGHT		DINNER B & B PER PERSON PER WEEK		🛏 4
T C	MIN £	MAX £	MIN £	MAX £	OPEN
	6	8	70	84	1—12

Farmhouse

Pentre Farm*

Llanfair, Lampeter
Dyfed SA48 8LE
Tel: (057045) 313

CATEGORIES

| 3 | 3 | 2 |

Pentre is a dairy and live stock farm of 300 acres overlooking Teifi Valley. The 19th century stone-built farmhouse has large, comfortable bedrooms and spacious lounge with inglenook fireplace and oak beams. Meals are home-cooked using fresh farm produce. We welcome children and offer fishing and shooting to guests.

	B & B PER PERSON PER NIGHT		DINNER B & B PER PERSON PER WEEK		🛏 3
T C	MIN £	MAX £	MIN £	MAX £	OPEN
	7	7.50	75	82	4—9

Hotels

Brynfield Hotel

Brynfield Road, Langland Bay,
Swansea, West Glamorgan
Tel: (0792) 66208

CATEGORIES: 3 3 5

Country house hotel. 2 acres secluded grounds. Car park. Uninterrupted view of headland and sea. Most bedrooms have sea views and private bathrooms. Residential and restuarant licence. Cocktail bar. Short walk to beach, golf course, tennis. Mini Break Weekends early/late season. No pets.

[C]	B & B PER PERSON PER NIGHT		DINNER B & B PER PERSON PER WEEK		🛏 11
	MIN £	MAX £	MIN £	MAX £	OPEN
	18	19.40	88	108.60	1—12

Osborne Hotel

Rotherslade Road, Langland Bay
Gower, Swansea, SA3 4QL
Tel: (0792) 66274

CATEGORIES: 4 5 4

Cliff top situation overlooking peaceful Langland Bay with dramatic views across the Bristol Channel. Ideally located for touring Gower Peninsula, yet close to Swansea. Good restaurant and choice of bars. Colour TV, in all rooms. Full central heating. An Embassy hotel offering Hushaway Breaks, holidays throughout the year.

[T] [C]	B & B PER PERSON PER NIGHT		DINNER B & B PER PERSON PER WEEK		🛏 43
	MIN £	MAX £	MIN £	MAX £	OPEN
	16	19			1—12

Children stay at reduced rates, wherever you see this symbol.

[C]

Guest House

Henfaes Guest House*

4 Rotherslade Road, Langland
Mumbles, Swansea, West Glamorgan
SA3 4QN
Tel: (0792) 66003

CATEGORIES: 3 3 2

Judith and Brian Kingdom welcome you to their friendly and comfortable guest house, with Langland Bay only a short distance. Beautiful bedrooms, all with tea-making facilities. Children sharing family rooms—free accommodation. Convenient for golf, tennis, surfing, fishing etc. Autumn and Spring Breaks a speciality.

[T] [C]	B & B PER PERSON PER NIGHT		DINNER B & B PER PERSON PER WEEK		🛏 8
	MIN £	MAX £	MIN £	MAX £	OPEN
	6	8	58	78	1—12

Hotel

Laugharne Holiday Park*

Laugharne
Dyfed
Tel: (099421) 275

CATEGORIES: 3 3 5

Under new ownership and completely renovated. 16 bedrooms situated in bungalows all with private showers and colour television. Dylan Thomas Bar. Restaurant with fine views, serving table d'hote and à la carte meals. Lounge with colour television. Indoor heated pool. Entertainment in summer. Dogs welcome. Breaks available at attractive rates.

[T] [C]	B & B PER PERSON PER NIGHT		DINNER B & B PER PERSON PER WEEK		🛏 16
	MIN £	MAX £	MIN £	MAX £	OPEN
	12.65	17.25	72	110	4—12

Hotel

The Hand Hotel

Llanarmon Dyffryn Ceiriog
near Llangollen, Clwyd, LL20 7LD
Tel: (069 176) 666

CATEGORIES: 4 4 4

Situated in the beautiful Ceiriog Valley, the Hand, originally a 16th century farmhouse, is now a comfortably furnished, fully licensed, 3 star hotel with an à la carte restaurant. Enjoy walking, pony trekking, fishing, tennis, golf or tour North and Mid Wales and stay in the comfort of the Hand.

[T] [C]	B & B PER PERSON PER NIGHT		DINNER B & B PER PERSON PER WEEK		🛏 14
	MIN £	MAX £	MIN £	MAX £	OPEN
	18	25	150	165	1—12

Hotel

Llanina Arms Hotel

Llanarth, New Quay
Dyfed
Tel: (0545) 580220

CATEGORIES: 3 2 5

The hotel lies on the main A487 Aberystwyth to Cardigan road, 1½ miles from New Quay. There are 15 bedrooms all with radio and baby alarms. There is a large function hall with entertainment most nights. The restaurant offers a comprehensive menu for young and old alike.

[C]	B & B PER PERSON PER NIGHT		DINNER B & B PER PERSON PER WEEK		🛏 15
	MIN £	MAX £	MIN £	MAX £	OPEN
	7	10.50	77	102	1—12

Llanarthney
SOUTH WALES

Farmhouse

Glantowy Farm*

Llanarthney, Carmarthen
Dyfed SA32 8JU
Tel: (05584) 275

CATEGORIES

1	3	1

This 140 acre dairy farm, near the market town of Llandeilo and Carmarthen is easily accessible to the coast and countryside, e.g., Gower coast, Pembrokeshire National Park, Brecon Beacons National Park. Many castles, walks in vicinity and salmon and trout fishing on Towy river. Evening meals available in village.

C	B & B PER PERSON PER NIGHT		DINNER B & B PER PERSON PER WEEK		2
	MIN £	MAX £	MIN £	MAX £	OPEN
	6	6.50			1—12

Llanbedr
MID WALES

Hotels

Ty Mawr Hotel*

Llanbedr
Gwynedd
Tel: (034 123) 440

CATEGORIES

4	4	4

Fully licensed country house situated in Snowdonia National Park near the sea and mountain. 10 bedrooms with bath·en-suite and colour TV. Tastefully furnished and set in a lovely garden. Real ale and excellent food served. With open fires and central heating to ensure a warm and friendly stay.

C	B & B PER PERSON PER NIGHT		DINNER B & B PER PERSON PER WEEK		10
	MIN £	MAX £	MIN £	MAX £	OPEN
	10	11.50	105	115.50	1—12

This symbol means you can book through your local travel agent.

Victoria Hotel

Llanbedr, Gwynedd
LL45 2LD
Tel: (034123) 213

CATEGORIES

2	3	1

The hotel stands on the banks of the River Artro and is ideally situated enabling visitors to enjoy some of the most beautiful countryside in Wales. Golf, river and lake fishing, pony trekking all within easy reach. You may even wish to relax in the delightful garden.

C	B & B PER PERSON PER NIGHT		DINNER B & B PER PERSON PER WEEK		5
	MIN £	MAX £	MIN £	MAX £	OPEN
	11	12.50	102	112	1—12

Farmhouses

Alltgoch

Llanbedr, Gwynedd
LL45 2NA
Tel: (034 123) 229

CATEGORIES

3	2	2

Working farm in quiet setting, 2 miles from Llanbedr village, 3 miles from the sea. Wash basins in bedrooms, central heating, TV in sitting room. Children under 11 years at reduced rates. Food mostly home produced. Car recommended. Plenty of parking space.

C	B & B PER PERSON PER NIGHT		DINNER B & B PER PERSON PER WEEK		3
	MIN £	MAX £	MIN £	MAX £	OPEN
	4.75	5	52.50	56	5—9

Gwyn Fryn Farm*

Llanbedr
Gwynedd
Tel: (034123) 381

CATEGORIES

3	2	2

Two hundred year old farmhouse set in picturesque surroundings. Ideally placed for touring Snowdonia. 8 miles Barmouth, 2 miles Harlech. Half mile from the beach. Fishing, golf, craft village and slate caverns all within easy reach.

C	B & B PER PERSON PER NIGHT		DINNER B & B PER PERSON PER WEEK		3
	MIN £	MAX £	MIN £	MAX £	OPEN
	6.50		70		5—9

Llanbedrog
NORTH WALES

Hotel

Glyn Garth Hotel

Llanbedrog, near Abersoch
Gwynedd LL53 7UB
Tel: (075 884) 268

CATEGORIES

3	3	5

On Abersoch road A499 with Llanbedrog beach only a few minutes' walk away. Well situated for touring the peninsula by car or on foot. A warm welcome and comfortable surroundings assured. Catering of outstanding quality and value. Table d'hote or à la carte menus.

C	B & B PER PERSON PER NIGHT		DINNER B & B PER PERSON PER WEEK		11
	MIN £	MAX £	MIN £	MAX £	OPEN
	8.50	11	98	110	3—10

Llanberis
NORTH WALES

Map ref: Ae4
Starting point for Snowdon by Mountain Railway. Sits in pass of Llanberis between lakes Padarn and Peris. Llanberis Lake Railway, Museum of the Slate Industry,

Padarn Country Park and C.E.G.B. interpretive centre for giant underground power station, distract you from views unequalled in Britain.

Hotels

Erw Fair Hotel*

High Street
Llanberis, Gwynedd 4HA L55
Tel: (0286) 870238

CATEGORIES		
3	3	4

Centrally situated in Llanberis. Perfect for Snowdonia and North Wales. Single, double and family rooms; special rates for children and parties. Hot and cold water and shaver points in all bedrooms, some with private shower. Tea and coffee-making facilities. Television lounge. Licensed restaurant à la carte menu. Central heating. Parking on forecourt.

C	B & B PER PERSON PER NIGHT		DINNER B & B PER PERSON PER WEEK		🛏 9
	MIN £	MAX £	MIN £	MAX £	OPEN
	6	8	55	75	1—12

Gallt y Glyn Hotel*

Llanberis
Gwynedd LL55 4EL
Tel: (0286) 870370

CATEGORIES		
3	4	4

A charming old house in own grounds outside village. Superb mountain views. Perfect centre for walking, climbing, golf, fishing, sandy beach etc. Accommodation: from rooms with showers, family rooms, to "Alpine dormitories" each sleeping 6 bunks with own shower, hot and cold water and toilet. Excellent food, warmth and hospitality. Recommended Good Hotel Guide. Car park. no pets.

T	B & B PER PERSON PER NIGHT		DINNER B & B PER PERSON PER WEEK		🛏 10
C	MIN £	MAX £	MIN £	MAX £	OPEN
	12.25	13.05	108	114	1—12

Grosvenor Hotel*

High Street, Llanberis
Gwynedd LL55 4HB
Tel: (0286) 871491

CATEGORIES		
3	3	5

Licensed hotel and restaurant at foot of Snowdon. Ideal for mountains and coast. Traditional home-cooking, speciality Welsh dishes, relaxed atmosphere; children welcome. Private showers, tea-making facilities, ample parking. Instruction available for rock-climbing, mountain walking, canoeing, board-sailing, etc. Weekly or daily basis. Qualified staff. Specialist equipment provided.

T	B & B PER PERSON PER NIGHT		DINNER B & B PER PERSON PER WEEK		🛏 4
C	MIN £	MAX £	MIN £	MAX £	OPEN
	7.50	9.50	85	95	1—12

Mount Pleasant Hotel*

High Street, Llanberis
Gwynedd LL55 4HA
Tel: (0286) 870395

CATEGORIES		
3	3	5

At the foot of Snowdon. Llanberis is an ideal centre for walking, climbing and touring North Wales. The hotel has double, twin and family rooms with hot and cold water, and tea-making facilities; Some with showers. Separate dining room, TV lounge and bar. Open at Christmas.

C	B & B PER PERSON PER NIGHT		DINNER B & B PER PERSON PER WEEK		🛏 7
	MIN £	MAX £	MIN £	MAX £	OPEN
	7.50	9	73	84	1—12

Royal Victoria Hotel*

Llanberis
Gwynedd LL55 4TY
Tel: (0286) 870253

CATEGORIES		
4	4	4

The hotel is located in the heart of Snowdonia and is an ideal centre for touring North Wales. 118 rooms; 60 with private facilities. All bedrooms have tea and coffee-making facilities. Special Bargain Breaks available on request.

	B & B PER PERSON PER NIGHT		DINNER B & B PER PERSON PER WEEK		🛏 118
	MIN £	MAX £	MIN £	MAX £	OPEN
	12	14	127.40	141.40	1—12

Guest Houses

Beech Bank Guest House*

High Street, Llanberis
Gwynedd LL55 4EN
Tel: (0286) 870414

CATEGORIES		
3	1	1

Small, homely guest house, with friendly service, at quiet end of village overlooking Llyn Padarn and mountains. All bedrooms have hot and cold water, shaver points, fitted carpets and central heating. Large dining room with separate tables. Full Welsh breakfast. Private parking. Convenient for buses, shops and restaurants.

C	B & B PER PERSON PER NIGHT		DINNER B & B PER PERSON PER WEEK		🛏 3
	MIN £	MAX £	MIN £	MAX £	OPEN
	5.50	6.50			1—12

Farmhouses

Esgair Farm*

Esgair, Llanbrynmair
Powys SY19 7OU
Tel: (06503) 205

CATEGORIES		
1	3	2

Farm house and 188 acre working farm situated in picturesque countryside with beautiful views of valley and surrounding mountains. Car essential but great opportunity for walking. Half a mile off main coast road. Plain, home cooking in a happy home atmosphere. Children welcome. Ample car parking.

C	B & B PER PERSON PER NIGHT		DINNER B & B PER PERSON PER WEEK		🛏 3
	MIN £	MAX £	MIN £	MAX £	OPEN
	5.50	6.50	52.50	58	5—10

Guides to North, Mid and South Wales

What to see and do in Wales's three holiday regions. Each guide has A-Z gazetteers, maps, beach information, activities and attractions.
Available from: Wales Tourist Board Department W.T.S. P.O. Box 1, CARDIFF CF1 2XN. Price: £1.00 each region, including postage and packing.

Map ref: La1
Farming centre at an important crossing of the Towy River. Ideal spot to search out hidden places in the valleys around—such as Carreg Cennen Castle, Talley Abbey and traditional evening entertainment up the road at Llas Glansevin, Llangadog.

Hotels

The Cawdor Arms Hotel*

Llandeilo
Dyfed SA19 6EN
Tel: (0558) 823500

CATEGORIES

| 5 | 4 | 4 |

Wales's only hotel to gain the coveted Red Star Award. A beautifully arranged Georgian Coaching Inn offering the highest standards of hotel-keeping. All apartments with private facilities; international cuisine and personal service reminiscent of a by-gone era. Ideal for touring some of Britain's outstanding and historic countryside.

T C	B & B PER PERSON PER NIGHT		DINNER B & B PER PERSON PER WEEK		🛏 18
	MIN £	MAX £	MIN £	MAX £	OPEN
	26		210		1—12

The Kings Head Hotel

Bridge Street, Llandeilo
Dyfed SA19 6BN
Tel: (0558) 822388

CATEGORIES

| 5 | 4 | 5 |

The Kings Head is a 17th century hotel providing a very relaxing and comfortable atmosphere. The restaurant in a part of the building dating from the 13th century, cooks only the finest fresh food with home-made pies and patès. Fresh lobsters and fillet steaks stuffed with pearl onions and Stilton cheese. Children and pets are welcome.

C	B & B PER PERSON PER NIGHT		DINNER B & B PER PERSON PER WEEK		🛏 7
	MIN £	MAX £	MIN £	MAX £	OPEN
	9.75	14	99	150	1—12

Maesteilo Mansion Country House Hotel*

Capel Isaac
Llandeilo, Dyfed
Tel: (05584) 510

CATEGORIES

| 3 | 3 | 4 |

A family owned country house. Immense character, superbly situated in 16 acres; magnificent views across rural valley. Residential licence. Swimming pool, local fishing, riding etc. Honeymoons a speciality. Luxury, outstanding cuisine our hallmark. All rooms with bathrooms, Colour television, Tea and coffee facilities. Regret no children or pets. Bargain Breaks.

T	B & B PER PERSON PER NIGHT		DINNER B & B PER PERSON PER WEEK		🛏 8
	MIN £	MAX £	MIN £	MAX £	OPEN
	12.50	20	136	189	1—12

Guest Houses

Bryn-y-Wawr*

Pen-y-Banc, Llandeilo
Dyfed SA19 7SU
Tel: (0558) 822419

CATEGORIES

| 1 | 3 | 2 |

Small, family-run guest house, 1½ miles from Llandeilo —¾ mile off A40 road. Panoramic views, ample parking. Hot and cold water in bedrooms. Fire certificate. Lounge with colour TV. Full central heating. Ideal base for touring both coast and countryside. Open all the year.

C	B & B PER PERSON PER NIGHT		DINNER B & B PER PERSON PER WEEK		🛏 4
	MIN £	MAX £	MIN £	MAX £	OPEN
	5.50	6	63	70	1—12

Llwyndewi

Trapp near Llandeilo
Dyfed SA19 6TT
Tel: (0269) 850362

CATEGORIES

| 1 | 3 | 2 |

Situated in the peace and quiet of the Brecon Beacons National Park. The farmhouse is ideally situated for horse riding, pony trekking, fishing, golf and walking. Full central heating. Family, double and single rooms. Lounge with colour TV. Dining room. Open all the year.

T C	B & B PER PERSON PER NIGHT		DINNER B & B PER PERSON PER WEEK		🛏 4
	MIN £	MAX £	MIN £	MAX £	OPEN
	6.50	7.50	64.75	68.25	1—12

Farmhouse

Parc Mawr

Cwmdu, Llandeilo
Dyfed SA19 7NW
Tel: (0558) 492

CATEGORIES

| 1 | 2 | 2 |

Centrally heated farmhouse. Exposed beams and log fire. Carpeted throughout. In beautiful valley with panoramic views. 86 acre farm with woodland and small river. Play area for children; also poultry, rabbits, ducks to feed. Ideal centre for touring mountains and coasts. Many places of interest to visit.

C	B & B PER PERSON PER NIGHT		DINNER B & B PER PERSON PER WEEK		🛏 3
	MIN £	MAX £	MIN £	MAX £	OPEN
	5	6	49	54	4—10

Hotel

The Lion Hotel

Llandinam, Powys
SY17 5BY
Tel: (068684) 233

CATEGORIES

| 2 | 3 | 3 |

Small, family hotel; 5 bedrooms only. Home cooking. Situated on the banks of River Severn. With 4 miles fly fishing, ½ mile coarse fishing (day permits available). Private sauna. Stair lift. Full central heating. Situated in small village. Main road between Newtown and Llangurig A470. Ideal tourist centre.

C	B & B PER PERSON PER NIGHT		DINNER B & B PER PERSON PER WEEK		🛏 5
	MIN £	MAX £	MIN £	MAX £	OPEN
	7.75	7.75	87.50	94.50	1—12

For autumn to spring breaks send for our free Great Little Breaks booklet.

Map ref: Gb6
Market town where A40 road enters the Vale of Towy from the east. 8 miles away is scenic Llyn Brianne whose dam holds water to supply Swansea. Good touring centre for Brecon Beacons and Cambrian Mountains roads.

Hotel

Picton Court Hotel*

Llandovery
Dyfed SA20 0JT
Tel: (0550) 20320

CATEGORIES: 3 3 3

Informal, family-run, fully modernised and licensed country house hotel in 10 acres with own river. Offering good food and personal service. Completely rural, yet only ⅓rd mile from Llandovery's main street. Single, double and family rooms. Residents lounge, cosy bar and dining room with separate tables.

C	B & B PER PERSON PER NIGHT		DINNER B & B PER PERSON PER WEEK		10
	MIN £	MAX £	MIN £	MAX £	OPEN
	11	13			1—12

Guest Houses

Llwyncelyn Guest House*

Llandovery
Dyfed SA20 0EP
Tel: (0550) 20566

CATEGORIES: 3 3 2

Delightful riverside setting. Town centre 10 minutes' walk. Full central heating. Homely atmosphere; ample parking. No pets. Closed Christmas. Attractions include Brecon Beacons National Park, Llyn Brianne Reservoir, castles, forts, gold mines, fishing, pony trekking. The famous Red Kite and Twm Shon Cati's Cave.

C	B & B PER PERSON PER NIGHT		DINNER B & B PER PERSON PER WEEK		6
	MIN £	MAX £	MIN £	MAX £	OPEN
	8.70	10.40	96.60	106.95	1—12

Y Neuadd

Pentretygwyn, Llandovery
Dyfed
Tel: (0550) 20603

CATEGORIES: 3 3 2

Situated in the peaceful hamlet of Pentretygwyn, only 3 miles from Llandovery. The house, built in the eighteenth century as a manse, is uniquely sited in over an acre of garden bordered by two little brooks. Double bedrooms with private toilets, showers, radios, razor points. Superb touring centre.

T C	B & B PER PERSON PER NIGHT		DINNER B & B PER PERSON PER WEEK		5
	MIN £	MAX £	MIN £	MAX £	OPEN
	8	10	90	100	3—10

Farmhouses

Dan-y-Parc

Cynghordy, Llandovery
Dyfed SA20 0LD
Tel: (0550) 20401

CATEGORIES: 1 2 2

A comfortably furnished, centrally heated farmhouse with 14 acres of pasture and woodland, overlooking picturesque valley. Excellent walking country and within easy reach by car of Llyn Brianne, gold mines, Brecon Beacons. Good home cooking from fresh produce when available. Accommodation in 1 family, 1 twin bedded and 1 single room. All with hot and cold water and shaver points.

C	B & B PER PERSON PER NIGHT		DINNER B & B PER PERSON PER WEEK		3
	MIN £	MAX £	MIN £	MAX £	OPEN
	5.50	7	55	70	1—12

'Galltybere'

Rhandirmwyn, Llandovery
Dyfed SA20 0PH
Tel: (05506) 218

CATEGORIES: 1 2 1

Situated in the beautiful upper Towy Valley, this sheep farm is ideally placed for touring, walking, fishing, bird and nature reserves. Close to the Llyn Brianne Reservoir. Nine miles north of Llandovery. For further details, write to Mrs. Williams, SAE please.

T C	B & B PER PERSON PER NIGHT		DINNER B & B PER PERSON PER WEEK		4
	MIN £	MAX £	MIN £	MAX £	OPEN
	6.50	8			3—10

Pantllech

Rhandirmwyn, Llandovery
Dyfed SA20 0NG
Tel: (05506) 261

CATEGORIES: 3 3 2

In the beautiful upper Towy Valley, on the edge of the Brecon Beacons National Park. Superb scenery, quiet and unspoilt. Bird-watching and good walking country. Trout and salmon fishing and riding available nearby. Good food and plenty of it.

C	B & B PER PERSON PER NIGHT		DINNER B & B PER PERSON PER WEEK		3
	MIN £	MAX £	MIN £	MAX £	OPEN
	6	7	60	70	1—12

Map ref: Ge3
Spa town whose architecture betrays the more expansive, restful and generous life style of yester-year when families of means took the waters as a cure for everything from gout to rheumatism. Now more active visitors come: Pony trekking, fishing in the towns lake, golf, walking and touring. Bowling Festivals and tennis—and the high standards in hotels—are a welcome link with earlier days.

Children stay at reduced rates, wherever you see this symbol.

Hotel Commodore

Spa Road, Llandrindod Wells
Powys LD1 5ER
Tel: (0597) 2288

CATEGORIES: 4 5 4

Privately owned in centre spa town. 55 rooms; all en-suite, radio intercom. Tea-making facilities. 2 squash courts, indoor heated pool, sauna, solarium, spa bath. Children's adventure area, 50" TV/Video. Free golf Monday to Friday. Special family terms. Large car park.

T	B & B PER PERSON PER NIGHT		DINNER B & B PER PERSON PER WEEK		55
C	MIN £	MAX £	MIN £	MAX £	OPEN
	17	19	135	150	1—12

Glen Usk Hotel*

South Crescent, Landrindod Wells
Powys LD1 5DH
Tel: (0597) 2085

CATEGORIES: 4 4 4

Attractive Victorian hotel situated in the centre of Mid Wales's premier spa resort. The friendly, informal atmosphere generated by the long-established local management makes the Glen Usk an attractive overnight stop or a base for exploring the delights of the area. Equally attractive are the budget-beating tariff and special packages available.

T	B & B PER PERSON PER NIGHT		DINNER B & B PER PERSON PER WEEK		80
C	MIN £	MAX £	MIN £	MAX £	OPEN
	16.50				1—12

Greenway Manor Hotel*

Crossgates, Llandrindod Wells
Powys LD1 6RF
Tel: (059787) 230

CATEGORIES: 3 3 5

This is a Tudor-style gentleman's residence set in 15 acres of pasture and woodland. A comfortable and friendly family-run hotel with licensed restaurant providing a varied grill and à la carte menu; also a good stock of table wines. Open all year for bed, breakfast and evening dinner. Ideally situated for the tourist, fisherman, pony trekkers, or those who just want to get away from it all. Centrally heated plus open log fires. Pleasant and comfortable bedrooms. Small wedding and private parties catered for.

T	B & B PER PERSON PER NIGHT		DINNER B & B PER PERSON PER WEEK		7
C	MIN £	MAX £	MIN £	MAX £	OPEN
	12.50		107		1—12

Griffin Lodge Hotel & Restaurant

Temple Street, Llandrindod Wells
Powys LD1 5HF
Tel: (0597) 2432

CATEGORIES: 3 2 2

Come and stay in our small hotel in the beautiful, sweeping hills of Mid Wales. Good food and wine. AA* RAC* Traveller's Britain etc.

C	B & B PER PERSON PER NIGHT		DINNER B & B PER PERSON PER WEEK		10
	MIN £	MAX £	MIN £	MAX £	OPEN
	9		98		1—12

Hampton Hotel

Temple Street, Llandrindod Wells
LD1 5HF
Tel: (0597) 2585

CATEGORIES: 3 3 4

Family-run hotel in the heart of Mid Wales. Comfortable and friendly atmosphere created by the resident proprietors, Derek and Vera Kermode. Most rooms with private bathrooms. Radio. Babysitting. Private car park. Welsh Male Voice Choir entertains most Mondays throughout season. Bowling, golf, fishing, pony trekking, all available locally.

T	B & B PER PERSON PER NIGHT		DINNER B & B PER PERSON PER WEEK		30
C	MIN £	MAX £	MIN £	MAX £	OPEN
	9	10	92		1—12

Hotel Metropole*

Temple Street, Llandrindod Wells
Powys LD1 5DY
Tel: (0597) 2881/2 Telex: 35237

CATEGORIES: 4 5 4

Situated in the heart of beautiful Mid Wales. The Metropole is the ideal base for people exploring the area. Experienced friendly hospitality and service, with good food and fine wines. Residents may enjoy free golf (Monday to Friday) and free fishing, or swimming in the hotel's own outdoor pool.

T	B & B PER PERSON PER NIGHT		DINNER B & B PER PERSON PER WEEK		141
C	MIN £	MAX £	MIN £	MAX £	OPEN
	14	21.80	138.25	157.50	1—12

C **Children stay at reduced rates, wherever you see this symbol.**

T **This symbol means you can book through your local travel agent.**

The Park Motel*

Crossgates, Llandrindod Wells
Powys LD1 6RF
Tel: (059 787) 201

CATEGORIES: 3 3 5

Set in 3 acres amidst the beautiful Mid Wales countryside, near Elan Valley Reservoirs and centrally situated for touring. Accommodation in modern, luxury self-contained centrally heated chalets. Licensed restaurant open all day for meals and snacks. Lounge bar with colour TV; swimming pool. RAC** Pets welcome. Resident proprietors.

	B & B PER PERSON PER NIGHT		DINNER B & B PER PERSON PER WEEK		7
T **C**	MIN £	MAX £	MIN £	MAX £	OPEN
	8	11	84	103	1—12

Guest Houses

'Berwyn'

Wellington Road, Llandrindod Wells
Powys LD1 5NB
Tel: (0597) 2192

CATEGORIES: 1 2 2

Small, comfortable guest house. Single, double and family rooms with special rates for children. Lounge with colour TV. Dining room with separate tables. Evening meal by prior arrangement. Central heating in all rooms. Parking available.

	B & B PER PERSON PER NIGHT		DINNER B & B PER PERSON PER WEEK		3
C	MIN £	MAX £	MIN £	MAX £	OPEN
	6	7	58	66	5—10

Clifton Guest House & Restaurant*

Clifton House, Wellington Road
Llandrindod Wells, Powys LD1 5NB
Tel: (0597) 2527

CATEGORIES: 1 3 5

Small, friendly Guest House. Comfortable bedrooms including family room. Good home cooking including 'Welsh' breakfast, luncheon, dinner and snacks all day. Licensed. One of finest small wine lists in Mid Wales. Ideal touring centre. For good food, honest wine and friendly service visit the Clifton House.

	B & B PER PERSON PER NIGHT		DINNER B & B PER PERSON PER WEEK		6
C	MIN £	MAX £	MIN £	MAX £	OPEN
	6.25	7.50	54.25	85	1—12

Corven Hall*

Howey, Llandrindod Wells
Powys LD1 5RE
Tel: (0597) 3368

CATEGORIES: 3 3 2

Corven Hall is a family-run, licensed country guest house set in its own grounds, amid the beautiful scenery of Radnorshire. The house is noted for comfort and home cooking. Private game and coarse fishing, golf, pony trekking and hill walking in the area. Children welcome. Ample parking.

	B & B PER PERSON PER NIGHT		DINNER B & B PER PERSON PER WEEK		6
C	MIN £	MAX £	MIN £	MAX £	OPEN
	6.50	7.50	62	68	1—12

Howey Hall Guest House

Howey, Llandrindod Wells
Powys LD1 5PT
Tel: (0597) 2879

CATEGORIES: 1 2 2

We offer you a warm welcome with a high standard of comfort and home cooking in our small Georgian country house, set in its own grounds. Just off the A483 road. Excellent centre for golf, fishing, riding and walking. Licensed.

	B & B PER PERSON PER NIGHT		DINNER B & B PER PERSON PER WEEK		3
C	MIN £	MAX £	MIN £	MAX £	OPEN
	6.50	7.50	72	80.50	4—10

Southlea*

Craig Road, Llandrindod Wells
Powys LD1 5HS
Tel: (0597) 3163

CATEGORIES: 3 3 2

Comfort and good home cooking in a friendly atmosphere. Price includes tea or coffee served in colour TV lounge each evening. Early breakfast and packed lunches available. We have a cot, high-chair, toys and will babysit. Large reductions for children sharing. We'll make your stay a pleasant one.

	B & B PER PERSON PER NIGHT		DINNER B & B PER PERSON PER WEEK		5
C	MIN £	MAX £	MIN £	MAX £	OPEN
	6	7	50	60	1—12

Ty Clyd Guest House*

Park Terrace, Llandrindod Wells
Powys LD1 6AY
Tel: (0597) 2122

CATEGORIES: 3 3 2

A very pleasant house. Situated in a quiet cul-de-sac overlooking Rock Park. Comfortable bedrooms with hot and cold water, washbasins, shaver points. Central heating throughout. A cosy dining room where a variety of home-cooked meals are served. Large guests' lounge with colour TV. Fire Certificate granted. Highly recommended. Near shops, trains, buses, bowls, tennis etc.

	B & B PER PERSON PER NIGHT		DINNER B & B PER PERSON PER WEEK		8
T **C**	MIN £	MAX £	MIN £	MAX £	OPEN
	5.75	6.25	48	53	1—12

Farmhouses

Bryn Nicholas Farm*

Gwystre, Llandrindod Wells
Powys LD1 6RW
Tel: (059 787) 447

CATEGORIES: 3 3 2

Enjoy a warm Welsh welcome in peaceful Mid Wales. Ideal for touring, walking. Single, double and twin rooms; all with hot and cold water, shaver point and tea-making facilities. Lounge with colour television. Dining room with separate tables. Full central heating.

	B & B PER PERSON PER NIGHT		DINNER B & B PER PERSON PER WEEK		4
T **C**	MIN £	MAX £	MIN £	MAX £	OPEN
	6	7	70	77	4—10

Bryn Thomas

Penybont, Llandrindod Wells
Powys
Tel: (059 787) 302

CATEGORIES: 1 3 3

100 yards from River Ithon. Fishing on the farm; pony rides free. It is a mixed farm with cattle, sheep, poultry, pony and working sheepdogs.

	B & B PER PERSON PER NIGHT		DINNER B & B PER PERSON PER WEEK		2
C	MIN £	MAX £	MIN £	MAX £	OPEN
	5	6	56	63	5—11

Gwystre Farm*

Gwystre, Llandrindod Wells
Powys LD1 6RN
Tel: (0397 87) 316

CATEGORIES: 1 2 2

Mixed farm: 160 acres. Situated in the lakeland of Wales, 8 miles from Elan Valley Reservoir. Guests welcome to walk around the farm. 1 double, 1 family room. Reduced terms for children. Quiet and peaceful surroundings. 50 yards off the main A44 road.

	B & B PER PERSON PER NIGHT		DINNER B & B PER PERSON PER WEEK		2
C	MIN £	MAX £	MIN £	MAX £	OPEN
	6	6.50	65	70	3—9

 **Tourist Information Centres are listed at back of book.**

Three Wells Farm*

Howey, Llandrindod Wells, Powys
LD1 5PB
Enquiries to: Mr. & Mrs. R. Bufton
Tel: (0597) 2484

CATEGORIES: 3 3 2

This 50 acre mixed working farm, ideally situated for touring Mid Wales countryside. Residential licence. Fully centrally heated. Fitted carpets in all bedrooms with wash basins, 4 with en-suite private showers. Good food. Large dining room, bar, lounge, TV room. Private fishing; morning tea. Full English breakfast. Ron and Margaret Bufton.

| T | B & B PER PERSON PER NIGHT | | DINNER B & B PER PERSON PER WEEK | | 🛏 8 |
C	MIN £	MAX £	MIN £	MAX £	OPEN
	6	7.50	60	70	1—12

Llandudno

Map ref: Bb3
The premier coastal resort of North Wales enjoying an unrivalled position on a lowland peninsula between two fine headlands, the Great and Little Ormes. Between the town's two beaches lie fine shopping streets and a wealth of hotels and guest houses. A grand pier, walks and gardens as well as a Cabin Lift and beginning of the century tramway, make it a town of character. For the active there is yachting from the promenade, three 18-hole golf courses, a swimming pool and donkey rides. There are quieter pursuits as well as nightly cabaret, bingo, cinema and band concerts, though a certain decorum stems from the fine Edwardian-style architecture of many of the buildings. As a touring centre it is convenient for coast and mountains.

Hotels

April Court Private Hotel*

10 St. Davids Place, Llandudno
LL30 2UG
Tel: (0492) 77898

CATEGORIES: 1 3 2

Small hotel, tastefully decorated and furnished with fitted carpets. Shower points hot and cold in all rooms. Attractive front dining room. Relaxing front lounge with colour TV. Children welcome. Reductions for retired citizens. Enclosed car park rear property. Full Fire Certificate granted. Five minutes to shops and both beaches.

C	B & B PER PERSON PER NIGHT		DINNER B & B PER PERSON PER WEEK		🛏 7
	MIN £	MAX £	MIN £	MAX £	OPEN
	6	6.50	47	47	4—10

Ashfields Hotel*

Deganwy Avenue, Llandudno
LL30 2YB
Tel: (0492) 79220

CATEGORIES: 2 3 3

A family-run private hotel offering good food and comfortable accommodation. TV lounge, attractive dining room with separate tables. Cocktail bar. Car park. Access to rooms at all times. Situated on the level, close to promenade, shops and all entertainments. Write or telephone for colour brochure and terms.

C	B & B PER PERSON PER NIGHT		DINNER B & B PER PERSON PER WEEK		🛏 11
	MIN £	MAX £	MIN £	MAX £	OPEN
	6.50	7	59	64	1—12

The Bay Court Hotel*

North Parade, Promenade, Llandudno
Gwynedd LL30 2LP
Tel: (0492) 77356

CATEGORIES: 4 4 4

Superb seafront position opposite pier entrance, gardens and beach. The Bay Court Hotel is highly recommended for excellent cuisine, fine service and friendly atmosphere. Well appointed rooms, numerous with shower and toilet. All with television. Generous children's reduction. Colour television, lounge, residents' bar. Centrally heated. SAE please for our colour brochure.

| T | B & B PER PERSON PER NIGHT | | DINNER B & B PER PERSON PER WEEK | | 🛏 10 |
C	MIN £	MAX £	MIN £	MAX £	OPEN
	7.50	8.50	72	86	3—11

Baytree Hotel*

Promenade, Llandudno
Gwynedd LL30 2LP
Tel: (0492) 75858 Telex: 61467

CATEGORIES: 3 4 4

First class hotel occupying an enviable promenade position. Excellent views of Llandudno's beautiful crescent-shaped bay. Close to shops and entertainment. Luxurious Victorian-style velvet furnishing in lounge, ballroom, bar, dining room. Lift, sauna, solarium. Bedrooms with colour TV, radio, teasmade. En-suite rooms available. A welcome awaits you from Stan and June Dickens. SAE for brochure. M.C.F.A.

| T | B & B PER PERSON PER NIGHT | | DINNER B & B PER PERSON PER WEEK | | 🛏 44 |
C	MIN £	MAX £	MIN £	MAX £	OPEN
	10.50	12	105	122	2—11

Bedford Hotel

Central Promenade, Llandudno
Gwynedd LL30 1BN
Tel: (0492) 76647

CATEGORIES

| 3 | 3 | 4 |

Detached seafront hotel with ample parking space. Centrally situated between the Great and Little Orme. Most rooms with seaview, some en-suite. TV lounge. Central heating in all public rooms. Under the supervision of Mr. and Mrs. Carciero and Mr. and Mrs. Galeotti, North Wales chef of the year 1980/81. RAC* AA*.

T C	B & B PER PERSON PER NIGHT		DINNER B & B PER PERSON PER WEEK		28
	MIN £	MAX £	MIN £	MAX £	OPEN
	7.50	9.50	84	105	1—12

Bella Vista Private Hotel*

72 Church Walks, Llandudno
Gwynedd LL30 2HG
Tel: (0492) 76855

CATEGORIES

| 3 | 3 | 2 |

Situated within two minutes' walk of the beach, promenade and shops. The hotel is centrally heated. All bedrooms have fitted vanity units with mirror, lights and shaver points. Some rooms with private shower. Cocktail bar, colour TV lounge. Fire Certificate. Closed mid December-mid January. Private car park.

C	B & B PER PERSON PER NIGHT		DINNER B & B PER PERSON PER WEEK		12
	MIN £	MAX £	MIN £	MAX £	OPEN
	8.05	8.65	80.50	84.50	1—12

Belvedere Hotel*

Central Promenade, Llandudno
Gwynedd LL30 1AR
Tel: (0492) 76388

CATEGORIES

| 3 | 3 | 2 |

Situated in centre of Bay, close to all amenities: Express Coach park, railway station, Conference Centre. Family rooms available (reductions for children). Also ground floor and single bedrooms. Colour television. Licensed. Separate tables in dining room. Hot and cold water. Bar snacks at lunch time. Under personal supervision of proprietors.

C	B & B PER PERSON PER NIGHT		DINNER B & B PER PERSON PER WEEK		18
	MIN £	MAX £	MIN £	MAX £	OPEN
	6.50	9.50	57	77	4—10

Bodysgallen Hall Hotel*

near Llandudno, Gwynedd
North Wales, LL30 1RS
Tel: (0492) 84466/7
Telex: 8951493 MONTEK G

CATEGORIES

| 6 | 5 | 4 |

This historic 17th century house has been restored to the highest standards to provide all the comfort, evocative of the best traditions of a country house. Each room has a private bathroom, central heating, colour TV and direct-dial telephone. We specialise in serving traditional British dishes.

T C	B & B PER PERSON PER NIGHT		DINNER B & B PER PERSON PER WEEK		32
	MIN £	MAX £	MIN £	MAX £	OPEN
	25	35	224	259	1—12

Branksome Hotel*

Lloyd Street, Llandudno
LL30 2YP
Tel: (0492) 75989

CATEGORIES

| 3 | 4 | 4 |

Nicely situated, licensed family-run hotel only minutes from both shores, therefore convenient for all amenities. Fully centrally heated, choice of lounges, games room, ground floor rooms (some en-suite). Parking. Christmas programme, Mini Breaks available also conferences and functions catered for. Be sure of a warm welcome at The Branksome. Brochure on request.

T C	B & B PER PERSON PER NIGHT		DINNER B & B PER PERSON PER WEEK		55
	MIN £	MAX £	MIN £	MAX £	OPEN
	7.50	10	77	90	1—12

Branstone*

Llewelyn Avenue, Llandudno
Gwynedd LL30 2ER
Tel: (0492) 76448

CATEGORIES

| 3 | 3 | 3 |

Comfortable, family-run hotel. Ideally situated: 2 minutes' walk to pier and town centre. Excellent service and cuisine. Full English breakfast, 5-course dinner. Own keys, residential licence, lounge with colour television. Bedlights, hot and cold water, shavers, heating all rooms. Mid-week bookings. Open all year and Christmas. Fire Certificate. Reduced rates for children.

C	B & B PER PERSON PER NIGHT		DINNER B & B PER PERSON PER WEEK		8
	MIN £	MAX £	MIN £	MAX £	OPEN
	6.50	8	63	67	1—12

Brigstock Private Hotel*

1 St. Davids Place, Llandudno
Gwynedd LL30 2UG
Tel: (0492) 76416

CATEGORIES

| 3 | 3 | 3 |

Situated on the level between the promenade and the popular West Shore. Brigstock offers a comfortable, friendly, holiday atmosphere. Convenient for shops and entertainments, yet quiet and restful. Single, double and family accommodation. AA and RAC listed. Residential licence. Car Park. Fire Certificate. Proprietors Janette and Ray Fisher.

C	B & B PER PERSON PER NIGHT		DINNER B & B PER PERSON PER WEEK		10
	MIN £	MAX £	MIN £	MAX £	OPEN
	7.50	8	70	75	4—10

Brig-y-Don

Central Promenade, Llandudno
Gwynedd
Tel: (0492) 77319

CATEGORIES

| 3 | 3 | 2 |

Few hotels can boast of a more magnificent setting than Brig-y-Don on the seafront, close to shops and cinemas. Comfortable lounges and bar. All the comforts of home under the personal supervision of Mrs. MacLean. Colour brochure available on request.

T C	B & B PER PERSON PER NIGHT		DINNER B & B PER PERSON PER WEEK		32
	MIN £	MAX £	MIN £	MAX £	OPEN
		8		70	4—10

Brinkburn Hotel

Grand Promenade, Llandudno
Gwynedd LL30 2NR
Tel: (0492) 76886

CATEGORIES

| 2 | 3 | 4 |

Ideally situated on the Grand promenade with superb views of the sea, Great and Little Orme. The principal shopping facilities are within a few yards. Some bedrooms en-suite, most with sea views. 3 lounges, comfortable bar. Car park. Lifts to all floors. Brochure on request.

T C	B & B PER PERSON PER NIGHT		DINNER B & B PER PERSON PER WEEK		42
	MIN £	MAX £	MIN £	MAX £	OPEN
	9	14	80	115	4—10

Broadway Hotel*

Mostyn Broadway, Llandudno
Gwynedd
Tel: (0492) 76398

CATEGORIES | 2 | 2 | 3

Residential and restaurant licence. Situated only 100 yards from the magnificent promenade and seafront, for which Llandudno is so famed. Shopping is very convenient from the Broadway. Cinemas and places of entertainment are all within easy walking distance. Relax in one of our two lounges, bar and dance floor.

T C	B & B PER PERSON PER NIGHT		DINNER B & B PER PERSON PER WEEK		42
	MIN £	MAX £	MIN £	MAX £	OPEN
	6.50		55	65	4—10

Bromwell Court Hotel*

Promenade, Llandudno
Gwynedd LL30 1BB
Tel: (0492) 78416

CATEGORIES | 4 | 4 | 4

AA** Bromwell Court, Promenade, Llandudno Telephone: (0492) 78416. Luxurious and elegantly furnished hotel. Most bedrooms have bathrooms or shower en-suite. Some have colour television, radios and tea and coffee making-facilities in all bedrooms.. Centrally heated throughout. Special winter breaks. Victorian-style cocktail lounge. Member of Minotels. Resident proprietors Mrs. O. and Mrs. D. R. Ruddle.

T C	B & B PER PERSON PER NIGHT		DINNER B & B PER PERSON PER WEEK		12
	MIN £	MAX £	MIN £	MAX £	OPEN
	10.75	12	107	112.40	1—12

Bron Orme Hotel

Church Walks, Llandudno
Gwynedd LL30 2HL
Tel: (0492) 76735

CATEGORIES | 3 | 3 | 2

Ideally situated in loveliest part of Llandudno. Bron Orme offers all that you would expect from a good class hotel. AA* RAC* Comfortable lounge with colour TV. Licensed. Beautiful home-cooked meals. Friendly atmosphere, personal service assured. Fire Certificate. Moderate terms. Please write or telephone for brochure.

T C	B & B PER PERSON PER NIGHT		DINNER B & B PER PERSON PER WEEK		11
	MIN £	MAX £	MIN £	MAX £	OPEN
	6.70	7.70	66.50	73.50	3—10

Bryn Derwen Hotel

34 Abbey Road, Llandudno
Gwynedd LL30 2EE
Tel: (0492) 76804

CATEGORIES | 3 | 4 | 3

A family-run hotel where hospitality is a major consideration. The Chef/owner has had many years of experience in hotels and as a college lecturer. Substantial reductions for children. Solarium for that perfect tan. Car park conveniently located for town and both main beaches.

T C	B & B PER PERSON PER NIGHT		DINNER B & B PER PERSON PER WEEK		13
	MIN £	MAX £	MIN £	MAX £	OPEN
	8.30	9.30	72.80	79.80	4—10

Bryn-y-Bia Lodge Hotel*

Craigside, Llandudno
Gwynedd LL30 3AS
Tel: (0492) 49644

CATEGORIES | 4 | 4 | 4

Unique in character and situation. This highly recommended hotel stands on the coastal road near to the sea. Convenient for all amenities, yet having the tranquility of spacious grounds with ample parking. All bedrooms have bathroom en-suite, colour TV and teasmade. Full cental heating. Comfortable lounges. Residential licence.

T C	B & B PER PERSON PER NIGHT		DINNER B & B PER PERSON PER WEEK		19
	MIN £	MAX £	MIN £	MAX £	OPEN
	10	15	95	135	1—12

Carmel Private Hotel*

17 Craig y Don Parade, Promenade
Llandudno LL30 1BG
Tel: (0492) 77643

CATEGORIES | 3 | 3 | 2

Ideally situated on the promenade. Friendly family-run hotel specialising in comfort and good food, well cooked. Convenient conference centre, entertainments, transport and tours. All bedrooms (some with toilet and shower) have fitted carpets. Bed-head lights and shaving points, full central heating. Free car park. Highly recommended.

C	B & B PER PERSON PER NIGHT		DINNER B & B PER PERSON PER WEEK		10
	MIN £	MAX £	MIN £	MAX £	OPEN
	6.75	7.75	64.25	83.50	3—12

Clarence Hotel*

Gloddaeth Street, Llandudno
Gwynedd LL30 2DD
Tel: (0492) 76485 Telex: 61254

CATEGORIES | 3 | 4 | 4

One of Llandudno's leading hotels, this two star hotel has 74 comfortably furnished bedrooms, a spacious restaurant serving fine food and wines, a choice of two warm and friendly bars with entertainment. Lift to all floors. Night porter. Colour TV lounge. Family rooms available. Special Short Break terms.

T C	B & B PER PERSON PER NIGHT		DINNER B & B PER PERSON PER WEEK		74
	MIN £	MAX £	MIN £	MAX £	OPEN
	11	14	102	110	4—10

Cornerways Hotel*

2 St. Davids Place, Llandudno
LL30 2UG
Tel: (0492) 77334

CATEGORIES | 3 | 3 | 3

Free car park. Large, comfortable lounge with ample seating. Dining room with separate tables. Modern bedrooms are all on 2 floors only. Fire Certificate granted. Hotel open most of the year. Brochure on request.

T C	B & B PER PERSON PER NIGHT		DINNER B & B PER PERSON PER WEEK		11
	MIN £	MAX £	MIN £	MAX £	OPEN
	7	7.50	70	75	1—12

Children stay at reduced rates, wherever you see this symbol.

C

Craig-Ard Hotel*

Arvon Avenue, Llandudno
Gwynedd LL30 2DY
Tel: (0492) 77318

CATEGORIES

2	3	3

Beautifully situated with attractive garden only a minutes' walk from pier, promenade and main shopping centre. Residential licence with comfortable lounge bar. Heated throughout. Ground floor and single room available. Separate TV and Reading Lounge. Private car park for 12 cars—unrestricted parking in avenue. Ideal for touring Snowdonia. Central for golf courses, sailing, riding and swimming pool. Illustrated colour brochure and tariff on request. Small wedding and private parties catered for. Under the constant personal supervision of resident proprietors, Mr. & Mrs. E. Watkins.

	B & B PER PERSON PER NIGHT		DINNER B & B PER PERSON PER WEEK		18
T **C**	MIN £	MAX £	MIN £	MAX £	OPEN
	8.20	10.50	71.50	87.50	4—10

Craiglands

7 Carmen Sylva Road, Craig-y-Don
Llandudno, Gwynedd
Tel: (0492) 75090

CATEGORIES

3	3	2

Small, select hotel close to promenade and all amenities. Colour TV lounge. All bedrooms tastefully decorated with central heating, tea and coffee-making facilities. Good food and comfort assured. Fire Certificate granted.

	B & B PER PERSON PER NIGHT		DINNER B & B PER PERSON PER WEEK		5
C	MIN £	MAX £	MIN £	MAX £	OPEN
	6.50	7.50	66.50	70	3—10

Cranleigh Hotel*

Great Orme's Road, West Shore
Llandudno, Gwynedd LL30 2AR
Tel: (0492) 77688

CATEGORIES

3	4	4

The Cranleigh, for a very happy holiday experience. Delightful situation only yards from West Shore beach, and convenient all amenities. Attractive accommodation, (some en-suite rooms). Teamaking facilities. Centrally heated throughout. Choice cuisine, personal service and hospitality. Special rates for children. Dogs welcome. Cosy bar. Own enclosed car park.

	B & B PER PERSON PER NIGHT		DINNER B & B PER PERSON PER WEEK		13
T **C**	MIN £	MAX £	MIN £	MAX £	OPEN
	8.50	12.10	85	111.15	4—10

Deganwy Castle Hotel*

Deganwy, Gwynedd
LL31 9DA
Tel: (0492) 83358

CATEGORIES

4	4	4

AA* RAC* Egon Ronay recommended. Superbly situated overlooking Conwy Castle, estuary and background of Snowdonia. Extensive golfing and fishing facilities nearby. Ideal touring centre. Free car parking. Gardens. Rooms en-suite. Excellent cuisine featuring local specialities. Entertainment. Bargain Breaks. Christmas Programme. Open all year. Resident proprietors, Mr. and Mrs. D. A. Campbell.

	B & B PER PERSON PER NIGHT		DINNER B & B PER PERSON PER WEEK		35
T **C**	MIN £	MAX £	MIN £	MAX £	OPEN
	10	20	119	154	1—12

Drummond Hotel

Trinity Square, Llandudno
Gwynedd LL30 2RB
Tel: (0492) 76417

CATEGORIES

3	3	4

Near railway station and coach station. Car park. Pleasant lawns, cosy bar. Colour TV, lounge, excellent food and service. Radio/intercom and tea-making all bedrooms. Close to promenade and shopping centre. Reduced terms for children-choice of menu.

	B & B PER PERSON PER NIGHT		DINNER B & B PER PERSON PER WEEK		22
C	MIN £	MAX £	MIN £	MAX £	OPEN
	9.20		82.80		4—10

Dunoon Hotel*

Gloddaeth Street, Llandudno
Gwynedd LL30 2DW
Tel: (0492) 77078

CATEGORIES

4	4	4

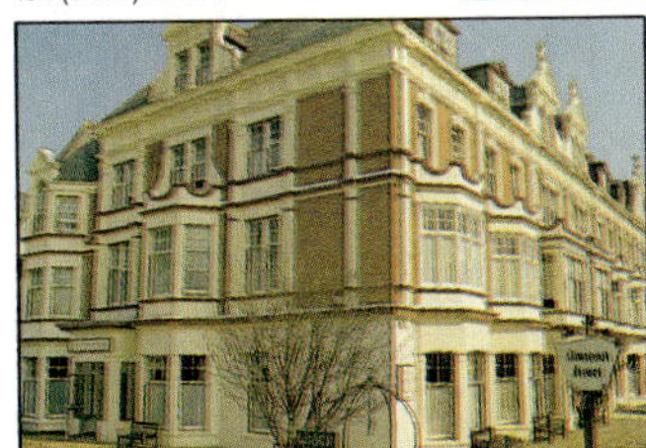

Family-owned and operated over 35 years with reputation for hospitality and value-for-money. Dunoon offers comfortable bedrooms, most with private bath, all with TV, central heating. Tea and coffee-making facilities. Oak panelled public rooms. Spacious dining room, games room, lift. Car park.

	B & B PER PERSON PER NIGHT		DINNER B & B PER PERSON PER WEEK		59
T **C**	MIN £	MAX £	MIN £	MAX £	OPEN
	9	15	85	130	2—11

Empire Hotel*

Church Walks, Llandudno
Gwynedd LL30 2HE
Tel: (0492) 79955 Telex: 617161

CATEGORIES

6	5	6

Family-run hotel, central position near to promenade, shops and amenities. All bedrooms with bath and colour TV. Some family suites with mini kitchens. Indoor heated swimming pool. Roof garden bars, restaurant, grill room. Car parks, lifts; dancing every Saturday. Ideal base for touring Snowdonia. Mini breaks. Closed Christmas and New Year.

	B & B PER PERSON PER NIGHT		DINNER B & B PER PERSON PER WEEK		56
T **C**	MIN £	MAX £	MIN £	MAX £	OPEN
	15	25	150	200	1—12

Esplanade Hotel*

Glan-y-Mor Parade, The Promenade
Llandudno, Gwynedd
Tel: (0492) 76687/77100

CATEGORIES

4	4	4

Centrally situated on seafront; convenient for shops and entertainment. En-suite rooms available with colour TV, teasmade, trouser press, radio, telephone. Full central heating. Parking for residents. Lift, Cocktail bar, two lounges, pool and games room. Free golf. Buttery bar. Conference facilities and group terms. RAC* and AA* Brochure on request.

	B & B PER PERSON PER NIGHT		DINNER B & B PER PERSON PER WEEK		60
T **C**	MIN £	MAX £	MIN £	MAX £	OPEN
	10	16	105	140	1—12

Family Holidays Association Limited

Cae Mor Hotel, Promenade
Llandudno, Gwynedd LL30 1SR
Tel: (0492) 48375

CATEGORIES

| 3 | 3 | 3 |

Both specially equipped for families. Large lounge, games room, separate TV lounge. Mothers' kitchen: washing, drying, airing, ironing facilities. Hot and cold water all bedrooms, razer points, baby-listening. Bar (residents only), free car parking. All welcome. Reasonable prices. Free colour brochure: F. W. T. Phillips, General Manager, Family Holidays Association Limited, Meadowcroft Hotel, Llanncerch Road East, Rhos-on-Sea, Colwyn Bay, Clwyd LL28 4DF.

C	B & B PER PERSON PER NIGHT		DINNER B & B PER PERSON PER WEEK		33
	MIN £	MAX £	MIN £ 82.48	MAX £ 86.23	OPEN 4—9

The Grafton Hotel*

Promenade, Llandudno
Gwynedd LL30 1BG
Tel: (0492) 76814

CATEGORIES

| 4 | 4 | 4 |

"Be like the rest and book the best" It could cost far less than you expect and offers excellent accommodation. All bedrooms having colour television, tea/coffee-making facilities and of course, bath or shower and toilet en-suite. Ideal for that special occasion—honeymoon, anniversary.

T C	B & B PER PERSON PER NIGHT		DINNER B & B PER PERSON PER WEEK		21
	MIN £	MAX £ 11.60	MIN £	MAX £ 105	OPEN 2—11

Headlands Hotel*

Hill Terrace, Llandudno
Gwynedd LL30 2LS
Tel: (0492) 77485

CATEGORIES

| 4 | 4 | 4 |

Peaceful position overlooking bay. Excellent cuisine, 18 bedrooms, 12 en-suite, with colour TV. All with tea/coffee-making facilities. Licensed AA* RAC* Ashley Courtenay recommended. 2-day breaks, mid-week bookings. Open Easter-November. Centrally heated. Special reductions children. Brochure from C. A. Lonsdale, F.H.C.I.M.A. Box WSW 83, or Mrs. W. A. Lonsdale.

T C	B & B PER PERSON PER NIGHT		DINNER B & B PER PERSON PER WEEK		18
	MIN £ 11.50	MAX £ 18	MIN £ 102	MAX £ 130	OPEN 4—11

Heath House*

Central Promenade, Llandudno
Gwynedd LL30 1AT
Tel: (0492) 78956

CATEGORIES

| 3 | 4 | 3 |

Family-run seafront hotel, with residents' car park and close to bus and train terminals. We offer you value-for-money holidays. Our guidelines are comfort, cleanliness, good food with ample meals and a varied menu. Full central heating, air conditioned dining rooms, double glazing. Cabaret, dance floor. Lounge bar. Baby-listening service and facilities. AA listed.

T C	B & B PER PERSON PER NIGHT		DINNER B & B PER PERSON PER WEEK		21
	MIN £ 8.50	MAX £ 10	MIN £ 87.50	MAX £ 93.50	OPEN 1—12

Hen Dy Hotel*

10 North Parade, Llandudno
Gwynedd LL30 2LP
Tel: (0492) 76184

CATEGORIES

| 3 | 3 | 4 |

Licensed, family hotel. Situated opposite the pier. Magnificent view of the bay. Distinctive dining room, wine list on request. Radio, intercom in all bedrooms. Fully centrally heated. Television lounge. Full Fire Certificate granted. Small coach parties accommodated and conference delegates welcome. Mid-week bookings and Weekend Breaks. Open for Christmas.

T C	B & B PER PERSON PER NIGHT		DINNER B & B PER PERSON PER WEEK		15
	MIN £ 8	MAX £ 10.50	MIN £ 66.50	MAX £ 79.80	OPEN 3—12

Kinmel Private Hotel*

The Central Promenade, Llandudno
Gwynedd
Tel: (0492) 76171

CATEGORIES

| 2 | 3 | 2 |

Centrally situated on promenade close to shops, train and bus stations. Comfortable TV lounge, foyer bar. Many rooms with sea view. Beach only 25 yards away, leisure centre and theatre 500 yards. Cinemas close by.

C	B & B PER PERSON PER NIGHT		DINNER B & B PER PERSON PER WEEK		17
	MIN £ 8.50	MAX £ 9.50	MIN £ 77	MAX £	OPEN 4—10

Knowsley Hotel

North Parade, Llandudno
LL30 2LP
Tel: (0492) 76025

CATEGORIES

| 3 | 3 | 2 |

Prime position opposite pier. Family-run, established 15 years. Rear car park. Central heating. Lounge with colour TV, olde worlde Cocktail bar. Reduced terms for children. Full Fire Certificate. Open April to beginning of October.

C	B & B PER PERSON PER NIGHT		DINNER B & B PER PERSON PER WEEK		15
	MIN £ 11	MAX £ 13	MIN £ 88	MAX £ 102	OPEN 3—10

Leamore Hotel*

40 Lloyd Street, Llandudno
Gwynedd LL30 2BE
Tel: (0492) 75552

CATEGORIES

| 3 | 3 | 3 |

Central position, small family-run hotel. We offer excellent food, comfort and hospitality. Full central heating. Licensed bar. Tea-making facilities in all the bedrooms. AA RAC One star.

T C	B & B PER PERSON PER NIGHT		DINNER B & B PER PERSON PER WEEK		12
	MIN £ 8	MAX £ 9	MIN £ 75	MAX £ 82	OPEN 1—12

Lockyers

Central Promenade, Llandudno
Gwynedd LL30 2SX
Tel: (0492) 76053

CATEGORIES

| 3 | 4 | 4 |

Lockyers Hotel is a building of Victorian character which has been tastefully modernised and furnished. Full central heating, some rooms en-suite. All with colour TV and video system. Lift to all floors. Centrally situated on the seafront, close to shops and amenities. Function, conference room available.

T C	B & B PER PERSON PER NIGHT		DINNER B & B PER PERSON PER WEEK		54
	MIN £ 11.50	MAX £	MIN £ 105	MAX £ 120	OPEN 4—10

Marine Hotel*

Vaughan Street, Llandudno
Gwynedd LL30 1AN
Tel: (0492) 77521

CATEGORIES: 4 5 4

With fine sea views, this large and comfortable hotel has 79 bedrooms, many with private bath and all with telephone, radio, colour TV and tea/coffee-making facilities. Ideal for family holidays. Car park. Weekend and Mid-week Bargain Breaks and High-Time Holidays available. Small conferences accommodated.

T C	B & B PER PERSON PER NIGHT		DINNER B & B PER PERSON PER WEEK		79
	MIN £	MAX £	MIN £	MAX £	OPEN
	17.75	20			1—12

Mayfair Private Hotel*

4 Abbey Road, Llandudno
Gwynedd LL30 2EA
Tel: (0492) 76170

CATEGORIES: 4 4 3

We are a pleasantly situated family-managed hotel, AA and RAC listed. Providing good service and home cooking. For your comfort we provide well-stocked lounge and bar. Separate colour TV lounge. Full central heating. Single, double and family rooms; some with private bathroom. Hotel close to all amenities.

C	B & B PER PERSON PER NIGHT		DINNER B & B PER PERSON PER WEEK		13
	MIN £	MAX £	MIN £	MAX £	OPEN
	6.75	8.50	70	77	1—12

The Mermaid Private Hotel*

120 Mostyn Street, Llandudno
Gwynedd LL30 2SW
Tel: (0492) 75119

CATEGORIES: 3 3 2

Looking for a friendly place to stay? The Mermaid, 120 Mostyn Street, Llandudno, telephone (0492) 75119. Fire Certificate. Top quality menus. (Chef proprietor). Cosy bar. Showers. Colour TV lounge. Near beach, Happy Valley, Great Orme. Please send SAE for brochure to: Erik or Mary Hansen.

T C	B & B PER PERSON PER NIGHT		DINNER B & B PER PERSON PER WEEK		8
	MIN £	MAX £	MIN £	MAX £	OPEN
	6.50	7.25	62.50	66.90	1—12

New Style Imperial Hotel*

Promenade, Llandudno
Gwynedd LL30 1AP
Tel: (0492) 77466

CATEGORIES: 3 5 5

Our facilities include a sauna, solarium and exercise room, 145 comfortable bedrooms, all of which have radio, telephone, tea/coffee-making facilities and colour TV, (most have private bathrooms). Our remarkably good value tariff starts from just £13.95 per person, per night. Brochure from Mr. W. S. Lofthouse.

T C	B & B PER PERSON PER NIGHT		DINNER B & B PER PERSON PER WEEK		150
	MIN £	MAX £	MIN £	MAX £	OPEN
	13.95	17.95	132.30	135	1—12

North Western

Vaughan Street, Llandudno
Gwynedd
Tel: (0492) 77694

CATEGORIES: 3 4 4

This elegant, superbly situated hotel is convenient for shopping, as it stands in the main shopping area and close to the beach and entertainments. Some bedrooms are en-suite. Lift to all floors, central heating in some bedrooms and public rooms, teasmade. Small functions, conference facilities catered for. Brochure on request.

T C	B & B PER PERSON PER NIGHT		DINNER B & B PER PERSON PER WEEK		54
	MIN £	MAX £	MIN £	MAX £	OPEN
	10	12	88	110	1—12

Nuneham House Hotel

12 South Parade, Llandudno
Gwynedd
Tel: (0492) 77369

CATEGORIES: 2 3 3

Friendly, family-run hotel overlooking the Great Orme and pier. Central to all amenities. Comfortable lounge with colour TV. Modern, furnished bedrooms, hot and cold water, shaving points, bed lights all rooms. Pleasant dining room; separate tables. Access to bedroom and lounge at all times. Special rates for senior citizens.

C	B & B PER PERSON PER NIGHT		DINNER B & B PER PERSON PER WEEK		14
	MIN £	MAX £	MIN £	MAX £	OPEN
	6.50	7.50	59.50	66	3—11

Oak-Alyn Hotel

Deganwy Avenue, Llandudno
Gwynedd LL30 2YB
Tel: (0492) 76497

CATEGORIES: 3 4 4

Llandudno Oak Alyn Hotel. RAC* AA* Do you want your holiday hotel clean, comfortable, with central heating, choice of dishes at meal times? Ample car parking. Situated town centre, the Oak Alyn has all these and more. For details ring Llandudno 70497 or write to Barbara Jones.

T C	B & B PER PERSON PER NIGHT		DINNER B & B PER PERSON PER WEEK		15
	MIN £	MAX £	MIN £	MAX £	OPEN
	7	8.75	65	87.50	2—12

Plas Fron Deg*

48 Church Walks, Llandudno
Gwynedd
Tel: (0492) 77267

CATEGORIES: 4 4 5

Sunday Times Taste of Britain Award Winner: Wales 1982.

A dramatically beautiful hotel standing in terraced gardens. Modernised to very high standards of comfort, yet retaining the character of this historic building. Excellent gourmet menu in relaxing, tastefully furnished dining room. Well-stocked bar, lounge. Resident proprietors provide friendly, yet efficient service and a real taste of gracious living.

T C	B & B PER PERSON PER NIGHT		DINNER B & B PER PERSON PER WEEK		10
	MIN £	MAX £	MIN £	MAX £	OPEN
	10		98		1—12

Queens Hotel

Promenade, Llandudno
Gwynedd
Tel: (0492) 77218

CATEGORIES

| 2 | 3 | 4 |

Situated in the centre of Llandudno's beautiful promenade. The Queens Hotel is central for all amenities, shops, entertainment, bus and train stations. Some bedrooms are en-suite, all with heating for your comfort. Two bars, conference and function facilities available. Car parking for all residents. Brochure available on request.

	B & B PER PERSON PER NIGHT		DINNER B & B PER PERSON PER WEEK		75
T	MIN £	MAX £	MIN £	MAX £	OPEN
C	11.50	13.50	89	110	1—12

Ravenhurst Hotel*

West Shore, Llandudno
Gwynedd LL30 2BB
Tel: (0492) 75525

CATEGORIES

| 3 | 4 | 4 |

Situated on West Shore with views of sea and mountains. Residential licence. Radios, tea-making equipment in all bedrooms. Ground floor bedrooms and private bathrooms available. Morning coffee, afternoon tea served. Separate TV lounge. Car park. Ideal for touring North Wales. Golf, sailing, indoor swimming, riding, all nearby.

	B & B PER PERSON PER NIGHT		DINNER B & B PER PERSON PER WEEK		24
T	MIN £	MAX £	MIN £	MAX £	OPEN
C	10	13.50	98	114	2—10

Regent Court Hotel

Promenade, Llandudno
Gwynedd
Tel: (0492) 76853/83711

CATEGORIES

| 4 | 4 | 4 |

Beautifully positioned in the centre of Llandudno's glorious promenade, we offer the best in holiday accommodation. Luxury hotel. Indoor heated swimming pool. Sauna, solarium, games room, dancing, entertainment. Bar, lift, car park. Central heating throughout. Private bathrooms. Radios, teasmade, Mini Weekend Breaks.

	B & B PER PERSON PER NIGHT		DINNER B & B PER PERSON PER WEEK		49
T	MIN £	MAX £	MIN £	MAX £	OPEN
C	9.50	12.50	101	122.50	3—11

Richmond Hotel*

B. T. Williams
St. Georges Place, Llandudno
Gwynedd LL30 2NR
Tel: (0492) 76347

CATEGORIES

| 3 | 3 | 4 |

Family-run hotel which offers a high standard of comfort. Lift, residents' bar, television lounge, enclosed sun verandah. Over 50% of our luxurious bedrooms have bathroom suites. Father and son are qualified chefs. Many guests have been visiting the Richmond for over 25 years. Why not join them!

	B & B PER PERSON PER NIGHT		DINNER B & B PER PERSON PER WEEK		26
T	MIN £	MAX £	MIN £	MAX £	OPEN
C	9.50	9.50	86.50		4—10

Risboro Hotel*

Clement Avenue, Llandudno
Gwynedd LL30 2ED
Tel: (0492) 76343

CATEGORIES

| 4 | 4 | 4 |

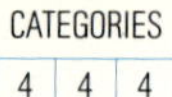

Convenient for all amenities, seafront, shops, minutes from hotel. 57 bedrooms all with en-suite facilities. Colour TV. Tea and coffee-making facilities. Large lounges. Ballroom, conference suite. Sauna, solarium, jacuzzi, spa pool and health club. Games room. Full chef cuisine. Open Christmas. Myles-Irving resident proprietors.

	B & B PER PERSON PER NIGHT		DINNER B & B PER PERSON PER WEEK		57
T	MIN £	MAX £	MIN £	MAX £	OPEN
C	10	12	100	130	1—12

Rochdale Hotel

10 Deganwy Avenue, Llandudno
Gwynedd LL30 2YB
Tel: (0492) 76481

CATEGORIES

| 3 | 3 | 3 |

A private, family-run, licensed hotel offering good fresh food and a home-from-home friendly atmosphere. On the level, close to all amenities. Free parking on our forecourt. Hot and cold water, shaver points and the most comfortable of beds in all rooms. Special rates for children.

	B & B PER PERSON PER NIGHT		DINNER B & B PER PERSON PER WEEK		14
C	MIN £	MAX £	MIN £	MAX £	OPEN
	7.50	8	65.50	70	3—10

Rocksley Private Hotel*

Promenade, Craig-y-Don
Llandudno, Gwynedd
Tel: (0492) 76626

CATEGORIES

| 1 | 3 | 2 |

Close to the Conference and Leisure Centre and all amenities. Single, twin, family and double rooms. Large ground floor bedroom with adjacent toilet. Dining room, lounge with TV, also on the ground floor. Partial central heating. Large car park. Reservations from any day. Mr & Mrs E. Buckley.

	B & B PER PERSON PER NIGHT		DINNER B & B PER PERSON PER WEEK		10
C	MIN £	MAX £	MIN £	MAX £	OPEN
	6.25	6.50	61.25	63	4—9

---

i **Tourist Information Centres are listed at back of book.**

C **Children stay at reduced rates, wherever you see this symbol.**

St. George's Hotel

Llandudno
Gwynedd LL30 2LG
Tel: (0492) 77544 Telex 61520

CATEGORIES: 6 6 6

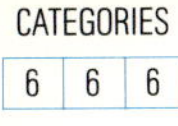

One of Wales's finest hotels, transformed since the take-over by Mr. & Mrs. Michael Forte in 1977. Every effort has been made to retain the beautiful, original, classic design, but also introducing the best of modern amenities. All bedrooms have private bathroom, shower, TV, teasmade. Double glazing, central heating. A choice of bars with snack facilities. Car parking. Sea view rooms available.

T / C	B & B PER PERSON PER NIGHT		DINNER B & B PER PERSON PER WEEK		91
	MIN £	MAX £	MIN £	MAX £	OPEN
	19	24	168	192.50	1—12

St Hilary Hotel

16 Promenade, Craig-y-Don
Llandudno LL30 1DZ
Tel: (0492) 75551

CATEGORIES: 3 3 2

Situated on the seafront, commanding magnificent views of Llandudno Bay and the Great and Little Orme Headlands. Squash and indoor swimming available. 3 minutes from hotel. Bedrooms are of a high standard, all with tea-making facilities and heating. Colour TV, lounge. Excellent home cooking.

C	B & B PER PERSON PER NIGHT		DINNER B & B PER PERSON PER WEEK		10
	MIN £	MAX £	MIN £	MAX £	OPEN
	6.50	6.75	70	73.50	3—10

St. Kilda Private Hotel*

Central Promenade, Llandudno
Gwynedd LL30 2XS
Tel: (0492) 76348

CATEGORIES: 2 3 3

Premier position: central promenade. Shops, amusements, indoor pool within walking distance. Lounge overlooking sea. Welsh Bar. Games room. Passenger lift. Bedrooms have strip lights, shaving sockets, TV, radio and electric fires. Options of breakfast, lunch and dinner in ground floor dining room. "Our family looking after your family."

C	B & B PER PERSON PER NIGHT		DINNER B & B PER PERSON PER WEEK		37
	MIN £	MAX £	MIN £	MAX £	OPEN
	8.50	9.50	72	80	3—10

The St. Tudno Hotel

North Parade, Llandudno
Gwynedd LL30 2LP
Tel: (0492) 76309

CATEGORIES: 4 4 4

Highly recommended for excellent cuisine and hospitality. This luxury, family-run hotel has all rooms with private bathroom, colour television, fridge, tea facilities. Lift, new Garden Room, restaurant, Victorian bar lounge. Unrivalled seafront position opposite pier. Our personal attention ensures a memorable holiday. Children welcome, generous reductions (our brochure with pleasure).

T / C	B & B PER PERSON PER NIGHT		DINNER B & B PER PERSON PER WEEK		21
	MIN £	MAX £	MIN £	MAX £	OPEN
	13	19	102	155	3—11

Sandilands Hotel*

Dale Road, West Shore
Llandudno, Gwynedd LL30 2B6
Tel: (0492) 75555

CATEGORIES: 3 3 3

Situated on sunny West Shore, seconds from beach. Friendliness pervades this bright and comfortable hotel. Attractive cocktail bar, spacious dining room, comfortable lounge. Fully fitted bedrooms. Cleanliness, quality and quantity of food assured. Free car park. Access to hotel all day. Brochure from Fred and Margaret French, resident proprietors.

C	B & B PER PERSON PER NIGHT		DINNER B & B PER PERSON PER WEEK		11
	MIN £	MAX £	MIN £	MAX £	OPEN
	7.35	8.40	69.50	76	4—10

Sandringham Hotel*

West Parade, West Shore
Llandudno, Gwynedd LL30 2BD
Tel: (0492) 76513/76447

CATEGORIES: 3 4 3

This detached, licensed, seafront hotel has unrivalled views of the Snowdonia Range and Anglesey. Full central heating. Most bedrooms on first floor with seaview, TV, radio-alarm, some en-suite. Choice of meals, bar lunches, sun conservatory. Parking for residents. A warm welcome awaits you from Mr & Mrs Kavanagh. SAE for brochure. AA and RAC listed.

T / C	B & B PER PERSON PER NIGHT		DINNER B & B PER PERSON PER WEEK		18
	MIN £	MAX £	MIN £	MAX £	OPEN
	9	10	87.50	98	3—11

Somerset Hotel*

St. George's Crescent
The Promenade, Llandudno
Gwynedd LL30 2LF
Tel: (0492) 76540

CATEGORIES: 3 3 4

A family-run hotel with your comfort in mind. On the seafront, near to the pier and also the shopping centre. Large car park, free for residents. TV lounge, cocktail bar. Lift to all floors. Many rooms with bath, shower, toilet, colour TV a warm welcome awaits you from Brenda and Grahame Winter.

T / C	B & B PER PERSON PER NIGHT		DINNER B & B PER PERSON PER WEEK		36
	MIN £	MAX £	MIN £	MAX £	OPEN
	9.50	11.50	95	110	4—10

Sunnymede Hotel*

West Parade, West Shore
Llandudno, Gwynedd LL30 2BD
Tel: (0492) 77130

CATEGORIES: 3 4 4

Sunnymede is a privately owned and run AA and RAC One star hotel on the front of West Shore. Delightfully appointed bedrooms some with bath en-suite. Ground floor rooms, all with tea-making facilities and radios. Two super lounges. Large, private car park. Breaks available at attractive rates.

T / C	B & B PER PERSON PER NIGHT		DINNER B & B PER PERSON PER WEEK		18
	MIN £	MAX £	MIN £	MAX £	OPEN
	9	11	90	110	3—11

Tan Lan Hotel*

West Shore, Llandudno
North Wales LL30 2AR
Tel: (0492) 75981

CATEGORIES: 3 4 4

Lovely position in Llandudno's West Shore. This privately owned hotel offers quality throughout. Licensed, AA* and RAC.* Choice of menu, central heating ground and first floor bedrooms only. Private bathrooms available. Easy parking. Tea-making facilities all bedrooms, television in some. Ideal situation for touring nearby castles and Snowdonia.

T / C	B & B PER PERSON PER NIGHT		DINNER B & B PER PERSON PER WEEK		19
	MIN £	MAX £	MIN £	MAX £	OPEN
	10.50	11.80	92.50	101.50	3—10

Thorpe House*

3 St. David's Road, Llandudno
Gwynedd LL30 2UL
Tel: (0492) 77089

CATEGORIES

1	4	3

Hot and cold water and shaver points in all bedrooms. Single, double and family rooms with special rates for children. Lounge with colour television. Dining room with separate tables. Full central heating. Fire Certificate. Ideally situated for golf, fishing horse riding, walking, beaches and touring Snowdonia.

T	B & B PER PERSON PER NIGHT		DINNER B & B PER PERSON PER WEEK		11
C	MIN £	MAX £	MIN £	MAX £	OPEN
	6.50	7.50	56	63	1—12

Uxbridge Hotel*

Clonmel Street, Llandudno
Gwynedd LL30 2LE
Tel: (0492) 77383

CATEGORIES

2	3	3

Welcome to our family-run, licensed hotel just off the main promenade. Ideally situated for sea and shops, also touring Snowdonia. Some bedrooms with showers and family bedrooms with reduced rates for children. Pleasant dining room and bar, lounge with colour television. Partial central heating. Fire Certificate granted.

T	B & B PER PERSON PER NIGHT		DINNER B & B PER PERSON PER WEEK		12
C	MIN £	MAX £	MIN £	MAX £	OPEN
	8	9	65	75	1—12

Wellington Private Hotel*

opposite Pier, Promenade
Llandudno, Gwynedd LL30 2LP
Tel: (0492) 76709

CATEGORIES

3	3	2

Family-run, private hotel in prime position at the "right end" of promenade. Views over whole bay. Adjacent Happy Valley and shopping centre. Electric kettles available. Bathing on four star beach opposite. Well recommended food. Friendly service and every comfort guaranteed. Send SAE for brochure. Hotel established 1933 by present owners.

C	B & B PER PERSON PER NIGHT		DINNER B & B PER PERSON PER WEEK		12
	MIN £	MAX £	MIN £	MAX £	OPEN
	7	7.50	60	68	5—9

Westdale Hotel*

37 Abbey Road, Llandudno
Gwynedd LL30 2EH
Tel: (0492) 77996

CATEGORIES

2	3	2

Quietly situated with open views of the southern face of Great Orme. Opposite are the famous Haulfre Gardens and nearby is the promenade and the panoramic West Shore. Short walk from pier, pavilion, shops, beaches and amusements. Privately-run with personal service from resident proprietors. Excellent varied menu.

T	B & B PER PERSON PER NIGHT		DINNER B & B PER PERSON PER WEEK		12
C	MIN £	MAX £	MIN £	MAX £	OPEN
	6.75	7.50	61	64	4—10

White Court Hotel

2 North Parade, Llandudno
Gwynedd LL30 2LP
Tel: (0492) 76719

CATEGORIES

2	3	3

White Court Hotel, North Parade, Llandudno, Gwynedd, telephone number (0492) 76719. Situated on North Parade making us close to all amenities. A delightful family-run hotel with friendly atmosphere. Radio/intercom, baby-listening. Toilets all floors, ground floor bedroom, TV lounge. Separate bar lounge. Fire Certificate. Joan and Cliff Wright.

C	B & B PER PERSON PER NIGHT		DINNER B & B PER PERSON PER WEEK		16
	MIN £	MAX £	MIN £	MAX £	OPEN
	7	8	59.50	73.60	3—10

The Woodlee Hotel*

West Shore, Llandudno
Gwynedd LL30 2BP
Tel: (0492) 77702

CATEGORIES

3	4	3

Situated on level on Llandudno's lovely West Shore. Famed for its views and sunsets. Convenient for golf, fishing, walking and touring Snowdonia. Bedrooms on two floors. Radios, tea-making facilities, central heating, separate dining tables with excellent cuisine. Fire Certificate. Children welcome. Car parking readily available. Party enquiries welcome.

T	B & B PER PERSON PER NIGHT		DINNER B & B PER PERSON PER WEEK		22
C	MIN £	MAX £	MIN £	MAX £	OPEN
	9.50	11.50	87	95.50	3—10

Guest Houses

Asgard House

4 Charlton Street, Llandudno
Gwynedd LL30 2AA
Tel: (0492) 76893

CATEGORIES

1	2	2

Comfortable, licensed guest house conveniently situated for rail and coach services, beach and town centre. Colour TV, lounge separate from licensed bar. Single, double and family rooms with reductions for children. Hot drinks available all day.

C	B & B PER PERSON PER NIGHT		DINNER B & B PER PERSON PER WEEK		9
	MIN £	MAX £	MIN £	MAX £	OPEN
	5.50	6.50	52.50	59.50	4—10

Belmont

18 Clifton Road
Llandudno, Gwynedd
Tel: (0492) 77179

CATEGORIES

2	3	3

A small, homely guest house situated within easy walking distance of both shores and town centre. Highly recommended for good food and friendly atmosphere. Separate tables in dining room. Colour TV Lounge. Hot and cold water in all rooms. Razor point, part central heating, own keys. Fire Certificate. Parking nearby, Dinner 1p.m. Sunday. Access to house all day.

C	B & B PER PERSON PER NIGHT		DINNER B & B PER PERSON PER WEEK		7
	MIN £	MAX £	MIN £	MAX £	OPEN
	5.50	6.50	49	53	3—10

Braemar Guest House*

5 St. David's Road, Llandudno
Gwynedd LL30 2UL
Tel: (0492) 76257

CATEGORIES

3	3	3

Situated in select residential area. Mid-way both shores on the level for shops, beach, entertainment. Family-run hotel that offers all home comforts. Highly recommened for service and food. Central heating, colour TV, lounge. Separate tables in dining room. Open all year. SAE please for brochure. Fire Certificate granted.

T	B & B PER PERSON PER NIGHT		DINNER B & B PER PERSON PER WEEK		7
C	MIN £	MAX £	MIN £	MAX £	OPEN
	6.50	7.50	55	60	1—12

Bryn Hazel Guest House*

10 Harcourt Road, Craig-y-Don
Llandudno LL30 1TU
Tel: (0492) 75098

CATEGORIES

2	3	2

Small, friendly guest house situated in quiet tree-lined road, close to park, bowling green, tennis courts. A short distance from beach, shops, entertainment. Single, double, family rooms available, all with hot and cold water. Lounge with colour TV. Part central heating. Fire Certificate granted. Open Christmas.

T	B & B PER PERSON PER NIGHT		DINNER B & B PER PERSON PER WEEK		6
C	MIN £	MAX £	MIN £	MAX £	OPEN
	5.50	6.50	50	56	1—12

Corwen Guest House

126 Mostyn Street
Llandudno, Gwynedd
Tel: (0492) 75452

CATEGORIES

| 3 | 3 | 2 |

Ideal for short and weekend breaks, all through the year. Situated in Llandudno's main shopping street. Tastefully furnished rooms; excellent food in comfortable dining room. Good value with personal service—bedrooms have central heating, colour televisions and tea-making facilities. Full Fire Certificate. Access and visa cards accepted.

	B & B PER PERSON PER NIGHT		DINNER B & B PER PERSON PER WEEK		4
T C	MIN £	MAX £	MIN £	MAX £	OPEN
	7	8	63	70	1—12

Crewood Guest House*

77 Mostyn Avenue, Craig-y-Don
Llandudno, Gwynedd LL30 1DZ
Tel: (0492) 76366

CATEGORIES

| 3 | 3 | 2 |

Highly recommended, small guest house pleasantly situated close to promenade and all entertainment. Excellent cuisine, separate tables in dining room, lounge with colour TV. Hot and cold water in every bedroom. All-day access. Reduced rates for children sharing parents' room. Midweek bookings accepted.

	B & B PER PERSON PER NIGHT		DINNER B & B PER PERSON PER WEEK		6
C	MIN £	MAX £	MIN £	MAX £	OPEN
	6.50	7	59	63	5—10

Elgin Lodge*

14 Abbey Road, Llandudno
Gwynedd LL30 2EA
Tel: (0492) 78486

CATEGORIES

| 3 | 3 | 2 |

Pleasant location close to all amenities. Small private car park. Central heating. Reduction for children sharing parents' rooms. Open all year except Christmas. Fire Certificate. Comfortable lounge with colour TV. Our aim is to make you want to come again.

	B & B PER PERSON PER NIGHT		DINNER B & B PER PERSON PER WEEK		8
C	MIN £	MAX £	MIN £	MAX £	OPEN
	6	6.50	56	60	1—11

This symbol means you can book through your local travel agent.

Glenvine*

45 Church Walks
Llandudno, Gwynedd
Tel: (0492) 75850

CATEGORIES

| 2 | 2 | 3 |

A homely guest house situated at foot of Great Orme. Recommended for good food. Children welcome, reduced rates. Free baby-sitting, large garden with swings etc., Panoramic views. Separate tables in dining room. Own keys. Colour TV lounge. Our aim is to please. SAE for brochure and tariff.

	B & B PER PERSON PER NIGHT		DINNER B & B PER PERSON PER WEEK		5
T C	MIN £	MAX £	MIN £	MAX £	OPEN
	6	7	56	63	2—10

Hawarden Villa

27 Chapel Street
Llandudno
Tel: (0492) 75447

CATEGORIES

| 2 | 2 | 2 |

3 minutes from sea, hot and cold water all rooms. Access to rooms all day. Television lounge, dining room with separate tables, part central heating, car parking at the rear. Full Fire Certificate.

	B & B PER PERSON PER NIGHT		DINNER B & B PER PERSON PER WEEK		8
C	MIN £	MAX £	MIN £	MAX £	OPEN
	6		56		4—10

Kimberley Guest House

38 St. Mary's Road, Llandudno
Gwynedd LL30 2UE
Tel: (0492) 76573

CATEGORIES

| 3 | 3 | 3 |

Kimberley is run by a husband and wife team, whose aim is to offer a comfortable family-style atmosphere, simple cooked food, with just a touch of elegance in the decor. Special attention given to elderly guests by proprietor's wife, who is a State Registered Nurse.

	B & B PER PERSON PER NIGHT		DINNER B & B PER PERSON PER WEEK		5
C	MIN £	MAX £	MIN £	MAX £	OPEN
	5.50	6	50	57	1—12

Melrose

41 St. Mary's Road, Llandudno
Gwynedd LL30 2UE
Tel: (0492) 76712

CATEGORIES

| 1 | 2 | 1 |

Modern guest house situated in select, central area. Separate tables, comfortable lounge, colour TV. Hot and cold water, spring interiors, bed lights, razor plugs. Access to rooms all day: own key. Fire Certificate. Please send SAE for brochure to Mrs. S. Heritage.

	B & B PER PERSON PER NIGHT		DINNER B & B PER PERSON PER WEEK		5
C	MIN £	MAX £	MIN £	MAX £	OPEN
	5.50	6.50			4—10

Oakwood*

21 St. David's Road, Llandudno
Gwynedd LL30 2UH
Tel: (0492) 79208

CATEGORIES

| 3 | 3 | 2 |

A well-appointed Guest house situated on the level, close to both shores and all amenities. Ample road parking. High standard of personal service and home cooking in a friendly, relaxed atmosphere. Hot and cold water, shaver points and bedside lamps in all bedrooms. Colour TV lounge, plus separate reception lounge. Public telephone. Full access at all times. Children welcome (reduced terms when sharing)— free baby-listening service. Full central heating. Fire Certificate. Garden furniture for guests' use.

	B & B PER PERSON PER NIGHT		DINNER B & B PER PERSON PER WEEK		6
C	MIN £	MAX £	MIN £	MAX £	OPEN
	5.50	6.50	56	63	4—9

St. Helier Guest House*

10 Clifton Road,
Llandudno, Gwynedd
Tel: (0492) 78379

CATEGORIES

| 3 | 3 | 2 |

Access to rooms all day: own keys. Hot and cold water all bedrooms. Shaver points and bed lights. Children welcome. Baby-sitting service. Reduced terms for children. Very comfortable lounge. Full central heating. Full fire precautions. Highly recommended. Member of Llandudno Hotels Association. Centrally situated, close to all amenities.

	B & B PER PERSON PER NIGHT		DINNER B & B PER PERSON PER WEEK		7
C	MIN £	MAX £	MIN £	MAX £	OPEN
	6	7	50.75	56	4—9

Victoria House*

415 Victoria Street
Llandudno, Gwynedd
Tel: (0492) 79920

CATEGORIES

| 2 | 3 | 3 |

2 singles, 4 doubles, 3 family rooms. Radios in each room. 2 public bathrooms. Bed and breakfast from £4.95 to £5.50 (single), £9.90 to £11 (double). Bed and breakfast, evening meal from £7 to £7.50 per night. Evening meal from 6 p.m.-7 p.m.

	B & B PER PERSON PER NIGHT		DINNER B & B PER PERSON PER WEEK		9
T C	MIN £	MAX £	MIN £	MAX £	OPEN
	4.95	5.50	36.75	52.50	1—12

Walsall House

4 Chapel Street, Llandudno
Gwynedd LL30 2SY
Tel: (0492) 75279

CATEGORIES: 1 2 2

Small, private guest house in a good residential area, central to all amenities. Bedrooms are comfortably furnished and each have hot and cold water and shaver points. Own key with freedom of access at all times. Resident's lounge with colour TV. Good, varied menu. Fire precautions installed.

C	B & B PER PERSON PER NIGHT		DINNER B & B PER PERSON PER WEEK		8
	MIN £	MAX £	MIN £	MAX £	OPEN
	5	6	42	52	4—10

Llandudno Junction
NORTH WALES

Farmhouse

Garth Fawr Farm*

Llangystennin, Llandudno Junction
Gwynedd LL31 9JF
Tel: (0492) 44646

CATEGORIES: 3 3 1

A pleasant farmhouse offering 3 comfortable rooms and a warm welcome. Hot and cold water, shaver points and central heating in all rooms. Lounge with colour TV and dining room with separate tables. Situated mid-way between Colwyn Bay, Conwy and Llandudno, at the gateway to Snowdonia.

C	B & B PER PERSON PER NIGHT		DINNER B & B PER PERSON PER WEEK		3
	MIN £	MAX £	MIN £	MAX £	OPEN
	6	6.50			4—10

Llandysul
MID WALES

Farmhouse

Pant-y-Croi

Llandysul
Dyfed
Tel: (055 934) 613

CATEGORIES: 3 3 2

Farmhouse, specialising in calf-rearing. Situated in picturesque valley with close-running river, ideal for fishing, pony trekking nearby. Easy reach of Carmarthen and Cardigan coast. Ideal facilities for children, and pets welcome. Beautiful countryside all around and very quiet but village only 2 miles away.

C	B & B PER PERSON PER NIGHT		DINNER B & B PER PERSON PER WEEK		3
	MIN £	MAX £	MIN £	MAX £	OPEN
	6.50	7.50	59.50	66.50	3—10

Llanelli
SOUTH WALES

Hotels

Ashburnham Hotel*

Pembrey, near Burry Port
Dyfed SA16 0TH
Tel: (05546) 2328/2442

CATEGORIES: 3 3 5

Small, comfortable hotel quietly situated opposite the well-known Ashburnham Golf Course, with fine views over Carmarthen Bay. Within easy reach of splendid coastline and Pembrey Country Park. Centrally heated throughout. Colour TV lounge. Ample parking. Tudor-style restaurant and spacious bar. Weekend terms offered.

T C	B & B PER PERSON PER NIGHT		DINNER B & B PER PERSON PER WEEK		11
	MIN £	MAX £	MIN £	MAX £	OPEN
	11.50	12.50	87.50	95	1—12

Stradey Park Hotel*

Furnace, Llanelli
Dyfed SA15 4HA
Tel: (05542) 58171 Telex 48521

CATEGORIES: 4 5 5

Built round an old manor house, this hotel standing above Llanelli has 77 bedrooms, all with private bath, telephone, radio, colour TV, and tea/coffee-making facilities. Central heating and ample car parking. Weekend and Mid-Week Bargain Breaks available. Good centre for touring the Gower Peninsula.

T C	B & B PER PERSON PER NIGHT		DINNER B & B PER PERSON PER WEEK		80
	MIN £	MAX £	MIN £	MAX £	OPEN
	19.25				1—12

Guest Houses

The Croft Hotel

89 Queen Victoria Road
Llanelli, Dyfed SA15 2TR
Tel: (05542) 4539

CATEGORIES: 3 3 2

3 minutes to shops, buses and beach. Hot and cold water and shaver points in all bedrooms. Single, double and family rooms with special rates for children. Lounge with colour television. Dining room with separate tables. Full central heating. Fire Certificate granted. Free car park. Licensed bar.

C	B & B PER PERSON PER NIGHT		DINNER B & B PER PERSON PER WEEK		17
	MIN £	MAX £	MIN £	MAX £	OPEN
	7	7	60	60	1—12

Llanfairfechan
NORTH WALES

Hotel

Chatham House Hotel

Penmaenmawr Road
Llanfairfechan, Gwynedd LL33 0PN
Tel: (0248) 680138

CATEGORIES: 3 4 2

Jackie and Bill Bintley offer you a warm welcome to their comfortable hotel, situated close to the beach and surrounded by beautiful countryside and the Snowdonia National Park. Comfortable lounge and dining room with bar overlooking the sea with views of Anglesey. Large car park. Packed lunches available.

T C	B & B PER PERSON PER NIGHT		DINNER B & B PER PERSON PER WEEK		9
	MIN £	MAX £	MIN £	MAX £	OPEN
	6	7.50	58	65	1—12

Llanfair-ynghornwy
NORTH WALES

Guest House

The Old Rectory

Llanfairynghornwy, Isle of Anglesey
Gwynedd LL65 4LH
Tel: (0407 88) 741

CATEGORIES: 3 3 3

Georgian rectory situated in countryside of outstanding natural beauty, near rocky coves and sandy bays. A quiet and unspoilt corner of Anglesey. Two tennis courts and sheltered, sunny swimming pool. Garden ideal for picnic lunches. Home cooking using fresh garden and local produce. Lounge with colour television, games room with table tennis. All bedrooms en-suite. Golf, sailing, riding, fresh and sea water fishing nearby. Tennis a special feature (coaching available). Families welcome.

T C	B & B PER PERSON PER NIGHT		DINNER B & B PER PERSON PER WEEK		6
	MIN £	MAX £	MIN £	MAX £	OPEN
	9		94.50		1—12

Tourist Information Centres are listed at back of book.

Llanfyllin

Hotels

Bodfach Hall*

Llanfyllin
Powys SY22 5HS
Tel: (069184) 272

CATEGORIES

| 4 | 4 | 4 |

Privately owned and operated. We offer unsophisticated comfort and a sincere welcome to our visitors. Our lovely old house is secluded in 4 acres of gardens well off the road. Only 9 bedrooms, most with bathrooms. Good homely food, interesting wine list. Llanfyllin is an ideal touring centre.

C	B & B PER PERSON PER NIGHT		DINNER B & B PER PERSON PER WEEK		🛏 9
	MIN £	MAX £	MIN £	MAX £	OPEN
	14		122.50		3—10

Cain Valley Hotel

High Street, Llanfyllin
Powys
Tel: (069 184) 366

CATEGORIES

| 4 | 4 | 5 |

The hotel is a small country inn with a reputation for good food; rich in beams and cosy atmosphere. The building dates more than 350 years. The wood beam staircase is a show-piece as are the old paintings on glass in the oak panelled lounge bar. Central heating throughout. Summer Breaks available, July, August, September—£14.50 dinner, bed and breakfast, per person per night. Minimum stay 2 nights. Winter Breaks also available.

T	B & B PER PERSON PER NIGHT		DINNER B & B PER PERSON PER WEEK		🛏 12
C	MIN £	MAX £	MIN £	MAX £	OPEN
	12	14.50	70	95	1—12

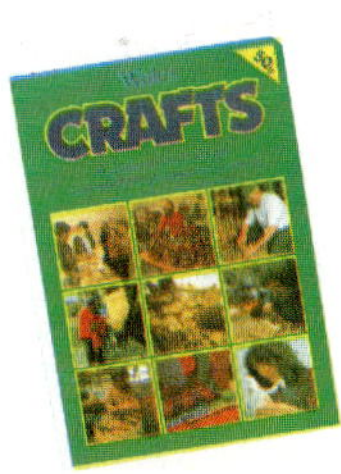

Crafts

Attractive, completely revised guide to craft workshops in Wales – including woollen mills, potteries, slate, stone and woodcarvers, jewellery, metal and leatherworkers. Available from: Wales Tourist Board Department W.T.S. P.O. Box 1, CARDIFF CF1 2XN. Price: 65p including postage and packing.

Farmhouses

Cyfie Farm*

Llanfihangel, Yng Ngwynfa
Llanfyllin, Powys SY22 5JE
Tel: (069184) 451

CATEGORIES

| 4 | 3 | 2 |

178 acre hill farm (sheep, cattle). Welsh long house of character. Inglenook fireplace, quaint beamed rooms. Stable attached. Tastefully converted into bedroom with shower/toilet en-suite together with ground floor, lounge, colour TV. Short drive Lake Vyrnwy, Bala. 1 hour sea. True farm life atmosphere with warm welcome. Excellent farm fare.

T	B & B PER PERSON PER NIGHT		DINNER B & B PER PERSON PER WEEK		🛏 3
C	MIN £	MAX £	MIN £	MAX £	OPEN
	7.50		75	82	1—12

Waen Uchaf

Bwlch-y-Cibau, Llanfyllin
Powys SY22 5LT
Tel: (069184) 577

CATEGORIES

| 3 | 2 | 2 |

Quietly situated country house with marvellous views, offering peace, comfort, warmth and a variety of good home-produced fresh food. Excellent fishing, golf, touring and walking area. Free riding and shooting available. No pets. Illustrated brochure.

T	B & B PER PERSON PER NIGHT		DINNER B & B PER PERSON PER WEEK		🛏 3
C	MIN £	MAX £	MIN £	MAX £	OPEN
	9.20	12	75	80	1—12

Llangadog

Guesthouse

"Cefn Cilgwyn"*

Llangadog
Dyfed SA19 9LF
Tel: (05503) 493

CATEGORIES

| 3 | 3 | 2 |

Centuries old country house with all modern comforts. Situated in beautiful, wooded valley bordering Brecon Beacons National Park. Garden, ample parking in cobbled yard. Home-grown and local produce. Personal attention. Central heating. Ideal for walking, birdwatching, fishing, golf, pony trekking. Families welcome. Cot, highchair, baby-sitting. Brochure available.

T	B & B PER PERSON PER NIGHT		DINNER B & B PER PERSON PER WEEK		🛏 2
C	MIN £	MAX £	MIN £	MAX £	OPEN
	7	8			1—12

Farmhouse

Cynyll Farm

Llangadog
Dyfed SA19 9BB
Tel: (05503) 316

CATEGORIES

| 1 | 2 | 2 |

76 acre dairy farm 1 mile from Llangadog. Salmon and trout fishing, pony trekking within locality. Central for touring Brecon Beacons, Llyn Brianne Dam, Gold mine, various lakes, caves and castles. Black mountains visible from farmhouse. Good food: fresh, home-grown vegetables, milk cream and free-range eggs.

C	B & B PER PERSON PER NIGHT		DINNER B & B PER PERSON PER WEEK		🛏 4
	MIN £	MAX £	MIN £	MAX £	OPEN
	5	6.50	45	50	4—10

Llangammarch Wells

Hotel

Lake Hotel

Llangammarch Wells
Powys LD4 4BS
Tel: (05912) 202

CATEGORIES

| 4 | 4 | 4 |

50 acres private grounds. 9-hole golf course, putting green, tennis court. Two and a half acre trout lake. Riding and trekking available. Five and a half miles trout and salmon fishing. All bedrooms: colour television and tea-making facilities. Billiard room. Fine country cuisine. Dogs and children are welcome.

T	B & B PER PERSON PER NIGHT		DINNER B & B PER PERSON PER WEEK		🛏 29
C	MIN £	MAX £	MIN £	MAX £	OPEN
	12	18	100	150	1—12

Don't forget that 1983 is Festival of Castles Year in Wales with events planned for all the major historic sites.

Farmhouse

Nant Fadog Farm

Rhosheirch, Llangefni
Isle of Anglesey, Gwynedd LL77 7RJ
Tel: (0248) 722123

CATEGORIES

| 1 | 2 | 2 |

The 170 acre farm is situated 2 miles from Llangefni, the main market town of Anglesey. Car is essential but we are within easy reach of all beaches. We have a safe play area for young children and a large lawn ideal for various games.

C	B & B PER PERSON PER NIGHT		DINNER B & B PER PERSON PER WEEK		2
	MIN £	MAX £	MIN £	MAX £	OPEN
	5	6	59.50	63	1—12

Hotel

Burrows Hall Hotel and Trekking Centre

Llangennith, Gower
West Glamorgan SA3 1HU
Tel: (044127) 221

CATEGORIES

| 1 | 3 | 2 |

Surrounded by fine, unspoilt beaches in an area of outstanding natural beauty. Licensed country hotel. 20 bedrooms, w.c. Sea views. Well-stocked bar. Excellent food. Pleasant service. Two lounges, games room. Trekking centre adjoining: sensible ponies for those who wish to explore on horseback. Disciplined dogs welcome. Brochure available.

T C	B & B PER PERSON PER NIGHT		DINNER B & B PER PERSON PER WEEK		20
	MIN £	MAX £	MIN £	MAX £	OPEN
	7	7	75	85	1—12

Inn

The Stag Hotel*

Llangernyw, Abergele
Clwyd LL22 8PP
Tel: (074576) 213

CATEGORIES

| 3 | 3 | 4 |

17th century inn. Full of charm and well renowned throughout North Wales for both its good food, and its relaxing olde worlde atmosphere. Offers very comfortable accommodation with all modern amenities. Within easy reach of the whole of Snowdonia and all the coastal resorts.

	B & B PER PERSON PER NIGHT		DINNER B & B PER PERSON PER WEEK		5
	MIN £	MAX £	MIN £	MAX £	OPEN
	8.34	10.93	95	120	1—12

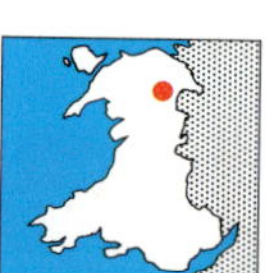

Map ref: Ec1
Beauty spot in the deep, wooded Vale of Llangollen. Beneath towering castle-crowned hills, beside the sparkling, tumbling river Dee. Offa's Dyke Path follows the rim of the vale. There is a brightly painted steam railway in the town, Llangollen Canal— with its Canal Museum—winds up to Horseshoe Falls where remains of Valle Crucis Abbey, and Eliseg's 9th century pillar, remind us of by-gone days. But the annual July week-long International Musical Eisteddfod is the town's high spot.

Hotels, Inns

The Britannia Inn*

Horseshoe Pass, Llangollen
Clwyd LL20 8DW
Tel: (0978) 860144

CATEGORIES

| 3 | 4 | 4 |

Residential free house. Egon Ronay Grade 1 accommodation. This 15th century inn provides all modern amenities and is an ideal centre for walking, touring or just relaxing. A comprehensive menu is served throughout the inn. Autumn to Spring Bargain Break holidays available. Resident owners, Maureen and Cyril Ashton.

	B & B PER PERSON PER NIGHT		DINNER B & B PER PERSON PER WEEK		6
	MIN £	MAX £	MIN £	MAX £	OPEN
	12	15	125	150	1—12

Bryn Derwen Hotel*

Abbey Road, Llangollen
Clwyd LL20 8EF
Tel: (0978) 860583 Telex 837595

CATEGORIES

| 4 | 3 | 4 |

Homely hotel in tranquil surroundings, overlooking the River Dee and Berwyn Mountains. Single, double and family rooms with special rates for children including intercom baby-listening service. Most bedrooms have private bathrooms and TV. Full central heating, television lounge, cellar bar, sauna and solarium facilities. High class cuisine to suit every pocket. Centrally situated for golf, pony trekking, tennis, canoeing, rambling, squash, bowls, shooting, fishing, touring and even relaxing. Nostalgic steam trains and horse-drawn barges pass the hotel. Breaks available at attractive rates.

T C	B & B PER PERSON PER NIGHT		DINNER B & B PER PERSON PER WEEK		14
	MIN £	MAX £	MIN £	MAX £	OPEN
	12.50	13	110	126	1—12

Chainbridge Hotel*

Berwyn, Llangollen
North Wales LL20 8BS
Tel: (0978) 860215

CATEGORIES

| 5 | 4 | 5 |

Nestling in the peaceful Vale of Llangollen on the banks of the Dee, combines traditional character with every modern comfort. Ideal for walking, fishing, golfing. Excellent cuisine in a restaurant with a panoramic view, overlooking the river. Candlelight dinner dance Saturday evenings.

T	B & B PER PERSON PER NIGHT		DINNER B & B PER PERSON PER WEEK		35
C	MIN £	MAX £	MIN £	MAX £	OPEN
	12	17.50	115	150	1—12

The Conquering Hero Inn

Rhewl, Llangollen
Clwyd
Tel: (0978) 860 647

CATEGORIES

| 1 | 2 | 3 |

Breathtaking views and farmyard smells. Fishing permits available for huge salmon and trout in adjacent River Dee. Very steep walks. O.S. maps sold at the bar. Real ale, real food, real fire, real sheep. Roads are snow-free in summer months.

T	B & B PER PERSON PER NIGHT		DINNER B & B PER PERSON PER WEEK		3
C	MIN £	MAX £	MIN £	MAX £	OPEN
	5	8	30	50	1—12

Hand Hotel*

Bridge Street, Llangollen, Clwyd
North Wales LL20 8PL
Tel: (0978) 860303 Telex 61160

CATEGORIES

| 5 | 5 | 5 |

Set on a bank of the river Dee, the Hand Hotel retains its tradition of hospitality to the traveller founded in the old coaching days: only the comfort has been improved. Ample car parking. A warm and welcoming atmosphere and a fine restaurant complement the excellent facilities. Value Breaks available all year.

T	B & B PER PERSON PER NIGHT		DINNER B & B PER PERSON PER WEEK		59
C	MIN £	MAX £	MIN £	MAX £	OPEN
	19.25	22			1—12

Royal Hotel

Bridge Street, Llangollen
Clwyd LL20 8PG
Tel: (0978) 860202

CATEGORIES

| 5 | 4 | 4 |

Situated on the banks of the River Dee by the bridge. This hotel has 33 comfortable bedrooms, many with mountain views and all with private bath, telephone, radio, colour TV and tea/coffee-making facilities. Special bargain breaks available. Ideal base for touring North Wales.

T	B & B PER PERSON PER NIGHT		DINNER B & B PER PERSON PER WEEK		33
C	MIN £	MAX £	MIN £	MAX £	OPEN
	29.75				1—12

Ty'n-y-Wern Hotel

Llangollen, Clwyd
LL20 7PH
Tel: (0978) 860252

CATEGORIES

| 3 | 3 | 4 |

Charming, old country house hotel in spacious grounds amid beautiful scenery, close to Eisteddfod town of Llangollen. Restaurant seats 48. Two attractive bars, TV and tea-making facilities in bedrooms. Open to non-residents. Golf ½ mile, fishing River Dee 200 yards, pony trekking ½ mile. Fire Certificate.

C	B & B PER PERSON PER NIGHT		DINNER B & B PER PERSON PER WEEK		10
	MIN £	MAX £	MIN £	MAX £	OPEN
	13	15	126	140	3—12

The Wild Pheasant Hotel

Berwyn Road, Llangollen
Clwyd LL20 8AD
Tel: (0978) 860629

CATEGORIES

| 5 | 4 | 4 |

An hotel with olde worlde charm, modern amenities set in 17 acres of its own pasture and rough grazing land with wild pheasants and grazing horses to add to the country scene. 11 bedrooms; nine with private shower or bathroom; colour TV, private telephone; radio, intercom and tea/coffee-making facilities.

T	B & B PER PERSON PER NIGHT		DINNER B & B PER PERSON PER WEEK		11
C	MIN £	MAX £	MIN £	MAX £	OPEN
	17	22	140	160	1—12

Guest Houses

Abbey Grange*

Llangollen
Clwyd
Tel: (0978) 860753

CATEGORIES

| 3 | 3 | 2 |

Situated 1½ miles outside Llangollen at the foot of the spectacular Horseshoe Pass. Surrounded by fields, it offers an idyllic setting for your holiday. All rooms have hot and cold water. Licensed residents' bar. Centrally heated. Colour television. Car parking. 5 family rooms; 1 with private bathroom.

T	B & B PER PERSON PER NIGHT		DINNER B & B PER PERSON PER WEEK		5
C	MIN £	MAX £	MIN £	MAX £	OPEN
	7	8	70	80	1—12

"Mia-Casa"*

Grange Road, Llangollen
Clwyd LL20 8AQ
Tel: (0978) 860491

CATEGORIES

| 1 | 1 | 1 |

Modern bungalow situated in peaceful setting with panoramic views. Only 5 minutes walk from Langollen town. Salmon, trout and grayling fishing on Welsh Dee. Loan, tackle and instructions arranged. TV, lounge, ample parking Hospitality second to none. Adults only.

	B & B PER PERSON PER NIGHT		DINNER B & B PER PERSON PER WEEK		2
	MIN £	MAX £	MIN £	MAX £	OPEN
	6.50	7.50			1—12

T **This symbol means you can book through your local travel agent.**

The Old Vicarage Guest House

Vicarage Road, Llangollen
Clwyd LL20 8HF
Tel: (0978) 861000 Telex: 860973

CATEGORIES: 2 2 3

Glorious scenery. Touring, trekking, walking, excursions close to town. Quiet, secluded, large gardens. Singles, doubles, twins, family dormitory bedrooms. Hot and cold water; showers available. Open 12 months. Residents' kitchen with hot drinks tray. Residents' lounge, colour TV, children's reductions, baby-sitter. Animals welcome. Ample parking. Leisure centre 4 miles.

	B & B PER PERSON PER NIGHT		DINNER B & B PER PERSON PER WEEK		9
T	MIN £	MAX £	MIN £	MAX £	OPEN
C	6	6.50	55	60	1—12

Farmhouse

Tyn Llan Farmhouse

Llantysilio, Llangollen
Clwyd
Tel: (0978) 860 566

CATEGORIES: 3 2 1

13th century oak-beamed farmhouse, well maintained and extensive garden, set in beautiful Welsh countryside, situated 2 miles outside Llangollen on B5103 road. Mountain walks, fishing in nearby River Dee. Peaceful and quiet. Excellent accommodation: hot and cold water all rooms, lounge, dining room, TV, parking.

	B & B PER PERSON PER NIGHT		DINNER B & B PER PERSON PER WEEK		3
C	MIN £	MAX £	MIN £	MAX £	OPEN
	5.50	6.50			3—10

Inn

Red Lion Hotel

Llangorse, Brecon
Powys LD3 71
Tel: (08 7484) 238

CATEGORIES: 3 4 5

Charming olde worlde inn offering excellent accommodation: 5 bedrooms with bathrooms en-suite, 5 with showers. Two oak-beamed bars with a range of unusual wine, real ale; delicious bar food. Superb resuarant with à la carte and table d'hote menus. Resident proprietors: Wendy and Brian Hibbard. Mid week and Weekend Breaks throughout the year. Egon Ronay, Arthur Eperon, Relais Routiers recommended. AA RAC listed.

	B & B PER PERSON PER NIGHT		DINNER B & B PER PERSON PER WEEK		10
C	MIN £	MAX £	MIN £	MAX £	OPEN
	10	15	112	135	1—12

Farmhouses

Middle–Penllanafal*

Llangorse, Brecon, Powys
LD3 7UN
Tel: (087 484) 307

CATEGORIES: 1 2 2

Middle Penllanafal is a working farm with sheep, cattle and ponies (one for children to ride round farm). Ideally placed for touring Brecon Beacons with walking, pony-riding, golf, fishing and boating; all this adding up to a super holiday, with good food, all freshly cooked by Sandra Hamer.

	B & B PER PERSON PER NIGHT		DINNER B & B PER PERSON PER WEEK		3
T	MIN £	MAX £	MIN £	MAX £	OPEN
C	6		66.50	73	4—10

Upper Penllanafal*

Llangorse, Brecon
Powys
Tel: (0874 84) 206

CATEGORIES: 1 2 3

Working farm, 260 acres. 1 mile off the Abergavenny-Talgarth road. Close to Black Mountains and Brecon Beacons. Trekking locally. There is fishing and sailing at Llangorse Lake. I extend a warm welcome to everyone and specialise in good farmhouse cooking using fresh farm produce. Children welcome. SAE for early reply.

	B & B PER PERSON PER NIGHT		DINNER B & B PER PERSON PER WEEK		2
C	MIN £	MAX £	MIN £	MAX £	OPEN
	42	45	63	70	4—9

Hotel

Pentre Arms Hotel*

Llangrannog, Cardiganshire
Dyfed SA44 6SW
Tel: (023978) 229 and 483

CATEGORIES: 3 3 3

Fully licensed AA and RAC listed residential inn. Situated alongside safe, sandy beach in this picturesque village. Centrally heated and all bedrooms with hot and cold water, shaving points. Ideally situated for bathing, visiting woollen mills and numerous other local crafts; also the many beauty spots which abound in the area. Horse riding, golf, fishing etc., available in the vicinity. Daily/weekly terms and also 'short breaks'. SAE for brochure. Proprietors: Mr. & Mrs. D. M. Wilson.

	B & B PER PERSON PER NIGHT		DINNER B & B PER PERSON PER WEEK		16
C	MIN £	MAX £	MIN £	MAX £	OPEN
	8.50	13.50	85	105	3—10

Farmhouse

Hendre

Llangrannog, Llandysul
Dyfed SA44 6AP
Tel: (023 978) 342

CATEGORIES: 3 3 2

100 acre dairy farm, keeping turkeys and poultry, situated in delightful countryside, 2 miles from Llangrannog's sandy beach. A warm Welsh welcome awaits you in the attractive and comfortable farmhouse. We serve excellent food, using fresh farm produce. Nearby are lovely cliff-top walks, castles, coracles, markets and much more.

	B & B PER PERSON PER NIGHT		DINNER B & B PER PERSON PER WEEK		3
C	MIN £	MAX £	MIN £	MAX £	OPEN
	7	8.50	70	85	4—10

Inns

The Blue Bell Inn*

Llangurig,
Powys SY18 6SG
Tel: (05515) 254

CATEGORIES: 3 3 4

A fine centre for touring Mid Wales. The Blue Bell is a 16th century inn on the River Wye with olde worlde charm carefully retained. Rooms are well appointed and cuisine widely recommended for its excellence. Real ale is served in the frindly bars, also choice of bar meals.

	B & B PER PERSON PER NIGHT		DINNER B & B PER PERSON PER WEEK		10
T	MIN £	MAX £	MIN £	MAX £	OPEN
C	11	14	125	145	1—12

Glansevern Arms Hotel

Pantmawr, Llangurig
Llanidloes, Powys
Tel: (05515) 240

CATEGORIES: 4 3 4

This homely little 18th century inn has lovely views of the River Wye and nearby Tarenig Forest. Individually decorated, cottage-type bedrooms are fully centrally heated, cosy and comfortable, as are the bars and lounge. The inn is renowned for its food and fine wines. Closed 1 week at Christmas.

	B & B PER PERSON PER NIGHT		DINNER B & B PER PERSON PER WEEK		6
C	MIN £	MAX £	MIN £	MAX £	OPEN
	11.25	13	115	140	1—12

Children stay at reduced rates, wherever you see this symbol.

Llangynfelyn

Guest House

Rock House*

Llangynfelin, Machynlleth
Powys SY24 5LN
Tel: (097086) 617

CATEGORIES		
3	2	2

Overlooking Cors Fochno and near Ynyslas Nature Reserve, Ynyshir Bird Sanctuary and Borth. Good centre for hills, countryside and seaside. Fishing, golf, pony trekking etc., locally. Comfortable rooms with hot and cold water, shaver points and tea-making facilities. Home cooking and cheerful service. Children and pets welcome.

T C	B & B PER PERSON PER NIGHT		DINNER B & B PER PERSON PER WEEK		3
	MIN £	MAX £	MIN £	MAX £	OPEN
	6	7	60	70	1—12

Llanidloes

Hotel

Trewython Arms Hotel*

Great Oak Street, Llanidloes
Powys
Tel: (05512) 2214

CATEGORIES		
3	3	3

The hotel is situated next to the Laura Ashley shop in an attractive market town, alongside the River Severn. Children stay free when sharing parents' room (meals extra). Ideal for fishing the local rivers and reservoirs. Pony trekking and sailing available in the area. Countryside ideal for walking.

T C	B & B PER PERSON PER NIGHT		DINNER B & B PER PERSON PER WEEK		11
	MIN £	MAX £	MIN £	MAX £	OPEN
	8.50	11	91	105	1—12

Farmhouse

Esgairmaen Farm

Y Fan, Llanidloes
Powys
Tel: (05516) 272

CATEGORIES		
1	2	1

312 acre mixed farm. 1 double, 1 family room, 1 bathroom. Bed and breakfast from £6 per person. Open January-December. Enquiries: Mrs. L. R. Rees.

	B & B PER PERSON PER NIGHT		DINNER B & B PER PERSON PER WEEK		2
	MIN £	MAX £	MIN £	MAX £	OPEN
	6				1—12

Llannefydd

Inn

Hawk & Buckle Inn*

Llannefydd, near Denbigh
Clwyd LL16 5ED
Tel: (074 579) 249

CATEGORIES		
4	4	3

An old village inn, sitting high on the slopes of the Denbigh hills with panoramic views over the vale of Clwyd and sea. Modern extensions to this old, beamed free house, provide pleasant, centrally heated rooms with private bathrooms, TV and tea-making facilities. Bargain Breaks throughout the year.

T	B & B PER PERSON PER NIGHT		DINNER B & B PER PERSON PER WEEK		10
	MIN £	MAX £	MIN £	MAX £	OPEN
	12.50	18	119	133	1—12

Llanrhaeadr
(Llanrhaeadr yng Nginmerch)

Hotel

Bryn Morfydd Hotel

Llanrhaeadr, near Denbigh
Clwyd LL16 NP
Tel: (074578)313

CATEGORIES		
6	6	6

The North Wales Conference Centre with a bonus, set within the hotel grounds, is a uniquely interesting 9-hole, par 3 golf course with magnificent views. The Princess Golf Course is complimented by en-suite bedrooms, all with colour TV, telephone. Swimming pool, tennis court. Excellent cuisine: restaurant or bar meals. Convenient for North Wales or north west visitors.

T C	B & B PER PERSON PER NIGHT		DINNER B & B PER PERSON PER WEEK		25
	MIN £	MAX £	MIN £	MAX £	OPEN
	15	23	160	190	1—12

Cestyll '83 – 1983 is the year of the castles.

Llanrhaeadr ym Mochnant

Guest House

Plas-yn-Llan

Llanrhaeadr ym Mochnant
near Oswestry, Salop
Tel: (069 189) 236

CATEGORIES		
3	3	2

Llanrhaeadr is situated in an area of great natural beauty. Plas-yn-Llan is a large 17th century house in the centre of the village with oak-beamed rooms and a cobbled courtyard. Children welcome, log fires and home cooking a speciality. Pony trekking, walking, fishing, spinning courses, country pubs.

T C	B & B PER PERSON PER NIGHT		DINNER B & B PER PERSON PER WEEK		5
	MIN £	MAX £	MIN £	MAX £	OPEN
	6	7	56	63	1—12

Llanrhystud

Hotel

Plas Gwyn Hotel

Llanrhystud, near Aberystwyth
Dyfed
Tel: (09748) 206

CATEGORIES		
3	3	4

Under new ownership. 10 miles south of Aberystwyth on main A487 coast road. 5 minutes sea. Georgian mansion in own grounds overlooking Cardigan Bay. Hot and cold water in all bedrooms. Single, double and family rooms. Children welcome. Separate restaurant, fully licensed bars. TV lounge. Ample parking. Fire Certificate granted.

C	B & B PER PERSON PER NIGHT		DINNER B & B PER PERSON PER WEEK		10
	MIN £	MAX £	MIN £	MAX £	OPEN
	10	12	120	140	1—12

Llanrwst

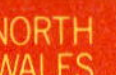

Map ref: Bb6
Towering pine and oak forests, still mountain lakes, the silvery Conwy singing its way under a 17th century Inigo Jones 3-arched bridge; these are the memories you keep of Llanrwst.

Hotels

Corn-U-Copia Court Hotel

Bridge Street, Llanrwst
Gwynedd
Tel: (0492) 640275

CATEGORIES

| 2 | 3 | 2 |

Corn-U-Copia Court Hotel, Bridge Street, Llanrwst, originally a 16th century post house that has been converted into a comfortable hotel, catering for bed, breakfast and other meals. All rooms have hot and cold water, colour TV. Lounge, pool room. Reduced rates for children. Pets welcome.

C	B & B PER PERSON PER NIGHT		DINNER B & B PER PERSON PER WEEK		12
	MIN £	MAX £	MIN £	MAX £	OPEN
	8	9	80	90	1—12

Maenan Abbey Hotel*

Maenan, Llanrwst
Gwynedd LL26 OUL
Tel: (049 269) 247 and 230

CATEGORIES

| 5 | 4 | 5 |

19th century country house situated in spacious gardens. Well appointed bedrooms, most with bathrooms or showers. Fire Certificate granted. Ideally situated for touring Snowdonia and the North Wales coast. Restaurant open to non-residents. A la carte and table d'hote menus. AA** and RAC**

T	B & B PER PERSON PER NIGHT		DINNER B & B PER PERSON PER WEEK		14
C	MIN £	MAX £	MIN £	MAX £	OPEN
	14.50	19.50	154	196	1—12

Meadowsweet Hotel*

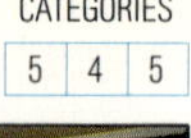

Station Road, Llanrwst
Gwynedd LL26 ODS
Tel: (0492) 640732

CATEGORIES

| 5 | 4 | 5 |

A privately owned licensed and centrally heated hotel overlooking Betws-y-Coed. Each bedroom has a private toilet and shower, as well as TV and GPO telephone. Manx kippers, finnan haddocks and black puddings around at breakfast time. And our dinner menu has earned us recommendation in all the top food guides. Special rates for children. Superb Christmas and New Year house parties. Unquestionably one of the finest hotels in Wales.

T	B & B PER PERSON PER NIGHT		DINNER B & B PER PERSON PER WEEK		10
C	MIN £	MAX £	MIN £	MAX £	OPEN
	12	17	120	170	1—12

Plas Maenan Hotel*

Maenan, Llanrwst
Gwynedd LL26 OYR
Tel: (049 269) 232

CATEGORIES

| 5 | 4 | 5 |

Popularly known as "The Welsh Hotel". BTA commended. AA*** Mentioned Good Hotel Guide. Country cooking, oak-panelled restaurant, harp music, genuine welcome, enthusiastic local staff. 15 bedrooms with cheerful decor, bathroom, colour television, telephone, central heating, drinks tray. Low season bargains. Splendid Snowdonia view. School children accommodated free.

T	B & B PER PERSON PER NIGHT		DINNER B & B PER PERSON PER WEEK		15
C	MIN £	MAX £	MIN £	MAX £	OPEN
	13	15.25	106.50	129.50	1—12

Victoria Hotel*

Llanrwst, Gwynedd
North Wales
Tel: (0492) 640022

CATEGORIES

| 3 | 3 | 4 |

4 miles from Betws-y-Coed overlooking the old Inigo Jones bridge with superb views of Snowdonia National Park. The ideal centre to avoid the traffic and high prices. This friendly hotel where visitors return year after year to enjoy the beauty of Snowdonia, the nearby coast, unspoilt Gwydyr Forest and lakes, and of course, good food with a choice of menu. Reserve by Access. 7 day licence. Ample parking.

T	B & B PER PERSON PER NIGHT		DINNER B & B PER PERSON PER WEEK		18
C	MIN £	MAX £	MIN £	MAX £	OPEN
	8.30		94		3—12

Farmhouse

Mrs. M. Owen*

Bodrach Farm, Llanrwst
Gwynedd LL26 ONY
Tel: (0492) 640 326

CATEGORIES

| 1 | 2 | 2 |

The farm is about 5 miles from the market town of Llanrwst, in a quiet spot with good view of country side and within easy reach of Snowdonia ranges and Bodnant Garden and the coastal towns Colwyn Bay, Llandudno and Rhyl.

C	B & B PER PERSON PER NIGHT		DINNER B & B PER PERSON PER WEEK		2
	MIN £	MAX £	MIN £	MAX £	OPEN
	6	7	56	60	4—11

Llansilin

Farmhouse

Ysgwennant*

Llansilin
Oswestry SY10 7JL
Tel: (069170) 411

CATEGORIES

| 1 | 3 | 2 |

Only 7 miles from Oswestry, but set in a beautiful Welsh valley. Ysgwennant is an Elizabethian farmhouse. It is an ideal centre for touring, walking or pony trekking. Much of the food is home-produced and all home-cooked. The welcome is warm.

C	B & B PER PERSON PER NIGHT		DINNER B & B PER PERSON PER WEEK		3
	MIN £	MAX £	MIN £	MAX £	OPEN
	5	5	45	45	4—10

Tourist Information Centres are listed at back of book.

Llanwrtyd Wells

Hotels

Abernant Lake Hotel

Llanwrtyd Wells
Powys LD5 4RR
Tel: (05913) 250

CATEGORIES: 4 | 4 | 4

Set in own 18 acres and surrounded by spectacular mountain scenery, Abernant is the ideal spot for exploring Mid Wales. Own swimming pool, boating/fishing lake, playground and programme of competitions and entertainments (in season). Special facilities (and prices) for children including supervised nursery and baby-listening.

	B & B PER PERSON PER NIGHT		DINNER B & B PER PERSON PER WEEK		56
T C	MIN £	MAX £	MIN £	MAX £	OPEN
	17.50	21	182	190	1—12

Carlton Court Hotel

Dolecoed Road
Llanwrtyd Wells, Powys
Tel: (05913) 494

CATEGORIES: 3 | 2 | 5

Enjoy lovely holiday. Old fashioned prices at this most attractive, friendly hotel. Home-cooking. Cocktail bar, residents' sun lounge, patio, colour TV. Residents' telephone. Sauna, centrally heated. Choose single, double, twin-bedded, family rooms. With hot and cold water. Fitted carpets throughout. Relax infront of traditional log fire, listen to electric organ. Ideal centre for tourist. Bird-watching, pony trekking, fishing or walking in picturesque areas. Come and see the heart of Wales in all its beauty. Fire Certificate. SAE brochure.

	B & B PER PERSON PER NIGHT		DINNER B & B PER PERSON PER WEEK		8
T C	MIN £	MAX £	MIN £	MAX £	OPEN
	7.50	10.50	69.50	80	4—1

Victoria Wells Holiday Centre

Llanwrtyd Wells
Powys LD5 4SY
Tel: (05913) 334

CATEGORIES: 3 | 2 | 4

Set in beautiful, unspoiled countryside, ideal for all family including pets. 10 centrally heated Scandinavian chalets. Good food served in licensed restaurant. Swimming pool, riding, fishing, bird-watching (red kite); beautiful walks, scenic drives. Summer holidays, Winter/Spring Breaks.

	B & B PER PERSON PER NIGHT		DINNER B & B PER PERSON PER WEEK		20
T C	MIN £	MAX £	MIN £	MAX £	OPEN
	8.50	13	94.50	129.50	3—11

Guest House

Lasswade House*

Station Road, Llanwrtyd Wells
Powys
Tel: (05913) 515

CATEGORIES: 3 | 3 | 5

Spacious accommodation furnished to high standard of comfort. À la carte dinner menu, licensed. Some rooms TV, all with hot and cold water and tea facilites. 3 bathrooms or showers to serve 7 bedrooms. Set in scenic countryside with ready access to trekking, fishing, walking, excellent bird-watching. Central Wales railway line.

	B & B PER PERSON PER NIGHT		DINNER B & B PER PERSON PER WEEK		7
C	MIN £	MAX £	MIN £	MAX £	OPEN
	8	9	82	92	1—12

Llanybydder

Farmhouses

Gwarcoed Einon

Llanwenog
Llanybyther, Dyfed
Tel: (054 555) 605

CATEGORIES: 1 | 2 | 2

Mixed livestock farm. Parking. Children welcome. Ironing facilities. Working farm. Reduced rates for children.

	B & B PER PERSON PER NIGHT		DINNER B & B PER PERSON PER WEEK		3
C	MIN £	MAX £	MIN £	MAX £	OPEN
	5	10	49	49	1—12

Rhiwson Isaf

Drefach, Llanybyther
Lampeter, Dyfed SA40 9TA
Tel: (0570) 480085

CATEGORIES: 1 | 3 | 2

Comfortable farmhouse set in peaceful surroundings on 100 acre dairy farm, only half a mile from nearest village and close to university and market town of Lampeter. Ideal location for touring West Wales and its coastline. Pony trekking, wildlife park, woollen mills, all within easy reach.

	B & B PER PERSON PER NIGHT		DINNER B & B PER PERSON PER WEEK		2
C	MIN £	MAX £	MIN £	MAX £	OPEN
	5.50	6	58	62	4—10

Llwyngwril

Hotel

Garthangharad Hotel

Llwyngwril
Gwynedd LL37 2UZ
Tel: (0341) 250484

CATEGORIES: 3 | 3 | 3

Small, family hotel in this picturesque coastal village. Ideal location for sailing, walking and pony trekking, sea fishing and golf. All these facilities can be booked by arrangement. A very friendly atmosphere exists in this olde worlde hotel which has recently been completely decorated throughout. Open all year.

	B & B PER PERSON PER NIGHT		DINNER B & B PER PERSON PER WEEK		3
C	MIN £	MAX £	MIN £	MAX £	OPEN
	8.50	9	75	80	1—12

Llwyn y Maen NORTH WALES

Hotel

Ashfield Country Hotel

Llwyn-y-Maen,
Trefonen, Near Oswestry
Shropshire SY10 9DD
Tel: (0691) 5200

CATEGORIES

| 4 | 4 | 3 |

Special offer: one week's holiday 1983—£90 per person, bed, breakfast, evening dinner, double or twin bedroom with private bathroom, tea-making facilities. Ashfield is situated on the North Wales border near Llangollen. Ideal for touring North and Mid Wales. Great Little Breaks available. SAE colour brochure to Mrs W. M. Lewis.

	B & B PER PERSON PER NIGHT		DINNER B & B PER PERSON PER WEEK		🛏 14
T **C**	MIN £	MAX £	MIN £	MAX £	OPEN
	9	15	80	140	1—12

Machynlleth MID WALES

Hotel

Wynnstay*

Maengwyn Street, Machynlleth
Powys SY80 8AE
Tel: (0654) 2003

CATEGORIES

| 3 | 3 | 4 |

A typically Welsh country town hotel with 31 comfortable bedrooms, some with private bath, and all with telephone, radio, colour TV and tea/coffee making facilities. Car park. Weekend and mid-week bargain breaks and "Hightime" holidays available. Excellent centre for touring central Wales and the coast.

	B & B PER PERSON PER NIGHT		DINNER B & B PER PERSON PER WEEK		🛏 31
T **C**	MIN £	MAX £	MIN £	MAX £	OPEN
	18.75	21.50			1—12

Guest House

Maenllwyd*

Newtown Road, Machynlleth
Powys SY20 8EY
Tel: (0654) 2928

CATEGORIES

| 3 | 3 | 2 |

Family run guest house with full central heating, hot and cold water and tea making facilities in all rooms. Lounge with colour television. Parking at rear of house. Reduced rates for children. Ideal centre for touring North and South Wales. Golf, fishing, walking nearby.

	B & B PER PERSON PER NIGHT		DINNER B & B PER PERSON PER WEEK		🛏 4
C	MIN £	MAX £	MIN £	MAX £	OPEN
	6.50	7.50	66	77	1—12

Farmhouses

Bacheiddon Farm*

Aberhosan, Machynlleth
SY20 8SG
Tel: (0654) 2229

CATEGORIES

| 1 | 1 | 2 |

Situated six miles from the market town of Machynlleth, we are in easy reach of the sea and of the Snowdonia National Park. All rooms in the farmhouse are comfortable. Guests are accommodated in two double bedrooms and one family bedroom, each with its own toilet and shower.

	B & B PER PERSON PER NIGHT		DINNER B & B PER PERSON PER WEEK		🛏 3
	MIN £	MAX £	MIN £	MAX £	OPEN
	7.50		84		4—10

Cefn Darowen

Cefn Darowen, Machynlleth
Powys SY20 4NS
Tel: (065 02) 336

CATEGORIES

| 1 | 2 | 1 |

Lies at end of small peaceful village amidst beautiful hill farm country central for touring North and Mid Wales and west coast, a country lovers paradise with excellent walking from the house. Oak beamed lounge —dining-room with excellent views. Quiet. Dogs by arrangement.

	B & B PER PERSON PER NIGHT		DINNER B & B PER PERSON PER WEEK		🛏 3
C	MIN £	MAX £	MIN £	MAX £	OPEN
	5	5			1—12

> ### Tourist Information Centres are listed at back of book.

Maentwrog NORTH WALES

Hotel

The Old Rectory

Maentwrog, Blaenau
Ffestiniog LL41 4HN
Tel: (076 685) 305/202

CATEGORIES

| 3 | 3 | 2 |

The Old Rectory stands in its own grounds in the Vale of Ffestiniog in the village of Maentwrog and is over 400 years old. Centrally heated annexe of bedrooms complete with own bathroom suite. Comfortable restaurant, residents lounge with colour TV, pool room and weekend live entertainment.

	B & B PER PERSON PER NIGHT		DINNER B & B PER PERSON PER WEEK		🛏 12
T **C**	MIN £	MAX £	MIN £	MAX £	OPEN
	10.50	15	105	140	1—12

Maesycrugiau MID WALES

Inn

Talardd Arms

Llanllwni, Pencader
Dyfed SA39 9DX
Tel: (055 935) 633

CATEGORIES

| 1 | 2 | 3 |

The Talardd Arms is a pleasant country inn, in the heart of the Teifi Valley. Ideally situated for fishing, pony trekking and visiting the beaches of New Quay, Aberaeron and Aberporth. Grill room with a wide choice of dishes, 2 bars, with friendly atmosphere.

	B & B PER PERSON PER NIGHT		DINNER B & B PER PERSON PER WEEK		🛏 3
C	MIN £	MAX £	MIN £	MAX £	OPEN
	7	8.50			1—12

> ### [C] Children stay at reduced rates, wherever you see this symbol.

Hotels

Castle Mead Hotel*

Manorbier, Tenby,
Pembrokeshire, Dyfed SA70 7TA
Tel: (083482) 358

CATEGORIES

| 4 | 4 | 4 |

A delightful quiet and restful hotel close to the sea.
Well appointed and with pleasant gardens overlooking
Manorbier Bay. Ideal touring centre with parking within
our own grounds. Central heating. Fire Certificate
granted. Residents bar and lounge. Private bathroom
with most rooms. RAC* and AA*

	B & B PER PERSON PER NIGHT		DINNER B & B PER PERSON PER WEEK		11
T C	MIN £	MAX £	MIN £	MAX £	OPEN
	11	13.50	103.50	116	3—10

Tudor Lodge Hotel

Jameston, Manorbier
Near Tenby, Dyfed SA70 7SS
Tel: (083 482) 320

CATEGORIES

| 3 | 3 | 5 |

An old character house of great interest in mature
grounds, mid-way between Tenby and Pembroke with a
reputation for its cuisine and service offering its guests
a warm and friendly welcome. Central to numerous
beaches, Norman castles, golf, fishing, riding, sailing.
Licensed bar, ample parking. Fire Certificate.

	B & B PER PERSON PER NIGHT		DINNER B & B PER PERSON PER WEEK		10
T	MIN £	MAX £	MIN £	MAX £	OPEN
	9.78	11.50	97.75	103.50	4—10

Guest House

The Lodge Coffee House*

Manorbier, near Tenby
Dyfed SA70 7TE
Tel: (083482) 495

CATEGORIES

| 3 | 1 | 3 |

Set in the middle of a picturesque village within five
minutes walking distance of the beach. The Lodge has
central heated rooms, each with hot and cold water,
shaver points and television. The dining room has
separate tables, serving good traditional fare which you
will enjoy.

	B & B PER PERSON PER NIGHT		DINNER B & B PER PERSON PER WEEK		3
C	MIN £	MAX £	MIN £	MAX £	OPEN
	6.75	7	65	68	1—12

Marloes — SOUTH WALES

Inn

The Lobster Pot

Marloes, Near Haverfordwest
Dyfed
Tel: (0254) 233

CATEGORIES

| 1 | 3 | 3 |

A fully licensed inn set in the heart of the
Pembrokeshire Coast National Park. Family run, with
pleasant dining room, colour TV lounge with a very
popular bar. A short walk to a selection of beautiful
beaches. For further details contact Beryl and Ray
Bardsley.

	B & B PER PERSON PER NIGHT		DINNER B & B PER PERSON PER WEEK		4
T C	MIN £	MAX £	MIN £	MAX £	OPEN
	7	8.50	65	80	1—12

Guest House

Foxdale*

Glebe Lane, Marloes
Nr Haverfordwest, Dyfed SA62 3AX
Tel: (064 65) 527

CATEGORIES

| 3 | 3 | 2 |

Situated in National Trust country with miles of coastal
footpaths and boat trips to Skomer Island. Family run
private house. HH commended. All rooms country views.
Central heating. TV lounge evening dinner. Reductions
children, ample parking. Telephone. Dining room with
separate tables. Single, Double and family rooms. On
entering Marloes turn first right by church. Foxdale first
white house on right in Glebe Lane.

	B & B PER PERSON PER NIGHT		DINNER B & B PER PERSON PER WEEK		3
C	MIN £	MAX £	MIN £	MAX £	OPEN
	6	8	63	77	1—10

Hotel

Gazelle Hotel

Glyngarth, Menai Bridge
Anglesey, Gwynedd LL59 5PD
Tel: (0248) 713364

CATEGORIES

| 3 | 3 | 4 |

Situated on the shores of the Menai Strait. Ideally
situated to explore the whole of Anglesey and also the
mountains of Caernarfonshire. Full central heating.
Residents lounge with colour TV. Large sun terrace
with views down the Strait. Ideal centre for both
yachting and sea fishing.

	B & B PER PERSON PER NIGHT		DINNER B & B PER PERSON PER WEEK		16
C	MIN £	MAX £	MIN £	MAX £	OPEN
	11.50	14.50	105	115	1—12

Farmhouse

Cefn Coch Farm

Llansadwrn, Menai Bridge
Anglesey, Gwynedd LL59 5SL
Tel: (0248) 810462

CATEGORIES

| 1 | 3 | 2 |

Comfortable, homely accommodation on 125 acre
mixed farm. Spacious rooms, guest's lounge with
colour TV. Ideally situated in area of outstanding
natural beauty near beaches, golf, sports centre etc.,
and easy reach of mountains. Pony available for riding
on farm. Children welcome, cots, baby-sitting. Early
suppers etc., available.

	B & B PER PERSON PER NIGHT		DINNER B & B PER PERSON PER WEEK		3
C	MIN £	MAX £	MIN £	MAX £	OPEN
	6		68		1—12

T

**This symbol
means you can
book through your
local travel agent.**

Hotels

Plas Newydd Hotel*

Cefn Coed, Merthyr Tydfil
Mid Glamorgan CF48 2PR
Tel: (0685) 2546 & 73945
Prop. 3050

CATEGORIES: 3 | 3 | 3

Private hotel of good standard. Car Park, lawn, lounge, bar. Central heating. TV room. Local shopping in Cefn Coed village; Merthyr Tydfil town centre 1¼ miles. Most sports available in the area. Within minutes of the Brecon Beacons National Park. Parties and functions a speciality. Most of South Wales is within one hour's drive.

C	B & B PER PERSON PER NIGHT		DINNER B & B PER PERSON PER WEEK		18
	MIN £	MAX £	MIN £	MAX £	OPEN
	7	7	66.50	66.50	1—12

Tregenna Hotel*

Park Terrace, Merthyr Tydfil
Mid. Glamorgan CF47 8RF
Tel: (0685) 3627

CATEGORIES: 4 | 4 | 4

Private car park. Residential area. Minutes from bus and railway station. 10 minutes by car to Brecon Beacon National Park and Brecon Mountain Railway. Seven bedrooms are chalet type with bathroom, all other bedrooms have hot and cold water or bathroom with shower. TV lounge. Lounge, bar, dining room with separate tables. Central heating. Fire Certificate granted.

T C	B & B PER PERSON PER NIGHT		DINNER B & B PER PERSON PER WEEK		22
	MIN £	MAX £	MIN £	MAX £	OPEN
	8	12.50	84	115	1—12

This symbol means you can book through your local travel agent.

Hotel and Inn

Ferry Inn*

Llanstadwell, Milford Haven
Pembrokeshire, Dyfed SA73 1EG
Tel: (0646) 600270

CATEGORIES: 3 | 3 | 4

Superb harbour view of Cleddau Bridge and B & I Ferry. Ideal for boating, canoeing, fishing. Adjacent to Coastal Path. Central for touring North and South Pembrokeshire. Full central heating, hot and cold water, shaving points in all bedrooms. Colour TV lounge, dining room seats 60 persons, separate tables. Hot and cold snacks served in bar and lounge.

C	B & B PER PERSON PER NIGHT		DINNER B & B PER PERSON PER WEEK		7
	MIN £	MAX £	MIN £	MAX £	OPEN
	8	10	80	100	1—12

Sir Benfro Hotel*

Herbrandston, Milford Haven
Dyfed, Wales SA73 3TD
Tel: (06462) 4242

CATEGORIES: 5 | 4 | 5

Sir Benfro Hotel, Herbrandston, Milford Haven, Dyfed, Set in pleasant rural surrounding within the Pembrokeshire Coast National Park and in easy reach of beaches. Own swimming pool and play area, pony riding, golfing, surfing and boating facilities nearby. Excellent parking facilities. Pleasant bar and restaurant.

C	B & B PER PERSON PER NIGHT		DINNER B & B PER PERSON PER WEEK		12
	MIN £	MAX £	MIN £	MAX £	OPEN
	14.38	18.98	201.25		1—12

Farmhouse

Woodson

Thornton, Milford Haven
Dyfed SA73 3UQ
Tel: (0437) 890 358

CATEGORIES: 3 | 2 | 2

17th century farmhouse with all modern amenities. Near St. Bride's Bay. Ideal touring, walking and beautiful beaches. Large spacious rooms with pleasant outlook. Excellent cuisine. Car parking on forecourt. Large lawns, ideal play area and/or sunbathing.

C	B & B PER PERSON PER NIGHT		DINNER B & B PER PERSON PER WEEK		5
	MIN £	MAX £	MIN £	MAX £	OPEN
	6.50	6.50		42	1—12

Hotel

Milton Manor Hotel*

Milton, Near Tenby
Dyfed SA70 8PG
Tel: (06467) 398

CATEGORIES: 4 | 4 | 5

Milton Manor Hotel a Georgian manor house in 7 acres set back from A477. 26 bedrooms mostly en-suite. Licensed bar, lounge separate, TV room. First class menus, wine our speciality. Bar snacks, packed lunches. Nursery. Teas available. Lovely beaches within easy reach. Open all year. Pets. Fire Certificate.

T C	B & B PER PERSON PER NIGHT		DINNER B & B PER PERSON PER WEEK		26
	MIN £	MAX £	MIN £	MAX £	OPEN
	12.15	15.75	107.50	137	1—12

Hotel

Chequers*

Northophall Village
Mold, Clwyd
Tel: (0244) 816181 Telex: 617112

CATEGORIES: 5 | 5 | 5

Former manor house in 40 acres wood and parkland. Ideal base for touring North Wales coast and Snowdonia also convenient for Mold Crown Court, Shire Hall and Theatr Clwyd. 30 bedrooms, all with private bathrooms, colour TV and teamakers. Ten minutes from M56 motorway.

T C	B & B PER PERSON PER NIGHT		DINNER B & B PER PERSON PER WEEK		30
	MIN £	MAX £	MIN £	MAX £	OPEN
		22	140	160	1—12

Farmhouse

Brithdir Mawr

Cilcain, Mold
Clwyd CH7 5PH
Tel: (0352 85) 351

CATEGORIES

| 1 | 3 | 2 |

Deep in the Welsh hills, Brithdir is a fascinating ancient farm house in an idyllic setting. The perfect centre for touring North-West Britain, with beautiful local walks on all sides. Good home cooking and a warm welcome await you.

C	B & B PER PERSON PER NIGHT		DINNER B & B PER PERSON PER WEEK		3
	MIN £	MAX £	MIN £	MAX £	OPEN
	7.50	7.50	65	65	3—11

Monmouth — SOUTH WALES

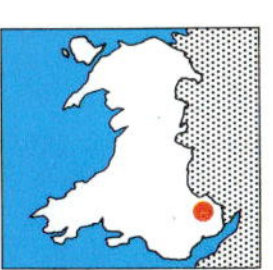

Map ref: Me1
Part of the glorious Wye Valley and Symonds Yat and sharing its scenery.

An ancient town with much character. Its fortified tower gate over the Monnow is notable. The Nelson Museum and other associations with him are interesting.

Hotels, Motels and Inns

Beaufort Arms

Agincourt Square, Monmouth
Gwent NP5 3BT
Tel: (0600) 2411

CATEGORIES

| 3 | 4 | 5 |

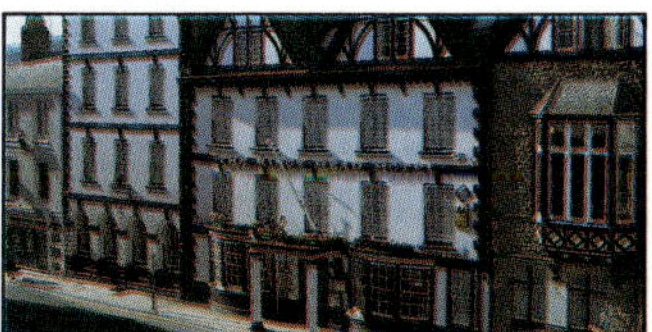

Historic regency inn in the town centre with 26 bedrooms, some with private bath and all with telephone, radio, colour TV and tea/coffee making facilities. Central heating, car park. Weekend and mid-week bargain breaks available. Fine touring centre for the Wye Valley and Forest of Dean.

T	B & B PER PERSON PER NIGHT		DINNER B & B PER PERSON PER WEEK		26
C	MIN £	MAX £	MIN £	MAX £	OPEN
	17.50	20.25			1—12

The King's Head Hotel

Agincourt Square, Monmouth
Gwent NP5 3DY
Tel: (0600) 2177

CATEGORIES

| 6 | 6 | 6 |

17th century coaching inn, tastefully modernised, situated in the centre of a small market town. It is an ideal touring centre for the Wye Valley and the Royal Forest of Dean. The surrounding countryside abounds with magnificent view-points, picnic areas, ancient castles, churches and abbeys. The hotel has 28 bedrooms, 26 with private bathroom. Restaurant, serving table d'hôte and extensive à la carte, Coachhouse grillroom, carvery and bars. Dinner, bed and breakfast, single, per week, including VAT on application.

T	B & B PER PERSON PER NIGHT		DINNER B & B PER PERSON PER WEEK		26
C	MIN £	MAX £	MIN £	MAX £	OPEN
	22	27			1—12

Leasbrook Country Hotel*

Dixton
Monmouth
Tel: (0600) 2831

CATEGORIES

| 3 | 4 | 5 |

Leasbrook is a privately-owned family run hotel standing in its own grounds adjacent to Monmouth Golf course just off A40, ideal for touring the Wye Valley. This is our home and we will do our best to make your stay comfortable, help you enjoy its restfulness, good food and happy atmosphere. We specialise in home grown produce. AA RAC listed.

C	B & B PER PERSON PER NIGHT		DINNER B & B PER PERSON PER WEEK		10
	MIN £	MAX £	MIN £	MAX £	OPEN
	11.50	15.50	115.50	143.50	1—12

Pengethley Hotel & Restaurant

near Ross-on-Wye
Herefordshire HR9 6LL
Tel: (098987) 211

CATEGORIES

| 6 | 4 | 5 |

Georgian country house hotel set in 15 acres of grounds with heated swimming pool, trout fishing lake. À la carte award winning restaurant and extensive wine cellar. Ideal golf, fishing, riding, walking, touring Black Mountains and Malverns. Mini breaks available any two days all the year.

T	B & B PER PERSON PER NIGHT		DINNER B & B PER PERSON PER WEEK		20
C	MIN £	MAX £	MIN £	MAX £	OPEN
	20	28	175	280	1—12

C

Children stay at reduced rates, wherever you see this symbol.

Queens Head Inn

St. James Street
Monmouth, Gwent
Tel: (0600) 2767

CATEGORIES

| 3 | 3 | 4 |

AA* RAC* recommended. Good beer guide. 6 bedroom accommodation all with bathroom, showers en-suite. Colour TV in all rooms. Fully central heated and double glazed. Tea and coffee making facilities. ½ mile from Monmouth Golf Course. Ideally situated for fishing, riding, walking. Special rates for children. Adjacent to Monmouth Leisure Centre which has swimming pool, badmington, tennis etc.

	B & B PER PERSON PER NIGHT		DINNER B & B PER PERSON PER WEEK		🛏 6
T C	MIN £	MAX £	MIN £	MAX £	OPEN
	11.50	13.50	90	100	1—12

The Rising Sun Inn & Motel*

Cinderhill Street, Monmouth
Gwent NP5 3EY
Tel: (0600) 3236 and 5577

CATEGORIES

| 4 | 3 | 5 |

One minute from shopping centre and bus routes. Easy access to historical monuments. Ample fishing, walks and leisure activities. All rooms have modern facilities. A la carte restaurant, games room with two full size snooker tables. Private car park garage available. Ten minutes from new golf course. Excellent service.

	B & B PER PERSON PER NIGHT		DINNER B & B PER PERSON PER WEEK		🛏 10
T	MIN £	MAX £	MIN £	MAX £	OPEN
	13.50	13.50			1—12

Don't forget that 1983 is Festival of Castles Year in Wales with events planned for all the major historic sites.

Talocher Farmhouse Hotel*

Wonastow Road
Monmouth, Gwent
Tel: (060083) 236

CATEGORIES

| 3 | 3 | 3 |

Situated in its own grounds on the hillside with superb views of the Welsh hills, 2 miles from Monmouth with fishing, walking, riding and golf nearby. Nine bedrooms. TV lounge, restaurant and bars. Large swimming pool with sauna, solarium and beauty salon. Ideal for long or short stays.

	B & B PER PERSON PER NIGHT		DINNER B & B PER PERSON PER WEEK		🛏 9
C	MIN £	MAX £	MIN £	MAX £	OPEN
	10	12	85	85	1—12

White Swan Hotel*

Priory Street, Monmouth
Gwent NP5 3BR
Tel: (0600) 2045

CATEGORIES

| 3 | 4 | 4 |

A 19 bedroom family hotel in the centre of Monmouth. Open all year, offering high standard of food and accommodation. Fully licensed restaurant open every day. Hot and cold water. Bar snacks available throughout the week. Resident proprietors David Lawton and John Jacobs. Closed Christmas.

	B & B PER PERSON PER NIGHT		DINNER B & B PER PERSON PER WEEK		🛏 19
T C	MIN £	MAX £	MIN £	MAX £	OPEN
	11				1—12

Guest Houses

Burton House

St. James Square, Monmouth
Gwent NP5 3DN
Tel: (0600) 3004

CATEGORIES

| 3 | 2 | 2 |

Period guest house, recently refurbished to high standard. Ideally situated for touring. Comfortable lounge, colour TV. Large rooms, full central heating, hot and cold water all rooms. Private parking. Special terms for children, pets welcome. Drying and ironing facilities. Evening meals by arrangement.

	B & B PER PERSON PER NIGHT		DINNER B & B PER PERSON PER WEEK		🛏 3
C	MIN £	MAX £	MIN £	MAX £	OPEN
	6	6.50	63	67.50	1—12

Tourist Information Centres are listed at back of book.

Ebberley Guest House*

St. James Square, Monmouth
Gwent NP5 3DN
Tel: (0600) 3602

CATEGORIES

| 3 | 3 | 3 |

Situated in pleasant square near centre of town. Comfortable lounge with colour TV if required. Pleasant dining room with separate tables, hot and cold water and shaving points in all rooms. Full central heating. A varied and interesting dinner menu (optional), morning tea and evening drinks available.

	B & B PER PERSON PER NIGHT		DINNER B & B PER PERSON PER WEEK		🛏 5
C	MIN £	MAX £	MIN £	MAX £	OPEN
	6	7	65	70	1—12

The Glen Farm

St. Maughans Green, Monmouth
Gwent NP5 3QG
Tel: (0600) 4728

CATEGORIES

| 2 | 1 | 1 |

1 double bedroom and 1 twin bedded room. Dairy farm 50 acres. From Monmouth, take B4233 through Rockfield. Turn right at S/P St. Maughans. Continue up hill to S/P St. Maughans Green. Then down hill past the houses to farm on left.

	B & B PER PERSON PER NIGHT		DINNER B & B PER PERSON PER WEEK		🛏 2
C	MIN £	MAX £	MIN £	MAX £	OPEN
	7				4—10

Lower Grove Farmhouse

Newcastle, Monmouth
Gwent NP5 4NT
Tel: (060 084) 243

CATEGORIES

| 1 | 3 | 2 |

Farmhouse set in a 6 acre small holding with ducks, geese, sheep, ponies and calves. In the midst of the beautiful Monnow Valley, 5 miles from Monmouth in an area full of beauty and historic interest. Open all year. Own swimming pool. Pets welcome. Ideal for walking and fishing holidays.

	B & B PER PERSON PER NIGHT		DINNER B & B PER PERSON PER WEEK		🛏 2
C	MIN £	MAX £	MIN £	MAX £	OPEN
	7				1—12

Montgomery — MID WALES

Farmhouses

Gwern-yr-Uchain Farm*

Llandyssil, Montgomery
Powys SY15 6HS
Tel: (068681) 298

CATEGORIES

| 3 | 2 | 2 |

Gwern-yr-Uchain is a 190 acre, cattle and sheep farm, situated in an elevated position with delightful views from every window. Children are especially welcome, with hens, ducks and a pony to interest them. Ideal base for touring Mid-Wales with fishing, golf, pony trekking and sports centre nearby.

	B & B PER PERSON PER NIGHT		DINNER B & B PER PERSON PER WEEK		🛏 3
T C	MIN £	MAX £	MIN £	MAX £	OPEN
	7	8	65	72	4—10

Little Brompton Farm*

Montgomery
Powys SY15 6MY
Tel: (068681) 371

CATEGORIES		
3	3	2

A 17th century 100 acre beef, sheep and arable farm. Traditionally furnished, many antiques. Several rooms have exposed beams. Guests may try their hand at spinning or making corn dollies. Country hospitality with good home produced food. Children very welcome. Offa's Dyke long distance footpath runs through the farm. Shooting available.

C	B & B PER PERSON PER NIGHT		DINNER B & B PER PERSON PER WEEK		3
	MIN £	MAX £	MIN £	MAX £	OPEN
	7.50		75		1—12

Morfa Nefyn NORTH WALES

Hotel

Bryn Noddfa Hotel

Morfa Nefyn, Pwllheli
Gwynedd LL53 6AD
Tel: (0758) 720843

CATEGORIES		
3	3	5

Close to Nefyn 18 hole golf links, lovely beaches suitable for swimming, boating, fishing and surfing and cliff walks. Most rooms have shower/toilet en-suite. Resident proprietors. Home grown vegetables, home made bread. Children welcomed and meals prepared for them at flexible times. À la carte and table d'hôte meals in restaurant. Informal meals in bar lounge. AA.*

C	B & B PER PERSON PER NIGHT		DINNER B & B PER PERSON PER WEEK		9
	MIN £	MAX £	MIN £	MAX £	OPEN
	8.50	9.50	54.50	60.50	1—12

An early holiday this year means you will be in need of another break before or after Christmas. Send for the Wales Tourist Board's free 'Great Little Breaks' 56-page booklet of fantastic Autumn to Spring holiday ideas.

Mumbles SOUTH WALES

Map ref: La4
Headland town, an extension west along the sandy bay of Swansea. Sailing and water-sports—water skiing and angling particularly—are first rate. Nearby are the sandy bays of Langland and Caswell, extending towards the scenic glories of Gower Peninsula, designated an Area of Outstanding Natural Beauty.

Hotels

Ael-y-Don Hotel*

Langland Bay Road,
Langland Bay, Mumbles
Gower, Swansea SA3 4QP
Tel: (0792) 66466

CATEGORIES		
3	4	3

The hotel is ideally situated in beautiful Langland Bay under the personal supervision of the proprietors, only 1½ miles from the village of Mumbles, with a variety of shops. Within easy reach of the renowned Gower beauty spots. Bathing direct from hotel. Reduction for children sharing parents room.

C	B & B PER PERSON PER NIGHT		DINNER B & B PER PERSON PER WEEK		17
	MIN £	MAX £	MIN £	MAX £	OPEN
	9.75		86.50		3—10

Anchor Bay Hotel

380/384 Mumbles Road, Mumbles
Swansea SA3 5TN
Tel: (0792) 69697

CATEGORIES		
3	3	3

Excellent small hotel, un-obstructed views of Swansea Bay beach opposite. Open all year. Hot and cold water, shaver points. Tea-makers in all bedrooms. Special rates for children. Colour television lounge residents. Full central heating. Private car park. Fire Certificate.

C	B & B PER PERSON PER NIGHT		DINNER B & B PER PERSON PER WEEK		20
	MIN £	MAX £	MIN £	MAX £	OPEN
	9.75	12	62.50	78	1—12

Glenview Hotel*

Glenview, 140 Langland Road,
Mumbles, Swansea SA3 4LU
Tel: (0792) 69244

CATEGORIES		
3	3	3

Comfortable family run hotel with friendly atmosphere and good home cooking. Adjacent to Underhill Park, and within a few minutes walking distance to sandy beaches of Rotherslade and Langland. Spacious rooms most with park views. Convenient for golf, tennis, fishing and touring Gower. Send SAE colour brochure— Mrs V Gwillim

C	B & B PER PERSON PER NIGHT		DINNER B & B PER PERSON PER WEEK		6
	MIN £	MAX £	MIN £	MAX £	OPEN
	7	11	65	85	4—10

Harbour Winds Hotel*

18 Overland Road,
Mumbles, Swansea
West Glamorgan SA3 4LP
Tel: (0792) 69298

CATEGORIES		
3	3	2

Situated in the village of Mumbles, Harbour Winds is a spacious residence of character set in its own grounds with ample private car parking facilities. Spacious lounges, colour TV. Historical oak-panelled dining room. Tea-making facilities in bedrooms; some bath, shower, toilet en suite. Children welcome. SAE brochure.

T C	B & B PER PERSON PER NIGHT		DINNER B & B PER PERSON PER WEEK		8
	MIN £	MAX £	MIN £	MAX £	OPEN
	9	10	63	70	4—10

Guest Houses

Quaintways Guest House

386 Mumbles Road, Norton
Swansea, Glam. SAE 357
Tel: (0792) 401486

CATEGORIES		
3	3	1

A small seafront guest house with a warm welcome and friendly atmosphere. Established over twenty years. Twin and double bedrooms, fully equipped, some with sea views. Tea making facilities. Access at all times. Comfortable TV Lounge. Pleasant garden. Parking at rear of house. Write or telephone—Mrs M L Carleton.

C	B & B PER PERSON PER NIGHT		DINNER B & B PER PERSON PER WEEK		4
	MIN £	MAX £	MIN £	MAX £	OPEN
	6.50	7			1—12

Tides Reach*

388 Mumbles Road
Mumbles, Swansea
Tel: (0792) 404877

CATEGORIES

3	3	2

We offer you a warm welcome and good food in our superbly situated sea-front guest house. We retain an air of old-world charm, whilst incorporating all modern comfort in our pleasant bedrooms. TV lounge with views over the bay. Close to holiday amenities. Children and pets welcome.

T / C	B & B PER PERSON PER NIGHT		DINNER B & B PER PERSON PER WEEK		🛏 5
	MIN £	MAX £	MIN £	MAX £	OPEN
	5.50	7.50	55	75	1—12

Myddfai — SOUTH WALES

Inn

The Plough Inn

Myddfai, Llandovery
Dyfed SA20 0NZ
Tel: (0550) 20643

CATEGORIES

3	3	5

Stay Inn—bed breakfast and evening meal—winter breaks. Shop Inn—local pottery and crafts. Eat Inn—sample our home-cooked food in the intimate restaurant or bars. Wide range of food at flexible prices. Drink Inn—our cosy public bar or character barn bar. Play Inn—separate games room—outstanding scenery in National Park.

C	B & B PER PERSON PER NIGHT		DINNER B & B PER PERSON PER WEEK		🛏 4
	MIN £	MAX £	MIN £	MAX £	OPEN
	8.50				1—12

Nantgwynant — NORTH WALES

Guest Houses

Glan Gwynant
Country Guest House*

Glan Gwynant, Nantgwynant
Gwynedd, North Wales LL55 4NW
Tel: (076686) 440

CATEGORIES

3	3	3

Well appointed select country guest house with panoramic views over Lake Gwynant. Quiet and secluded position. Private parking. Ideal base for touring North Wales both inland and its beautiful coasts. Activity and special interest holiday weeks. French, Portuguese, Spanish spoken. Regret no pets. SAE for brochure.

C	B & B PER PERSON PER NIGHT		DINNER B & B PER PERSON PER WEEK		🛏 5
	MIN £	MAX £	MIN £	MAX £	OPEN
	6	7	70	75	1—12

Llys Elen Guest House*

Nantgwynant near Beddgelert
Gwynedd LL55 4NW
Tel: (076686) 446

CATEGORIES

3	3	2

In the beautiful valley of Nantgwynant 3½ miles from Beddgelert surrounded by the mountains of Snowdonia and with views of Snowdon. Ideal centre for walking, climbing, fishing, riding, or just exploring North Wales. Hot and Cold water, shaver, points, tea and coffee facilities in all rooms, central heating, TV lounge. Fire Certificate.

C	B & B PER PERSON PER NIGHT		DINNER B & B PER PERSON PER WEEK		🛏 3
	MIN £	MAX £	MIN £	MAX £	OPEN
	6		63		1—12

Narberth — SOUTH WALES

Hotels, Motels and Inns

Plas Hyfryd
Hotel and Restaurant*

Moorfield Road, Narberth
Pembrokeshire
Tel: (0834) 860653

CATEGORIES

3	4	4

AA* family run hotel in 2 acres, garden with heated open-air pool. Narberth is ideally situated for easy access to coast and countryside. Family rooms available with reduced rates for children. Salmon fishing, gliding, riding, shooting can be arranged. Please write or phone for details.

T / C	B & B PER PERSON PER NIGHT		DINNER B & B PER PERSON PER WEEK		🛏 7
	MIN £	MAX £	MIN £	MAX £	OPEN
	13	13	116	116	1—12

Guest Houses

Welsh Kitchen*

Narberth
Dyfed
Tel: (0834) 860441

CATEGORIES

3	2	5

Licensed guest house and restaurant open all year round. Single, double, family rooms available, reduction for children. Lounge, colour TV laundry room. Central heating. Good home cooking.

C	B & B PER PERSON PER NIGHT		DINNER B & B PER PERSON PER WEEK		🛏 4
	MIN £	MAX £	MIN £	MAX £	OPEN
	5	7	49	70	1—12

C
Children stay at reduced rates, wherever you see this symbol.

Farmhouses

Highland Grange Farm
Guest House

Robeston Wathen, Narberth
Pembrokeshire Dyfed SA67 8EP
Tel: (0834) 860952

CATEGORIES

3	3	3

A warm welcome awaits you at this comfortable farmhouse situated 40 yards off A40 road overlooking the village. A mixed farm of 220 acres set amidst beautiful countryside offers unlimited opportunities for walking. 200 yards from local inn and 1 mile from Narberth. Naomi, a regular winner at the West Wales Catering Exhibition Salon Culinaire, provides excellent home cooking. 4 course dinner, plentiful and varied menu, garden produce. Family, double, twin and single bedrooms with washbasins. Suitable for disabled guests. Children welcome. Babysitting. Cot.

C	B & B PER PERSON PER NIGHT		DINNER B & B PER PERSON PER WEEK		🛏 4
	MIN £	MAX £	MIN £	MAX £	OPEN
	9		63		1—12

Jacob's Park

Narberth, Pembrokeshire
Dyfed SA67 8HA
Tel: (0834) 860525

CATEGORIES

3	3	2

Situated in the centre of the old county of Pembrokeshire within easy reach of sandy beaches, the Preseli Hills and the forest walk along the Cleddau estuary. Home cooking a speciality, a different meal served every day, mainly home produced. Evening beverage served free. SAE for brochure.

C	B & B PER PERSON PER NIGHT		DINNER B & B PER PERSON PER WEEK		🛏 3
	MIN £	MAX £	MIN £	MAX £	OPEN
	7	7.50	70	75	4—9

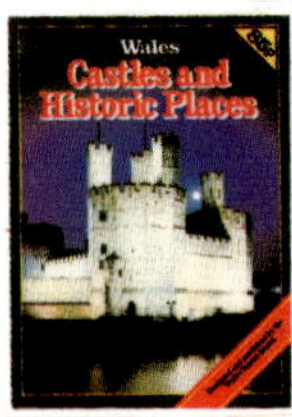

Castles and Historic Places

Invaluable in 1983, the year of the castles in Wales. This 92 page book guides you around over 120 castles and historic sites in Wales. There's also an introductory section on Welsh history.

Available from: Wales Tourist Board Department W.T.S. P.O. Box 1, CARDIFF CF1 2XN. Price: £1.10p including postage and packing.

Motel

Cimla Court Motel*

Cimla Road, Neath
West Glamorgan SA11 3TT
Tel: (0639) 3771/2639

CATEGORIES
| 3 | 5 | 5 |

The motel is situated on the edge of town with splendid views of the surrounding countryside. Just off M4 motorway and all main access routes to Swansea, etc. Ideal as central place to tour from. Conference and Banqueting facilities available. Bedrooms have colour TV and intercom.

	B & B PER PERSON PER NIGHT		DINNER B & B PER PERSON PER WEEK		27
T	MIN £	MAX £	MIN £	MAX £	OPEN
C	18.08	18.08	151	250	1—12

Hotel

Caeau Capel Hotel*

Rhodfar Mor, Nefyn
Gwynedd LL53 6EB
Tel: (0758) 720240

CATEGORIES
| 3 | 4 | 4 |

A small family hotel in its own grounds with tennis, putting green and gardens, ideally situated for beach, sailing and fishing. Convenient to 18-hole golf course, 21 bedrooms, some with private bathroom en-suite and balconies with sea views. Residential in the same family for over 50 years. Terms from £75.32 inclusive of Dinner, Bed and breakfast and VAT.

	B & B PER PERSON PER NIGHT		DINNER B & B PER PERSON PER WEEK		21
T	MIN £	MAX £	MIN £	MAX £	OPEN
C	8.62	11.50	75.32	108	4—9

This symbol means you can book through your local travel agent.

T

Guest House

Rose Hill Guest House*

Ffordd Dewisant, Nefyn
Pwllheli, Gwynedd LL53 6EA
Tel: (0758) 720530

CATEGORIES
| 2 | 3 | 2 |

Situated on the beautiful Lleyn Peninsula standing in its own grounds with ample parking. Two minutes to the safe sandy beach. Single, double and family rooms all with hot and cold and shaver points. Colour television. Special rates for children, sincere welcome in a friendly and informal atmosphere. Fire Certificate.

	B & B PER PERSON PER NIGHT		DINNER B & B PER PERSON PER WEEK		7
C	MIN £	MAX £	MIN £	MAX £	OPEN
	6.50	7.50	56		1—12

Hotels

Cawdor Hotel

Newcastle Emlyn
Dyfed SA38 9AJ
Tel: (0239) 710333

CATEGORIES
| 3 | 3 | 4 |

Situated in the beautiful Teifi valley town. The Cawdor offers everything you hope for. Good accommodation, comfortable residents TV lounge, wholesome food and friendliness. This hostelry provides bedrooms, some with private bathrooms or shower, intercom, radio, tea and coffee-making facilities. Central heating, launderette. Pool room.

	B & B PER PERSON PER NIGHT		DINNER B & B PER PERSON PER WEEK		24
C	MIN £	MAX £	MIN £	MAX £	OPEN
	18	21	85	93	1—12

Emlyn Arms Hotel

Bridge Street
Newcastle Emlyn, Dyfed
Tel: (0239) 710317

CATEGORIES
| 5 | 3 | 4 |

An original 18th century coaching house carefully modernised to give comfort whilst retaining character. There are 42 centrally heated bedrooms with TV. 2 bars and a restaurant serving à la carte and table d'hôte menus. Children are welcome and weekend breaks continue throughout the year.

	B & B PER PERSON PER NIGHT		DINNER B & B PER PERSON PER WEEK		39
T	MIN £	MAX £	MIN £	MAX £	OPEN
C	12	20	119	145.25	1—12

The Lamb Hotel

Llangeler, near Newcastle Emlyn
Dyfed
Tel: (0559) 370/567-576

CATEGORIES
| 3 | 3 | 4 |

Surrounded by beautiful countryside, small, comfortable hotel situated between Carmarthen and Cardigan on main A484 road, gateway to Cardigan coast. All bedrooms have private bath/toilet. Colour TV, tea-making facilities, choice 2 restaurants, under new ownership and family-run hotel. Resident band Saturday evenings, cabaret, Welsh nights during week. Personal supervision, proprietors Mr. & Mrs. E. Jones & Sons.

	B & B PER PERSON PER NIGHT		DINNER B & B PER PERSON PER WEEK		8
T	MIN £	MAX £	MIN £	MAX £	OPEN
C	14	16	84	90	1—12

Farmhouse

Llain Farm

Velindre, Llandysul
Dyfed SA44 5XT
Tel: (0559) 370683

CATEGORIES
| 1 | 2 | 2 |

Beautiful views of countryside surrounds the dairy farm between Carmarthen and Cardigan and is ideally placed for touring both the south and west coast. Pony trekking close by. Dining room, lounge, TV. Central heating.

	B & B PER PERSON PER NIGHT		DINNER B & B PER PERSON PER WEEK		2
C	MIN £	MAX £	MIN £	MAX £	OPEN
	6	7	60	70	4—10

Inns

The Golden Lion Inn*

East Street, Newport
Pembrokeshire, Dyfed SA42 0SY
Tel: (0239) 820321

CATEGORIES
| 3 | 3 | 5 |

Welcome to the Golden Lion Inn, Newport, Pembrokeshire, Dyfed. Accommodation ten rooms, children's bar, sauna, solarium, launderette. Real ales restaurant and bar meals. Fine Welsh fare and good company. Beer garden and barbeque. Ideal for beach, golfing, riding, walking, fishing. Always a welcome from Glyn and Penny Rees.

	B & B PER PERSON PER NIGHT		DINNER B & B PER PERSON PER WEEK		10
C	MIN £	MAX £	MIN £	MAX £	OPEN
	8	10	70	90	1—12

The Salutation Inn*

Felindre Farchog, Cardigan
Dyfed SA41 3UY
Tel: (0239) 820564

CATEGORIES

| 4 | 4 | 5 |

Traditional country inn with cosy bars, good food and bedrooms with private bath. Situated in village near river Nevern. Fishing, golf, pony trekking can be arranged for guests. Children stay free when sharing parents room, only meals charged for, junior menus. Facilities for disabled. Welsh singing. An Eagle Hotel.

T	B & B PER PERSON PER NIGHT		DINNER B & B PER PERSON PER WEEK		10
C	MIN £	MAX £	MIN £	MAX £	OPEN
	10.75	10.75	85	94.50	1—12

Newport
(Gwent)

SOUTH WALES

Map ref: Mc4
Steel and commercial centre at the mouth of the Usk river astride all roads and railways into South Wales. Shopping centre for the area, its museums and archaic, but fascinating, Transporter Bridge are worth attention. Tredegar House Country Park is chief among the many open spaces. Good centre for touring between Wye and the Eastern Valleys of Gwent.

Hotels and Motel

Celtic Manor Hotel*

The Coldra, Newport
Gwent NP6 2YA
Tel: (0633) 413000

CATEGORIES

| 6 | 6 | 6 |

Originally a private manor house, Celtic Manor has been tastefully converted to a most attractive 17 bedroom hotel. It is situated on the outskirts of Newport, close to junction 24 of the M4 motorway. The hotel offers 2 restaurants and bars, with first class cuisine and decor.

T	B & B PER PERSON PER NIGHT		DINNER B & B PER PERSON PER WEEK		17
C	MIN £	MAX £	MIN £	MAX £	OPEN
	27.50	38			1—12

Harris Hotel

34/36 Chepstow Road, Newport
Gwent NPT 8EA
Tel: (0633) 63367

CATEGORIES

| 3 | 4 | 4 |

Privately owned licensed restaurant hotel, situated at gateway to South Wales. Convenient for businessman and tourist. Easy access to industries, coast, countryside and several first-class golf courses. 7 minutes (walking) town centre. Menu varied and includes home made specialities. Parking facilities. M4 motorway exit 24.

T	B & B PER PERSON PER NIGHT		DINNER B & B PER PERSON PER WEEK		15
C	MIN £	MAX £	MIN £	MAX £	OPEN
	9.75	12			1—12

Ladbroke Mercury Hotel*

The Coldra, Newport
Gwent NP6 276
Tel: (0633) 412777 Telex 497205

CATEGORIES

| 6 | 5 | 6 |

The Ladbroke Mercury at Newport is set in attractive woodland just off the M4 motorway at Junction 24. The Garden Room restaurant offers an exciting menu while the hotel also has an attractive lounge bar and coffee shop. Rates: 2 night half-board weekend rates, £42-£46.

T	B & B PER PERSON PER NIGHT		DINNER B & B PER PERSON PER WEEK		125
C	MIN £	MAX £	MIN £	MAX £	OPEN
					1—12

Manor Hotel

147 Stow Hill, Newport
Gwent NPT 4HB
Tel: (0633) 64685

CATEGORIES

| 3 | 3 | 1 |

Just off M4 motorway within walking distance of town centre. Tastefully appointed, television lounge. Relax in beautiful garden and unwind. Central heating. Fire Certificate granted. Jo and Vernon welcome you and hope your visit will be a friendly and enjoyable experience, which you will remember and perhaps one day return again.

C	B & B PER PERSON PER NIGHT		DINNER B & B PER PERSON PER WEEK		7
	MIN £	MAX £	MIN £	MAX £	OPEN
	9.50	11			1—12

The New Inn Motel

Chepstow Road, Langstone
Newport Gwent NP6 2JN
Tel: (0633) 412426

CATEGORIES

| 5 | 4 | 6 |

Situated five miles from Newport in pleasant village on main A48 to Chepstow. All rooms with private bath or shower and toilet. TV, radio, teasmade, telephone. Residents lounge with colour TV and drinks dispenser. À la carte restaurant. Four bars. Ample parking. Close to Usk and Wye Valleys.

	B & B PER PERSON PER NIGHT		DINNER B & B PER PERSON PER WEEK		34
	MIN £	MAX £	MIN £	MAX £	OPEN
	20	25	172	350	1—12

Queens Hotel*

Bridge Street
Newport Gwent
Tel: (0633) 62992 Telex 858875

CATEGORIES

| 3 | 4 | 5 |

Recently refurbished. Town centre location, adjacent to railway station, cinema and places of interest and entertainment. Good position for touring Wye Valley, Brecon Beacons, Cardiff, South Wales Valleys. 43 bedrooms, all heated, with colour TV, most en-suite. Carving room, restaurant. Three bars. Conference facilities.

T	B & B PER PERSON PER NIGHT		DINNER B & B PER PERSON PER WEEK		43
C	MIN £	MAX £	MIN £	MAX £	OPEN
	18.50	27	165	215	1—12

Westgate Hotel

Commercial Street, Newport
Gwent NPT 1TT
Tel: (0633) 66244 Telex 498173

CATEGORIES: 4 6 5

An impressive building, the Westgate Hotel is situated in the main shopping centre of Newport. It is a fine touring centre for the lower Wye Valley and the Vale of Usk, famed for their beauty. All 70 bedrooms have radio, colour TV, telephone, tea and coffee making facilities.

T C	B & B PER PERSON PER NIGHT		DINNER B & B PER PERSON PER WEEK		70
	MIN £	MAX £	MIN £	MAX £	OPEN
	20	25	150	175	1—12

Guest House

St. Etienne Hotel*

162 Stow Hill, Newport
Gwent NPT 4FZ
Tel: (0633) 67695/62341

CATEGORIES: 3 3 1

Bed and breakfast. RAC listed. All rooms private showers, points and tea and coffee making facilities. Cooked breakfast in dining room, continental breakfast served in bedrooms. Lounge with colour television. Full central heating. Full Fire Certificate. Single, double and family rooms. Special rates for children.

C	B & B PER PERSON PER NIGHT		DINNER B & B PER PERSON PER WEEK		6
	MIN £	MAX £	MIN £	MAX £	OPEN
	11	12.75			1—12

Farmhouse

Brick House Farm

Redwick near Newport
Gwent NP0 3DX
Tel: (0633) 880230

CATEGORIES: 1 3 2

Delightful farmhouse accommodation in the quiet village of Redwick. Ideally placed for touring Wye Valley and Brecon Beacons. Cardiff and surrounding country. All rooms tastefully furnished with fitted carpets and central heating. Colour TV lounge, large dining room. Golf course nearby also fishing. Bed and breakfast, evening meal optional.

C	B & B PER PERSON PER NIGHT		DINNER B & B PER PERSON PER WEEK		3
	MIN £	MAX £	MIN £	MAX £	OPEN
		7		70	1—12

Map ref: Fc4
A butt of quay with sailing-days toll boards on the old net-house and anchored craft on the sands, tell of the tiny towns maritime past.

Hotels

The Black Lion Hotel*

New Quay
Dyfed SA45 9PT
Tel: (0545) 560209

CATEGORIES: 4 4 4

Georgian inn overlooking harbour and beaches. Most bedrooms with bathroom, all with colour TV and radio. Home cooking, good wine, real ale. 300 year old bar, beer garden with superb views. Winter packages and reduced terms for children. Run by the proprietors— Steve and Rhian Donohue. Brochure on request.

T C	B & B PER PERSON PER NIGHT		DINNER B & B PER PERSON PER WEEK		6
	MIN £	MAX £	MIN £	MAX £	OPEN
	12	13.50	115	125	1—12

Brynarfor Hotel*

New Road, New Quay
Dyfed SA45 9SB
Tel: (0545) 560358

CATEGORIES: 3 3 3

A restful impressive location with gardens overlooking Cardigan Bay. Village, sandy beach and quay are 5 minutes walk. Full central heating, large dining room with excellent home cooking. We have games room, TV and bar lounge. Circular tours of Mid-Wales from Brynarfor are extremely good. Private parking.

T C	B & B PER PERSON PER NIGHT		DINNER B & B PER PERSON PER WEEK		7
	MIN £	MAX £	MIN £	MAX £	OPEN
	8.50	12	75.60	97.65	1—12

New Quay Hotel*

New Quay
Dyfed SA45 9NN
Tel: (0545) 560282

CATEGORIES: 3 4 4

Situated on sea-front overlooking harbour and bay. Area offers safe sandy beaches, sailing, pony trekking, angling, golf, squash. Hotel, two lounge bars, wine bar. TV lounge. Restaurant. Centrally heated all bedrooms with hot and cold water, shaver point. Drinks facilities. Some with private shower and trouser press.

C	B & B PER PERSON PER NIGHT		DINNER B & B PER PERSON PER WEEK		11
	MIN £	MAX £	MIN £	MAX £	OPEN
	8.50	11	63	90	1—12

Queens Hotel*

Church Street, New Quay
Dyfed, West Wales SA45 9NX
Tel: (0545) 560678

CATEGORIES: 3 3 4

A small family run, AA listed hotel, situated 300 yards from beach and harbour. 8 bedrooms, 5 with shower and 2 family rooms, all rooms centrally heated, with colour television. Fully licensed, lounge, bar and à la carte restaurant. Hotel open throughout the year. Reduced rates during off-peak periods. Under personal supervision of proprietors.

T C	B & B PER PERSON PER NIGHT		DINNER B & B PER PERSON PER WEEK		8
	MIN £	MAX £	MIN £	MAX £	OPEN
	11.26	12.50	103	112	1—12

Guest House

Llain Cottage

Cross Inn, New Quay
Dyfed SA44 6NN
Tel: (0545) 560707

CATEGORIES
| 1 | 3 | 2 |

Peacefully situated amongst beautiful countryside with panoramic views towards Aberystwyth and the mountains. Ideal base for local beauty spots and beaches. All bedrooms have fitted wardrobes and vanity units with shaver lights. Two bedrooms available with private toilet. Bathroom has shower and bidet. Colour TV lounge. Large gardens.

	B & B PER PERSON PER NIGHT		DINNER B & B PER PERSON PER WEEK		5
C	MIN £	MAX £	MIN £	MAX £	OPEN
	7.50	8.20	76	82	3—9

New Radnor
MID WALES

Farmhouse

Lower House Farm

Llanfihangel, Nant Melan,
New Radnor, Presteigne
Powys LD8 2TN
Tel: (054 421) 224

FARMHOUSE AWARD

CATEGORIES
| 3 | 3 | 2 |

Lower house is a 310 acre mixed farm over which visitors may walk and watch the farming activities. Situated close to the Radnor Forest on Welsh Border, central for visiting the attractive towns of Presteigne and Knighton with fishing, golf, tennis and pony trekking available nearby. Guests always welcome at the historic Red Lion Inn, 50 yards away.

T		B & B PER PERSON PER NIGHT		DINNER B & B PER PERSON PER WEEK		3
C		MIN £	MAX £	MIN £	MAX £	OPEN
		5.50	6.50	60	69	1—12

Newtown
MID WALES

Map ref: Eb6
Former woollen weaving mills and a museum remain to remind us that Robert Owen 19th century Co-operative Association pioneer

was born here. Junction of many roads that approach this valley of the Severn, Newtown's main tourist role is as a touring centre.

Hotel

The Bear Hotel*

Broad Street, Newtown
Powys SY16 2LU
Tel: (0686) 26964

CATEGORIES
| 5 | 5 | 5 |

The Bear, dating back to Tudor times when it was a coaching inn, offers modern accommodation behind a traditional frontage. Children stay free when sharing parents room, only meals charged for, junior menus, early suppers. Dinner Dance every Saturday. Ideal centre for exploring Mid-Wales. An Eagle Hotel.

T		B & B PER PERSON PER NIGHT		DINNER B & B PER PERSON PER WEEK		38
C		MIN £	MAX £	MIN £	MAX £	OPEN
		12.70	13.70	106	119	1—12

Farmhouses

Dolymelinau Farm

Tregynon, Newtown
Powys SY16 3PS
Tel: (068 687) 287

CATEGORIES
| 1 | 3 | 2 |

A typically Welsh farm, centrally situated for touring Mid Wales. The spacious century old house has hot and cold basins, central heating, colour TV, lounge, cot, baby-sitting provided. Play area. For children swing, garden, golf, pony trekking and fishing locally. Parking available. Newtown 5 miles, Tregaron 2 miles.

	B & B PER PERSON PER NIGHT		DINNER B & B PER PERSON PER WEEK		2
C	MIN £	MAX £	MIN £	MAX £	OPEN
	5	5	56	56	5—9

Foel Farm

Anchor, Kerry
Newtown, Powys
Tel: (068 688) 600

CATEGORIES
| 1 | 2 | 2 |

Bed and breakfast in friendly surroundings, close to roadside 4½ miles from Kerry village. Quite nice wooded areas ideal for country walks. Evening meal optional good home cooking. Apply—Mrs. Mary Davies who will be on hand to help you.

	B & B PER PERSON PER NIGHT		DINNER B & B PER PERSON PER WEEK		3
C	MIN £	MAX £	MIN £	MAX £	OPEN
	5	5.25	47	49	1—12

Goitre

Kerry, Newtown
Powys SY16 4NA
Tel: (068 688) 248

CATEGORIES
| 1 | 2 | 2 |

Goitre is a 190 acre mixed farm set in a beautiful rural area of mid-Wales. The farm house is 100 years old, modernised but traditionally furnished. Fishing available and many scenic walks nearby. Ideal touring base offering a relaxed, friendly atmosphere along with good home-cooking.

	B & B PER PERSON PER NIGHT		DINNER B & B PER PERSON PER WEEK		3
C	MIN £	MAX £	MIN £	MAX £	OPEN
	8	66	70	1—12

Lower Gwestydd Farmhouse*

Llanllwchaiarn, Newtown
Powys SY16 3AY
Tel: (0686) 26718

CATEGORIES
| 3 | 3 | 2 |

FARMHOUSE AWARD

Lower Gwestydd is a 17th century black and white farmhouse with a wealth of oak beams and historical features. The main enterprises on this 200 acre farm are cattle, sheep and arable. Fishing, tennis, golf, pony trekking, sports centre nearby. Mrs. Jarman, Lower Gwestydd, Newtown, Powys, telephone 0686-26718.

T		B & B PER PERSON PER NIGHT		DINNER B & B PER PERSON PER WEEK		3
C		MIN £	MAX £	MIN £	MAX £	OPEN
		6.50	7	70	73.50	1—12

Penarth

Newtown
Powys SY16 3AN
Tel: (0686) 25760

CATEGORIES
| 3 | 2 | 2 |

Set in the heart of rural mid Wales, this unique 14th century farmhouse offers excellent cuisine and superb accommodation. Central heating and log fires compliment the warmth of character and atmosphere in this beautifully timbered Tudor building. For further information and brochure write or phone Mrs. Mary W. Higgs.

T		B & B PER PERSON PER NIGHT		DINNER B & B PER PERSON PER WEEK		3
C		MIN £	MAX £	MIN £	MAX £	OPEN
		7.50	9	80	100	1—12

Ogmore by Sea
SOUTH WALES

Guest House

Hazelwood

Ogmore by Sea, Bridgend
Mid Glamorgan CF32 0PW
Tel: (0656) 880789

CATEGORIES: 3 3 2

Large lounge with colour television overlooking Bristol Channel. Two double bedrooms with hot and cold water one single bedroom. Full central heating. Ideally situated for beach, bus stop, village shops, walking, golf, or touring Cardiff, Swansea, Gower coast and South Wales Valleys.

C	B & B PER PERSON PER NIGHT		DINNER B & B PER PERSON PER WEEK		2
	MIN £	MAX £	MIN £	MAX £	OPEN
	7	8	70	80	1—12

Oxwich
SOUTH WALES

Hotel

Woodside Hotel and Restaurant*

Oxwich Village, Gower
Swansea, West Glamorgan
Tel: (044 120) 315 or 309

CATEGORIES: 3 3 4

16th century cottage hotel. Two minutes walk from Oxwich beach. We have TV room, lounge, guest dining room. A residents bar. Excellent food and personal attention assured. Your hosts, Graham and Cherry Charlton. Restaurant also available for lunch, snacks, teas, etc. Self-catering accommodation also available.

C	B & B PER PERSON PER NIGHT		DINNER B & B PER PERSON PER WEEK		11
	MIN £	MAX £	MIN £	MAX £	OPEN
	10.50		94		3—10

Guest Houses

Driftwood*

Oxwich, Gower, Swansea
West Glamorgan SA3 1LS
Tel: (0792) 820405

CATEGORIES: 1 3 1

Small, friendly guest house with personal attention. Situated only 5 minutes' walk from beautiful Oxwich Beach. Hot and cold water and shaver points in all bedrooms. Dining room with separate tables. Comfortable lounge with colour television. Ample car parking. Full central heating all rooms. Special rates for children.

C	B & B PER PERSON PER NIGHT		DINNER B & B PER PERSON PER WEEK		3
	MIN £	MAX £	MIN £	MAX £	OPEN
	6.50	7.50			3—10

Surf Sound*

Oxwich, Gower
West Glamorgan
Tel: (044120) 333

CATEGORIES: 3 2 2

About five minutes walk from Oxwich bay. Safe bathing, surfing, and fishing. Hot and cold water and shaver points in all bedrooms. Some bedrooms with private bathrooms. Special rates for children. Lounge with coloured television. Dining room with separate tables. Full central heating. Fire Certificate granted. Licensed.

C	B & B PER PERSON PER NIGHT		DINNER B & B PER PERSON PER WEEK		6
	MIN £	MAX £	MIN £	MAX £	OPEN
	7	8	47	54	4—9

Farmhouse

Norton Farm

Oxwich, Gower
West Glamorgan SA3 1LT
Tel: (044 120) 241

CATEGORIES: 1 3 2

A comfortable furnished farmhouse. Full central heating. Separate dining room. Lounge with coloured TV. Tea making facilities in bedrooms. Norton Farm is central to all beaches in Gower. Oxwich Bay is very sandy and safe for bathing. Plenty of good walks in the area.

C	B & B PER PERSON PER NIGHT		DINNER B & B PER PERSON PER WEEK		2
	MIN £	MAX £	MIN £	MAX £	OPEN
		6		59.50	3—10

Parkmill
SOUTH WALES

Farmhouses

Lunnon Farm*

Parkmill, Gower, Swansea
West Glam. SA3 2EJ
Tel: (0792) 825205

CATEGORIES: 1 1 1

Lunnon Farm, Parkmill, Tel: Penmaen 205. One double bedroom, one family bedroom, public bathroom, separate toilet. Mixed dairy farm 100 acres (working) fresh farm produce. 1/2 mile from Parkmill and beach. Pony trekking, horse riding, near beautiful Gower Peninsula beaches and walks around. Bed and breakfast only available. Swansea 8 miles.

C	B & B PER PERSON PER NIGHT		DINNER B & B PER PERSON PER WEEK		2
	MIN £	MAX £	MIN £	MAX £	OPEN
	6	7	56	60	4—9

Cestyll '83 – 1983
is the year of the
castles.

Parc-le-Breos Farm Guest House & Riding Holiday Centre

Parkmill, Gower
West Glamorgan
Tel: (044-125) 636

CATEGORIES: 2 2 2

Comfortable farmhouse in the heart of Gower surrounded by beautiful countryside and beaches. Perfect for walking and riding. Home grown produce, safe lawn area for children. Games room, riding, holidays and occasional day rides available. SAE for brochure.

	B & B PER PERSON PER NIGHT		DINNER B & B PER PERSON PER WEEK		4
T					
C	MIN £	MAX £	MIN £	MAX £	OPEN
	6.50	7.50	9	10	1—12

Guides to North, Mid and South Wales

What to see and do in Wales's three holiday regions. Each guide has A-Z gazetteers, maps, beach information, activities and attractions.
Available from: Wales Tourist Board Department W.T.S. P.O. Box 1, CARDIFF CF1 2XN. Price: £1.00 each region, including postage and packing.

Map ref: Jd6
Fortress town with a castle, priory and walls of the late 11th century. Narrow streets where the ancient Pembroke Fair is held in Autumn strengthen the historic atmosphere. Convenient for every beach on the South Pembrokeshire peninsula and Milford Haven bridge to Preseli.

Hotels and Inn

Coach House Inn*

116 Main Street, Pembroke
Dyfed SA71 4HN
Tel: (0646) 684602

CATEGORIES

5	4	5

Situated in the main street of the history-steeped Pembroke town. An ideal centre for the National Park and the delightful old Pembrokeshire Coast. You'll find all the facilities you want for a memorable holiday. Easy access to B & I Ferry to Ireland. Credit cards. Access, Visa, American Express.

	B & B PER PERSON PER NIGHT		DINNER B & B PER PERSON PER WEEK		14
T C	MIN £	MAX £	MIN £	MAX £	OPEN
	14.50	16	118.50	143.50	1—12

Corston House Hotel

Axton Hill, Hundleton
Pembroke, Wales SA71 5HB
Tel: (064 681) 242

CATEGORIES

3	3	3

Georgian manor house—delightful situated in 27 acres, lawned gardens and woodlands. Plenty of beaches coastal walks, within 3 miles, 4 family sized, 8 double rooms, hot and cold, shaver lights, 4 bathrooms, 5 toilets, colour TV, lounge, fully licensed lounge bar, games room warm air, central heating open all year.

	B & B PER PERSON PER NIGHT		DINNER B & B PER PERSON PER WEEK		12
	MIN £	MAX £	MIN £	MAX £	OPEN
		9.50		75	1—12

The Court Hotel*

Lamphey
Pembroke SA71 5NT
Tel: (0646) 672273

CATEGORIES

5	4	5

Long or short bargain holidays at this delightful 3 star country hotel on Pembrokeshire coast. Children share free under 12 years. Own riding stables and heated pool. Golf, squash, sailing, rambling and the beaches nearby. Luxury rooms and excellent restaurant featuring local sea-food and produce. Honeymoon suites. Open Christmas and New Year. A Best Western Hotel.

	B & B PER PERSON PER NIGHT		DINNER B & B PER PERSON PER WEEK		14
T C	MIN £	MAX £	MIN £	MAX £	OPEN
	18.25		112	134.50	1—12

Hill House Inn*

Cosheston
Pembroke SA72 4UH
Tel: (0646) 684352

CATEGORIES

3	3	4

Fully licensed village inn situated in Pembrokeshire countryside. Just a few miles from several lovely beaches and National Trust Park. Open Christmas. Hot and cold water in all rooms, some rooms with en-suite showers. Attractive bars with pool table, dining room with dance floor.

	B & B PER PERSON PER NIGHT		DINNER B & B PER PERSON PER WEEK		6
C	MIN £	MAX £	MIN £	MAX £	OPEN
	10	14	70	98	1—12

Lion Hotel*

Main Street, Pembroke
Dyfed SA71 4JS
Tel: (0646) 684501

CATEGORIES

3	4	5

Family run hotel in centre of the attractive main street of Pembroke, 50 yards from the castle. TV room, restaurant, bars on premises. Ideal for those who like variety. A busy place. Good centre for exploring South Pembrokeshire. AA and RAC two star. Excellent cuisine.

	B & B PER PERSON PER NIGHT		DINNER B & B PER PERSON PER WEEK		26
T C	MIN £	MAX £	MIN £	MAX £	OPEN
	12.50	18	112	142	1—12

Wheeler's Old Kings Arms Hotel

Main Street
Pembroke Dyfed
Tel: (0646) 683611

CATEGORIES

5	3	5

Ancient coaching inn close to castle where King Henry VII was born. Friendly hospitality centred around the old kitchen. Restaurant accounts for year round popularity. The restaurant reflects the love of good food and wines of the supervising proprietors, much appreciated by patrons and their guests.

	B & B PER PERSON PER NIGHT		DINNER B & B PER PERSON PER WEEK		21
C	MIN £	MAX £	MIN £	MAX £	OPEN
	17.35	19.50			1—12

Guest House

High Noon Guest House*

Lower Lamphey Road, Pembroke
Dyfed SA71 4AB
Tel: (0646) 683736/681232

CATEGORIES

3	3	2

Situated 100 yards from the main street of the ancient walled town of Pembroke. Bedrooms have hot and cold water with shaver-points. Ample showers. Bathroom and toilet facilities. Full central heating. Good home cooking. Separate attractive dining room, colour TV lounge. Private car park. Open all year. Children welcome. Full Fire Certificate.

	B & B PER PERSON PER NIGHT		DINNER B & B PER PERSON PER WEEK		9
C	MIN £	MAX £	MIN £	MAX £	OPEN
	8	10	70	85	1—12

Hotel

Cleddau Bridge Hotel*

The Avenue, Pembroke Dock
Dyfed SA72 4B
Tel: (0646) 685961

CATEGORIES

6	4	5

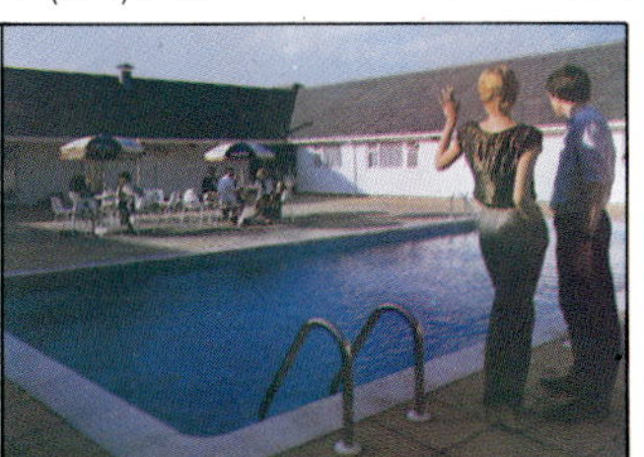

Family-owned hotel with luxury accommodation, all rooms with bath, phone, colour TV. Heated outdoor swimming pool with patio. Varied menu in the Royal Restaurant. Panoramic views of the Milford Haven waterway. Ideal centre for exploring Pembrokeshire. Multitude of beaches, castles and forts within 20 minutes drive. Welcome!

	B & B PER PERSON PER NIGHT		DINNER B & B PER PERSON PER WEEK		24
T C	MIN £	MAX £	MIN £	MAX £	OPEN
	15	25	142	162	1—12

Guest Houses

Ferry Guest House*

21 Pembroke Street
Pembroke Dock Dyfed SA72 6XH
Tel: (0646) 682558

CATEGORIES

3	3	2

Ideally suited for B & I Ferry, only two minutes from Terminal, within easy reach of shops, buses and trains. Hot and cold water and shaver points in all bedrooms. Single, double and family rooms with reduced rates for children. Lounge with television, separate dining room. Full central heating.

	B & B PER PERSON PER NIGHT		DINNER B & B PER PERSON PER WEEK		3
C	MIN £	MAX £	MIN £	MAX £	OPEN
	7				1—12

Roxana

Victoria Road, Pembroke Dock
Dyfed SA72 6XU
Tel: (0646) 682722

CATEGORIES

3	3	1

Close to B & I Ferry Port to Ireland and all amenities. Quiet area with parking.

	B & B PER PERSON PER NIGHT		DINNER B & B PER PERSON PER WEEK		3
	MIN £	MAX £	MIN £	MAX £	OPEN
	5	7			1—12

Hotels

Alan Leigh Hotel

14 Victoria Road, Penarth
South Glamorgan CF6 2EF
Tel: (0222) 701242

CATEGORIES

3	3	3

Ideally situated for all amenities, seafront close by. Cardiff 4 miles away, 6 golf clubs within 6 miles, 3 bowling clubs in Penarth. AA listed, RAC listed, licensed bar; ideally placed for a holiday in South Wales, with good home cooking and all modern facilities. Keys available at all times.

	B & B PER PERSON PER NIGHT		DINNER B & B PER PERSON PER WEEK		12
C	MIN £	MAX £	MIN £	MAX £	OPEN
	9.78	10.35	85	90	1—12

Glendale Hotel*

10 Plymouth Road, Penarth
South Glamorgan
Tel: (0222) 706701/708302

CATEGORIES

4	4	5

Ideally situated on the coast, three miles from Cardiff centre. Overlooking Alexandra Park, near Esplanade cliff walks. Golf course, tennis and swimming baths. Most rooms with private bathroom, all with television. Full central heating, TV lounge, cocktail bar. Conference room. Facilities for car parking. Special weekend breaks.

	B & B PER PERSON PER NIGHT		DINNER B & B PER PERSON PER WEEK		20
T C	MIN £	MAX £	MIN £	MAX £	OPEN
	10	14	105	135	1—12

Walton House Hotel*

37 Victoria Road, Penarth
South Galmorgan, CF6 2HY
Tel: (0222) 707782

CATEGORIES

4	4	4

Walton House is most favourably located within ten minutes walk of the sea front and a ten minute car journey from Cardiff. Colour television in all bedrooms. Excellent table d'hôte menus. Large car park. AA*, RAC* one star. Relais Routier. Details please contact Catherine Sutton B.A. Weekly rates on request.

	B & B PER PERSON PER NIGHT		DINNER B & B PER PERSON PER WEEK		14
T C	MIN £	MAX £	MIN £	MAX £	OPEN
	12	14			1—12

Guest Houses

Overthorpe Guest House

24 Plymouth Road, Penarth
South Glamorgan CF6 2DH
Tel: (0222) 700970

CATEGORIES

3	3	3

A friendly, Welsh welcome awaits you at this family guest house. Large lounge with colour TV. Within easy walking distance of sea-front, pier, promenade, shops, entertainment, buses and trains. Children and pets welcome. Baby-sitting service available. For further details write with SAE to Mrs. Anne Morse-Harries.

	B & B PER PERSON PER NIGHT		DINNER B & B PER PERSON PER WEEK		8
C	MIN £	MAX £	MIN £	MAX £	OPEN
	8.50	9.50	85	85	1—12

Starcross*

1 Archer Road, Penarth
South Glamorgan, CF6 2HW
Tel: (0222) 702718

CATEGORIES

1	3	3

Near town centre and railway station and within walking distance of beach and Cosmeston Country Park. Single, double and family room with special rates for children. Lounge with colour television, full central heating. Good plain cooking with home bread. Welcoming and friendly atmosphere.

	B & B PER PERSON PER NIGHT		DINNER B & B PER PERSON PER WEEK		3
C	MIN £	MAX £	MIN £	MAX £	OPEN
	7		70		1—12

Tourist Information Centres are listed at back of book.

Penmaen (Nicholaston)
SOUTH WALES

Hotel

Nicholaston House Hotel*

Penmaen, Gower, Swansea
West Glamorgan, SA3 2ML
Tel: (044 120) 312

CATEGORIES: 4 4 5

Centrally situated south side of Gower. Own grounds. Most bedrooms have private bathrooms. Also family bedrooms. Beautiful sea views. Excellent food, set or à la carte menu. Licensed restaurant. Central heating, snooker table, TV lounge, residents' lounge. Car park. Out of season breaks. Holiday flat also. SAE colour brochure to Jeanette Jenkins.

T C	B & B PER PERSON PER NIGHT		DINNER B & B PER PERSON PER WEEK		11
	MIN £	MAX £	MIN £	MAX £	OPEN
	10	13	90	110	2—12

Penmaenmawr
NORTH WALES

Guest House

Min-y-Don Guest House*

Min-y-Don, Conwy Road
Penmaenmawr, Gwynedd LL34 6BL
Tel: (0492) 623311

CATEGORIES: 1 3 3

Select, licensed guest house in pleasant surroundings, good food, service and cleanliness are assured. Comfortable bar, separate TV lounge and ample car parking space. 3 minutes from beach. Ideally situated for touring. Parties welcome, reductions for children sharing. Open all year. Full Fire Certificate. Sorry no pets.

C	B & B PER PERSON PER NIGHT		DINNER B & B PER PERSON PER WEEK		8
	MIN £	MAX £	MIN £	MAX £	OPEN
	5.50	6	49	52.50	1—12

Pennal
MID WALES

Guest House

Cwm Dwr*

Pennal, Machynlleth
Powys SY20 9DU
Tel: (065475) 610

CATEGORIES: 3 3 2

Cwm Dwr is a modernised slate cottage, peacefully situated in picturesque valley one mile from Pennal village, between Machynlleth and Aberdovey. Consisting of two double bedrooms and one single. Lounge and dining room, full central heating. Bed and breakfast, evening meal, excellent cuisine, personal attention. Sorry no pets.

C	B & B PER PERSON PER NIGHT		DINNER B & B PER PERSON PER WEEK		3
	MIN £	MAX £	MIN £	MAX £	OPEN
	5	8	63	84	1—12

Penybont (Powys)
MID WALES

Hotel

Severn Arms Hotel*

Penybont
Powys LD1 5UA
Tel: (059787) 224

CATEGORIES: 3 4 5

Noted for good food and comfortable accommodation all bedrooms having bathrooms en-suite with tea-making facilities provided. Comfortable residents lounge with colour TV. Full central heating installed. Ideal touring, walking, centre. 3½ miles fishing free to residents. Pony trekking available locally. Good parking, fully licensed. Brochure on request.

T C	B & B PER PERSON PER NIGHT		DINNER B & B PER PERSON PER WEEK		10
	MIN £	MAX £	MIN £	MAX £	OPEN
	9.50	11.50	98.50	110	1—12

Penybontfawr
NORTH WALES

Hotel

Plas Newydd Hotel

Pen-y-Bont Fawr, via Oswestry
Powys SY10 0NT
Tel: (069 174) 207

CATEGORIES: 3 3 3

Single, double and family rooms, some en-suite. TV lounge, central heating. In the beautiful Tanat Valley near the Berwyn Mountains, Lake Vyrnwy and Pistyll Rhaeadr Waterfall. Bala, Powis Castle and Welshpool and Llanfair. Light railway are all close by Snowdonia, Cader Idris, beaches and castles of North Wales are within easy reach by car.

C	B & B PER PERSON PER NIGHT		DINNER B & B PER PERSON PER WEEK		8
	MIN £	MAX £	MIN £	MAX £	OPEN
	9.90	10.90	95	102	3—10

Penygwryd
NORTH WALES

Hotel

Pen-y-Gwryd Hotel*

Nantgwynant, Gwynedd
LL55 4NT
Tel: (0286) 870211/870768

CATEGORIES: 3 3 4

The home of British mountaineering. Set in the majestic mountain scenery of North Wales. Ideal centre for walking and climbing, fishing, swimming etc. The haunt of famous authors, artists and mountaineers. Excellent local food, freshly baked rolls, Welsh lamb, local salmon, fresh vegetables etc. Good conversation. Games room.

C	B & B PER PERSON PER NIGHT		DINNER B & B PER PERSON PER WEEK		20
	MIN £	MAX £	MIN £	MAX £	OPEN
	11.40	12.40	132	140	12—10

C

Children stay at reduced rates, wherever you see this symbol.

This symbol means you can book through your local travel agent.

T

Farmhouse

The Croft*

Heol-y-Barna, Pontarddulais
Swansea SA4 1HG
Tel: (0792) 883654

CATEGORIES

| 1 | 3 | 2 |

Completely modernised farmhouse with fine views of surrounding countryside. Friendly atmosphere. Three double bedrooms, two with hot and cold water. Two bathrooms. Full central heating. Reductions for children. Pets by arrangement. Pony trekking nearby. Ideally situated for touring South Wales. 8 miles from Swansea and short drive to Gower beaches.

C	B & B PER PERSON PER NIGHT		DINNER B & B PER PERSON PER WEEK		🛏 3
	MIN £	MAX £	MIN £	MAX £	OPEN
	6	7.50	60	70	1—12

Hotel

Bron Dirion Hotel

Pontllyfni, Caernarfon
Gwynedd LL54 5EU
Tel: (028 686) 346

CATEGORIES

| 3 | 3 | 2 |

A 9-bedroomed charming 19th century family-owned hotel set in 8 acres of secluded grounds overlooking Caernarfon Bay. The hotel has a licensed bar, television lounge and excellent cuisine in the resturant. Ideally situated for family touring. Angling and golfing holidays with Snowdonia, Porthmadog and Anglesey all within easy reach. Many beautiful beaches locally.

C	B & B PER PERSON PER NIGHT		DINNER B & B PER PERSON PER WEEK		🛏 9
	MIN £	MAX £	MIN £	MAX £	OPEN
	8.50	9.50	70	80	3—10

Guest House

Plas Brynaerau Country House*

Pontllyfni, Caernarfon
Gwynedd LL54 5EP
Tel: (028 686) 210

CATEGORIES

| 1 | 4 | 5 |

Georgian house set in 6 acres. Sea views and balcony to main bedrooms. ½ mile from sea, 5 miles Caernarfon. Easy reach Lleyn Peninsula, Snowdonia, comfortable rooms. Antique paintings and small items for sale. Features superb gourmet restaurant. Full à la carte menu. Snacks also available. Fully licensed. Personal service from owners.

C	B & B PER PERSON PER NIGHT		DINNER B & B PER PERSON PER WEEK		🛏 4
	MIN £	MAX £	MIN £	MAX £	OPEN
	7.50	8.50	80.50	87.50	1—12

Guest House

Pantyfedwen

Pontrhydfendigaid, Ystrad Meurig
Dyfed SA25 6EN
Tel: (09745) 358

CATEGORIES

| 1 | 2 | 2 |

Old house of charm and character close to Strata Florida Abbey. The peace and tranquility enjoyed by the monks unsullied by the centuries. Ideal centre for walking, bird watching, fishing or just relaxing. Lounge with colour television, full central heating, extra log fires in winter. Warm welcome assured.

T / C	B & B PER PERSON PER NIGHT		DINNER B & B PER PERSON PER WEEK		🛏 2
	MIN £	MAX £	MIN £	MAX £	OPEN
	7	8	70	96	1—12

Farmhouse

Glan-Dwr Farm*

Pontshaen, Llandyssul
Dyfed SA44 4UA
Tel: (054 555) 255

CATEGORIES

| 3 | 3 | 4 |

Glan Dwr is a stone built farmhouse. Tastefully modernised. Retaining a wealth of character and charm. Set on a hillside overlooking Clettwr Fach Valley, with Glan Dwr as your base. Discover sandy bays, rugged coast. Enjoy the freedom of mountain, moorland, valleys.
BTA recommended country guest house.

T / C	B & B PER PERSON PER NIGHT		DINNER B & B PER PERSON PER WEEK		🛏 5
	MIN £	MAX £	MIN £	MAX £	OPEN
	8	9.25	75	82	1—12

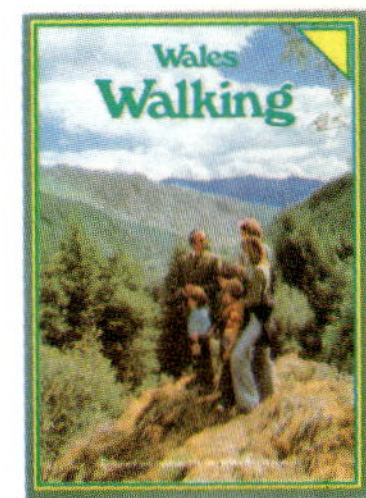

Walking
For 1983, a completely revised edition of this best-selling guide to Walking in Wales. Describes hundreds of way-marked and unway-marked walks designed for families and the more enthusiastic rambler.
Available from: Wales Tourist Board Department W.T.S. P.O. Box 1, CARDIFF CF1 2XN. Price: £1.35p including postage and packing.

Tourist Information Centres are listed at back of book.

For autumn to spring breaks send for our free Great Little Breaks booklet.

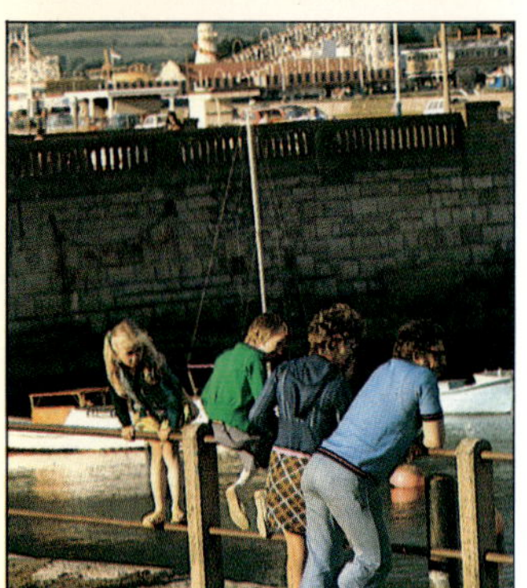

Map ref: Lc6
Happy Queen of the Glamorgan Coast, Porthcawl is an all the year round attraction. A 3,000 vehicle caravan park extends east, whilst west-wards the promenade is hotel-fronted. Golf at Royal Porthcawl, sea angling and surfing for boards and canoes, the giant funfair, small harbour and shopping centre, all add up to a holiday resort with something for everyone.

Hotels

Atlantic Hotel

West Drive, Porthcawl
Mid Glamorgan CF36 3LT
Tel: (065 671) 5011

CATEGORIES

| 5 | 4 | 5 |

The Atlantic directly overlooks the Bristol Channel, on the most natural part of Porthcawl seafront. It is conveniently situated near two excellent golf courses and the extensive beaches at Rest Bay. The town centre is within easy walking distance. The hotel is fully licensed and each bedroom has bathroom en-suite, colour television, radio/telephone, tea and coffee-making facilities. The restaurant offers superior cuisine and fine wines. Special weekend rates are available throughout the year.

	B & B PER PERSON PER NIGHT		DINNER B & B PER PERSON PER WEEK		15
T					
C	MIN £	MAX £	MIN £	MAX £	OPEN
	22	24	165	165	1—12

Brentwood Hotel*

Mary Street, Porthcawl
Mid-Glamorgan, CF36 3YN
Tel: (065671) 2725/6815

CATEGORIES

| 4 | 4 | 5 |

Situated in town centre, easy reach of shopping centre, night clubs. Beach only 2 minutes walk. Golf courses and bus station. Most rooms have showers or bathrooms en-suite. All with central heating, radios, baby listening, early morning call. Tea and coffee-making facilities, colour TV. Excellent cuisine. Bistro and cocktail bar. Parking available.

	B & B PER PERSON PER NIGHT		DINNER B & B PER PERSON PER WEEK		27
T					
C	MIN £	MAX £	MIN £	MAX £	OPEN
	11.50	17.50	110	140	1—12

Fairways Hotel*

Seafront, Porthcawl
Mid-Glamorgan
Tel: (065671) 2085

CATEGORIES

| 4 | 5 | 5 |

Delightful fully licensed family hotel. Sea front location, 27 bedrooms, the majority having en-suite and tea-making facilities. Single, double and family rooms available with special discount rates for children. Lift to all floors. Restaurant renowned for excellent cuisine. Ample car parking. Dogs welcome.

	B & B PER PERSON PER NIGHT		DINNER B & B PER PERSON PER WEEK		27
C	MIN £	MAX £	MIN £	MAX £	OPEN
	15	19	100	125	1—12

Maid of Sker Hotel

West Road, Nottage, Porthcawl
Mid Glamorgan CF36 3RT
Tel: (0656 71) 2172/43

CATEGORIES

| 6 | 4 | 4 |

The Maid of Sker, RAC, AA is pleased to offer ten luxury bedrooms with bathroom en-suite. Only minutes off M4 motorway but situated in quiet rural setting. Ideally suited for the business-man, holidaymakers, weekend travellers or golfer. Buffet lunches, à la carte restaurant and traditional Sunday Lunch.

	B & B PER PERSON PER NIGHT		DINNER B & B PER PERSON PER WEEK		10
T					
C	MIN £	MAX £	MIN £	MAX £	OPEN
	17.50	19.50	165	179	1—12

Minerva Private Hotel*

52 Esplanade Avenue, Porthcawl
Mid-Glamorgan, CF36 3YU
Tel: (065671) 2428

CATEGORIES

| 3 | 4 | 2 |

Adjacent sea and shops. Home cooking. Personal attention. Fire Certificate. Children and dogs catered for. Closed Christmas.

	B & B PER PERSON PER NIGHT		DINNER B & B PER PERSON PER WEEK		7
T					
C	MIN £	MAX £	MIN £	MAX £	OPEN
	6.50		66.50		1—12

Seaways Hotel*

Mary Street, Porthcawl
Mid Glamorgan CF36 3YA
Tel: (065671) 3510

CATEGORIES

| 3 | 3 | 4 |

A comfortable family run hotel within easy reach of beach and amenities. Two luxurious bars, table d'hôte and à la carte menus. Bar lunches, open all year. Fully licensed, many rooms with bath toilet colour television. All rooms with tea making facilities and radio alarm call. Credit cardholders welcome.

	B & B PER PERSON PER NIGHT		DINNER B & B PER PERSON PER WEEK		12
C	MIN £	MAX £	MIN £	MAX £	OPEN
	9	16	86.50	136.50	1—12

Guest House

Penoyre

29 Mary Street, Porthcawl
Mid Glamorgan, CF36 3YW
Tel: (065671) 4550

CATEGORIES

| 3 | 3 | 2 |

This clean, cosy guest house is only 2 minutes walk from the beach, the town centre swimming pools, the Grand Pavilion. The Coney Beach fun fair is within walking distance. For your comfort there is full central heating, TV lounge. A warm welcome awaits you from Ann and Jim Ormiston.

	B & B PER PERSON PER NIGHT		DINNER B & B PER PERSON PER WEEK		4
C	MIN £	MAX £	MIN £	MAX £	OPEN
	6.75	8	45	52	1—12

Map ref: Ae7
Main town of east Lleyn Peninsula, rail served by British Rail, Ffestiniog Narrow Gauge Railway and Welsh Highland Railway. Sandy bays extend to Black Rock sands and sailing from the harbour is popular. Nearby Aberglaslyn Pass beauty spot leads on to the lovely valleys about the foot of Snowdon.

Hotels

Bwlch-y-Fedwen Country House Hotel*

Penmorfa, Porthmadog
Gwynedd LL49 9RY
Tel: (0766) 2975

CATEGORIES: 4 4 3

17th century inn now fully modernised, but retaining original character with exposed stonework and beams. Antique furniture and dining by candlelight with traditional English and Welsh cooking, helps to keep this atmosphere for quiet relaxation of our guests. All bedrooms have private bathrooms with fitted carpets.

	B & B PER PERSON PER NIGHT		DINNER B & B PER PERSON PER WEEK		6
	MIN £	MAX £	MIN £	MAX £	OPEN
	12.75	15.25	115	127	4—10

Glaslyn Hotel*

Prenteg, Porthmadog
Gwynedd LL49 95P
Tel: (0766) 2861

CATEGORIES: 4 3 3

A family concern situated on the A498 road between Tremadog and Beddgelert. All bedrooms have private bathrooms and teasmade facilities. Family rooms available. TV lounge, two bars. Children's room and live entertainment up to six nights a week. Ideally situated for all leisure pastimes.

T C	B & B PER PERSON PER NIGHT		DINNER B & B PER PERSON PER WEEK		6
	MIN £	MAX £	MIN £	MAX £	OPEN
	7	8.50	66.50	77.50	1—12

Owen's Commercial and Residential*

71 High Street, Porthmadog
Gwynedd LL49 9EU
Tel: (0766) 2098

CATEGORIES: 3 2 3

Small family hotel. Table licence. Town centre. AA listed. TV lounge. Hot and cold water, central heating throughout. Children welcome. Fire Certificate. Residential proprietors, Lena and Edwin Owen. Popular yachting harbour and Ffestiniog narrow-gauge railway few minutes walk away. Within easy reach of lovely beaches and Snowdonia Mountain Range.

C	B & B PER PERSON PER NIGHT		DINNER B & B PER PERSON PER WEEK		12
	MIN £	MAX £	MIN £	MAX £	OPEN
	8.50	9.50	86	95	2—11

Royal Sportsman

High Street, Porthmadog
Gwynedd LL49 9HA
Tel: (0766) 2015/2030

CATEGORIES: 3 4 4

A comfortable small hotel with 21 bedrooms, some with private bath and all with telephone, radio, colour TV and tea/coffee making facilities. Car park. Weekend and mid-week bargain breaks and hightime holidays available. Good touring base for North Wales, Snowdonia and visiting the famous Ffestiniog Railway.

T C	B & B PER PERSON PER NIGHT		DINNER B & B PER PERSON PER WEEK		21
	MIN £	MAX £	MIN £	MAX £	OPEN
	18.75	21.50			1—12

Tan-yr-Onnen Hotel*

Ffordd Penamser, Porthmadog
Gwynedd
Tel: (0766) 2443

CATEGORIES: 4 3 2

Traditional cooking by the proprietors is a feature of the hotel. Welsh antiques, candle-lit dining room. All rooms with colour co-ordinates. Bar with railway relics and prints by Cuneo. Large garden with car park. All add up to one of the better hotels in the area.

C	B & B PER PERSON PER NIGHT		DINNER B & B PER PERSON PER WEEK		13
	MIN £	MAX £	MIN £	MAX £	OPEN
	11	11.50	115	120	1—12

Tourist Information Centres are listed at back of book.

Tyddyn Llwyn Hotel

Black Rock Road, Porthmadog
Gwynedd LL49 9UR
Tel: (0766) 2205

CATEGORIES: 3 4 6

Country House Hotel overlooking valley. Fully licenced, central heating. Magnificent views very high standard of comfort, food and personal attention. 10 bedrooms, Tudor Bar and Restaurant to seat 80 in solid oak panals and beams style. Miles of golden beach, golfing, climbing, tennis, fishing, yachting, riding all within 2 miles. 1982 rates quoted.

C	B & B PER PERSON PER NIGHT		DINNER B & B PER PERSON PER WEEK		10
	MIN £	MAX £	MIN £	MAX £	OPEN
	10	14.50	82.80		1—12

Guest Houses

'Borthwen'

Borth-y-Gest, Porthmadog, Gwynedd
LL49 9TP Tel: (0766) 2637
Enquiries: Mrs. G. M. Owen

CATEGORIES: 1 2 1

Ideal for bed and breakfast from £6.50. Attractive private house situated on sea front. Panoramic view of bay and mountains. Fully centrally heated. Hot and cold water in all bedrooms. Within easy reach of sandy coves. Parking.

C	B & B PER PERSON PER NIGHT		DINNER B & B PER PERSON PER WEEK		4
	MIN £	MAX £	MIN £	MAX £	OPEN
	6.50	7.50			3—10

Clogwyn Isa*

Morfa Bychan Road, Porthmadog
Gwynedd LL49 9RU
Tel: (0766) 2914

CATEGORIES: 1 2 2

House of character in own spacious grounds with superb views over estuary to Harlech Castle. Half mile Porthmadog High Street and Borth-y-Gest beaches. Two double bedded rooms, one twin, two with vanity units. A warm welcome with good home cooking. Ample parking. Dogs by prior arrangement.

T C	B & B PER PERSON PER NIGHT		DINNER B & B PER PERSON PER WEEK		3
	MIN £	MAX £	MIN £	MAX £	OPEN
	6.50	7	67	75	1—12

For autumn to spring breaks send for our free Great Little Breaks booklet.

Guest House*

49 Madog Street, Porthmadog
Gwynedd LL49 9BU
Tel: (0766) 3107

CATEGORIES: 1 1 2

Ideally situated for touring Snowdonia, visiting the Ffestiniog Railway and local beaches. Within easy reach of the town centre, buses and railway station. Homely atmosphere, children welcome. Central heating in all rooms, ample parking nearby. Open all the year round.

C	B & B PER PERSON PER NIGHT		DINNER B & B PER PERSON PER WEEK		4
	MIN £	MAX £	MIN £	MAX £	OPEN
	5.50	6.50	52.50	59.50	1—12

The Oakleys Guest House*

The Harbour, Porthmadog
Gwynedd LL49 9AS
Tel: (0766) 2482

CATEGORIES: 2 2 2

Situated on the harbour in Porthmadog. Licensed, an excellent base for visiting Snowdonia, Portmeirion and the beaches of Lleyn Peninsula, taking in Pwllheli, Abersoch and Criccieth. Fishing sea, trout and salmon. Golf course nearby. Spacious free car park. Comfortable lounge informal holiday atmosphere. Contact proprietors Mr. & Mrs. A. H. Biddle.

C	B & B PER PERSON PER NIGHT		DINNER B & B PER PERSON PER WEEK		8
	MIN £	MAX £	MIN £	MAX £	OPEN
	7.50	8.50	80	95	3—12

Portreuddyn Castle (Plas Portreuddyn)

Tremadoc, Porthmadog, Gwynedd
LL49 9SN
Tel: (0766) 2594

CATEGORIES: 3 2 2

Stone built house of character set in woodland. A family run guest house. Log fire and colour TV in lounge. Dining room overlooking mountains. Bedrooms have toilet and shower, hairdryer, teasmade and colour TV. Special diets catered for. Good choice of menu. Car parking space. Fire Certificate. SAE for brochure.

C	B & B PER PERSON PER NIGHT		DINNER B & B PER PERSON PER WEEK		4
	MIN £	MAX £	MIN £	MAX £	OPEN
	8.50	10	90	95	1—12

Treforris*

Garth Road, Porthmadog
Gwynedd LL49 9BN
Tel: (0766) 2853

CATEGORIES: 3 3 2

Homely guest house within easy reach of beach and mountains. Outdoor pursuits nearby include pony trekking, putting green and golf at Black Rock Sands, and local scenic walks. Steps to Borth-y-Gest beach are just down the road. Evening meal is optional. Separate sitting room and TV room with colour television.

C	B & B PER PERSON PER NIGHT		DINNER B & B PER PERSON PER WEEK		6
	MIN £	MAX £	MIN £	MAX £	OPEN
	6	6	66.50	66.50	1—12

Farmhouse

Cefn Uchaf Farm*

Garndolbenmaen, Porthmadog
Gwynedd LL51 9PJ
Tel: (076675) 239

CATEGORIES: 3 2 2

Cefn Uchaf is within easy reach of Porthmadog, beaches and Snowdonia Mountains, set in beautiful scenery with a panoramic view of Snowdonia. A modern centrally heated farmhouse, two rooms with private shower, teasmades, two lounges, colour TV. A 140 acre mixed livestock farm. Salmon and sea trout fishing available in season on grounds. Pony/donkey rides for children. For brochure write to: Mrs. R. A. Jones.

T C	B & B PER PERSON PER NIGHT		DINNER B & B PER PERSON PER WEEK		11
	MIN £	MAX £	MIN £	MAX £	OPEN
	6.50	7.50	65	75	1—12

Wales Tourist map

A real best seller. Detailed 5 miles/ 1 inch scale, also includes a wealth of tourist information, town plans, suggested tours and information centres.

Available from: Wales Tourist Board Department W.T.S. P.O. Box 1, CARDIFF CF1 2XN. Price: 65p including postage and packing.

Port Talbot
SOUTH WALES

Hotel

Twelve Knights Hotel

Margam Road, Margam
Port Talbot, SA13 2OB
Tel: (0639) 882381

CATEGORIES

| 5 | 4 | 5 |

11 bedrooms with colour TV telephone and tea/coffee making facilities. Close to M4 motorway junction 38, minutes away from Port Talbot. Tourists will appreciate the Twelve Knights proximity to the West Glamorgan coast-line, Gower Peninsula, Black Mountain and Margam Nature Park. Conference suite. Renowned for Knights "Carvery" restaurant.

	B & B PER PERSON PER NIGHT		DINNER B & B PER PERSON PER WEEK		11
T	MIN £	MAX £	MIN £	MAX £	OPEN
C	22	24.75	196	215.25	1—12

Prestatyn
NORTH WALES

Hotels

Bron-y-Bryn Country Lodge & Restaurant*

Bryniau, Dyserth, Prestatyn
Clwyd LL18
Tel: (0745) 570442

CATEGORIES

| 3 | 4 | 5 |

Secluded country hotel and restaurant (licensed) with beautiful panoramic sea views. Ideal touring centre for Chester, Snowdonia, Betws, Anglesey. 2½ miles Prestatyn's Ffrith beach. Nearby golf and squash courts, lovely country walks. Tea facilities. Personally supervised by resident owners. Car park. Fire Certificate. Bar, sun lounge, restaurant. TV.

	B & B PER PERSON PER NIGHT		DINNER B & B PER PERSON PER WEEK		4
T	MIN £	MAX £	MIN £	MAX £	OPEN
C	7.50	10.50	77	90	1—12

Bryn Gwalia Hotel*

17 Gronant Road, Prestatyn
Clwyd LL19 9DT
Tel: (07456) 2442

CATEGORIES

| 3 | 3 | 4 |

Nicely situated in Prestatyn, close to amenities and within walking distance of beach and championship golf course. A comfortable family run hotel, TV lounge, lounge bar with bar snacks combined with good home cooking. Ample car parking. The hotel is situated at the top of the High Street, turn left 100 yards. Brochure on request.

	B & B PER PERSON PER NIGHT		DINNER B & B PER PERSON PER WEEK		9
T	MIN £	MAX £	MIN £	MAX £	OPEN
C	10	15	90	120	1—12

Guest House

Hawarden House

13-15 Victoria Road, Prestatyn
LL19 7SW
Tel: (07456) 4226

CATEGORIES

| 2 | 3 | 2 |

Small homely guest house close to main rail and bus stations, shops, beach and all amenities. Single, double, twin and family rooms. Special rates for children. Lounge with colour television, dining room with separate tables. Full central heating. Fire Certificate.

	B & B PER PERSON PER NIGHT		DINNER B & B PER PERSON PER WEEK		6
C	MIN £	MAX £	MIN £	MAX £	OPEN
	6.50	8	66.50	77	1—12

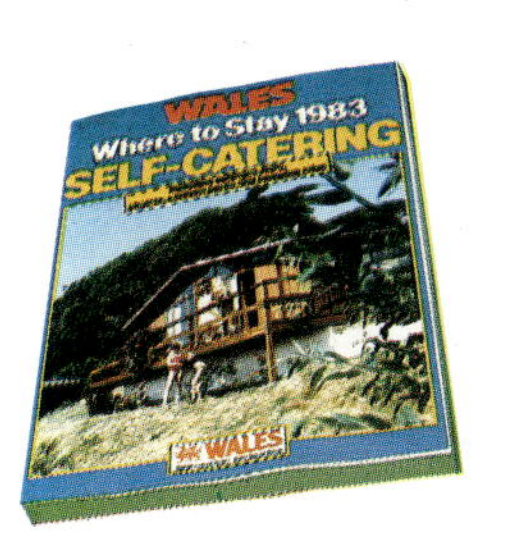

Pamper yourself on your main Wales holiday this year. But when you come back for that second, short break later in the year, remember we have a sister publication to this one. It's called "Where to Stay 1983 – Self Catering". Let us send you a copy. Details at back of book.

Presteigne
MID WALES

Hotels, Motels and Inns

The Bull Hotel*

St. David's Street, Presteigne
Powys LD8 7BP
Tel: (05-444) 488

CATEGORIES

| 3 | 3 | 4 |

A comfortable small hotel in the beautiful border country. Shower in every room. Central heating. Excellent centre for exploring Mid-Wales and walking Offa's Dyke. Bargain breaks available in Autumn to Spring. Known for good food and friendly service.

	B & B PER PERSON PER NIGHT		DINNER B & B PER PERSON PER WEEK		5
T	MIN £	MAX £	MIN £	MAX £	OPEN
	9.75	10.75	95	115	1—12

Radnorshire Arms

High Street, Presteigne
Powys LD8 2BE
Tel: (05444) 406

CATEGORIES

| 5 | 3 | 4 |

A black and white "Magpie" hotel dating from 1616 with Jacobean panelling and oak-beamed ceilings. 16 bedrooms with private bath, telephone, radio, colour television and tea/coffee-making facilities. Garage and car park. Pleasant garden. Special bargain breaks available.

	B & B PER PERSON PER NIGHT		DINNER B & B PER PERSON PER WEEK		16
T	MIN £	MAX £	MIN £	MAX £	OPEN
C	29.75				1—12

C Children stay at reduced rates, wherever you see this symbol.

Farmhouse

Gumma Farm

Presteigne
Powys LE8 2NP
Tel: (054 76) 243

CATEGORIES

| 1 | 3 | 3 |

350 acres stock rearing farm in beautiful Mid Wales, super for walking, bird watching, picnics. Situated in Offa's Dyke country. Near the border town of Presteigne. Good food, comfortable. Children welcome. Baby sitting. Within easy reach of 2 golf courses and horse riding. Nearest sea-side Aberystwyth.
Details and photograph on request.

C	B & B PER PERSON PER NIGHT		DINNER B & B PER PERSON PER WEEK		🛏 3
	MIN £	MAX £	MIN £	MAX £	OPEN
	6	8	70	84	5—10

Pumpsaint
SOUTH WALES

Farmhouse

Dolaucothi Farm

Pumpsaint, Llanwrda
Dyfed
Tel: (05585) 261

CATEGORIES

| 1 | 2 | 2 |

This 150 acre dairy farm in the midst of beautiful scenery on the A482 Lampeter/Llanwrda Road. A National Trust beauty spot within easy reach of coast and mountains. Trekking available nearby. Hot and cold in all rooms. Late night drink and Welsh cakes served. No dogs.

C	B & B PER PERSON PER NIGHT		DINNER B & B PER PERSON PER WEEK		🛏 4
	MIN £	MAX £	MIN £	MAX £	OPEN
	6.50	7	60	60	1—12

Pwllheli
NORTH WALES

Hotel

Seahaven Hotel*

18 West End Parade, Pwllheli
Gwynedd LL53 5PN
Tel: (0758) 2572

CATEGORIES

| 3 | 3 | 3 |

Overlooking sea and beach. Hot and cold water and shaver points in all rooms. Single, double and family rooms with reductions for children. Lounge with colour television. Licensed. Dogs welcome. Golf course within walking distance. Ideally suited for golf, walking, beaches and touring Snowdonia. Full Fire Certificate.

C	B & B PER PERSON PER NIGHT		DINNER B & B PER PERSON PER WEEK		🛏 10
	MIN £	MAX £	MIN £	MAX £	OPEN
	7	12	59	76	2—10

Farmhouses

Graeanfryn Farm*

Morfa Nefyn, nr Pwllheli
Gwynedd LL53 6YQ
Tel: (0758) 720455

CATEGORIES

| 2 | 2 | 2 |

Comfortable farm guest house, situated off main Pwllheli to Nefyn road, 1 mile Nefyn and Morfa-Nefyn beaches and golf links. Four bedrooms, three with hot and cold water, all modern conveniences. Separate lounge—dining room for each family. Good home produced, meals served. Evening Dinner. Bed and breakfast.

C	B & B PER PERSON PER NIGHT		DINNER B & B PER PERSON PER WEEK		🛏 4
	MIN £	MAX £	MIN £	MAX £	OPEN
	6	8	60	85	5—9

Gwynfryn Farm*

Pwllheli
LL53 5UF
Tel: (0758) 2536

CATEGORIES

| 2 | 2 | 1 |

Enjoy peaceful atmosphere ideal position only 1 mile from Pwllheli viewing sea. Within easy reach of sea, golf, tennis and numerous footpath passing through farm. Bedrooms well appointed, hot and cold only 4/5 visitors taken, parents can relax while children roam. Free range and organic produce served. Dinner served three or four nights per week, if required.

T C	B & B PER PERSON PER NIGHT		DINNER B & B PER PERSON PER WEEK		🛏 2
	MIN £	MAX £	MIN £	MAX £	OPEN
	5.50	7	9	12	1—12

Raglan
SOUTH WALES

Hotel

Beaufort Arms Hotel

Raglan, Gwent
NP5 2DY
Tel: (0291) 690412

CATEGORIES

| 3 | 3 | 5 |

Under new ownership and completely refurbished. Ideally situated adjacent A40 and A449 for touring and sporting facilities. A former coaching inn but now having all modern facilities. Full central heating. A la carte restaurant. TV in all bedrooms. Car parking on forecourt. Children welcome, but no pets.

T	B & B PER PERSON PER NIGHT		DINNER B & B PER PERSON PER WEEK		🛏 11
	MIN £	MAX £	MIN £	MAX £	OPEN
	14	18	110	124	1—12

Guest House

The Grange*

Clytha Road, Raglan
NP5 2YA
Tel: (0291) 690260

CATEGORIES

| 3 | 3 | 4 |

Elegant Victorian country house in 1½ acres of lawns and trees. Ideally situated for Wye Valley, Black Mountains, Brecon Beacons. Open all the year. Home grown vegetables, home baked bread. Log fires. Ample parking facilities. Private and wedding parties arranged. Local artists' paintings on display.

C	B & B PER PERSON PER NIGHT		DINNER B & B PER PERSON PER WEEK		🛏 3
	MIN £	MAX £	MIN £	MAX £	OPEN
	11.50		124.25		1—12

This symbol means you can book through your local travel agent.

Tourist Information Centres are listed at back of book.

Hotel

Bryn Tirion Hotel*

Red Wharf Bay, Isle of Anglesey
Gwynedd
Tel: (0248) 852366

CATEGORIES: 4 | 4 | 4

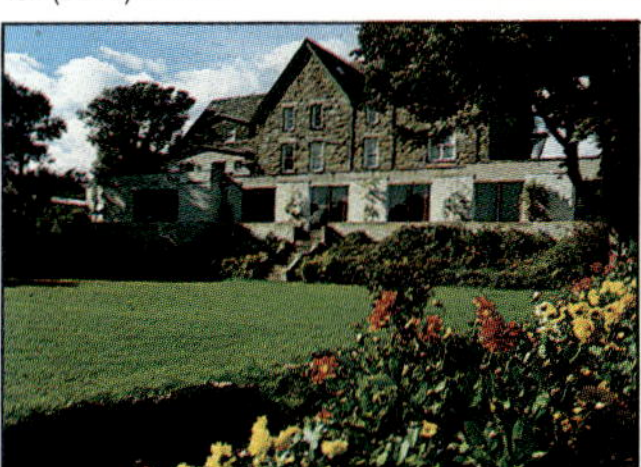

Magnificent views of the bay. Excellent centre for touring Anglesey, Snowdonia and North Wales. Most bedrooms with private bath and WC. Ample parking in hotel grounds. Good food and wines. Write or phone for brochure. Resident proprietors.

T C	B & B PER PERSON PER NIGHT		DINNER B & B PER PERSON PER WEEK		24
	MIN £	MAX £	MIN £	MAX £	OPEN
	12.75	13.50	102	108	4—10

Guest Houses

Gambo's End*

Reynoldston, Gower
Swansea SA3 1BR
Tel: (044 122) 467

CATEGORIES: 1 | 3 | 2

Clean, comfortable, friendly happy and restful atmosphere in pretty village surroundings. Centrally situated for all beaches, ideal countryside for walkers, good home cooking with varied cuisine. All modern conveniences, free on-site parking. Large lawn, many extra facilities. Pet dogs by arrangement.

C	B & B PER PERSON PER NIGHT		DINNER B & B PER PERSON PER WEEK		3
	MIN £	MAX £	MIN £	MAX £	OPEN
	6	7	63	70	4—9

Greenways*

Hills Farm, Reynoldston,
Gower, W. Glam SA3 1AE
Tel: (044122) 325
or (0792) 390125

CATEGORIES: 2 | 2 | 2

In beautiful countryside. Greenways is adjacent to Cefn Bryn, a walkers' paradise. Central to all Gower bays. Own garden produce. TV lounge. Pets by arrangement. Car Park. Evening dinner, bed and breakfast or bed and breakfast only. SAE Please.

C	B & B PER PERSON PER NIGHT		DINNER B & B PER PERSON PER WEEK		7
	MIN £	MAX £	MIN £	MAX £	OPEN
	6	7	60	65	3—10

Map ref: Gd2
Market town and node for the valleys of Elan and Claerwen nearby where the giant lakes provide water for Birmingham—and trout for the table. Good pony trekking centre and angling base for the lakes and Wye.

Hotels

The Castle Hotel

East St, Rhayader
Powys LD6 5DL
Tel: (0597) 810846

CATEGORIES: 1 | 2 | 6

A fully licensed freehouse. Ideal for pony trekking, fishing and touring. Intimate restaurant, extensive menu and wine list. Open to non-residents. Popular hot and cold snacks served in lounge bar. Special children's menu available. Large car park at rear of hotel. Fire Certificate granted.

C	B & B PER PERSON PER NIGHT		DINNER B & B PER PERSON PER WEEK		6
	MIN £	MAX £	MIN £	MAX £	OPEN
	8	10			1—12

Elan Hotel*

West Street, Rhayader
Powys LD6 5AF
Tel: (0597) 810373

CATEGORIES: 3 | 3 | 4

Hot and cold water and shaver points in all rooms. Lounge with colour TV. Single, double, twin and family rooms. Central heating. Fire Certificate granted. Free car park. Cocktail bar with residential and restaurant licence. Well thought out menus and tastefully cooked food for residents and non-residents.

C	B & B PER PERSON PER NIGHT		DINNER B & B PER PERSON PER WEEK		15
	MIN £	MAX £	MIN £	MAX £	OPEN
	8.25	9.50	92.75	110	1—12

Elan Valley Hotel*

Near Rhayader, Powys
Mid-Wales LD6 5HN
Tel: (0597) 810448

CATEGORIES: 3 | 4 | 4

Country hotel near Elan Valley lakes. Free trout fishing for residents staying one week. Radio, room call all bedrooms. AA* RAC* Fully licensed free house. Relais Routiers, Ashley Courtenay. Full heating. Fire Certificate. Private bathrooms available. Good home cooking and friendly atmosphere. Visited by H.M. Queen Elizabeth II.

T C	B & B PER PERSON PER NIGHT		DINNER B & B PER PERSON PER WEEK		12
	MIN £	MAX £	MIN £	MAX £	OPEN
	12	14	95	109	1—12

Guest Houses

Bryngwy*

Rhayader, Powys
LD6 5BN
Tel: (0597) 810463

CATEGORIES: 3 | 3 | 1

Country house well situated with lovely views, adequate free parking.

C	B & B PER PERSON PER NIGHT		DINNER B & B PER PERSON PER WEEK		3
	MIN £	MAX £	MIN £	MAX £	OPEN
	6	7			3—10

Glan-Rhyd-Wen

Elan Valley, Rhayader
Powys LD6 5HL
Tel: (0597) 810427

CATEGORIES: 2 | 1 | 2

A modern comfortable bungalow situated on the Elan Valley road, near the market town of Rhayader, overlooking the River Elan. Full central heating, colour TV lounge, licensed. Second to none for views and walks of the beautiful reservoirs and a favourite spot for bird-watching. 200 yards of free fishing available.

	B & B PER PERSON PER NIGHT		DINNER B & B PER PERSON PER WEEK		8
	MIN £	MAX £	MIN £	MAX £	OPEN
	5.50	6.50	65	75	1—12

Farmhouses

Beili Neuadd*

Rhayader
Powys LD6 5NS
Tel: (0597) 810211

CATEGORIES
4 2 2

16th century stone farmhouse. Beautifully situated in "The lakeland of Wales." An historical area of great natural beauty. The spacious, centrally-heated accommodation comprises single, double and twin-bedded rooms with two bathrooms. From Rhayader take B4518N road for 1½ miles turn right by TV mast, farm on L after ¼ miles.

T C	B & B PER PERSON PER NIGHT		DINNER B & B PER PERSON PER WEEK		5
	MIN £	MAX £	MIN £	MAX £	OPEN
	6.50	7.50	77	84	1—12

Downfield Farm*

Rhayader
Powys LD6 5PA
Tel: (0597) 810394

CATEGORIES
1 2 2

Downfield Farm is a mixed farm situated one mile east of Rhayader, set just back off A44 Crossgates road with good clean access. We extend a warm welcome to all our guests. Log and coal fires are lit if weather is cold. Lounge comfortable with colour TV.

C	B & B PER PERSON PER NIGHT		DINNER B & B PER PERSON PER WEEK		3
	MIN £	MAX £	MIN £	MAX £	OPEN
	6	6.50	66.50	70	2—11

Gigrin Farm*

South Street, Rhayader
Powys LD6 5BL
Enquiries to: Lena Powell
Tel: (0597) 810243

CATEGORIES
1 2 2

Gigrin is a 200 acre mixed farm of cattle, sheep and horses. The farm house is a 17th century Welsh Long house surrounded by hills and enjoying views overlooking Wye Valley. ½ mile south of Rhayader, 3 miles from Elan Valley. 3 double bedrooms. Brochure on request.

C	B & B PER PERSON PER NIGHT		DINNER B & B PER PERSON PER WEEK		3
	MIN £	MAX £	MIN £	MAX £	OPEN
	6	6.50	70	73.50	4—10

Farmhouse

Bryn Mawr Guest Farm*

Rhoscefnhir, Isle of Anglesey
Gwynedd LL75 8YT
Tel: (024870) 326

CATEGORIES
1 3 3

17th century farmhouse set in 12 acres grassland. Ideal for all ages. Games room, colour TV, double and family rooms. Central heating. Shaving points. Hot and cold water. Central for beaches, coves, sports centres, horse riding. Good home cooking. Pleasant atmosphere. Licensed bar. Fire Certificate. Special rates for children.

C	B & B PER PERSON PER NIGHT		DINNER B & B PER PERSON PER WEEK		6
	MIN £	MAX £	MIN £	MAX £	OPEN
	6.50	7.50	66.50	73.50	1—12

Farmhouse

Bryn Crin Farm

Rhosgadfan, Nr. Caernarfon
Gwynedd LL54 7HG
Tel: (0286) 830166

CATEGORIES
1 2 2

Quietly situated in 8 acres with magnificent views overlooking Caernarfon Bay and the Isle of Anglesey. Ample parking space. Two double rooms, one single, full central heating. Television. Large gardens and sun terrace for guests use. Ideally situated for Trekking, walking, touring Snowdonia or simply taking a restful holiday.

C	B & B PER PERSON PER NIGHT		DINNER B & B PER PERSON PER WEEK		3
	MIN £	MAX £	MIN £	MAX £	OPEN
	6.50	8.50	60	75	1—12

Hotels

Bay Hotel

Rhosneigr, Anglesey
Gwynedd LL64 5QW
Tel: (0407) 810332

CATEGORIES
3 3 3

Easily accessible by road and rail, excellent centre for sightseeing. Bathing direct from hotel. Broad beach. Indoor games room—billiards, table tennis.
Ideal location for:
Golf (18 holes) riding, fishing, boating, walking. Book now for summer holidays. Ideal for families. Finest food. Warm welcome. Write or telephone (0407) 810332.

C	B & B PER PERSON PER NIGHT		DINNER B & B PER PERSON PER WEEK		30
	MIN £	MAX £	MIN £	MAX £	OPEN
	12.50	17.50	110.50	124.50	3—10

Glan Neigr Hotel*

Rhosneigr
Gwynedd LL64 5JA
Tel: (0407) 810516

CATEGORIES
1 3 4

Now under new management the Glan Neigr is ideally situated to take advantage of all the facilities Rhosneigr has to offer—golf, riding, sea view and lake fishing, and is no more than a few minutes walk away from the sea front and beaches.

C	B & B PER PERSON PER NIGHT		DINNER B & B PER PERSON PER WEEK		7
	MIN £	MAX £	MIN £	MAX £	OPEN
	9.75	9.75	110	110	1—12

Hotel

Worms Head Cottage Hotel Ltd

Rhossili, near Swansea
West Glamorgan
Tel: (044 120) 512

CATEGORIES
3 4 4

The hotel is the most beautifully situated in Gower. It stands in a unique position on the cliff edge overlooking Rhossili Bay with the downs as a background. Bathing from sandy beaches. Walks and fishing are amenities to be enjoyed. RAC** and AA. **

C	B & B PER PERSON PER NIGHT		DINNER B & B PER PERSON PER WEEK		21
	MIN £	MAX £	MIN £	MAX £	OPEN
	9	10.25	88	97	1—12

Guest House

Sunnyside

Rhossili, Gower
West Glam SA3 1PL
Tel: (044 120) 596

CATEGORIES

| 1 | 3 | 2 |

Small private guest house, near sandy beaches. Dining room with separate tables. Good home cooking with garden produce. Lounge with colour television. Parking space. Reduction for children. Pets welcome access to rooms at all times. Ideally situated for riding, hang gliding and surfing. Beautiful coastal walks.

C	B & B PER PERSON PER NIGHT		DINNER B & B PER PERSON PER WEEK		3
	MIN £	MAX £	MIN £	MAX £	OPEN
	5	7	50	54	4—9

Rhostryfan — NORTH WALES

Farmhouse

Cae Garw

Rhostryfan near Caernarfon
Gwynedd LL54 7NH
Tel: (0286) 830287

CATEGORIES

| 3 | 2 | 2 |

Cae Garw is a small modern 36 acre farm. Rearing cattle, sheep, hens. Within easy reach of Snowdonia and Lleyn Peninsuls. Good farmhouse food provided, home-made bread and Bara Brith.

C	B & B PER PERSON PER NIGHT		DINNER B & B PER PERSON PER WEEK		3
	MIN £	MAX £	MIN £	MAX £	OPEN
	6	6.50	75	82	4—10

Rhyl — NORTH WALES

Map ref: Bd3
One of the three biggest and liveliest resorts on the North Wales coast, Rhyl's 2 miles of sandy-shore promenade is choc-full of interesting attractions—from the mammoth Sun Centre to the giant Royal Floral Hall. Every kind of recreation is here as well as sport: Golf, tennis and bowls, sailing—from Foryd Harbour—and sea angling, as well as good shopping. There is lively evening entertainment, daily competitions, theatre, cinemas and discotheques. Touring coaches leave daily for all North Wales beauty spots and attractions and the town is rail served.

Hotels, Motels and Inns

Grange Hotel

41 East Parade
Rhyl, Clwyd
Tel: (0745) 53174 or 55402

CATEGORIES

| 4 | 4 | 4 |

The Grange is delightfully situated overlooking the promenade gardens and opposite the new Suncentre. Brochure available showing this feature. A great number of our guests return again. Nevertheless our success depends upon the success and satisfaction of your visit. Car Park. Fire Certificate held. SAE for brochure.

T	B & B PER PERSON PER NIGHT		DINNER B & B PER PERSON PER WEEK		26
C	MIN £	MAX £	MIN £	MAX £	OPEN
	9	12	85	95	1—12

Hafod-y-Mor*

18-20 Palace Avenue, Rhyl
Clwyd LL18 1HS
Tel: (0745) 2566

CATEGORIES

| 3 | 3 | 3 |

Single, double, twin and family rooms, honeymoon suite, some en-suite facilities. Colour TV lounge, tea-making and TV in all bedrooms. Mid-week bookings and weekend breaks. Fire-cover. Parking. Residential licence and lounge bar. Open all year. SAE brochures.

T	B & B PER PERSON PER NIGHT		DINNER B & B PER PERSON PER WEEK		10
C	MIN £	MAX £	MIN £	MAX £	OPEN
	7	10	55	75	1—12

Pier Hotel*

23 East Parade, Rhyl
Clwyd LL18 3AL
Tel: (0745) 50280

CATEGORIES

| 3 | 3 | 2 |

The Pier Hotel provides a comfortable bed for every guest and newly wed. Reaches the standards of Tourist Board. There's fishing too off Foryd Ford. Convenient to promenade and beach, to roam. Clean and licensed. A super home. This marvellous house makes most select. Popular In Every Respect.

C	B & B PER PERSON PER NIGHT		DINNER B & B PER PERSON PER WEEK		12
	MIN £	MAX £	MIN £	MAX £	OPEN
	7.50	9	56	66	1—12

Sandringham Hotel*

West Parade, Rhyl
Clwyd LL18 1HH
Tel: (0745) 53986

CATEGORIES

| 3 | 3 | 4 |

Family run hotel situated on promenade. 24 bedrooms including family rooms all with tea/coffee making facilities. Electric fires, excellent cuisine, two bars serving real ale, organist weekends. Concession rates for senior citizens during May, June and September. Central for touring and all amenities.

T	B & B PER PERSON PER NIGHT		DINNER B & B PER PERSON PER WEEK		24
C	MIN £	MAX £	MIN £	MAX £	OPEN
	10	10.50	90	93	3—11

Sherbrook Hotel*

71 West Parade, Rhyl
Clwyd LL18 1HN
Tel: (0745) 31592

CATEGORIES

| 3 | 3 | 3 |

Modernised hotel situated on sea front. "Spiders Web" bar for residents only. All age groups catered for. Choice of menu for breakfast. Fire Certificate. Sauna room. Teasmades in all rooms.

C	B & B PER PERSON PER NIGHT		DINNER B & B PER PERSON PER WEEK		21
	MIN £	MAX £	MIN £	MAX £	OPEN
	8.60	9.75	62.50	70	2—11

Guest Houses

Accra Guest House*

12 Aquarium Street
Rhyl, Clwyd
Tel: (0745) 51129

CATEGORIES

| 2 | 2 | 2 |

B & B, evening meal, home cooking. Child minding. Licenced bar. One minute from sea front. Central to all amenities. Recommended by well-known paper. Apply Mr. and Mrs. Strickland, 12 Aquarium Street, Rhyl. Tel: (0745) 51129.

C	B & B PER PERSON PER NIGHT		DINNER B & B PER PERSON PER WEEK		8
	MIN £	MAX £	MIN £	MAX £	OPEN
	6	7	50	58	3—10

"Arncliffe"*

100 Crescent Road, Rhyl
Clwyd LL18 1LY
Tel: (0745) 53634

CATEGORIES

| 2 | 3 | 2 |

Jacqueline and Don invite you to come and try the friendly atmosphere at "Arncliffe." We are just 4 minutes from the promenade with free baby sitting and of course the best of food. Central for all amenities and within walking distance for all the night life of Rhyl.

C	B & B PER PERSON PER NIGHT		DINNER B & B PER PERSON PER WEEK		7
	MIN £	MAX £	MIN £	MAX £	OPEN
	6	6.50	56	60	2—11

Belmont Guest House*

4 Beechwood Road
Rhyl, Clwyd
Tel: (0745) 51483

CATEGORIES
| 3 | 3 | 2 |

Holiday or mini break? "Belmont" is a comfortable and friendly guest house, offering excellent food and service, situated off lovely East Parade with the beach and Sun Centre just around the corner. Full central heating. Resident's TV lounge. Reductions low season, also children sharing with parents! Brochure available.

T C	B & B PER PERSON PER NIGHT		DINNER B & B PER PERSON PER WEEK		🛏 6
	MIN £	MAX £	MIN £	MAX £	OPEN
	6.50	6.75	52	60	3—10

Gwynfa Guest House

6 Beechwood Road, Rhyl
Clwyd LL18 3EU
Tel: (0745) 53848

CATEGORIES
| 1 | 3 | 2 |

With the hotel treatment established nine years with regular seasonal trade for all age groups. Recommended Menu. Colour TV. Lounge—come and go as you please. Hot and cold water in all bedrooms. Showers. 25 yards from golden beaches. Flower gardens and the new indoor Sun Centre Complex, including 3 pools.

T C	B & B PER PERSON PER NIGHT		DINNER B & B PER PERSON PER WEEK		🛏 6
	MIN £	MAX £	MIN £	MAX £	OPEN
	6.25	7.25	59.50	68.25	4—10

Haywood Guest House*

12 Edward Henry Street, Rhyl
Clwyd LL18 1TE
Tel: (0745) 36087

CATEGORIES
| 3 | 3 | 2 |

Small family guest house 100 yards off promenade. Central for all amenities and Sun Centre. Colour TV lounge. Open all year, own keys. Also OAP's early and late season. Cots and high chairs available.

C	B & B PER PERSON PER NIGHT		DINNER B & B PER PERSON PER WEEK		🛏 5
	MIN £	MAX £	MIN £	MAX £	OPEN
	5.50	6.50	49	56	1—12

The Ingledene

6 Bath Street, Rhyl
Clwyd LL18 3EB
Tel: (0745) 4872

CATEGORIES
| 2 | 3 | 2 |

The Ingledene is AA listed. Central for shops etc. Short distance from promenade, Floral Hall and bowling greens. All bedrooms have hot and cold water, shaver points and facilities for guests to make their own hot drinks. Residential licence. Access to rooms at all times.

C	B & B PER PERSON PER NIGHT		DINNER B & B PER PERSON PER WEEK		🛏 11
	MIN £	MAX £	MIN £	MAX £	OPEN
	8	9	50	60	1—11

Joydene

13 Edward Henry Street
Rhyl LL18 1TE
Tel: (0745) 50459

CATEGORIES
| 3 | 3 | 2 |

Small friendly guest house. Close to beach and all amenities. Colour TV lounge. Hot and cold water and shaver points in all rooms. Dining room with separate tables. Friendly atmosphere. Come and go as you please. Own keys. Prices are inclusive. Special rates for senior citizens.

C	B & B PER PERSON PER NIGHT		DINNER B & B PER PERSON PER WEEK		🛏 7
	MIN £	MAX £	MIN £	MAX £	OPEN
	5.50	6.50	49	56	1—12

Ravenscroft Guest House

14-16 Bath Street, Rhyl
Clwyd LL18 3EB
Tel: (0745) 4210

CATEGORIES
| 3 | 3 | 2 |

Our 24th season, bed and breakfast, 4-course dinner 6 p.m. (Sunday 1p.m.). 3 minutes promenade, shops, 7 minutes from Sun Centre. Rooms for 2 to 4 persons. Hot and cold water. Lounge with colour TV. Fire Certificate. Front door and bedroom keys. Sorry no dogs. Daily Mirror 'Old Codgers' recommended. Ideal touring North Wales. SAE please.

C	B & B PER PERSON PER NIGHT		DINNER B & B PER PERSON PER WEEK		🛏 8
	MIN £	MAX £	MIN £	MAX £	OPEN
	6.60	7	55	55	1—12

Toomargoed*

31-33 John Street, Rhyl
Clwyd LL18 1PP
Tel: (0745) 4103

CATEGORIES
| 2 | 3 | 3 |

Toomargoed, 31-33 John Street, Rhyl, tel: 0745-4103. Licensed. Separate colour TV lounge, dining room, own tables. Full English breakfast, 4-course dinner. Single, double and family rooms with special rates for children and OAP's. 150 yards promenade. Ideally situated town, churches, amenities. Touring parties catered for. Enquiries and brochure, SAE M. H. & B. Herrington.

C	B & B PER PERSON PER NIGHT		DINNER B & B PER PERSON PER WEEK		🛏 14
	MIN £	MAX £	MIN £	MAX £	OPEN
	7	8.50	52	65	3—10

Wroxeter*

29 Warren Road, Rhyl
Clwyd LL18 1DR
Tel: (0745) 53904

CATEGORIES
| 3 | 3 | 3 |

The Wroxeter is under the personal supervision of your hosts, Derek and Jean Bamford. We have a very nice bar and TV lounge and large modern furnished bedrooms. The Wroxeter is situated on a quiet road close to the Marine Lake and Voryd Harbour. 5 minutes town centre.

C	B & B PER PERSON PER NIGHT		DINNER B & B PER PERSON PER WEEK		🛏 7
	MIN £	MAX £	MIN £	MAX £	OPEN
	6		46		1—12

Hotel

Ruthin Castle*

Ruthin
Clwyd LL15 2NU
Tel: (08242) 2664 Telex 61169

CATEGORIES
| 5 | 5 | 4 |

Originally built as a fortress in 1282, this BTA Award-winning hotel stands in 35 acres of gardens and parkland which include ruins and dungeons. An ideal centre for touring North Wales. Own fishing, riding and golf available locally. The home of the original Mediaeval Banquet.

T C	B & B PER PERSON PER NIGHT		DINNER B & B PER PERSON PER WEEK		🛏 58
	MIN £	MAX £	MIN £	MAX £	OPEN
	21	23.50			1—12

Farmhouses

Bryn Awel*

Bontuchel, Ruthin
Clwyd LL15 2DE
Tel: (082 42) 2481

CATEGORIES
| 1 | 1 | 4 |

Set in beautiful scenery, 2 miles from the mediaeval town of Ruthin, in the Vale of Clwyd. Ideal for country walks. Fishing and horse riding nearby. Single, double and family rooms available. Easy reach of coastal resorts and Snowdon. No pets, but children are welcome.

C	B & B PER PERSON PER NIGHT		DINNER B & B PER PERSON PER WEEK		🛏 3
	MIN £	MAX £	MIN £	MAX £	OPEN
	5				1—12

Llanbenwch Farm*

Llanfair D.C., Ruthin
Clwyd LL15 2SH
Tel: (08242) 2340

CATEGORIES
| 3 | 3 | 2 |

Situated 3 miles from Ruthin on A525 (Wrexham road), it is a working farm. The oak beamed house conveniently situated for touring North Wales. Nice garden, good food assured. Bedrooms with washbasins, bathroom, two toilets. Dining room. Central heating. No dogs. Dinner, bed and breakfast.

C	B & B PER PERSON PER NIGHT		DINNER B & B PER PERSON PER WEEK		🛏 3
	MIN £	MAX £	MIN £	MAX £	OPEN
	5		49		2—11

Children stay at reduced rates, wherever you see this symbol.

St. Clears

Hotel

Black Lion Hotel*

St. Clears, Carmarthen
Dyfed SA33 4AA
Tel: (0994) 230700

CATEGORIES: 3 3 4

Small, friendly hotel run by family, 10 miles west of Carmarthen on main A40 road to Fishguard and Pembroke. Central for touring West Wales; easy access countryside and beaches. TV lounges, central heating, hot and cold shaver points all bedrooms, full dining-room facilities, bar snacks. AA, RAC recommended. Albert and Pat Lynch-Wilson.

	B & B PER PERSON PER NIGHT		DINNER B & B PER PERSON PER WEEK		🛏 11
T	MIN £	MAX £	MIN £	MAX £	OPEN
C	8	8.50	50	55	1—12

St. David's

SOUTH WALES

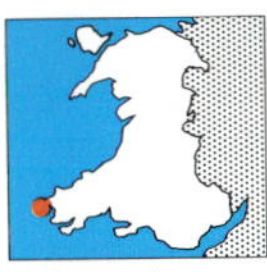

Map ref: Ja4 Cathedral City, probably the smallest in Britain. Little more than a village, it occupies a bracing situation on the western tip of South Wales. Islands and reefs lie offshore. Cliff scenery and sea-scapes abound, and the area is rich in both ancient and historic sites. St. David's Cathedral, squatting in a defile, is a gem and centre of pilgrimage through the ages. It has a selection of hotels, well sited, with an excellent reputation for food, wine and year round entertainment.

Hotels, Inns

City Inn*

New Street, St. David's
Pembrokeshire Dyfed
Tel: (0437) 720829

CATEGORIES: 3 3 5

Comfortable village pub/hotel, central to amenities of National Park. Cuisine ranges from cordon bleu to very good, depending upon mood of chef—my wife! Residents' lounge with colour T.V., and library to relax. Friendly, efficient service. General atmosphere informal and unpretentious—guests of similar disposition most welcome.

	B & B PER PERSON PER NIGHT		DINNER B & B PER PERSON PER WEEK		🛏 8
T	MIN £	MAX £	MIN £	MAX £	OPEN
C	6.50	9.50	60	85	1—12

Old Cross Hotel*

The Cross Square, St. David's
Dyfed SA62 6SP
Tel: (0437) 720387

CATEGORIES: 4 4 4

Situated in the centre of St. David's. All rooms with private bathrooms and tea or coffee making facilities. Fully licensed, with a bar and three lounges. We have a reputation for good food and offer both table d'hote and a la carte menus. Private car park for guests.

	B & B PER PERSON PER NIGHT		DINNER B & B PER PERSON PER WEEK		🛏 18
T	MIN £	MAX £	MIN £	MAX £	OPEN
C	11.50	16	120	152	3—11

St. Nons Hotel*

St. David's, Pembrokeshire
Dyfed SA62 6RJ
Tel: (0437) 720239

CATEGORIES: 4 4 5

All rooms private bath. Central heating throughout. A longstanding reputation for excellent food with friendly, efficient service. Fully licensed, with extensive, reasonably priced wine list. A full range of Bargain Breaks offered most of the year with special gastronomic weekends each month throughout the winter.

	B & B PER PERSON PER NIGHT		DINNER B & B PER PERSON PER WEEK		🛏 20
T	MIN £	MAX £	MIN £	MAX £	OPEN
C	12.50	14.50	125	148	1—12

Warpool Court Hotel*

St. David's
Pembrokeshire, Dyfed
Tel: (0437) 720300

CATEGORIES: 4 4 5

Overlooking the wild Atlantic on a remote peninsula of rugged beauty, steeped in ancient history. Inclusive fireside winter holidays with Welsh and classical music. In-house feature films and fine food. Memorable summer holidays lazing in the pool. Midsummer holiday offer.

	B & B PER PERSON PER NIGHT		DINNER B & B PER PERSON PER WEEK		🛏 25
T	MIN £	MAX £	MIN £	MAX £	OPEN
C	17.55	20.90	182.70	203	2—12

The Whitesands Bay Hotel*

Above Magnificent Whitesand Bay,
St. David's, Pembrokeshire
Dyfed SA62 6PT
Tel: (0437) 720403

CATEGORIES: 5 4 4

A three star country house hotel offering nearly every latest amenity: heated pool, sauna, solarium, launderette and coffee shop. Fully licensed. Luxury accommodation and excellent cuisine. Nearby sailing, fishing, riding, surfing and superb coastal walks. Free golf. The most westerly hotel in Wales.

	B & B PER PERSON PER NIGHT		DINNER B & B PER PERSON PER WEEK		🛏 25
T	MIN £	MAX £	MIN £	MAX £	OPEN
C	17	23	148	185	4—10

Guest Houses

Alandale Guest House*

43 Nun Street, St. David's,
Haverfordwest, Dyfed SA62 6NU
Tel: (0437) 720333

CATEGORIES: 3 3 2

Hot and cold water, shaver points and central heating in all six bedrooms; some rooms with sea view. Boat trips, horse riding, cliff walks two minutes from the famous Cathedral and shopping area. AA, and RAC listed. Lounge with colour TV, dining room with separate tables. Full current fire certificate.

	B & B PER PERSON PER NIGHT		DINNER B & B PER PERSON PER WEEK		🛏 6
C	MIN £	MAX £	MIN £	MAX £	OPEN
	6.75	7.25	70	75	2—11

Belmont Guest House*

Cross Square, St. David's
Pembrokeshire, Dyfed SA62 6SE
Tel: (043 788) 720264

CATEGORIES		
3	3	3

Ideally suited for Cathedral, shops, sandy beaches, coastal paths. We cater for non-smoking guests only. Bedrooms heated, well-furnished, wash basins, shaver points, cotton sheets. Comfortable guest lounge, colour TV, reading room. Excellent food. Personal attention of resident owners. Parking, play area. Fire Certificate. No pets. AA/RAC listed.

C	B & B PER PERSON PER NIGHT		DINNER B & B PER PERSON PER WEEK		8
	MIN £	MAX £	MIN £	MAX £	OPEN
	7.50	8.50	75	85	1—12

The Mount*

66 New Street, St. David's
Pembrokeshire, Dyfed SA62 6SU
Tel: (0437) 720276

CATEGORIES		
3	3	1

A 200 year old ex-farmhouse with character, a few minutes from city centre. Double and family rooms with reduced rates for children. Hot and cold water and shaver points in all bedrooms. Electric heating in rooms and electric blankets on beds. Colour TV lounge and private parking.

C	B & B PER PERSON PER NIGHT		DINNER B & B PER PERSON PER WEEK		4
	MIN £	MAX £	MIN £	MAX £	OPEN
	5	10			3—11

Redcliffe House*

17 New Street, St. David's
Pembrokeshire, Dyfed SA62 6SW
Tel: (0437) 720389

CATEGORIES		
3	3	2

Accommodation in spacious rooms; all modern conveniences. Hot and cold, shaver points, convector heating. Clean, comfortable beds. Good food and personal service offer visitors a most enjoyable holiday. The cathedral city of St. David's near the Pembrokeshire Coastal Path and beautiful sandy beaches. Well recommended. SAE for terms or telephone.

C	B & B PER PERSON PER NIGHT		DINNER B & B PER PERSON PER WEEK		5
	MIN £	MAX £	MIN £	MAX £	OPEN
	6		70		4—10

Tan y Ffynnon Guest House*

Whitesand Bay, St. David's
Pembrokeshire, Dyfed SA62 6PS
Tel: (0437) 720408

CATEGORIES		
3	3	2

Coastal footpath and beach only 2 minutes from this small guest house. Every comfort and good food provided. Home-made soups, a speciality. Bedrooms with hot and cold. Lounge with colour TV. Separate tables in dining room, central heating and Fire Certificate. Golf course and horse riding nearby. Send SAE please.

C	B & B PER PERSON PER NIGHT		DINNER B & B PER PERSON PER WEEK		5
	MIN £	MAX £	MIN £	MAX £	OPEN
	6.50	7.50	65	72	4—10

Wyncliffe*

Quickwell Hill, St. David's
Pembrokeshire, Dyfed SA62 6PO
Tel: (0437) 720447

CATEGORIES		
3	3	2

Wyncliffe is situated in a splendid position overlooking the Cathedral and valley to the coast beyond. In its own grounds away from traffic. Ample parking. Tea-making facilities in bedrooms. Hot and cold water, heated towel rails. High standard of cooking—choice of menu. Special rates for children.

C	B & B PER PERSON PER NIGHT		DINNER B & B PER PERSON PER WEEK		6
	MIN £	MAX £	MIN £	MAX £	OPEN
	6.50	7.50	77	84	4—9

Y Glennydd Guest House*

51 Nun Street, St. David's
Pembrokeshire, Dyfed
Tel: (0437) 720576

CATEGORIES		
3	4	3

Comfortable, centrally heated guest house. All rooms with hot and cold water. Overlooking Cathedral and two minutes from centre. Friendly atmosphere with good home cooking. Licensed. Lounge and separate TV lounge. Reduced rates in Spring and Autumn. AA and RAC listed. Write to Mrs Joan Darby for brochure and tariff.

C	B & B PER PERSON PER NIGHT		DINNER B & B PER PERSON PER WEEK		10
	MIN £	MAX £	MIN £	MAX £	OPEN
	6.25		66		1—12

Farmhouses

The Binchurn*

Trefin, Haverfordwest,
Pembrokeshire, Dyfed SA62 5AE
Tel: (03483) 264

CATEGORIES		
3	3	2

Large, fully modernised farmhouse. ¾ mile coastal footpath at Trefin. Ideally situated for touring Pembrokeshire. 200 acres mixed farm. Accommodation comprises 8 bedrooms, full central heating. Colour TV lounge, separate dining tables for family. Good home cooking. Open April to December. Children welcome. Dinner, bed and breakfast or bed and breakfast. St. David's 6 miles, Fishguard 7 miles. Within National Park. Terms on application.

T	B & B PER PERSON PER NIGHT		DINNER B & B PER PERSON PER WEEK		8
	MIN £	MAX £	MIN £	MAX £	OPEN
					4—12

Llety

Carnhedryn, Solva
Haverfordwest, Dyfed SA62 6XU
Tel: (034 83) 300

CATEGORIES		
1	2	2

A modern farmhouse with all modern amenities. Ideally placed within 2/3 miles of surrounding beaches. With hot and cold and shaver points in all bedrooms, single, double and family rooms, with special rates for children. Lounge with colour TV. Central heating. Car parking on forecourt.

C	B & B PER PERSON PER NIGHT		DINNER B & B PER PERSON PER WEEK		5
	MIN £	MAX £	MIN £	MAX £	OPEN
	5.50	6	52	55	5—10

Penysgwarne Farm*

Croesgoch, Haverfordwest
Dyfed SA62 5JX
Tel: (03483) 319

CATEGORIES		
3	3	2

Our farm offers a restful holiday away from crowded places, peace and quiet of beautiful countryside, walks, bays and beaches, within easy reach. The farm itself carries a dairy herd of a hundred Freisians also beef cattle.

T C	B & B PER PERSON PER NIGHT		DINNER B & B PER PERSON PER WEEK		12
	MIN £	MAX £	MIN £	MAX £	OPEN
	6.50	7	75	80	4—10

ℹ Tourist Information Centres are listed at back of book.

For autumn to spring breaks send for our free Great Little Breaks booklet.

Tregydd Farmhouse

Tregydd Farm, St. David's
Pembrokeshire, Dyfed SA62 6BZ
Tel: (0437) 721321

CATEGORIES | 1 | 3 | 2

Modern 200 acre dairy/mixed farm in Pembrokeshire National Park. Centrally situated on A487 St. David's/Fishguard road, 2¾ miles St. David's Cathedral City, 2¼ miles Solva harbour. Sandy beaches, footpaths, pony trekking, fishing with beautiful coastal scenery nearby. Farmhouse offers genuinely clean, homely, comfortable accommodation. Separate lounge/diner. Tarmacadam drive and frontage. WTB approved.

C	B & B PER PERSON PER NIGHT		DINNER B & B PER PERSON PER WEEK		🛏 3
	MIN £	MAX £	MIN £	MAX £	OPEN
	6				4—10

Trevaccoon

St. David's, Haverfordwest
Pembrokeshire Dyfed
Tel: (03483) 438

CATEGORIES | 3 | 2 | 2

A 17th century farmhouse with all modern amenities, ideally placed for beautiful beaches, coastal walks, boat trips etc. 1 mile from sea, all bedrooms with hot and cold, shavers, heating; fitted carpets throughout. TV lounge, dining room, separate tables. Car park, playing lawn. No pets. Children welcome. Farmhouse Award, Fire Certificate.

T C	B & B PER PERSON PER NIGHT		DINNER B & B PER PERSON PER WEEK		🛏 4
	MIN £	MAX £	MIN £	MAX £	OPEN
	6.50	7.50	66.50	73.50	3—10

Inn

Parsonage Farm Inn

St. Florence, Nr Tenby
Dyfed
Tel: (083 482) 436

CATEGORIES | 3 | 2 | 4

Welcome to the Parsonage, the award winning Inn of Wales. Situated in the "Bijou" village of St. Florence, the 300 year old Parsonage has been completely modernised yet still retains its original character. Single, double and family rooms available. Excellent parking facilities. TV lounge. Fully licensed, entertainment.

C	B & B PER PERSON PER NIGHT		DINNER B & B PER PERSON PER WEEK		🛏 10
	MIN £	MAX £	MIN £	MAX £	OPEN
	5.75	9			4—10

Farmhouse

New Mill*

Tregwynt, Nr St. Nicholas,
Letterston, Haverfordwest, Dyfed
Tel: (03485) 637

CATEGORIES | 1 | 2 | 2

Pretty Welsh farmhouse situated in peaceful valley, minutes walk from coastal path and unspoilt beach of Aberbach. For walkers, a natural night stop from Fishguard to St. David's. Hot and cold water each bedroom, colour TV; pets and children welcome. Exceptional cuisine from home-grown produce. Packed lunches and flasks filled.

C	B & B PER PERSON PER NIGHT		DINNER B & B PER PERSON PER WEEK		🛏 3
	MIN £	MAX £	MIN £	MAX £	OPEN
	6.50		70		1—12

Map ref: Ka4
This intriguing place name covers an area of splendid coastal scenery in Pembrokeshire Coast National Park and extending east towards Pendine and Laugharne. Near – neighbour to Tenby, its small harbour offers good sailing and sea angling and the sheltered waters, sail boarding, canoeing and dinghy racing. Packed with an enviable range of good hotels, which offer good food and wine and many evening entertainments. Though complete in itself Saundersfoot, offers excellent touring prospects to the bird-haunted stacks in the west, inland to a countryside and country towns richly castled by the Normans, or to the inland fiord of the Milford Haven.

Hotels

Claremont Hotel*

St. Brides Hill
Saundersfoot, South Pembrokeshire
Dyfed SA69 9NP
Tel: (0834) 813231

CATEGORIES | 3 | 4 | 3

RAC listed. Excellent standard of accommodation, food, wine and service. Ample free parking. Entertainment three nights weekly. Use of heated swimming pool in season. Separate tables. Full central heating, colour TV, lounge, licensed. Children welcome; sorry no pets. Please send for fully illustrated colour brochure to Pauline and Brian Hooper.

C	B & B PER PERSON PER NIGHT		DINNER B & B PER PERSON PER WEEK		🛏 21
	MIN £	MAX £	MIN £	MAX £	OPEN
	9	11	77	90	5—9

Coppet Hall Beach Hotel*

Saundersfoot, South Pembrokeshire
Dyfed SA69 9AJ
Tel: (0834) 813380

CATEGORIES | 3 | 3 | 3

Coppet Hall Beach Hotel, Saundersfoot, Dyfed. Telephone (0834) 813380. Licensed, private hotel situated at the side of Coppet Hall beach. One of Saundersfoot's most popular beaches. 5 minutes walk to shops and harbour. Bar lounge, colour TV lounge, family bedrooms. Free parking, children welcome. No pets.

T C	B & B PER PERSON PER NIGHT		DINNER B & B PER PERSON PER WEEK		🛏 21
	MIN £	MAX £	MIN £	MAX £	OPEN
	8.50	10	75	90	1—12

The Glen Beach Hotel*

Swallow Tree Woods
Saundersfoot, South Pembrokeshire
Dyfed
Tel: (0834) 813430

CATEGORIES

| 4 | 4 | 5 |

Set in acres of woodland with beach access. Delightful bedrooms all with en suite bathrooms. Restaurant with enviable reputation. Special Weekend Breaks, Christmas, Easter and Spring holidays. Fully licensed. Substantial reductions for children and group bookings. Open all year under personal supervision of proprietors Tony and Audrey Mullen.

		B & B PER PERSON PER NIGHT		DINNER B & B PER PERSON PER WEEK		13
T		MIN £	MAX £	MIN £	MAX £	OPEN
C		14	18	138	178	1—12

The Harbour Light Hotel*

2 High Street
Saundersfoot SA69 9EJ
Tel: (0834) 813496

CATEGORIES

| 3 | 3 | 2 |

Saundersfoot village centre, 120 yards sandy beach and harbour. Informality our theme with 'home from home' amenities. Tea-making facilities. Double glazing, heating, bar, baby-listening. Parking. Special family terms. AA/RAC listed. Sailing, fishing, riding, bowls, tennis, gliding, disco, all nearby. Many recommendations. Ring or write now! Please!

		B & B PER PERSON PER NIGHT		DINNER B & B PER PERSON PER WEEK		11
T		MIN £	MAX £	MIN £	MAX £	OPEN
C		8.00		77		1—11

Merlewood Hotel

Saundersfoot, Nr. Tenby
Pembrokeshire, Dyfed SA69 9NP
Tel: (0834) 812421

CATEGORIES

| 3 | 4 | 3 |

AA and RAC listed. Modern, private hotel, family-run. Excellent cuisine, heated swimming pool in season, children's playground, 9 hole putting green, pool table etc. Ample free parking. All day bar service; entertainment three nights weekly. Please send for fully illustrated colour brochure to Dennis and Irene Williams.

	B & B PER PERSON PER NIGHT		DINNER B & B PER PERSON PER WEEK		21
C	MIN £	MAX £	MIN £	MAX £	OPEN
	9	11	82	98	2—11

St. Brides Hotel*

Saundersfoot, South Pembrokeshire
Dyfed SA69 9NH
Tel: (0834) 812304 Telex: 48350

CATEGORIES

| 5 | 5 | 5 |

Superb situation overlooking Carmarthen Bay. Clifftop, air-conditioned restaurant with dramatic views. Lobster, local fish, flàmbe dishes. Kaptain Katz luxurious drinks salon. Heated pool. All bedrooms with private bath/shower, colour TV, telephone, radio, tea-makers. Activity holidays. Children sharing parents' room accommodated free, meals only charged.

		B & B PER PERSON PER NIGHT		DINNER B & B PER PERSON PER WEEK		49
T		MIN £	MAX £	MIN £	MAX £	OPEN
C		16.50	19.50	140	165	1—12

Swn-y-Mor Hotel*

4 Cambrian Terrace
Saundersfoot, South Pembrokeshire
Dyfed SA69 9ER
Tel: (0834) 813201

CATEGORIES

| 1 | 3 | 4 |

In the centre of the village, one minute from beach, Swn-y-Mor Hotel, 4 Cambrian Terrace, telephone 813201. The highest reputation for food and service; established over fifteen years. Children very welcome. Lounge with colour TV. Fire Certificate granted. Phone or write for brochure.

	B & B PER PERSON PER NIGHT		DINNER B & B PER PERSON PER WEEK		8
C	MIN £	MAX £	MIN £	MAX £	OPEN
		8.50	65	80.50	4—10

Guest Houses

"Cherry Tree Lodge"*

Jeffreston, Kilgetty
South Pembrokeshire, Dyfed
Tel: (06467) 667

CATEGORIES

| 3 | 3 | 2 |

Saundersfoot, Tenby, National Park beaches and castles are within easy reach from country guest house set in rural area. Colour TV lounge with olde worlde beams and Jøtal woodstove. Separate tables. Ample car parking in grounds. Children welcome. Full English breakfast and 4-course dinner. Good home cooking.

	B & B PER PERSON PER NIGHT		DINNER B & B PER PERSON PER WEEK		5
C	MIN £	MAX £	MIN £	MAX £	OPEN
	6	6	65	65	4—10

Cestyll '83 – 1983 is the year of the castles.

Edgecombe Guest House*

The Ridgeway, Saundersfoot
South Pembrokeshire, Dyfed
Tel: (0834) 812810

CATEGORIES

| 3 | 3 | 2 |

Family guest house 200 yards beach and village. Ideal centre for touring. Single, double and family rooms; special rates for children. Lounge with colour TV, licensed bar and restaurant. Parking. Baby-sitting. Access and Vista cards accepted. SAE please or phone (0834) 812810.

	B & B PER PERSON PER NIGHT		DINNER B & B PER PERSON PER WEEK		11
C	MIN £	MAX £	MIN £	MAX £	OPEN
	6.98	9.28	57.50	80.50	1—12

The Grange*

Wooden, Saundersfoot
South Pembrokeshire, Dyfed
Tel: (0834) 812809

CATEGORIES

| 2 | 3 | 3 |

Between Tenby and Saundersfoot, ideal location for surrounding beaches and tourist attractions. Lawned play area for children and ample parking in grounds. Comfortable TV lounge and pleasant bar lounge; separate dining tables. All bedrooms central heating, hot and cold, shaver points and some have private toilets/shower. Special terms for children.

	B & B PER PERSON PER NIGHT		DINNER B & B PER PERSON PER WEEK		6
C	MIN £	MAX £	MIN £	MAX £	OPEN
	5	7	50	69	1—12

Sandy Hill Guest House*

Tenby Road, Saundersfoot, South
Pembrokeshire, Dyfed SA69 9DR
Tel: (0834) 813165

CATEGORIES

| 3 | 3 | 2 |

Sandy Hill guest house, Tenby Road, Saundersfoot. Bed/Breakfast and dinner. Swimming pool. Tea and coffee facilities in all rooms. Also colour television in all rooms; licensed bar. Separate tables. Ample car parking. Open all year round.

	B & B PER PERSON PER NIGHT		DINNER B & B PER PERSON PER WEEK		5
C	MIN £	MAX £	MIN £	MAX £	OPEN
	7	8	70	84	1—12

Hotel

White House Hotel*

Sennybridge
Brecon, Powys LD3 8RP
Tel: (087482) 396

CATEGORIES: 3 3 5

Relaxing country holiday. Magnificent mountain scenery. Hotel recommended by Relais Routiers. Ideal centre for scenic drives, walking, fishing, pony trekking and tourist attractions. Dinner, bed and breakfast from £75 week. Summer breaks—2 days £30, 5 days £70. Special terms for the elderly, £60 week March, April, October and 10% off summer rates. Free brochure pack available. Mastercard, Access, Barclaycard, VISA accepted.

T C	B & B PER PERSON PER NIGHT		DINNER B & B PER PERSON PER WEEK		7
	MIN £	MAX £	MIN £	MAX £	OPEN
	8.75	9.25	75	92.50	1—12

Hotel

Harbour House Hotel*

Lower Solva, Haverfordwest
Pembrokeshire, Dyfed
SA62 6UT
Tel: (0437) 721267

CATEGORIES: 4 3 5

Small, family-run hotel on the Coastal Path, overlooking the beautiful harbour. Friendly service, excellent cuisine, bar, well-appointed rooms with private shower, toilet, TV, tea/coffee-maker. Weekly terms available. Special Spring and Autumn Weekend Breaks.

C	B & B PER PERSON PER NIGHT		DINNER B & B PER PERSON PER WEEK		4
	MIN £	MAX £	MIN £	MAX £	OPEN
	10	13.50	112	135	1—12

Guest House

Hendre House*

Llandeloy, Solva
Haverfordwest, Dyfed
Tel: (03483) 270

CATEGORIES: 3 3 2

Secluded manor house in own extensive grounds; acres of garden, woods, with indoor 32 ft swimming pool. 3 miles to coast; provides a high standard of accommodation for a limited number of guests. Excellent food prepared and cooked by proprietor. Hot and cold in all rooms. Dining room, lounge (colour TV), morning room etc.

C	B & B PER PERSON PER NIGHT		DINNER B & B PER PERSON PER WEEK		3
	MIN £	MAX £	MIN £	MAX £	OPEN
	6	10	84	98	5—10

Farmhouses

Gwar-y-Coed Uchaf*

Solva, Haverfordwest
Dyfed SA62 6TR
Tel: (0437) 721330

CATEGORIES: 1 2 3

Modern, comfortable farmhouse in peaceful surroundings with panoramic views of sea, mountains and countryside. Traditional farmhouse cooking, wine, home-killed meat and poultry and local vegetables and fish. Quiet beaches, fishing, surfing, pony trekking, country walks, all available locally. Children will love the pet lambs, goat, poultry. Ample parking.

C	B & B PER PERSON PER NIGHT		DINNER B & B PER PERSON PER WEEK		2
	MIN £	MAX £	MIN £	MAX £	OPEN
	5	6.50	59.50	70	1—12

"Upper Vanley"*

Llandeloy, Solva
Haverfordwest, Dyfed
Tel: (03483) 418

CATEGORIES: 3 2 2

Upper Vanley is a 120 acre dairy farm with pedigree herd, situated in centre of St. David's peninsula. Nearest beach—Newgale Sands, 2½ miles. Guests are served a variety of traditional farmhouse cooking, including home-baked bread. Vegetarians catered for. Bicycles for hire. Central heating. Fire Certificate. W.T.B Farmhouse Award.

T C	B & B PER PERSON PER NIGHT		DINNER B & B PER PERSON PER WEEK		5
	MIN £	MAX £	MIN £	MAX £	OPEN
	5	6.50	56	70	1—12

Hotel

Heatherslade Bay Hotel

1 West Cliff, Southgate
Gower, Near Swansea
West Glamorgan
Tel: (044128) 3328

CATEGORIES: 3 3 4

Gloriously situated on the cliff top, overlooking a sandy cove. All rooms en-suite with colour TV. Fully licensed dining room and restaurant with lounge bar. Family rooms available with reduced prices for children. We guarantee home cooking at its best.

C	B & B PER PERSON PER NIGHT		DINNER B & B PER PERSON PER WEEK		17
	MIN £	MAX £	MIN £	MAX £	OPEN
	11	13	99.50	112	4—10

Guest House

"Heatherlands,"*

1 Hael Lane, Southgate
Gower, Swansea
West Glamorgan SA3 2AP
Tel: (044 128) 3256

CATEGORIES: 3 1 1

Modern chalet-type residence on Pennard Cliffs. Lovely bays approached by road or cliff walks with safe bathing. Comfortable bedrooms with hot and cold. Reduced rates for children if sharing. Lounge with colour TV, dining room with separate tables. Central heating. Fire Certificate granted. Parking. Regret no pets.

C	B & B PER PERSON PER NIGHT		DINNER B & B PER PERSON PER WEEK		3
	MIN £	MAX £	MIN £	MAX £	OPEN
	6	6.50			4—9

Map ref: La4
Home town of poet, Dylan Thomas, seaport, commercial centre and holiday resort Swansea has a Welshness it is proud of. Good hotels complement good shopping; it has an indoor food and Welsh-produce market, the envy of other towns. First class rugby, football and cricket are a rare combination, offered by Swansea. Possessor of fine parks and open spaces and especially along the sandy bay, it also sports a modern Leisure Centre, Industrial and Maritime Museum and is developing a good yachting marina. Westwards lies the yachting centre of Mumbles and the sandy bays of Gower Peninsula.

Hotels

Alexander Private Hotel*

3 Sketty Road, Uplands, Swansea
West Glamorgan SA2 0EU
Tel: (0792) 470045

CATEGORIES

| 4 | 4 | 2 |

Family-run hotel. Full central heating. All bedrooms have TV, radio, tea/coffee-making facilities. Most bedrooms have private bath/shower and toilet. Friendly, licensed bar. Well equipped games room—snooker, pool, table tennis, darts etc. Ideally situated for city centre. Gower Peninsula St. Helen's rugby/cricket ground and parks etc.

	B & B PER PERSON PER NIGHT		DINNER B & B PER PERSON PER WEEK		7
T	MIN £	MAX £	MIN £	MAX £	OPEN
C	8	10	80	85	1—12

Brynteg Hotel*

1 Higher Lane
Langland, Swansea
West Glamorgan SA3 4NS
Tel: (0792) 66820

CATEGORIES

| 3 | 2 | 2 |

Homely, licensed family hotel close to beach, golf and tennis. Easy access to Swansea and Gower. Central heating and hot and cold water in all bedrooms. Excellent personal service and home cooking. Pleasant colour TV lounge and cocktail bar. Autumn and Spring Breaks. Write or phone Carl and Judy Huntley.

	B & B PER PERSON PER NIGHT		DINNER B & B PER PERSON PER WEEK		10
T	MIN £	MAX £	MIN £	MAX £	OPEN
C	8.05	8.63	60.95	74.75	1—12

The Dolphin Hotel*

Whitewalls, Swansea
West Glamorgan SA1 3AB
Tel: (0792) 50011 Telex 48128

CATEGORIES

| 5 | 5 | 4 |

Modern city centre hotel in Swansea's new shopping and leisure centre development and the new Marina. A three star hotel, all rooms with private bath, colour TV, telephone. Complimentary tea/coffee. 24 hour porterage. Licensed bars and restaurant. Ideal base for touring the Gower Peninsula. Bargain weekend breaks and family rates offered.

	B & B PER PERSON PER NIGHT		DINNER B & B PER PERSON PER WEEK		66
T	MIN £	MAX £	MIN £	MAX £	OPEN
C	9.50	22.50	100	150	1—12

Dragon Hotel*

39 The Kingsway, Swansea
West Glamorgan SA1 5LS
Tel: (0792) 51074 Telex 48309

CATEGORIES

| 6 | 6 | 6 |

Modern City Centre Hotel. Easy access to the Shops and Leisure Centre. Only 20 minutes from the beautiful Gower Coast. A la carte restaurant plus coffee shop. Four bars with different ambience. All bedrooms have private bath, colour TV, radio, telephone and tea and coffee making facilities. Special Bargain Breaks available.

	B & B PER PERSON PER NIGHT		DINNER B & B PER PERSON PER WEEK		118
T	MIN £	MAX £	MIN £	MAX £	OPEN
C	36				1—12

Langland Court Hotel*

Langland Court Road
Langland Bay, Swansea
Glamorgan SA3 4TD
Tel: (0792) 68505

CATEGORIES

| 4 | 4 | 4 |

Fully licensed Tudor-style country house with lots of character, standing in its own grounds. Oak panelled entrance hall and dining room. Traditional cuisine at its best. Log fires in the winter. Dinner dance most Saturday evenings. Mini Breaks. Meetings, conferences. Ideally situated for touring the Gower Coast.

	B & B PER PERSON PER NIGHT		DINNER B & B PER PERSON PER WEEK		20
T	MIN £	MAX £	MIN £	MAX £	OPEN
C	15	30	135	200	1—12

Llwyn Helyg Hotel*

Ffynone Road, Ffynone
Swansea SA1 6BT
Tel: (0792) 465735

CATEGORIES | 5 | 4 | 5

One of Swansea's most imposing residences. Converted into a luxury hotel, run by the proprietor. All rooms have private facilities, telephone, television/radio room. Service always a pleasure. Car park within hotel grounds. Ideal for business or holidays. Fully licensed bar and restaurant. Open all year.

	B & B PER PERSON PER NIGHT		DINNER B & B PER PERSON PER WEEK		🛏 11
T C	MIN £	MAX £	MIN £	MAX £	OPEN
	15	15	125	125	1—12

Mansel Hotel

Mansel Street, Swansea
West Glamorgan SA1 5TN
Tel: (0792) 52818

CATEGORIES | 3 | 3 | 1

Under new ownership; completely refurbished. Central heating in all rooms; lounge with colour TV. Some rooms with private facilities. City centre, within a couple of minutes walk to all entertainments and restaurants and near the sea. Fire Certificate and personal attention.

	B & B PER PERSON PER NIGHT		DINNER B & B PER PERSON PER WEEK		🛏 9
	MIN £	MAX £	MIN £	MAX £	OPEN
	6.50	8	45.50	60	1—12

Pantycelyn Hotel

Seafront, Swansea
West Glamorgan
Tel: (0792) 51325 or 466899

CATEGORIES | 2 | 4 | 4

Overlooking expanse of Swansea Bay, the start of the beautiful Gower Coast. 38 bedrooms, all with radio/intercom, baby-listening; many with bathroom, teasmade, television. Ground floor bedrooms, lift. Disabled welcome. Special childrens rates. Groups (up to 60) specially catered for. Excellent Welsh cooking with fresh produce. Pool, function rooms. Licensed etc.

	B & B PER PERSON PER NIGHT		DINNER B & B PER PERSON PER WEEK		🛏 38
C	MIN £	MAX £	MIN £	MAX £	OPEN
	10.35	13.80	94.30	123.05	1—12

St. Anne's Private Hotel*

6 Gore Terrace, Swansea
West Glamorgan SA1 5DN
Tel: (0792) 50914

CATEGORIES | 1 | 3 | 2

Ideally situated in quiet surroundings near the heart of Swansea, looking towards The Mumbles. The picturesque Gower Peninsula only minutes away by car. Colour television lounge; single, double and family bedrooms. Front door key. Fire Certificate. Excellent cuisine. Tea Garden. AA listed. Proprietors extend a warm Welsh welcome.

	B & B PER PERSON PER NIGHT		DINNER B & B PER PERSON PER WEEK		🛏 8
T C	MIN £	MAX £	MIN £	MAX £	OPEN
	6	7	60	66	1—12

St David's Hotel*

15 Sketty Road
Uplands, Swansea
West Glamorgan SA2 0EU
Tel: (0792) 473814

CATEGORIES | 3 | 4 | 2

A small, licensed hotel, convenient for Gower's beaches and countryside, yet only a mile from Swansea's modern centre. All bedrooms have TV, radio and intercom; most have private bathroom or shower. Centrally heated, of course. You are assured of good food and good company at the St. David's.

	B & B PER PERSON PER NIGHT		DINNER B & B PER PERSON PER WEEK		🛏 12
T C	MIN £	MAX £	MIN £	MAX £	OPEN
	8.50		75		1—12

Tregare Hotel*

9 Sketty Road
Uplands, Swansea
West Glamorgan SA2 0EU
Tel: (0792) 470608: Reception
(0792) 466753: Guests

CATEGORIES | 4 | 3 | 2

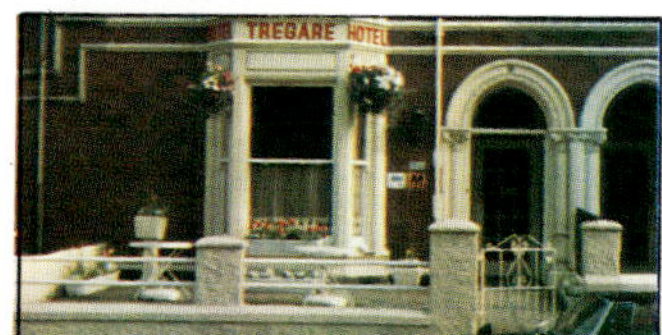

Comfortable, fully centrally heated hotel on main road (A4118) to the Gower Peninsula, yet within easy reach of the city centre. Bus service to all parts. Car Park. Fire certificate. Licensed cocktail bar (snacks served until 11p.m.). Separate lounge with colour TV, (TV sets in all bedrooms). Most bedrooms have private bath or shower with w.c. All bedrooms have radio, shaver sockets and hot and cold water. Family rooms available. Brochure and terms on request.

	B & B PER PERSON PER NIGHT		DINNER B & B PER PERSON PER WEEK		🛏 11
C	MIN £	MAX £	MIN £	MAX £	OPEN
	6	8	57	80.50	1—12

Guest Houses

Acorns Guest House*

176 Gower Road
Sketty, Swansea
West Glamorgan
Tel: (0792) 201345

CATEGORIES | 2 | 3 | 2

Conveniently situated on main Gower road. Approximately 2 miles from city centre and beaches. Comfortable lounge with colour TV. Separate bar and dining room. Hot and cold water in all rooms. Evening meals available on request. Private car park. Fire Certificate. Cordial welcome by resident proprietors Olive and John Gray

	B & B PER PERSON PER NIGHT		DINNER B & B PER PERSON PER WEEK		🛏 8
C	MIN £	MAX £	MIN £	MAX £	OPEN
	8	9.50	73.50	84	1—12

Beachway Guest House

8 Bryn Road
Brynmill, Swansea
West Glamorgan SA2 0AR
Tel: (0792) 466557

CATEGORIES | 2 | 3 | 2

Well recommended guest house offering the best in the guest house tradition. Good food, comfort and friendly service. Bedrooms with hot and cold water, heating, colour TV lounge, separate dining room, shower, bath facilities, unrestricted access to lounge, bedrooms. Convenient for city centre; near seafront and parks. Brochure. Terms on request.

	B & B PER PERSON PER NIGHT		DINNER B & B PER PERSON PER WEEK		🛏 8
C	MIN £	MAX £	MIN £	MAX £	OPEN
	6	6.50	56	56	1—12

Belmont Guest House*

2 Mirador Crescent
Uplands, Swansea
West Glamorgan SA2 0QX
Tel: (0792) 466812

CATEGORIES | 1 | 2 | 2

Private car park, Tourist Board listed. Quiet location; within minutes of bus routes to all amenities. Near lovely parks. Homely atmosphere. Good food, comfortable lounge, colour television, central heating. Open all year. Highly recommended by previous guests. Singles, doubles, twin and family rooms. Full Fire Certificate granted.

	B & B PER PERSON PER NIGHT		DINNER B & B PER PERSON PER WEEK		🛏 8
C	MIN £	MAX £	MIN £	MAX £	OPEN
	6.50	7.50	63	77	1—12

Channel View Guest House

17 Bryn Road
Brynmill, Swansea
West Glamorgan SA2 0AR
Tel: (0792) 466834

CATEGORIES

| 2 | 3 | 1 |

A first class guest house, highly recommended for excellent food and service, overlooking St. Helen's Rugby/Cricket field, 2 minutes seafront. Close to city centre, University, parks, leisure centre, Brangwynne Hall. Ideally situated for touring Gower and Wales. AA listed. Fire Certificate. Please write or phone for free brochure.

C	B & B PER PERSON PER NIGHT		DINNER B & B PER PERSON PER WEEK		6
	MIN £	MAX £	MIN £	MAX £	OPEN
	6	6.50	52	56	1—12

Devon View Guest House

396 Oystermouth Road, Swansea
West Glamorgan SA1 3UL
Tel: (0792) 462008

CATEGORIES

| 1 | 1 | 2 |

A family-run guest house, recommended for comfort, food and service. Opposite beach and well situated for touring. Close to city centre, Brangwyn Hall and University. Colour TV lounge, bed, breakfast; evening meal (opt.). Parking nearby. Party reductions. Further details terms from resident proprietress— Mrs Janice Grigg.

C	B & B PER PERSON PER NIGHT		DINNER B & B PER PERSON PER WEEK		6
	MIN £	MAX £	MIN £	MAX £	OPEN
	7		65		1—12

Mirador Guest House*

14 Mirador Crescent
Uplands, Swansea
West Glamorgan SA2 0QX
Tel: (0792) 466976

CATEGORIES

| 1 | 2 | 2 |

Comfortable, homely guest house, close to city centre and easy access to parks, leisure centre, Mumbles and Gower Coast. Bed and breakfast, evening meal optional. Heating and hot and cold water in all bedrooms, razor points, residents colour TV lounge. Access to rooms at all times. Fire Certificate. Unrestricted parking. Weekly dinner, bed and breakfast rates on application.

C	B & B PER PERSON PER NIGHT		DINNER B & B PER PERSON PER WEEK		7
	MIN £	MAX £	MIN £	MAX £	OPEN
	6	6.50			1—12

St Helen's Guest House*

St Helen's Crescent, Swansea
West Glamorgan SA1 4NX
Tel: (0792) 460065

CATEGORIES

| 3 | 2 | 2 |

Compact, detached house adjacent to City Guildhall. Under personal supervision of the proprietor, Mrs. M. Evans. Comfortable, luxurious twin and family bedrooms. Excellent food and service. Residents' lounge and colour television. Fully centrally heated. Easy car parking; few minutes from the beach and St. Helen's Cricket and Rugby ground. Bath and shower facilities. Within walking distance of city centre. Open all year round. Near bus routes. AA approved.

C	B & B PER PERSON PER NIGHT		DINNER B & B PER PERSON PER WEEK		6
	MIN £	MAX £	MIN £	MAX £	OPEN
	8	10	84	100	1—12

Uplands Court Guest House*

134 Eaton Crescent, Uplands
Swansea, West Glamorgan SA1 4QS
Tel: (0792) 473046 and 466992

CATEGORIES

| 3 | 3 | 2 |

Situated in a quiet crescent, just off main Swansea/Gower road. Convenient for city centre, Swansea Bay, University, Guildhall and sports venues. A very high standard of cleanliness, comfort, good food and service. TV, radios, intercoms in all bedrooms. Guest lounge with colour TV. Fire certificate; adequate parking. AA and RAC listed.

C	B & B PER PERSON PER NIGHT		DINNER B & B PER PERSON PER WEEK		8
	MIN £	MAX £	MIN £	MAX £	OPEN
	7	8	77	86	1—12

Farmhouse

Coynant Farm*

Felindre, Swansea
West Glamorgan
Tel: (0269) 5640 and 2064

CATEGORIES

| 3 | 4 | 2 |

Near Gower's beaches, peaceful farmhouse amidst 150 tranquil acres. Fascinating livestock farm conveniently situated to visit the many local attractions. Magnificent walking country. Lake fishing and riding. Comfortable bedrooms with hot and cold. Log fires, fresh farm produce, good food and a warm welcome awaits visitors all year round. AA, RAC.

T C	B & B PER PERSON PER NIGHT		DINNER B & B PER PERSON PER WEEK		5
	MIN £	MAX £	MIN £	MAX £	OPEN
	7.50	8	69.50	73.50	1—12

Farmhouses

Bronllys Court

Bronllys, Brecon, Powys LD3 0LF
Enquiries to: Mrs L. M. Hopkins
Tel: (0874) 711362

CATEGORIES

| 3 | 2 | 2 |

Situated on A438 road, half-way between Hay and Brecon. An old farmhouse tastefully furnished with ample parking facilities. A convenient centre for touring Brecon Beacons, Dan-yr-Ogof Caves, Black Mountains, Wye Valley, Mid Wales, Elan Valley etc., Boating, swimming and pony trekking available nearby.

	B & B PER PERSON PER NIGHT		DINNER B & B PER PERSON PER WEEK		4
	MIN £	MAX £	MIN £	MAX £	OPEN
	6		70		4—11

Penyrheol Farm*

Talgarth
Brecon, Powys
Tel: (0874) 711409

CATEGORIES

| 1 | 2 | 2 |

Penyrheol is a hill farm of 140 acres at the foot of Mynydd Troed. Situated between the Black Mountains and the Brecon Beacons near Talgarth and Llangorse, off the A479 road. All bedrooms have washbasins. Travellers' Britain mentions my cooking. We have a TV, Cot and children's pony for guests.

T C	B & B PER PERSON PER NIGHT		DINNER B & B PER PERSON PER WEEK		2
	MIN £	MAX £	MIN £	MAX £	OPEN
	6	6.50	60	65	3—10

SOUTH
WALES

Farmhouse

Llanddetty Hall Farm

Talybont-on-Usk, Brecon
Powys LD3 7YR
Tel: (087487) 267

CATEGORIES

| 3 | 1 | 2 |

170 acre family in National Park's Usk Valley, accessible to Brecon Beacons and Black Mountains. Bus route, villages within walking distance via canal tow path. Area ideal for walking, trekking, golf, fishing, motoring etc. Local OS maps available. Warm welcome, good food, comfortable accommodation in 17th century farmhouse.

C	B & B PER PERSON PER NIGHT		DINNER B & B PER PERSON PER WEEK		3
	MIN £	MAX £	MIN £	MAX £	OPEN
	5.50	6.50	65	70	4—10

Talyllyn

MID
WALES

Hotels

Minffordd Hotel*

Talyllyn, Tywyn
Gwynedd LL36 9AJ
Tel: (065473) 665

CATEGORIES

| 4 | 4 | 4 |

Welcome to Minffordd, once an old coaching inn. Unwind and relax in a friendly and comfortable atmosphere. Featured by the leading Hotel and Food Guides. Savour our excellent dinner, after spending the day discovering the dramatic beauty of Cader Idris and the Dysynni Valley. Minffordd is full of character and charm. Most bedrooms are en-suite with bathroom. A cheery log fire flickers in the old parlour. The prices below are inclusive of both service and VAT. Brochure and tariff from Mr Bernard Pickles.

C	B & B PER PERSON PER NIGHT		DINNER B & B PER PERSON PER WEEK		7
	MIN £	MAX £	MIN £	MAX £	OPEN
	14	16	143.50	157.50	4—10

Pen-y-Bont Hotel*

Tal-y-Llyn, Tywyn
Gwynedd LL36 9AJ
Tel: (065 477) 285

CATEGORIES

| 3 | 3 | 4 |

16th century coaching inn situated west shore of lake. All rooms have bathroom with shower, television, teasmade. Olde worlde, beamed restaurant, serving local specialities. Separate lounge bar, overlooking lake. Tables outside to enjoy the magnificent view. Ideal centre for hill walking, golfing, fishing, pony trekking or just 'taking it easy'.

C	B & B PER PERSON PER NIGHT		DINNER B & B PER PERSON PER WEEK		6
	MIN £	MAX £	MIN £	MAX £	OPEN
	6.90	9.90	75.95	109.55	3—11

Tynycornel Hotel

Talyllyn, Tywyn
Gwynedd LL36 9AJ
Tel: (065 477) 282

CATEGORIES

| 5 | 4 | 5 |

Tynycornel has been in the same family for 58 years. On the shores of our private lake which offers free fly fishing for trout to guests. Sailing, canoeing, windsurfing available July and August. Beautiful scenery with good food and friendly service our priority. Family rooms. Fire Certificate.

C	B & B PER PERSON PER NIGHT		DINNER B & B PER PERSON PER WEEK		15
	MIN £	MAX £	MIN £	MAX £	OPEN
	16	20	150	190	2—12

Farmhouse

Dolffanog Fach

Talyllyn, Tywyn
Gwynedd LL36 9AJ
Tel: (065473) 235

CATEGORIES

| 2 | 3 | 2 |

Dolffanog is situated near Talyllyn Lake at the foot of Cader Idris range on the B4405 road between Minffordd Junction and Talyllyn Lake. Comfort and good home cooking. Fire Certificate held. Ample car parking. Hot and cold water in bedrooms. Lounge for guests. Reduction for children under ten years.

C	B & B PER PERSON PER NIGHT		DINNER B & B PER PERSON PER WEEK		4
	MIN £	MAX £	MIN £	MAX £	OPEN
	5.50	6	56	59.50	4—10

C

Children stay at reduced rates, wherever you see this symbol.

Tenby

SOUTH
WALES

Map ref: Je6
Few would grudge Tenbys claim to the title of prettiest resort on the west coast of Britain. It has a dry climate, excellent hotels and a position in the renowned Pembrokeshire Coast National Park. Unspoiled, it occupies a headland between two fine sandy beaches. Offshore is Caldey Island, home of seals, seagulls and monks who press perfume from the Island's flowers for visitors from the mainland. Ancient town walls and gatehouses, an old spired church and stub of quay, guarding bobbing boats, present backdrops for holiday pictures that neighbours will envy. Sailing and seasports are dominant, but there is plenty of day and evening entertainment as well.

Hotels, Motels

Belvedere Hotel*

Serpentine Road, Tenby
Pembrokeshire
Dyfed SA70 8DD
Tel: (0834) 2549

CATEGORIES

| 3 | 3 | 3 |

Situated on the main Carmarthen road into Tenby, only 10 minutes from beach and town. Ample car parking. Central heating throughout, cocktail bar. TV lounge, large attractive garden. Afternoon teas. A warm welcome awaits you and your children from Viv and John. AA and RAC listed.

T	B & B PER PERSON PER NIGHT		DINNER B & B PER PERSON PER WEEK		16
C	MIN £	MAX £	MIN £	MAX £	OPEN
	8	10.50	77	95	4—10

Buckingham Hotel*

Esplanade, Tenby
Pembrokeshire
Dyfed
Tel: (0834) 2622 or 2693

CATEGORIES

| 4 | 4 | 5 |

Superbly situated overlooking beach. A quiet, relaxing hotel offering fine food, wine and service. 30 rooms, central heating, beverage facilities, many private bath and colourful lounge and dining room. Wonderful views, where discerning guest can enjoy a wide choice of menus. Three-day breaks available throughout season.

	B & B PER PERSON PER NIGHT		DINNER B & B PER PERSON PER WEEK		25
T	MIN £	MAX £	MIN £	MAX £	OPEN
C	10	12.50	100	—	2—11

Castle View Private Hotel*

The Norton, Tenby
Pembrokeshire
Dyfed
Tel: (0834) 2666

CATEGORIES

| 2 | 3 | 2 |

Family hotel on sea front. Large family bedrooms; children welcome; convenient for amusements, cinema coach or train station. All bedrooms have hot and cold with razor points. Separate tables in large dining room; no petty restrictions as all guests have their own keys. Licensed. School parties welcome.

	B & B PER PERSON PER NIGHT		DINNER B & B PER PERSON PER WEEK		19
T	MIN £	MAX £	MIN £	MAX £	OPEN
C	6.90	11.50	64.50	96.50	1—12

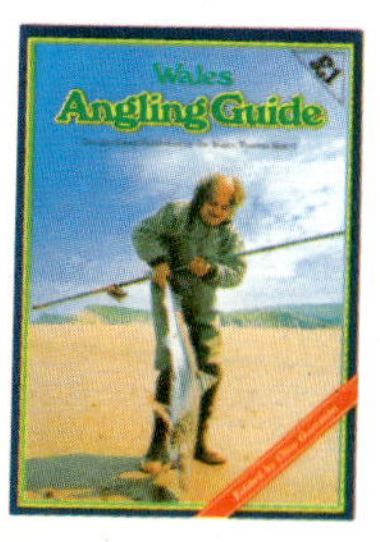

Angling
112 page guide packed with information and advice for visiting sea, game and coarse fishermen.
Available from: Wales Tourist Board Department W.T.S. P.O. Box 1, CARDIFF CF1 2XN. Price: £1.25p including postage and packing.

Clarence House Hotel*

Esplanade, Tenby
Pembrokeshire
Dyfed SA70 7DU
Tel: (0834) 4371

CATEGORIES

| 3 | 4 | 4 |

Sunny South Shore, centre seafront, beach-steps. Seagull lounge bar, patio, stone-wall, rose garden. Seaview lounges, TV, library; cavern dancing. Recommended cuisine; ground floor dining room. Lift all floors. Electrically heated bedrooms. Compact suites—private w.c./shower. Fridge, colour TV. Special family reductions tariff, B & B , Dinner B & B. Children's playroom, table tennis, coin wash/dry. Personal supervision by owners. Fire certified. Easy walking distances for harbour, golfcourse, entertainment, shopping, rail/coach, car parking. Write or telephone—free colour brochures/tariffs.

	B & B PER PERSON PER NIGHT		DINNER B & B PER PERSON PER WEEK		55
T	MIN £	MAX £	MIN £	MAX £	OPEN
C	6	15	63	126	4—10

The Croft Hotel*

The Croft, Tenby
Pembrokeshire
Dyfed SA70 8AP
Tel: (0834) 2576

CATEGORIES

| 3 | 3 | 3 |

Situated overlooking the picturesque harbour amidst the peaceful beauty of Carmarthen Bay with sun patio and private steps to beach. Owned by a caring family experienced in providing friendly service and good food. Cosy bar. Comfortable lounges (one with colour TV). All bedrooms have tea/coffee-making facilities. Private bathrooms available.

	B & B PER PERSON PER NIGHT		DINNER B & B PER PERSON PER WEEK		20
T	MIN £	MAX £	MIN £	MAX £	OPEN
C	8	10.50	98	104	4—10

This symbol means you can book through your local travel agent.

Fourcroft Hotel*

Croft Terrace, Tenby
Pembrokeshire
Dyfed SA70 8AP
Tel: (0834) 2516

CATEGORIES

| 4 | 4 | 4 |

Sea Front. Private garden with path to beach. Five minutes walk to town centre. 34 bedrooms with bathroom, central heating, tea/coffee maker, colour television, radio. Comfortable sea view lounges. Unique bar. Lift. Games room. Interesting cuisine. Good wine. Cheerful friendly service.

	B & B PER PERSON PER NIGHT		DINNER B & B PER PERSON PER WEEK		39
T	MIN £	MAX £	MIN £	MAX £	OPEN
C	10.50	12.50	115.50	122.50	4—10

Giltar Hotel*

The Esplanade, Tenby
Pembrokeshire
Dyfed SA70 7DU
Tel: (0834) 2507/3424

CATEGORIES

| 3 | 3 | 2 |

Christine and Miguel Gonzalez welcome you and your children to their informal seafront hotel overlooking the South Beach near town centre and facilities (golf, tennis). Sea view dining room; special children's rate and winter breaks. Residents' bar; late disco nightly. Babysitting; free parking. Spanish atmosphere; parties; children included. No VAT or service charge.

	B & B PER PERSON PER NIGHT		DINNER B & B PER PERSON PER WEEK		63
T	MIN £	MAX £	MIN £	MAX £	OPEN
C	10	17	90	135	1—12

Greenhills Hotel*

St. Florence, Tenby
Pembrokeshire
Dyfed SA70 8NB
Tel: (083482) 291

CATEGORIES

| 3 | 3 | 3 |

Greenhills family-run hotel. Licensed bar. Colour TV lounge, heated swimming pool. Hot and cold in all bedrooms. Tea-making facilities. Bar snacks. Children welcome at reduced rates. Traditional Welsh home cooking. Baby sitting facilities. Car parking. Local attractions. Beautiful coastline, fishing, swimming, surfing, wind surfing, boating, golf, nature walks.

	B & B PER PERSON PER NIGHT		DINNER B & B PER PERSON PER WEEK		26
C	MIN £	MAX £	MIN £	MAX £	OPEN
	7.25	9.25	60	70	1—12

Hafod-y-Werydd*

Heywood Lane, Tenby
South Pembrokeshire, Dyfed
SA70 8BU
Tel: (0834) 2501

CATEGORIES: 3 | 3 | 3

A family-run hotel in its own grounds. Free parking for all. Children sharing have concessionary rates. Pets welcome. Fully licensed. Separate TV lounge. Diets catered for. Ground and first floor bedrooms only. Parties catered for. Special rates September to May. SAE for brochure to Hafod-y-Werydd, Tenby, Pembrokeshire, Tel: (0834) 2501.

T C	B & B PER PERSON PER NIGHT		DINNER B & B PER PERSON PER WEEK		19
	MIN £	MAX £	MIN £	MAX £	OPEN
	7.50	10.50	60	85	1—12

Hallsville Hotel*

Victoria Street, Tenby
Pembrokeshire
Dyfed
Tel: (0834) 2410

CATEGORIES: 2 | 3 | 2

The Hallsville is within 100 yards of Tenby's beautiful South Beach and a short walk from the town. We have large, comfortable rooms: family, double and single. Cots available. Large TV lounge and pleasant, relaxing bar. The hotel is personally run by the proprietors. Fire Certificate. Send SAE for brochure.

T C	B & B PER PERSON PER NIGHT		DINNER B & B PER PERSON PER WEEK		11
	MIN £	MAX £	MIN £	MAX £	OPEN
	6.90	10.50	64.40	90	4—10

Heywood Lodge*

Heywood Lane, Tenby
Pembrokeshire
Dyfed SA70 8BN
Tel: (0834) 2684

CATEGORIES: 4 | 4 | 4

Situated in its own grounds the Lodge presents a peaceful country house atmosphere within walking distance of the town and beaches. Central heating, private parking for all residents. Some rooms with bath. Residential licence, good food presented with imagination and personal attention. Diets catered for. AA & RAC listed.

C	B & B PER PERSON PER NIGHT		DINNER B & B PER PERSON PER WEEK		14
	MIN £	MAX £	MIN £	MAX £	OPEN
	8.50	10.50	85	92	4—10

Heywood Mount*

Heywood Lane, Tenby
Pembrokeshire
Dyfed SA70 8DA
Tel: (0834) 2087

CATEGORIES: 2 | 3 | 3

Set in peaceful surroundings but within easy walking distance to beaches, town and all amenities. TV lounge, bar, lounge, central heating. Free parking. Coach parties and block bookings, special tariff. Family-run hotel by mother and daughter, Mrs. L. Walters, Mrs. J. Andrews for colour brochure SAE please.

C	B & B PER PERSON PER NIGHT		DINNER B & B PER PERSON PER WEEK		22
	MIN £	MAX £	MIN £	MAX £	OPEN
	8	10.50	70	90	1—12

Hildebrand Hotel*

Victoria Street, Tenby
Pembrokeshire
Dyfed SA70 7DY
Tel: (0834) 2403

CATEGORIES: 3 | 3 | 2

Close to beach and car park. Town harbour, golf course, (reduced green fees), all within easy walking distance. Well appointed bedrooms, all with radio/intercom, tea/coffee-making facilities and heating; some with shower and toilets. For further details send for colour brochure to Veronica and Jim Martin.

T C	B & B PER PERSON PER NIGHT		DINNER B & B PER PERSON PER WEEK		12
	MIN £	MAX £	MIN £	MAX £	OPEN
	7.50	12.50	69	92	2—12

Hotel Doneva*

The Norton, Tenby
Pembrokeshire
Dyfed SA70 8AB
Tel: (0834) 2460

CATEGORIES: 3 | 3 | 3

Comfortable, friendly, family, licensed hotel in own grounds, 4 minutes from North Beach and town centre with own large, free car park. Personally supervised by Proprietors, Lui and Bette Vick. All meals served to high standard at separate tables. Colour TV lounge, central heating. Special early season rates. Full Fire Certificate.

C	B & B PER PERSON PER NIGHT		DINNER B & B PER PERSON PER WEEK		14
	MIN £	MAX £	MIN £	MAX £	OPEN
	7.50	8.50	65	87	3 10

The Imperial Hotel

The Paragon, Tenby
Pembrokeshire
Dyfed SA70 7HR
Tel: (0834) 3737

CATEGORIES: 3 | 5 | 5

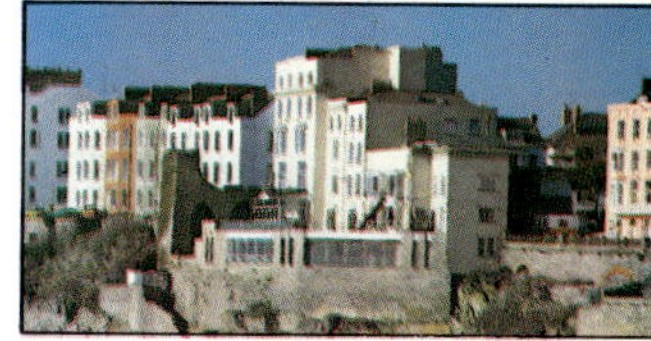

Magnificent cliff-top position, overlooking the South Beach towards St. Catherine's and Caldy Island. Lift to all floors, private steps to beach. Car park, garage, tennis court. Colour TV, radio and telephone in all bedrooms. Dinner/dance most Friday/Saturdays. Holiday Bargain Breaks available all year. Open for Christmas and New Year.

T C	B & B PER PERSON PER NIGHT		DINNER B & B PER PERSON PER WEEK		48
	MIN £	MAX £	MIN £	MAX £	OPEN
	15	25	129.50	168	2—12

Kinloch Court Hotel*

Queens Parade, Tenby
Pembrokeshire
Dyfed SA70 7EG
Tel: (0834) 2777

CATEGORIES

4	4	3

Adjacent beach and golf course. Most rooms with en-suite facilities. Ample parking. Own grounds. Comfortable licensed bar. Separate TV lounge, games room, central heating. Children welcome. Few minutes town and harbour. Personal attention. The family hotel which really cares. Please write or telephone for colour brochure.

T	B & B PER PERSON PER NIGHT		DINNER B & B PER PERSON PER WEEK		12
C	MIN £	MAX £	MIN £	MAX £	OPEN
	8.50	10.50	80	97	4—10

Marlborough House*

South Cliff Street, Tenby
Pembrokeshire
Dyfed SA70 7EA
Tel: (0834) 2961

CATEGORIES

3	3	3

Sue and Ken Lunn extend a warm welcome and assure you of an enjoyable holiday. Good food, comfortable rooms, and our well-stocked Treasure Chest Bar for a nightcap or two or three

C	B & B PER PERSON PER NIGHT		DINNER B & B PER PERSON PER WEEK		12
	MIN £	MAX £	MIN £	MAX £	OPEN
	6	8	69	80	1—12

Newton Croft Private Hotel

8 The Croft, Tenby
Pembrokeshire
Dyfed
Tel: (0834) 2631

CATEGORIES

3	3	2

Situated overlooking Carmarthen bay with private garden leading down to beach. Rooms available with private bathrooms or showers. Personal service. Licensed. Tea-making facilities available. Well cooked food. Children welcomed. 1971 Fire Act complied with.

C	B & B PER PERSON PER NIGHT		DINNER B & B PER PERSON PER WEEK		15
	MIN £	MAX £	MIN £	MAX £	OPEN
	8	10	70	98	3—10

Children stay at reduced rates, wherever you see this symbol.

C

Ocean Hotel

The Croft, Tenby
Pembrokeshire
Dyfed SA70 8AP
Tel: (0834) 2476

CATEGORIES

3	3	3

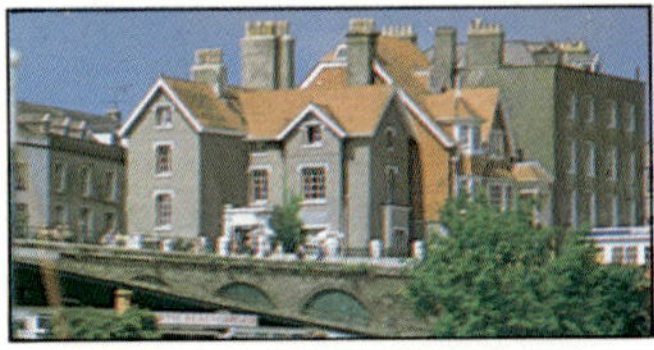

The hotel with marvellous views. The entrance to the beach is just opposite. Bathing from hotel. A friendly, comfortable family-run hotel enjoying on of the finest positions in Tenby. Having beautiful views of the picturesque harbour, North Beach and Carmarthen Bay with a combination of the highest standards of cuisine and comfort. Attractive lounge with colour television, bar. Reductions for children. Special terms early and late bookings.

C	B & B PER PERSON PER NIGHT		DINNER B & B PER PERSON PER WEEK		7
	MIN £	MAX £	MIN £	MAX £	OPEN
	10	12	75	85	1—12

The Old Rectory*

Gumfreston, Tenby
Pembrokeshire
Dyfed SA70 8RA
Tel: (0834) 3440 or 2487

CATEGORIES

3	4	4

1878 old rectory in two acres of grounds, 1¼ miles from Tenby, overlooking Caldey Island and Carmarthen Bay. Ample parking. Central heating, hot and cold in all bedrooms, shaving sockets. Tea/coffee-making facilities: some rooms with private bathrooms, toilet en suite. TV lounge, hall lounge, lounge bar, restaurant and residential licence.

C	B & B PER PERSON PER NIGHT		DINNER B & B PER PERSON PER WEEK		13
	MIN £	MAX £	MIN £	MAX £	OPEN
	12.75	14.50	108	117	3—10

Pembroke Hotel

Warren Street, Tenby
Pembrokeshire
Dyfed SA70 7JX
Tel: (0834) 3670

CATEGORIES

3	2	3

Situated just outside Tenby's 13th century town walls, yet within a short walk of the shopping centre and golden beaches and harbour. Full central heating; some rooms with showers. Parking for 6 cars. Packed lunches on request. Cocktail Bar. TV lounge.

C	B & B PER PERSON PER NIGHT		DINNER B & B PER PERSON PER WEEK		14
	MIN £	MAX £	MIN £	MAX £	OPEN
	7	8.50	63	73.50	1—12

Penally Manor Hotel*

Tenby, Pembrokeshire
Dyfed SA70 7PZ
Tel: (0834) 2668

CATEGORIES

4	4	3

Beautifully renovated family-run licensed hotel in wooded grounds overlooking Tenby Golf Course and beach. Full central heating. Most rooms private WC, radio/alarm, sea views. Heated swimming pool, paddling pool, play areas. Bar lunches. Barbeques. Dancing. Excellent cuisine. 50% reduction children sharing. Special terms for babies. Optional children's early dinner. Baby-listening. Parking. Fire certified. Mini Breaks.

T	B & B PER PERSON PER NIGHT		DINNER B & B PER PERSON PER WEEK		16
C	MIN £	MAX £	MIN £	MAX £	OPEN
	7.50	12	69	99	1—12

Red House Hotel*

Heywood Lane, Tenby
Pembrokeshire
Dyfed SA70 8JN
Tel: (0834) 2770

CATEGORIES

4	4	4

No parking problems; situated in its own spacious grounds, only ten minutes walk from the beach and town. Outdoor heated pool. Fully centrally heated for all year comfort. Residential licence, tennis court, TV lounge. Write or telephone for colour brochure. Resident Proprietors, Mr. and Mrs. J. W. Lewis. AA listed.

T	B & B PER PERSON PER NIGHT		DINNER B & B PER PERSON PER WEEK		25
C	MIN £	MAX £	MIN £	MAX £	OPEN
	7.50	10	79	95	4—10

Tourist Information Centres are listed at back of book.

Ripley St. Mary's Hotel*

St. Mary's Street, Tenby
Pembrokeshire
Dyfed SA70 7HN
Tel: (0834) 2837

CATEGORIES

| 3 | 3 | 3 |

Highly recommended licensed hotel in quiet floral street in centre of Tenby. 75 yards sea front and Paragon Gardens. Car parks, shops, churches all amenities within short walking distance. Attractive lounge and residents bar. Well appointed bedrooms all with tea/coffee facilities. Six with private bathrooms. We are proud of our reputation for hospitality and home cooking. For details of long or short breaks contact: Alan W. S. Mace.

T C	B & B PER PERSON PER NIGHT		DINNER B & B PER PERSON PER WEEK		14
	MIN £	MAX £	MIN £	MAX £	OPEN
	8	10	85	95	2—11

The Royal Gate House Hotel

White Lion Street, Tenby
South Pembrokeshire
Dyfed SA70 7ET
Tel: (0834) 2255

CATEGORIES

| 3 | 3 | 4 |

Exquisitely situated overlooking Tenby harbour, with all modern amenities. Central for town and transport terminals. Terms from £13 B & B daily. Ideal for fishing, golf, sailing and water-skiing. Reductions for children sharing parents' room. For further information contact Mr. Graham Fry.

C	B & B PER PERSON PER NIGHT		DINNER B & B PER PERSON PER WEEK		65
	MIN £	MAX £	MIN £	MAX £	OPEN
	13	18	115	132	1—12

This symbol means you can book through your local travel agent.

Royal Lion Hotel

High Street, Tenby
Dyfed
Tel: (0834) 2127

CATEGORIES

| 3 | 3 | 4 |

This 300 year old Coaching Inn now a modernised privately owned hotel has a lift to all floors, Cocktail Bar, seaview dining room and, for late night meals, enjoy the imaginative 'Lions Den' Restaurant originally the White Lion Inn. Wine cellars. Rooms with seaview and private bathroom available. All rooms centrally heated and with TV.

C	B & B PER PERSON PER NIGHT		DINNER B & B PER PERSON PER WEEK		36
	MIN £	MAX £	MIN £	MAX £	OPEN
	12	17	100	130	4—10

St. Davids Hotel*

The Croft, Tenby
Pembrokeshire, Dyfed
Tel: (0834) 2721

CATEGORIES

| 3 | 3 | 3 |

Beautifully situated overlooking Carmarthen bay and Tenby's picturesque harbour. Private cliff garden with pathway to beach. Most bedrooms have en-suite all with tea/coffee making facilities and central heating, colour TV lounge and cocktail bar. Wide choice of family rooms. Reductions for children sharing. Parties/group bookings welcome.

T C	B & B PER PERSON PER NIGHT		DINNER B & B PER PERSON PER WEEK		15
	MIN £	MAX £	MIN £	MAX £	OPEN
	7.50	10.50	70.50	95	1—12

Sea Breezes Private Hotel*

18 The Norton, Tenby
South Pembrokeshire
Dyfed SA70 8AA
Tel: (0834) 2753

CATEGORIES

| 3 | 3 | 3 |

Cosy, comfortable "Sea Breezes" with 18 bedrooms and residential licence. Just 100 yards from North Beach and town. An abundance of bathrooms, central heating, and tea-makers in all rooms; some with private bathrooms and TV. Large TV lounge, bar lounge and Cabin Bar for your complete relaxation. Fire Certificate granted.

T C	B & B PER PERSON PER NIGHT		DINNER B & B PER PERSON PER WEEK		18
	MIN £	MAX £	MIN £	MAX £	OPEN
	6.50	8.50	70	85	3—11

Southbourne Hotel

South Cliff Gardens, Tenby
South Pembrokeshire
Dyfed
Tel: (0834) 2186

CATEGORIES

| 3 | 4 | 4 |

Close to the town centre, beaches, golf course and bowling green. Rooms have tea-making facilities, hot and cold water, shaver points. Private bathroom available. Open all year including Christmas. Special rates for off-season breaks.

T C	B & B PER PERSON PER NIGHT		DINNER B & B PER PERSON PER WEEK		25
	MIN £	MAX £	MIN £	MAX £	OPEN
	8	10	60	80	1—12

Strathmore Hotel*

23 Victoria Street, Tenby
South Pembrokeshire
Dyfed
Tel: (0834) 2323

CATEGORIES

| 3 | 3 | 3 |

Open all the year. 60 yards from South Beach. All usual amenities. Especially for people who enjoy good food. Free colour brochure (stamp appreciated). Tel: (0834) 2323.

C	B & B PER PERSON PER NIGHT		DINNER B & B PER PERSON PER WEEK		12
	MIN £	MAX £	MIN £	MAX £	OPEN
	7	8	60	80	1—12

Sundowner Motel

Twy Cross, Saundersfoot
South Pembrokeshire
Dyfed
Tel: (0834) 813390

CATEGORIES

| 4 | 3 | 4 |

Modern motel holiday accommodation. Easy walk to 5 beaches in Pembrokeshire National Park. Good access and parking. Single, twin and family suites with private shower/toilet facilities and colour TV. 2 bars, restaurant, heated pool, sauna and large play area. Children half price under twelve. 10% discount. 7 nights or longer.

C	B & B PER PERSON PER NIGHT		DINNER B & B PER PERSON PER WEEK		20
	MIN £	MAX £	MIN £	MAX	OPEN
	11.50	14.50	100	120	1—12

Cestyll '83 – 1983 is the year of the castles.

Tall Ships

Victoria Street, Tenby
South Pembrokeshire
Dyfed
Tel: (0834) 2055

CATEGORIES: 2 3 2

A warm welcome awaits you aboard the "Tall Ships".
A small, private hotel just 50 yards from Tenby's
popular South Beach. Short distance to bowling/putting
greens, town centre and entertainments. Radio,
shaving sockets in all double, twin and family rooms.
Parking nearby. Licensed bar. Friendly service.
Fire certificate.

T C	B & B PER PERSON PER NIGHT		DINNER B & B PER PERSON PER WEEK		14
	MIN £	MAX £	MIN £	MAX £	OPEN
	6.90	10.50	64.40	90	1—12

Victoria Hotel

Victoria Street, Tenby
South Pembrokeshire
Dyfed SA70 7DY
Tel: (0834) 2191

CATEGORIES: 1 2 2

Victoria is a small, family hotel situated very near
beach and car park. Short walk bowling green, tennis
court, golf course, shops. Hot and cold water in all
bedrooms, shaving points. Large, comfortable lounge
with colour TV. Separate tables in dining room. Bed,
breakfast, dinner.

C	B & B PER PERSON PER NIGHT		DINNER B & B PER PERSON PER WEEK		9
	MIN £	MAX £	MIN £	MAX £	OPEN
	6.50	7	50	60	1—12

Guest Houses

Ashby House*

24 Victoria Street, Tenby
South Pembrokeshire SA70 7DY
Tel: (0834) 2867

CATEGORIES: 3 3 3

Superbly situated 60 yards from the South Beach and
two minutes to the town centre. Single, double and
family rooms all with hot and cold water and shaver
points. Reduced rates for children. Table licence,
lounge with colour televiion. Large public car park
directly behind house.

C	B & B PER PERSON PER NIGHT		DINNER B & B PER PERSON PER WEEK		10
	MIN £	MAX £	MIN £	MAX £	OPEN
	7	8.50	68	78	4—9

Courtney Guest House*

4 South Cliffe Street
Tenby, South Pembrokeshire
Dyfed SA70 7EB
Tel: (0834) 2397

CATEGORIES: 3 3 2

Situated only a few minutes walk from South Beach
and town centre. Courtney is convenient to bowling,
tennis court and golf link. Public car park 100 yards.
Pleasant lounge with TV, full use of rooms permitted
at all times. High standard catering and excellent
varied menu.

C	B & B PER PERSON PER NIGHT		DINNER B & B PER PERSON PER WEEK		
	MIN £	MAX £	MIN £	MAX £	OPEN
	5.75	6.50	59.50	68	1—12

The Forge Guest House*

New Hedges
Tenby, South Pembrokeshire
Dyfed SA70 8TL
Tel: (0834) 2366

CATEGORIES: 2 3 2

Bed and breakfast or bed, breakfast and evening dinner.
Recently built, small, family guest house, central for
beaches and shops. Tenby 1 mile—Saundersfoot
1½ miles. Spring interiors, hot and cold water and
shaver points in all rooms. Lounge with colour TV.
Dining room with separate tables. Children welcome
with baby-sitting service. Free parking on premises.
Access to rooms at all times. Fire Certificate approved.
SAE for brochure to Mrs Christine Rogers.

C	B & B PER PERSON PER NIGHT		DINNER B & B PER PERSON PER WEEK		6
	MIN £	MAX £	MIN £	MAX £	OPEN
	9	10	70	79	5—9

Haytor

Narberth Road, Tenby, South
Pembrokeshire, Dyfed SA70 8HT
Tel: (0834) 2772

CATEGORIES: 2 1 1

Haytor, Narberth Road, Tenby, South Pembrokeshire,
Dyfed. Quiet and secluded standing in large garden.
Easy walking distance beach and town centre. Single,
double and family rooms. Bed and breakfast, free
parking.

C	B & B PER PERSON PER NIGHT		DINNER B & B PER PERSON PER WEEK		5
	MIN £	MAX £	MIN £	MAX £	OPEN
	8				5—9

Highlands Farm Guest House

Manorbier, Newtown
Tenby, South Pembrokeshire
Dyfed SA70 8PX
Tel: (083482) 481

CATEGORIES: 3 3 2

Highlands is a pleasant country guest house, situated
in 12 acres of the Pembrokeshire Coast National Park.
Convenient for many beaches and other recreational
activities. Comfortably furnished guests' lounge with
panoramic views of countryside. Family tables in dining
room, hot and cold water in all bedrooms. House
centrally heated. Licensed. Ample parking space. Ideal
for family holiday (babysitting can be arranged). Write
or telephone for brochure.

C	B & B PER PERSON PER NIGHT		DINNER B & B PER PERSON PER WEEK		6
	MIN £	MAX £	MIN £	MAX £	OPEN
	7.50	8	68	74	6—10

**Tourist Information
Centres are listed at
back of book.**

Hill Cottage Guest House*

Heywood Lane
Tenby, South Pembrokeshire
Dyfed SA70 8BG
Tel: (0834) 2548

CATEGORIES: 1 2 2

Family, double rooms; hot and cold water in all rooms;
colour TV lounge; separate tables in dining room.
About 10 minutes walk to beaches, shops and near
railway station. Children welcome at reduced rates.
Access to rooms at all times. Car park nearby. Send
SAE for brochure.

C	B & B PER PERSON PER NIGHT		DINNER B & B PER PERSON PER WEEK		5
	MIN £	MAX £	MIN £	MAX £	OPEN
	5.50	6.50	56	62	4—10

Ivy Bank Guest House

Harding Street
Tenby, South Pembrokeshire
Dyfed SA70 7LL
Tel: (0834) 2311

CATEGORIES: 1 3 2

A great holiday awaits you at this small, family-run
guest house. We offer good home cooking and friendly
attention in a relaxed atmosphere. Close to all beaches,
few minutes to railway station. Easy car parking. Fire
Certificate held. SAE please for brochure to Shirley or
Dudley Scotcher.

C	B & B PER PERSON PER NIGHT		DINNER B & B PER PERSON PER WEEK		9
	MIN £	MAX £	MIN £	MAX £	OPEN
	5	7	60	68	1—12

Oxford Lodge Guest House*

Lower Frog Street
Tenby, South Pembrokeshire
Dyfed SA70 7HT
Tel: (0834) 2934

CATEGORIES: 3 3 2

Situated within Tenby's historic town walls. Close to
beach and shops. We offer holidays in a friendly
atmosphere. Colour TV in pleasant lounge. Separate
dining room tables. Reduced terms for senior citizens
early and late season. Fire Certificate. For brochure
please send SAE to Mrs Pat Phillips.

T C	B & B PER PERSON PER NIGHT		DINNER B & B PER PERSON PER WEEK		7
	MIN £	MAX £	MIN £	MAX £	OPEN
	7	8	53	63	4—9

St. Oswalds

Picton Terrace, Tenby,
South Pembrokeshire
Dyfed SA70 7DR
Tel: (0834) 2130

CATEGORIES: 2 3 2

Private parking. Some private bathrooms. 50 yards to
sea front, few minutes walk to town. Bowling, putting
greens and tennis courts opposite. Hot and cold water,
shaver points and bedside lights. Separate tables in
dining room. Reduced terms for children sharing
parents' room. Full Fire Certificate.

T C	B & B PER PERSON PER NIGHT		DINNER B & B PER PERSON PER WEEK		13
	MIN £	MAX £	MIN £	MAX £	OPEN
	7	9	69	95	5—9

"Sutherlands"*

3 Picton Road, Tenby
South Pembrokeshire
Dyfed SA70 7DP
Tel: (0834) 2522

CATEGORIES: 2 2 2

Tastefully furnished and converted. Reductions for senior citizens. Small, family guest house within easy reach of beaches, shops, car parks. Public golf course and putting/bowling greens. Home cooking; children specially catered for. Hot and cold water in all rooms. Separate dining tables; colour TV, Shower room. Friendly, informal atmosphere.

C	B & B PER PERSON PER NIGHT		DINNER B & B PER PERSON PER WEEK		🛏 6
	MIN £	MAX £	MIN £	MAX £	OPEN
	6	7	50	60	1—12

The Mead

Manorbier, Newtown, Near Tenby,
South Pembrokeshire
Dyfed SA70 8QU
Tel: (083 482) 267

CATEGORIES: 2 3 2

The Mead is situated in the quiet countryside, close to beaches and sporting activities. Good home cooking, home-grown garden vegetables served when in season. Colour TV, separate dining tables, large lounge with inglenook fireplace. Lawn with garden furniture. Ample parking. Fire Certificate.

C	B & B PER PERSON PER NIGHT		DINNER B & B PER PERSON PER WEEK		🛏 5
	MIN £	MAX £	MIN £	MAX £	OPEN
	7	9	68	74	5—10

Tides Reach*

St. Julian Street, Tenby,
South Pembrokeshire
Dyfed SA70 7BD
Tel: (0834) 2614

CATEGORIES: 3 2 1

Family-run guest house in superb position overlooking castle and South Beach. Lovely Georgian house with spacious, airy rooms; private steps to beach. 100 yards from picturesque harbour. Evening snacks provided if required. Tea and coffee on request during day. Local proprietors have detailed knowledge of town and surrounding area.

C	B & B PER PERSON PER NIGHT		DINNER B & B PER PERSON PER WEEK		🛏 4
	MIN £	MAX £	MIN £	MAX £	OPEN
	6.50	8			3—10

Tintern
SOUTH WALES

Hotels, Inn

Beaufort Hotel

Tintern, Chepstow,
Gwent NP6 6SF
Tel: (029) 18202

CATEGORIES: 6 4 4

Delightful country "inn", situated in peaceful Wye Valley opposite Tintern Abbey. All rooms with bath/shower, colour TV, and central heating. Excellent restaurant and friendly bar. 'Hush-away' Breaks available throughout the year. Includes horse riding holidays. An Embassy Hotel.

T	B & B PER PERSON PER NIGHT		DINNER B & B PER PERSON PER WEEK		🛏 27
C	MIN £	MAX £	MIN £	MAX £	OPEN
	17.50	20			1—12

The Fountain Inn*

Trellech Grange, Tintern, Chepstow,
Gwent NP6 6QW
Tel: (029 18) 303

CATEGORIES: 3 3 5

17th century inn, secluded countryside location, 2 miles from Tintern Abbey. Touring centre for historic castles, forest and country walks. Local horse and pony riding. Full central heating, log fires. Country restaurant for à la carte or grill meals. Bedrooms have tea-making facilities and TV. Egon Ronay recommended. AA* RAC*.

T	B & B PER PERSON PER NIGHT		DINNER B & B PER PERSON PER WEEK		🛏 4
C	MIN £	MAX £	MIN £	MAX £	OPEN
	8.75	8.75	135	135	1—12

The Old Farmhouse Hotel*

Llandogo, Near Tintern, Chepstow,
Gwent NP54 TL
Tel: (0594) 530303 and 530527

CATEGORIES: 4 4 5

17th century farmhouse/modern hotel, set in the wooded slopes of the Wye Valley overlooking the river. Fully licensed bars and Les Routiers-recommended restaurant. Ample car parking serves the hotel. Rooms and hotel chalets have private bathrooms. Most have tea-making facilities, radio/intercom and colour TV. The resident proprietors extend a warm welcome.

T	B & B PER PERSON PER NIGHT		DINNER B & B PER PERSON PER WEEK		🛏 24
C	MIN £	MAX £	MIN £	MAX £	OPEN
	16	20	92	140	1—12

Royal George

Tintern, Near Chepstow,
Gwent NP6 6SF
Tel: (02918) 205 and 503

CATEGORIES: 5 4 4

A comfortable 17th century inn near the famous ruined Abbey. Most of the 19 bedrooms have private bath, and all have telephone, radio, colour TV, and tea and coffee-making facilities. Central heating, car park. Bargain Breaks available. Ideal touring base for the Wye Valley.

T	B & B PER PERSON PER NIGHT		DINNER B & B PER PERSON PER WEEK		🛏 19
C	MIN £	MAX £	MIN £	MAX £	OPEN
	20.25	23			1—12

Children stay at reduced rates, wherever you see this symbol.

Guest House

Parva Farmhouse*

Tintern, Near Chepstow,
Gwent NP6 68Q
Tel: (02918) 411
Telex: 498280 (PARVA F)

CATEGORIES

| 3 | 4 | 2 |

Beautifully situated by the River in the Wye Valley:
glorious views. A 17th century licensed farmhouse
renowned for its good home country cooking. AA
and RAC approved. Large comfortable TV lounge,
central heating, 4 bathrooms. Horse riding,
trout/salmon fishing available. For further details
contact Rod and Gilly Baverstock.

T C	B & B PER PERSON PER NIGHT		DINNER B & B PER PERSON PER WEEK		6
	MIN £	MAX £	MIN £	MAX £	OPEN
	8	9	80	85	1—12

Trearddur Bay
NORTH WALES

Map ref: Aa3
Holy Island, joined
by causeway and
railway bridge to
the Isle of Anglesey,
is an islet of three faces: high cliffs,
water-filled creeks and sandy bays.
Hotels front the sea at the main
bay, Trearddur, where a tangle of
rocky outcrops, separated by fine
sand, provide shade and shelter for
busy children wielding sand
buckets and spades.

Hotels

The Beach Hotel*

Trearddur Bay, Holyhead,
Isle of Anglesey, Gwynedd LL65 2YT
Tel: (0407) 860125 and 860332
Telex: 61529

CATEGORIES

| 5 | 5 | 6 |

The hotel is synonymous with all that is quality on the
island. Delightful accommodation, delicious food,
friendly service. Facilities include squash courts, the
'Sanctuary' Health and Beauty Centre with sun rooms,
sauna, jacuzzi pool. Boutique, Steak House; own pub.
Sophisticated discoteque club. Golf available.

T C	B & B PER PERSON PER NIGHT		DINNER B & B PER PERSON PER WEEK		26
	MIN £	MAX £	MIN £	MAX £	OPEN
	15	17	135		1—12

The Fairway Private Hotel*

Trearddur Bay, Isle of Anglesey,
Gwynedd LL65 2UD
Tel: (0407) 860255

CATEGORIES

| 3 | 4 | 2 |

The Fairway is a small family hotel on B4545 road
between beach and golf club. Ideal for family holidays,
honeymoons, quiet weekends off-season. Golf, sailing,
fishing, diving, pony trekking and pleasant coastal
walks. Residential licence. Private parking.
AA RAC listed. Personally supervised by the owner,
Mrs Mair Lees.

C	B & B PER PERSON PER NIGHT		DINNER B & B PER PERSON PER WEEK		7
	MIN £	MAX £	MIN £	MAX £	OPEN
	8.05	11.50	80.50	104.65	1—12

High Ground Hotel*

off Ravenspoint Road, Trearddur Bay,
Isle of Anglesey, Gwynedd LL65 2YY
Tel: (0407) 860 078

CATEGORIES

| 3 | 4 | 3 |

Unique marine residence. Direct access beach. Superb
food. Luxury accommodation. Tea/coffee-making
facilities in all bedrooms. Licensed bar. AA listed.
Highly recommended. No restrictions. Fire Certificate.
SAE for brochure: Mrs. A. S. Rivington, High Ground
Hotel, Ravenspoint Road, Trearddur Bay, Anglesey.
Phone (0407) 860 078. Wheelchair facilities. Ramp.
All prices fully inclusive.

T C	B & B PER PERSON PER NIGHT		DINNER B & B PER PERSON PER WEEK		7
	MIN £	MAX £	MIN £	MAX £	OPEN
	8.50	9	94.50	101.50	1—12

Trearddur Bay Hotel

Holyhead, Isle of Anglesey,
Gwynedd LL65 2UN
Tel: (0407) 860301 Telex: 61609

CATEGORIES

| 5 | 5 | 5 |

Situated in own grounds, next to beach. Fully licensed.
Spacious lounge, large restaurant. Indoor heated
swimming pool. Ample parking for cars. TV's, radios,
and phones in all bedrooms. Special terms for
weekends and weekly terms available, except for
August, Christmas and Easter. Dogs accommodated at
Manager's discretion.

T C	B & B PER PERSON PER NIGHT		DINNER B & B PER PERSON PER WEEK		28
	MIN £	MAX £	MIN £	MAX £	OPEN
	16	30	140	190	1—12

Guest Houses

"Hafod y Twyni"*

Penrallt Road, Trearddur Bay
Isle of Anglesey
Gwynedd LL65 2UG
Tel: (0407) 860631

CATEGORIES

| 1 | 3 | 2 |

Hafod y Twyni is a modern bungalow situated in quiet
cul-de-sac in village with double, twin and single
rooms. Central heating, hot and cold water, wash
basins, shaver points, TV lounge. Parking space.
Sea views. Near beaches, golf, sailing, fishing
facilities, nature reserves and Holyhead Town.
Excellent centre for touring and walking.

C	B & B PER PERSON PER NIGHT		DINNER B & B PER PERSON PER WEEK		3
	MIN £	MAX £	MIN £	MAX £	OPEN
	5.50	7	60	68	4—9

Moranedd Guest House*

Trearddur Road, Trearddur Bay,
Isle of Anglesey, Gwyneed
Tel: (0407) 860324

CATEGORIES

| 3 | 3 | 1 |

A well furnished guest house set in ¾ acre garden in
quiet cul-de-sac. Near beach and golf club. Hot and
cold water and shaver points in all bedrooms. Central
heating throughout. Lounge with colour TV, dining room
with separate tables.

C	B & B PER PERSON PER NIGHT		DINNER B & B PER PERSON PER WEEK		8
	MIN £	MAX £	MIN £	MAX £	OPEN
	6	6			5—10

Trefeglwys MID WALES

Farmhouse

The Old Ffinnant*

Trefeglwys, Caersws,
Powys SY17 5QY
Tel: (05516) 263

CATEGORIES		
1	2	2

Stay in comfort in a 17th century farmhouse. Cordon bleu cooking and suite of private rooms. One party taken at a time. Come with friends or family. Complete privacy and personal service. Beautiful countryside. Easy reach of pony trekking, fishing, golf, wonderful walking; 25 miles from coast. Dogs welcome.

	B & B PER PERSON PER NIGHT		DINNER B & B PER PERSON PER WEEK		🛏 2
	MIN £	MAX £	MIN £	MAX £	OPEN
	8	8	112	112	1—12

Tregaron MID WALES

Hotel

Talbot Hotel

The Square, Tregaron,
Dyfed SY25 6JL
Tel: (097 44) 208

CATEGORIES		
3	3	4

One of the oldest and best known hotels in West Wales. Fully licensed freehouse, tourist centre. Excellent fishing: river and lakes. Approximately 10 square miles nature reserve which is an ornithologist's paradise with many rare birds. Pony trekking centre with picturesque walks, mountain scenery and the Brianne Dam.

C	B & B PER PERSON PER NIGHT		DINNER B & B PER PERSON PER WEEK		🛏 14
	MIN £	MAX £	MIN £	MAX £	OPEN
	8		98		4—10

Farmhouses

Brynblodau

Llwynygroes, Tregaron,
Dyfed SY25 6PY
Tel: (057045) 344

CATEGORIES		
1	2	2

A traditional Welsh farmhouse offering comfortable accommodation and good food. Ideal family holiday on a working farm. Golf, pony trekking, fishing nearby. Rough shooting on farm. Coast 20 minutes. Scenic tours and walks within easy reach. No pets indoors please. Holiday especially suitable for couples or parents with young children.

C	B & B PER PERSON PER NIGHT		DINNER B & B PER PERSON PER WEEK		🛏 1
	MIN £	MAX £	MIN £	MAX £	OPEN
	6		72	77	5—10

Neuaddlas*

Tregaron, Dyfed SY25 6LG
Wales
Tel: (09744) 380

CATEGORIES		
3	2	2

1½ miles Tregaron main A484 road to Aberystwyth. This peaceful scenic haven for bird watching, rambling and fishing, overlooks Cors Caron Nature Reserve and Cambrian Mountains. Ideal for touring coast, woollen mills, scenic railways, riding. Golf club 6 miles and many places of interest. Country home cooking. Suitable disabled. Parties catered for. Wales Farmhouse Award. Fire Certificate held. Heated, plus log fire. Hot and cold water in bedrooms. 2 bathrooms. Private guest lounge. Weekly, daily. Children welcome.

T	B & B PER PERSON PER NIGHT		DINNER B & B PER PERSON PER WEEK		🛏 5
C	MIN £	MAX £	MIN £	MAX £	OPEN
	7	7.50	75	82	1—12

Aberdwr Guest Farmhouse*

Abergwesyn Road, Tregaron,
Dyfed
Tel: (09744) 255

CATEGORIES		
3	3	2

Aberdwr is situated on the river bank and in scenic, mountainous surroundings. Approximately ½ mile from the market town of Tregaron. Pony trekking, fishing, bird-watching, nature walks. All bedrooms with hot and cold water; washing facilities. A large, comfortable lounge with television; separate tables in dining room. SAE for brochure.

C	B & B PER PERSON PER NIGHT		DINNER B & B PER PERSON PER WEEK		🛏 7
	MIN £	MAX £	MIN £	MAX £	OPEN
	6	7	70	77	4—10

Treherbert SOUTH WALES

Hotel

Dunraven Hotel

Dunraven Street, Treherbert,
Mid-Glamorgan CF47 5BH
Tel: (0443) 771329

CATEGORIES		
2	3	5

Near Brecon Beacons National Park. Ideal for touring and sporting holidays. Single, double and family rooms; some with bath. Hot and cold water and shaver points in all bedrooms. Lounge with colour television, full à la carte restaurant. Fire Certificate granted. Homely welcoming atmosphere. Open Christmas.

C	B & B PER PERSON PER NIGHT		DINNER B & B PER PERSON PER WEEK		🛏 16
	MIN £	MAX £	MIN £	MAX £	OPEN
	7.50	8.50	12.50	13.50	1—12

Tresaith MID WALES

Hotel

Glandwr Manor Hotel

Tresaith, Cardigan,
Dyfed SA43 2JH
Tel: (0239) 810197

CATEGORIES		
3	3	3

Situated in 5 acres of the beautiful Tresaith Valley. 6 minutes' walk to superb, sandy beach with safe bathing. Comfortable bar with beamed ceiling; open log fire. The restaurant offers a good selection of food and wine with fresh cream desserts always on the menu. Fire Certificate.

C	B & B PER PERSON PER NIGHT		DINNER B & B PER PERSON PER WEEK		🛏 8
	MIN £	MAX £	MIN £	MAX £	OPEN
	9.78		86.25		1—12

Tremle

Tresaith, Cardigan,
Dyfed SA43 2JQ
Tel: (0239) 810283

CATEGORIES

| 1 | 2 | 2 |

Friendly, family accommodation only 250 yards from safe, sandy beach, with Post Office, shop, refreshments, cafe and inn. Glorious coastal views and waterfall. Ideal touring centre. Hot and cold water in bedrooms, shaver points. Lounge, colour TV. Half price children under 12. Parking.

C	B & B PER PERSON PER NIGHT		DINNER B & B PER PERSON PER WEEK		🛏 3
	MIN £	MAX £	MIN £	MAX £	OPEN
	5.50	6	55	60	4—10

Tudweiliog — NORTH WALES

Hotel

Lion Hotel

Tudweiliog, Pwllheli,
LL53 8ND
Tel: (075 887) 244/325

CATEGORIES

| 2 | 2 | 3 |

Friendly inn near a coast of outstanding natural beauty on the lovely Lleyn Peninsula. Three golf courses within 12 miles. Hot and cold water in all the pleasant rooms. Heating as required. Large beer garden with play area.

C	B & B PER PERSON PER NIGHT		DINNER B & B PER PERSON PER WEEK		🛏 5
	MIN £	MAX £	MIN £	MAX £	OPEN
		9.50		85	1—12

Tywyn — MID WALES

Map ref: Db5
On the flat coastal plain between the Dysynni river and Aberdovey rises Tywyn—literally 'sand dune'. Diligent hotels and guest houses

"gild the lily" of a holiday at Tywyn by adding comfort, good food and wine to natures gifts of fine sands, clear seas and a panorama of the Cader Idris range. Talyllyn Narrow Gauge Railway takes you on a magical journey into that panorama.

Hotels

Gorlan Hotel

6 Marine Parade, Tywyn
Gwynedd LL36 0DE
Tel: (0654) 710404

CATEGORIES

| 3 | 3 | 4 |

Gorlan Hotel, 6, Marine Parade, Tywyn, Gwynedd. This family-run hotel is open all year round. Double and family rooms. Special rates for children. Lounge with colour television. Dining room with separate tables. Bar lounge. Special Winter Breaks. Please apply for brochure with our competitive terms. Pets welcome.

T C	B & B PER PERSON PER NIGHT		DINNER B & B PER PERSON PER WEEK		🛏 7
	MIN £	MAX £	MIN £	MAX £	OPEN
	7	7.50	77	80.50	1—12

The Greenfield Private Hotel*

Tywyn, Gwynedd
LL36 9AD
Tel: (0654) 710354

CATEGORIES

| 3 | 3 | 4 |

Centrally situated close to cinema, shops, sandy beach, bus and rail stations. Heated swimming pool; large car park opposite. Licensed bar, lounge with colour TV. Choice of menu. Ideally situated for golf, fishing, walking and touring Snowdonia. Reductions for children. Brochure on request from Brian and Cynthia Elson.

T C	B & B PER PERSON PER NIGHT		DINNER B & B PER PERSON PER WEEK		🛏 14
	MIN £	MAX £	MIN £	MAX £	OPEN
	8.25	9.25	76	85	2—11

Y-Ddraig-Goch (The Red Dragon)

Marine Parade, Tywyn
Gwynedd LL36 0DG
Tel: (0654) 710141

CATEGORIES

| 3 | 3 | 3 |

A modern hotel situated on the seafront. All rooms twin beds, TV, radio, tea and coffee facilities. Friendly, courteous service. Top floor restaurant with views over Cardigan Bay. Car park. Lift. Choice of bars. Tywyn home of Talyllyn Railway. 18 hole golf course, 10 minutes away at Aberdovey.

C	B & B PER PERSON PER NIGHT		DINNER B & B PER PERSON PER WEEK		🛏 12
	MIN £	MAX £	MIN £	MAX £	OPEN
	15	17	120	135	1—12

Guest Houses

Llwyn-y-Gog*

Ffordd Neifion, Tywyn
Gwynedd LL36 9ET
Tel: (0654) 711125

CATEGORIES

| 3 | 3 | 2 |

Private house overlooking large school field. 3 minutes from station, swimming pool and cinema; 5 minutes from sandy beach. One twin and one double room. Separate dining room and colour TV lounge. Home cooking our speciality.

C	B & B PER PERSON PER NIGHT		DINNER B & B PER PERSON PER WEEK		🛏 2
	MIN £	MAX £	MIN £	MAX £	OPEN
	6	7	70	73	3—10

Min-y-Mor

7 Marine Parade, Tywyn
Gwynedd LL36 0DE
Tel: (0654) 710139

CATEGORIES

| 2 | 3 | 3 |

Situated on seafront; all amenities close at hand. Good beaches and safe bathing. Fire regulations incorporated. Hot and cold water in all bedrooms. Some private shower rooms. Colour TV lounge. Pleasant bar facilities. Personal supervision of owner— Kate Gatenby. SAE for details please. Open 1st April— 30th September inclusive. B & B single, per week including VAT £53.50 min. £60.50 max. Price of dinner depends on choice.

C	B & B PER PERSON PER NIGHT		DINNER B & B PER PERSON PER WEEK		🛏 6
	MIN £	MAX £	MIN £	MAX £	OPEN
	8	9			4—9

Monfa Guest House*

Pier Road, Tywyn
Gwynedd LL36 0AU
Tel: (0654) 710858

CATEGORIES

| 4 | 3 | 2 |

We aim to provide the foundation of an enjoyable holiday, comfortable accommodation, good food, friendly relaxed atmosphere. Shower or shower/toilet en-suite. Family and double rooms. Lounge with colour television. Table tennis. Central heating; unlicensed. Children reduced rates to age 15. Seafront 200 yards. Low price Winter Breaks.

T C	B & B PER PERSON PER NIGHT		DINNER B & B PER PERSON PER WEEK		8
	MIN £	MAX £	MIN £	MAX £	OPEN
	7.50	8.25	74.50	81.50	2—11

The Romarian

1 College Green, Tywyn
Gwynedd LL36 9BS
Tel: (0654) 711100

CATEGORIES

| 3 | 3 | 4 |

Situated with licensed restaurant close to shops, cinema and Narrow Gauge Railway. Hot and cold water in all single, double and family rooms. Special rates for children. Comfortable lounge with colour TV. Fire Certificate. Ideally situated for walking, golf, fishing, pony trekking, beaches and touring Snowdonia, and Mid Wales.

C	B & B PER PERSON PER NIGHT		DINNER B & B PER PERSON PER WEEK		6
	MIN £	MAX £	MIN £	MAX £	OPEN
	7	7.50	63	69	4—10

C

Children stay at reduced rates, wherever you see this symbol.

Hotels

Bridge Inn

Chainbridge, near Usk
Gwent NP5 1PP
Tel: (0873) 880243

CATEGORIES

| 3 | 3 | 4 |

Ideally situated mid-way Usk-Abergavenny. Riverside gardens, childrens playground. Fishing available. Hot and cold water in all rooms. Doubles, baths en-suite. Lounge with TV. Central heating. Fire Certificate granted. Games room. A la carte menu. Service until 10.30 p.m. Car park for 100. Caravan parking in grounds. Good food. Fine wine.

C	B & B PER PERSON PER NIGHT		DINNER B & B PER PERSON PER WEEK		6
	MIN £	MAX £	MIN £	MAX £	OPEN
	8	10	95	105	1—12

Glen-yr-Afon House*

Pontypool Road, Usk
Gwent NP5 1SY
Tel: (02913) 2302 or 3202

CATEGORIES

| 4 | 4 | 4 |

An elegant country house providing gracious service and fine home-cooked food in a warm, friendly atmosphere. In mature secluded grounds, close to Usk. Rooms tastefully decorated and furnished (most with private facilities). 3 comfortable lounges, one with TV, one a well stocked bar, and the third is a library.

C	B & B PER PERSON PER NIGHT		DINNER B & B PER PERSON PER WEEK		15
	MIN £	MAX £	MIN £	MAX £	OPEN
	17.25	18.40	138	151.80	1—12

For autumn to spring breaks send for our free Great Little Breaks booklet.

Nags Head Inn*

Twyn Square
Usk, Gwent
Tel: (02913) 2820

CATEGORIES

| 3 | 2 | 4 |

Egon Ronay recommended, 400 year old inn in centre of picturesque town square. Ample parking. Food home-made from fresh local produce. Local touring centre for beautiful Usk Valley, Wye Valley and Brecon Beacons National Park. Family inn free house amenities, fishing, gliding, grass skiing arranged.

	B & B PER PERSON PER NIGHT		DINNER B & B PER PERSON PER WEEK		6
	MIN £	MAX £	MIN £	MAX £	OPEN
	10	10	70		1—12

Guest House

Crown House*

2 Maryport Street, Usk
Gwent NP5 1AB
Tel: (029 13) 2388

CATEGORIES

| 3 | 2 | 1 |

Small, comfortable family guest house offering friendly personal service. Hot and cold water in all bedrooms. Full central heating. Special rates for children. Centrally situated in the older part of this historic town. Ideal base for touring Usk and Wye Valleys, Brecon Beacons, Border Castles and superb countryside. Weekly bed and breakfast rates from £45 to £49 (single).

T C	B & B PER PERSON PER NIGHT		DINNER B & B PER PERSON PER WEEK		3
	MIN £	MAX £	MIN £	MAX £	OPEN
	7	8			1—12

Hotel

Garth Derwen Hotel*

Buttington
Welshpool
Tel: (093 874) 238

CATEGORIES

| 3 | 4 | 4 |

Extremely comfortable, licensed country hotel in beautiful Welsh valley—bedrooms have individual decor and country views. Elegant 4-poster available. Wonderful touring centre with easy access to the coast, Powys Castle and local attractions; also fishing, golfing, pony trekking. Home cooking; large garden with tea patio; central heating; Fire Certificate. Closed Christmas and New Year.

T C	B & B PER PERSON PER NIGHT		DINNER B & B PER PERSON PER WEEK		9
	MIN £	MAX £	MIN £	MAX £	OPEN
	10.35	11.50	98.50	121.50	1—12

Guest House

Plas Cefn*

Buttington, Welshpool
Powys
Tel: (093874) 251

CATEGORIES

| 1 | 3 | 2 |

Lounge, good home-cooking, warm welcome, good views, 3-acre garden, parking, colour TV, central heating. Dining room: separate tables. Bedroom 1: hot & cold water, shaving point, bell. Teasmade with radio in one room. Bedroom 2: hot & cold water, shaving point, bell. Bedroom 3: hot and cold water, shaving point, bell. Bathroom, toilet and shower. 1½ miles Welshpool, Powis Castle. Monday market. Highly recommended.

C	B & B PER PERSON PER NIGHT		DINNER B & B PER PERSON PER WEEK		🛏 3
	MIN £	MAX £	MIN £	MAX £	OPEN
	6	7	45	56	1—12

Farmhouses

Bank Farm*

Middletown, Welshpool
Powys SY21 ATJ
Tel: (093874) 260

CATEGORIES

| 2 | 2 | 2 |

Situated on the main Shrewsbury to Welshpool road A458. The gateway to Mid Wales. Central for touring, swimming, fishing, walking on the nearby Breidden Hills. Good, wholesome home cooking made from fresh farm produce. Brochure available on request from Mrs. Elizabeth Bebb.

	B & B PER PERSON PER NIGHT		DINNER B & B PER PERSON PER WEEK		🛏 2
T					
C	MIN £	MAX £	MIN £	MAX £	OPEN
	6	7	65	75	3—10

Llettygynfach*

Kingswood, Forden, Welshpool
Powys SY21 8TU
Enquiries to: Mrs Kath Owens
Tel: (093876) 272

CATEGORIES

| 2 | 2 | 2 |

Llettygynfach is a family working farm. Good farmhouse food served in guests' dining room. Tea and coffee facilities in bedrooms. Full central heating. Ample hot water. Log fires in winter. Situated 5 miles South of Welshpool, 1 mile off A490 and B4388 roads in the Kingswood area of Forden.

	B & B PER PERSON PER NIGHT		DINNER B & B PER PERSON PER WEEK		🛏 2
T					
C	MIN £	MAX £	MIN £	MAX £	OPEN
	9	12	63	82	1—12

Tourist Information Centres are listed at back of book.

Whitland

Map ref: Ka2
Junction by rail for Tenby, Milford and Fishguard, Whitland on the river Taf (pronounced Tav) is a milk marketing town richly agricultural. Here King Hywel the Good in AD 930 codified the laws of Wales in an Abbey then called "Ty Gwyn ar Daf", (white house on the Taf) as the town is still called today by its Welsh-speaking inhabitants.

Picture : Pembrokeshire Coast

Hotel

Waungron Mansion*

Country Hotel and Home Farm
Whitland, Pembrokeshire
Dyfed SA34 0QX
Tel: (0994) 240232 and 240451

CATEGORIES

| 3 | 3 | 3 |

Situated off the main road within easy reach of Pembrokeshire's fine sandy beaches and National Park beauty spots. Activities nearby include Riding School, pony trekking, golf, fishing, tennis and sailing. Licensed. Farmhouse cooking. Bar meals available. Colour television. Free use of ponies for children. Colour brochure available.

C	B & B PER PERSON PER NIGHT		DINNER B & B PER PERSON PER WEEK		🛏 9
	MIN £	MAX £	MIN £	MAX £	OPEN
	6.50	7.50	65	70	1—12

Farmhouses

Bryn Emlyn Farm*

Llanboidy, Whitland,
Pembrokeshire
Dyfed SA34 0LJ
Tel: (09946) 391

CATEGORIES

| 3 | 2 | 2 |

Large dairy farm situated on hilltop with fabulous views of undulating farmland in all directions. Ideal for touring Pembrokeshire and Preseli hills. Bedrooms have hot and cold water and shaver points. Central heating throughout. Dining room with family tables. Guests' lounge with TV. Ample parking.

	B & B PER PERSON PER NIGHT		DINNER B & B PER PERSON PER WEEK		🛏 3
T					
C	MIN £	MAX £	MIN £	MAX £	OPEN
	7.50	8	75	82	4—10

Goitre Isaf Farm

Llanboidy, Whitland, Pembrokeshire
Dyfed SA34 0DL
Tel: (09946) 286

CATEGORIES

| 3 | 2 | 2 |

The farmhouse is a delightful mixture of olde worlde charm and all modern amenities. Situated 7 miles from Laugharne, home of poet, Dylan Thomas. It is within easy reach of Pembrokeshire National Park, Cardigan Bay, Carmarthen Bay and the Preseli Hills. Fitted carpets, central heating, log fires, home produce.

C	B & B PER PERSON PER NIGHT		DINNER B & B PER PERSON PER WEEK		🛏 1
	MIN £	MAX £	MIN £	MAX £	OPEN
	7.50	8.50	73.50	80.50	3—10

Maencochyrwyn Farm*

Maencochyrwyn, Login, Llanboidy
Whitland, Dyfed SA34 0TN
Tel: (099 47) 283

CATEGORIES

| 1 | 2 | 2 |

Maencochyrwyn Farm is situated in a quiet, rural area within easy reach of Tenby, Pendine Sands, Saundersfoot, Pembrokeshire Coast and the picturesque Preseli Mountains. The farmhouse has all modern amenities: fitted carpets throughout and colour TV lounge.

C	B & B PER PERSON PER NIGHT		DINNER B & B PER PERSON PER WEEK		🛏 2
	MIN £	MAX £	MIN £	MAX £	OPEN
	6	8	68	82	4—10

Maesyllan Farm

Login, Whitland, Pembrokeshire
Dyfed SA34 0XA
Tel: (09912) 374

CATEGORIES

| 1 | 2 | 2 |

Modern farm house. Log fire and colour TV in lounge. Separate tables for each family. Our aim is to provide an enjoyable holiday in a comfortable relaxed atmosphere. Panoramic views over surrounding country side. Free fishing. Also pony trekking locally. Conveniently situated for touring South West Wales.

C	B & B PER PERSON PER NIGHT		DINNER B & B PER PERSON PER WEEK		🛏 3
	MIN £	MAX £	MIN £	MAX £	OPEN
	5.50	7	63	70	6—10

Waungron Farm Hotel*

Waungron Isaf, Whitland
Pembrokeshire, Dyfed SA34 0QX
Tel: (0994) 240682

CATEGORIES

| 4 | 4 | 4 |

A family run, AA listed, modernised farm in an agricultural region, providing the ideal location for a superb holiday. Within easy reach of attractive fishing villages, sandy beaches and Dylan Thomas' Boathouse. All bedrooms with private bath/shower and tea/coffee making facilities. Full central heating, colour TV. Choice of twin, double or 4-poster beds. Disabled guests welcome. Reduced rates for children sharing parents' room. Licensed. Recipient of Henley Award 1981. Winners of 'Come to Britain Trophy 1981—Certificate of distinction'. Brochure and full details from the Welsh speaking proprietors, Ray and Jean Daniels.

C	B & B PER PERSON PER NIGHT		DINNER B & B PER PERSON PER WEEK		13
	MIN £	MAX £	MIN £	MAX £	OPEN
		11		83	1—12

Wiston SOUTH WALES

Farmhouse

Heathfield Lodge

Wiston, Haverfordwest
Pembrokeshire, SA62 4PT
Tel: (043782) 200

CATEGORIES

| 1 | 2 | 2 |

This modern farm bungalow is an ideal place to spend a peaceful holiday with spacious lawns and panoramic views. Central to all beaches. Car essential. Children welcome. Sorry no pets. Mostly home produced food. Baby-sitting if needed.

C	B & B PER PERSON PER NIGHT		DINNER B & B PER PERSON PER WEEK		3
	MIN £	MAX £	MIN £	MAX £	OPEN
		6.50		70	5—9

This symbol means you can book through your local travel agent.

Wolfscastle SOUTH WALES

Hotel

Wolfscastle Country Hotel & Restaurant*

Wolfscastle, near Haverfordwest
North Pembrokeshire
Tel: (043 787) 225

CATEGORIES

| 3 | 3 | 4 |

We specialise in good food. Rooms with private bathroom all with colour TV, central heating. 2 squash courts, tennis court. 15 minutes from the beautiful Pembrokeshire coastline. Haverfordwest 10 minutes—ideally situated for fishing, golf, riding, walking, beaches, touring and relaxing.

T	B & B PER PERSON PER NIGHT		DINNER B & B PER PERSON PER WEEK		12
C	MIN £	MAX £	MIN £	MAX £	OPEN
	12	18	130	175	1—12

Wrexham NORTH WALES

Hotel

Crest Hotel

Yorke Street, Wrexham
LL13 8LP
Tel: (0978) 53431 and Telex: 61674

CATEGORIES

| 6 | 5 | 5 |

Situated in the heart of North Wales's most important town, an excellent base from which to tour the whole region. All bedrooms have private bathroom and colour television, radio and tea/coffee-making facilities. There is a comfortable restaurant and popular bar, and free car parking.

T	B & B PER PERSON PER NIGHT		DINNER B & B PER PERSON PER WEEK		80
C	MIN £	MAX £	MIN £	MAX £	OPEN
	32.50				1—12

For autumn to spring breaks send for our free Great Little Breaks booklet.

Farmhouses

Buck Farm*

Hanmer, Clwyd
SY14 7LX
Tel: (094874) 339

CATEGORIES

| 3 | 3 | 3 |

Tudor farmhouse on A525 road. 7 miles Wrexham, Whitchurch; 15 miles Llangollen, Chester, Shrewsbury. Well placed for exploring mountains and valleys of North Wales and the Marcher counties: Cheshire and Shropshire. Our own wholemeal breads, granola, 100% pork sausages, lamb, organic vegetables, Jersey dairy products. Vegetarian, special diets on request. Transport, tours, bicycles. Yoga weekends. French, some German. Reductions for children. AA listed.

T	B & B PER PERSON PER NIGHT		DINNER B & B PER PERSON PER WEEK		4
C	MIN £	MAX £	MIN £	MAX £	OPEN
	7	8	80	93	1—12

Plas Maen*

Cefn-y-Bedd
Near Wrexham
Tel: (0978) 760355

CATEGORIES

| 1 | 2 | 1 |

Comfortable farmhouse accommodation, convenient to Chester, and ideal touring centre for North Wales and the coast.

	B & B PER PERSON PER NIGHT		DINNER B & B PER PERSON PER WEEK		3
	MIN £	MAX £	MIN £	MAX £	OPEN
	6.50	8			1—12

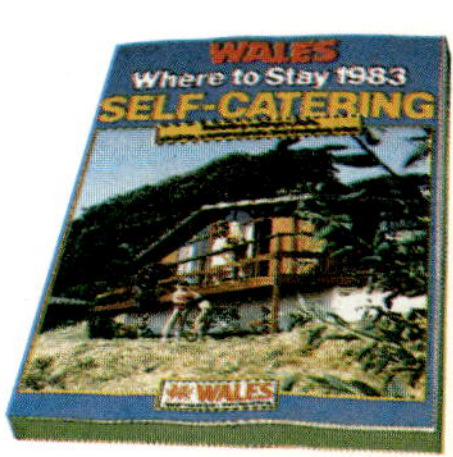

Pamper yourself on your main Wales holiday this year. But when you come back for that second, short break later in the year, remember we have a sister publication to this one. It's called "Where to Stay 1983 – Self Catering". Let us send you a copy. Details at back of book.

Activity Holidays in Wales

Below is a selection of activity and special interest holidays, many of them inclusive packages, with accommodation and tuition provided. Where it has been possible to verify the establishment according to WTB classification or minimum standards, this has been done. Outdoor pursuits centres, field study centres, canal cruisers and other holiday accommodation where no WTB standards are yet available, will not have been visited. Please, therefore, check all prices and facilities when making your booking.

Goat keeping for beginners

The Colinsdown Herd of Dairy Goats

Pengawsai Fach
Whitland, Dyfed
Tel: (0994) 240659

Cover a year's work in one week and enjoy yourselves doing it, with the aid of lectures, slides and practical demonstrations. Camp on the farm or stay locally. Interesting places to visit in your spare time and all within a few miles of Pengawsai Fach. Send for brochure and accommodation list. Prices on application.

T	TERMS PER PERSON PER WEEK	GOAT KEEPING FOR BEGINNERS	16
C	MIN £	MAX £	OPEN 4—10

Multi-activity Centres

Brookside House Hotel and Country Club

Bronygarth
Nr Oswestry
Tel: (0691) 773288

CATEGORIES

4	5	4

Brookside, Bronygarth, Wales-Shropshire border. Country house 4 acres, 3 hard tennis courts (1 floodlit) 2 glass-backed squash courts, heated swimming pool, solarium, sports, shops. Resident tennis and squash, professional coaches. Golf, riding, fishing, shooting nearby. Licensed, luxury accommodation. Home cooking. Glorious views. Any 2 nights. Double, bed and breakfast £35.00 inc. Ensuite. (Details (0691) 773288)

C	TERMS PER PERSON PER WEEK	SQUASH	7
		TENNIS	
		SWIMMING	
	MIN £ 84	RIDING	OPEN
	MAX £ 84	WALKING	1—12

Craig-y-Dderwen*

Country House Hotel,
Betws-y-Coed,
Gwynedd LL24 0AS
Tel: (06902) 293

CATEGORIES

4	4	5

Beautiful stone-built country house hotel set in three acres of its own gardens on banks of river Conway in the heart of Snowdonia. Well equipped bedrooms, private bathrooms. Licensed bar, central heating, first class restaurant offering Welsh and French cuisine of the highest standard. Free golf, pony trekking, fishing, shooting, canoeing and much more. Send for colour brochure to Mr WTS Palmer, Craig-y-Dderwen, Country House Hotel, Betws-y-Coed, Gwynedd LL24 0AS. Dinner, bed and breakfast rates given.

T	TERMS PER PERSON PER WEEK	FISHING	22
		SHOOTING	
		GOLF	
C	MIN £ 99	MAX £ 125 / PONY TREKKING	OPEN 1—12

Tourist Information Centres are listed at back of book.

Maesmawr Hall Hotel*

Caersws
Powys SY17 5SF
Tel: (068 684) 255/410

CATEGORIES

4	4	5

16th century country house hotel set in 5½ acres. 20 bedrooms most with private bath or shower. Fully licensed. Log fires and central heating. Renowned for friendliness and personal attention. Golf, shooting, fishing and bridge available. Mini breaks all year. Always open to resident and non-residents Luncheons, morning coffee, bar snacks, home-made afternoon teas dinner served every day, ideal centre for touring, AA** RAC** An Inter Hotel.

T	TERMS PER PERSON PER WEEK	GOLF	19
		SHOOTING	
		FISHING	
C	MIN £ 107	MAX £ 144 / BRIDGE	OPEN
		PONY TREKKING	1—12

Minerva Outdoor Ventures

Rhongyr and Penyrheol Centres
Penycae, South Wales
Tel: (063977) 757

Minerva's two farmhouse centres run multi-activity holidays for young people. Our highly experience team of staff are able to offer canoeing, riding, caving, climbing, gorge-walking, archery, rifle shooting, plus a host of evening activities. The centres have hot showers, central heating, shop and really good food. Accommodation is in bedrooms and dormitories. Courses available for individuals, schools and industrial groups. Prices include the use of all specialist equipment. Overseas groups welcome.

T	TERMS PER PERSON PER WEEK	CANOEING	12
		RIDING	
		CAVING	
	MIN £ 65	MAX £ 110 / CLIMBING	OPEN
		GORGE-WALKING	1—12

Children stay at reduced rates, wherever you see this symbol.

C

Mount Severn*

Llanidloes
Powys SY18 6PP
Tel: (05512) 2344

CATEGORIES

4	3	3

The beautiful country hotel, surrounded by extensive gardens and woodland through which flows the River Severn, offers superb accommodation and a range of exciting activities for individuals and families. The multi-activity weeks include walking, canoeing, climbing, pony trekking, and orienteering. Sporting and drying facilities, single, double and family rooms, all with private bathrooms, special weeks/weekends, arranged for groups. Off-season weekends, short breaks, bed and breakfast.

	TERMS PER PERSON PER WEEK	WALKING	
T		CLIMBING	11
		CANOEING	
C	MIN £	MAX £	PONY TREKKING	OPEN
	53	115	ORIENTEERING	1—12

The Red Ridge Activity Centre

Plas-y-Drain, Cefn Coch
Welshpool, Powys SY21 0AZ
Tel: (0938) 810821

Offering accommodation on the seasonally erected campsite or in the newly modernised farmhouse with bedrooms and dormitory. Plas-y-Drain provides an excellent base for multi-activity holidays and embraces the Red Ridge School of sailing and canoeing with first class facilities on the beautiful and extensive waters of Llyn Clywedog. Courses to suit schools and youth groups, overseas language students, further education establishments as well as individuals.

	TERMS PER PERSON PER WEEK	SAILING CANOEING, ETC	
T			16
C	MIN £	MAX £	OPEN
	65	95	1—12

For autumn to spring breaks send for our free Great Little Breaks booklet.

Pony trekking and Riding

Cwmyoy Pony Trekking Centre

Daren Farm
Cwmyoy, Abergavenny.
Enquiries to: Mr A. R. Smith
The Cornmill, Llanthony
Abergavenny, Gwent NP7 7NN
Tel: (087382) 565

Trekking in the beautiful Black Mountains on ponies of Britain and Pony Trekking Society of Wales—approved ponies. Caravans, camping and accommodation arranged. Weeks, weekends, day or half day rides available, also evening rides in May and June. Daily rate £6.50; £4.00 per ½ day. Please send SAE for brochure

	TERMS PER PERSON PER WEEK	PONY TREKKING	
			16
	MIN £	MAX £	OPEN
	39	39	3—10

Lion Royal Hotel & Trekking Centre

West Street
Rhayader, Powys LO6 5AB
Tel: (0597) 810202

CATEGORIES

3	3	4

Rhayader is a quiet little market town, uncommercialised, unspoilt, in times when such places are rapidly disappearing. Situated on the river Wye, in the loveliest countryside in Mid Wales, it is the ideal centre for those who enjoy hill walking, fishing, pony trekking or simply relaxing in peace and quiet. For over 400 years the Lion Royal has accommodated such people. Today resident proprietors Elwyn and Mary Collard extend a warm welcome.

	TERMS PER PERSON PER WEEK	PONY TREKKING	
T		FISHING	20
C	MIN £	MAX £	HILL WALKING	OPEN
	105	105		1—12

Trefach Pony Trekking Centre

Mynachlog-Ddu, Clynderwen
Dyfed SA66 7RU
Tel: (09947) 457/565

CATEGORIES

1	2	3

Riding over the beautiful Preseli mountains in the Pembrokeshire Coast National Park. Well kept good quality ponies for you to personally look after and trek on. End of week Gymkhana. Spacious farmhouse accommodation with good wholesome home cooking. Inexperienced and experienced riders catered for. Unaccompanied children welcomed.

	TERMS PER PERSON PER WEEK	PONY TREKKING	
			5
	MIN £	MAX £	OPEN
	85	100	3—12

Tregaron Pony Trekking Centre

Tanybryn, Tregaron Dyfed Tel: (09744) 634

Come and ride over some of Wales's most beautiful countryside. Experienced and novice riders catered for. Weekly or daily treks available. Accommodation arranged in local guest houses. Dinner, bed and breakfast plus packed lunches. Approved by British Horse Society and Ponies of Britain. Full board rates quote.

	TERMS PER PERSON PER WEEK	PONY TREKKING	
			16
	MIN £	MAX £	OPEN
		81	5—9

Study Centres

Coleg Harlech

Harlech
Gwynedd LL46 2PU
Tel: (0766) 780363

CATEGORIES

3	2	4

Adult college in Snowdonia National Park, overlooking Royal St David's golf links and superb safe beach. Facilities for badminton, table tennis and squash. First-class theatre with summer season. Tennis courts and indoor swimming pool nearby. Summer schools in Welsh language, orchestral playing, architecture, history, computer studies and natural history. Language laboratory, conference and teaching facilities available for groups. Single and double rooms. Full central heating, superb base for field trips.

	TERMS PER PERSON PER WEEK	WELSH LANGUAGE	
C		ORCHESTRAL PLAYING	16
		ARCHITECTURE	
	MIN £	MAX £	HISTORY	OPEN
	90		COMPUTER STUDIES, etc	7—9

Plas Tan y Bwlch

Maentwrog, Blaenau
Ffestiniog, Gwynedd LL41 3YU
Tel: (076 685) 324/334

CATEGORIES

1	2	3

The Snowdonia National Park Study Centre offers a wide range of courses including natural history, archaeology, history, photography, painting, industrial archaeology and mountain walking, revealing the fascinating background to this unique area. The courses will interest active walkers of all ages and last 3 days (long weekend) to 1 week.
Accommodation is in a spacious, well-appointed and comfortable country house set in superb surroundings in the heart of the National Park. Full board and tuition rates given.

	TERMS PER PERSON PER WEEK	MOUNTAIN WALKING	
C		NATURAL HISTORY	36
		ARCHAEOLOGY	
	MIN £	MAX £	INDUST. ARCHAEOLOGY	OPEN
	88	120	HISTORY, etc	1—12

The maps which follow divide Wales into twelve sections, each with a slight overlap. The grid overlaying each map will help you find the town or village of your choice for against the entry for each of them in this book is a reference number indicating the section of map and grid square. Simply turn up the appropriate map sheet, look for the grid square quoted in the code and pick out the place itself in that square. The maps are at 5 miles or 8 kilometres to one inch scale. The small map on the right of this column represents the former 13 counties of Wales; the new counties, which total 6, are shown on the adjacent map.

Key to symbols on maps

- Airport or Airfield
- Building of historic association or architectural interest
- Castle or defensive works
- Cathedral, abbey, priory or notable Christian site
- Country Park
- Early Christian monument
- Walk: Nature Trails, Forest Trails, Long distance walks, Town Trails and Heritage Trails
- Prehistoric site of importance
- Roman site
- Sea Fishing boats
- Surfing beach
- Tourist Information Centre
- Underwater swimming facilities
- Water Skiing
- Yacht or boat club

Wales—Maps

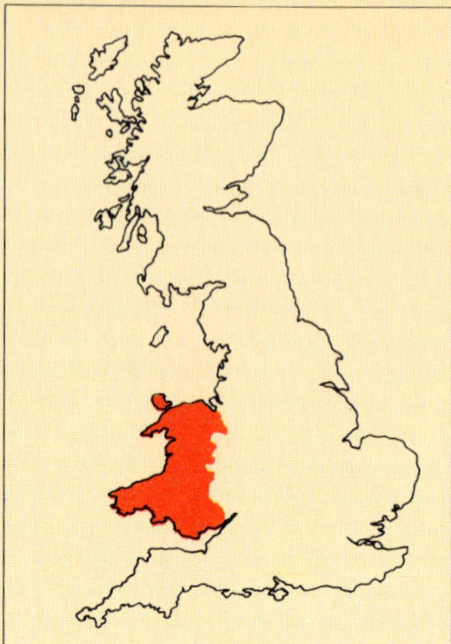

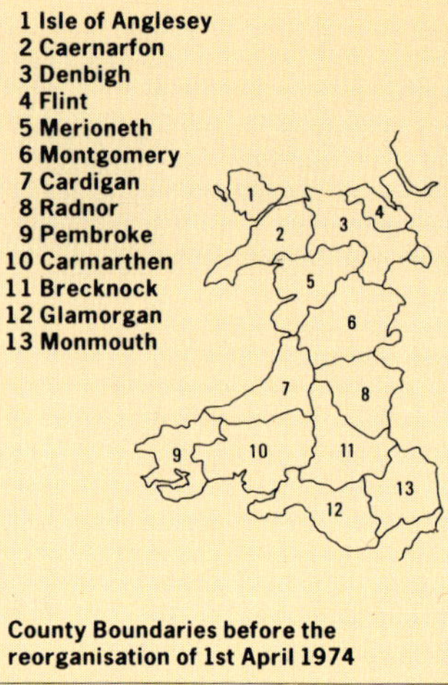

County Boundaries before the reorganisation of 1st April 1974

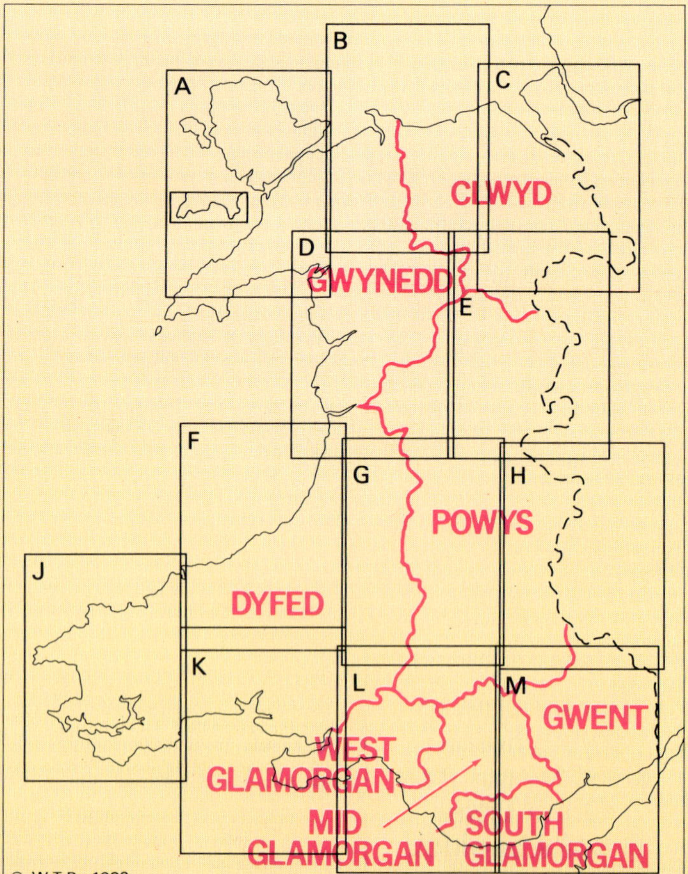

© W.T.B. 1982

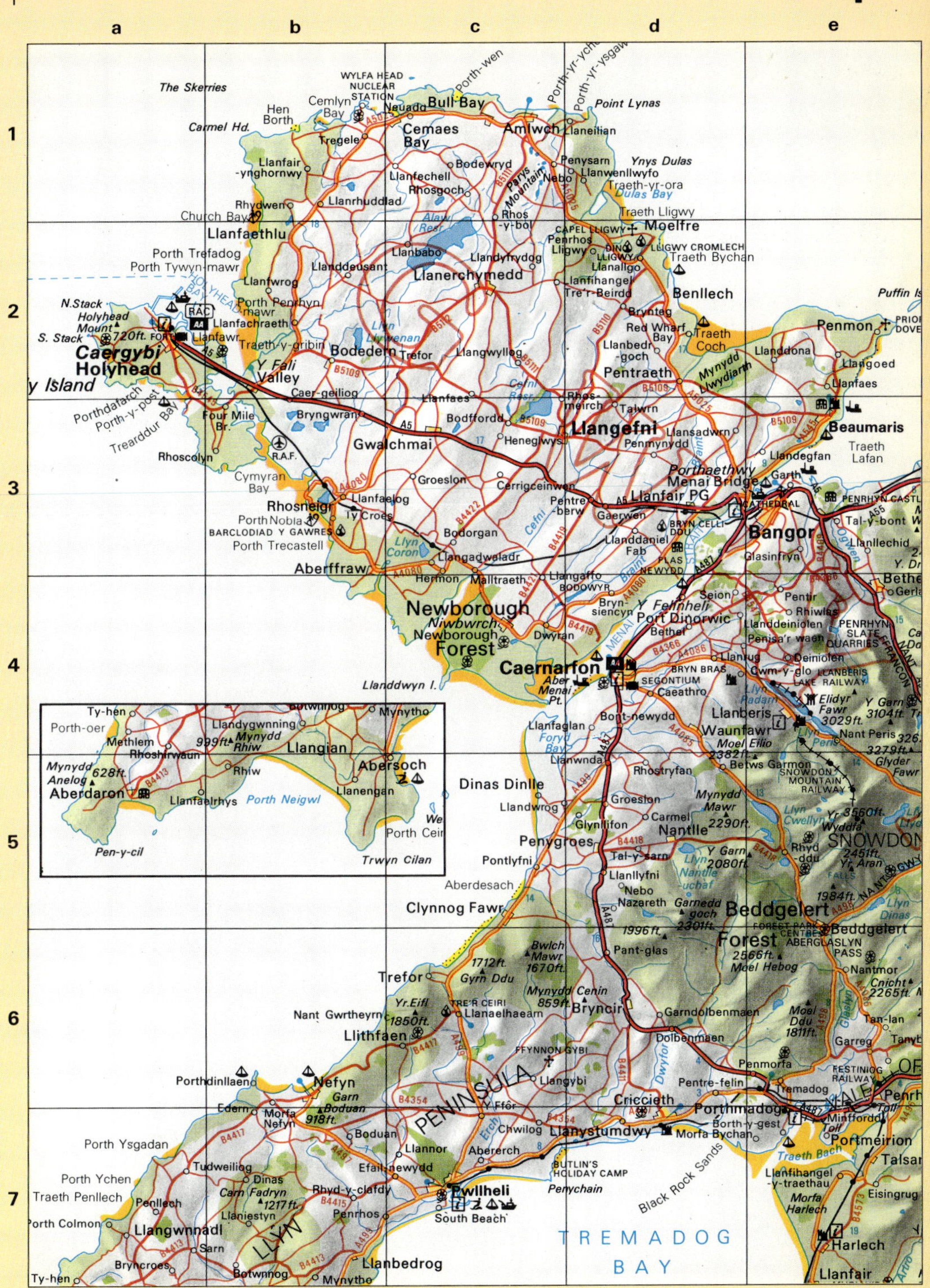

Map A

Map B
N
Miles 0 1 2 3 4 5
Kilometres 0 1 2 3 4 5 6 7 8
a b c d e
1
2
Excursions Llandudno-Isle of Man
Excursions Llandudno-Liverpool
3
Point of A
Gt. Ormes Hd.
GT. ORME TRAMWAY
CABIN LIFT
North Shore
Toll
Little Ormes Hd.
Penrhyn Bay
Kinmel Bay
Gronant
Gwesbyr
Meliden
Prestatyn
Llanasa
Island
Llandudno
West Shore
NORTH WALES G.C.
Llandrillo -yn-rhos
Rhos on Sea
Colwyn Bay
Towyn
Rhyl
Trelawnyd
MAEN ACHWYF
RY, WELL, ECOTE
CONWY BAY
Deganwy
Morfa Conwy
MAESDU G.C.
Llandudno Junc.
Old Colwyn
Pensarn
Abergele
BODRHYDDAN HALL
Dyserth
FALLS
Marian
Llyn Helyg
Gorse
Conwy
ZOO
Llandulas
A547
Rhuddlan
Bodelwyddan
A55
4
Penmaenmawr
Gyffin
Llansantfraid Glan Conwy
Llaneilian -yn-rhos
Rhyd-y-foel
St. George
Bodelwyddan
Rhuallt
St. Asaph
Caerwys
Tremeirchion
Capelulo
Moel-llys
Llanfairfechan
Pentre-felin
BODNANT GARDENS
Dolwen
Moelfre 1038ft. -isaf
Wern-fach
Cefn Meiriadog
Bodfari
Aber Carreg Fawr
Moelfre 1423ft.
Llangelynnin
Tal-y-fan 2001ft.
Tyn-y-groes
Graig
Betws -yn-rhos 1299ft.
Moelfre -uchaf
Llannefydd
Trefnant
Moel Wnion 1903ft.
Ro-wen
Moel Gyffylliog
Pen-y-mwdwl 1178ft.
Llanfair Talhaearn
Henllan
Denbigh
Waen
Drum 2529ft.
Tal-y-catn
Caerhun
Eglwys Bach
Pentre
Bryn-rhyd-yr-arian
FRIARY
Llandyrnog
Foel Fras 3092ft.
Llanbedr-y Cennin
Llangernyw
Groes
TOWN WALLS
2484ft. rosgl
Tal-y-Bont
Llansannan
Llanrhaeadr Dyffryn Clwyd
Llanynys
esda
Yr Aryg 2876ft.
Dolgarrog
Pont Dolgarrog
5
Foel Grach 3485ft.
Llyn Eigiau
Llanddoged
Pandy-Tudur
Bylchau
Nantglyn
1128ft.
Rhewl
arnedd dafydd 3424ft.
Trefriw
Pentre Tafarn-y-fedw
Gwytherin
1696ft.
Capel Curig
Llanrwst
GWYDIR UCHAF FOREST VISITOR CENTRE
Moel Seisiog 1534ft.
Cyffylliog
Bontuchel
SWALLOW FALLS
Nebo
Llyn Alwen
Mynydd Hiraethog
1703ft.
Clocaenog
Efenechtyd
Clocaenog
ryfan 3010ft.
Glyder Fach
y-hyll
Betws-y-coed
Capel Garmon
1742ft.
CRONFA ALWEN FOREST VISITOR CENTRE
Brenig Reservoir
Forest
Clawdd Newydd
6
Moel Siabod 2861ft.
Pont -y-pant
CAIRN
1557ft.
Pont Alwen
BOD PETRUAL FOREST VISITOR CENTRE
Pont Petryal
Derwen
Gwydyr Forest
Dolwyddelan
Pentrefoelas
Cefn-brith
Llanfihangel Glyn Myfyr
Penmachno
Y Foel
Rhydlydan
Glasfryn
Melin-y-wig
1274ft.
1083ft.
Llanel
Ro-Wen 1961ft.
Garn Prys 1747ft.
Cerrigydrudion
B5105
GLODDFA GANOL
LLECHWEDD SLATE CAVERNS
Ysbyty Ifan
Mwdwl Eithin 1543ft.
Betws Gwerfil Goch
Gwyddelwern
7
STWLAN DAM
Moelwyn Mawr 2527ft.
Blaenau Ffestiniog
Bethania
Gylchedd 2059ft.
Cader Bentlyn 2194ft.
Maerdy
Tyn-y-cefn
Four Crosses
B5437
Moelwyn Bach 2334ft.
Dduallt
Ffestiniog
Migneint
Arennig Fach
Carnedd-y-Filiast
Foel Goch 2004ft.
Llangwm
Dwyryd
Corwen

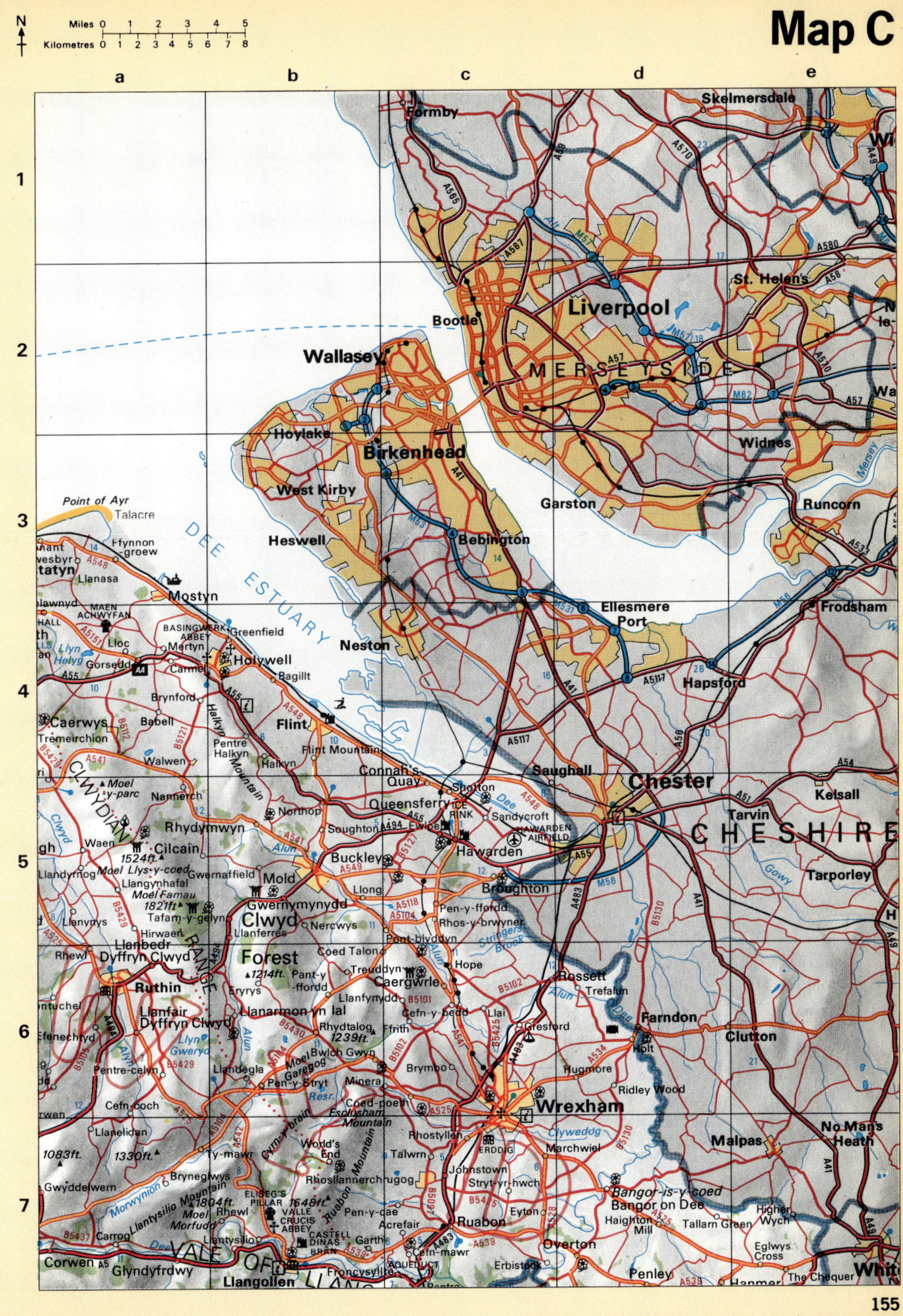

Map C
Miles
Kilometres
a
b
c
d
e
Skelmersdale
Formby
Bootle
Liverpool
St. Helen's
Wallasey
MERSEYSIDE
Hoylake
Birkenhead
Widnes
West Kirby
Garston
Runcorn
Point of Ayr
Talacre
Heswell
Bebington
DEE ESTUARY
Frodsham
hant vesbyr
Ffynnongroew
tatyn
Llanasa
Mostyn
Ellesmere Port
MAEN ACHWYFAN
Greenfield
Neston
lawnllo
BASINGWERK ABBEY
th
HALL
Llyn Helyg
Lloc
Mertyn
Holywell
LS
Gorsedd
Carmel
Bagillt
Hapsford
Caerwys
Brynford
Babell
Halkyn
A5117
Tremeirchion
Pentre Halkyn
Flint
A5
Walwen
Halkyn
Flint Mountain
Saughall
Chester
Kelsall
ri
Moel y-parc
Nannerch
Northop
Connah's Quay
CHESHIRE
CLWYDIAN
Rhydymwyn
Queensferry
Spotton
ICE RINK
Sandycroft
Tarvin
gh
Waen
Cilcain
Soughton
Ewloe
HAWARDEN AIRFIELD
1524ft.
Moel Llys-y-coed
A55
Tarporley
Llandyrnog
Gwernaffield
Mold
Buckley
Hawarden
Llangynhafal
Llong
Broughton
Llanymys
Moel Famau 1821ft.
Tafam-y-gelyn
Clwyd
Gwernymynydd
Pen-y-ffordd
Rhos-y-brwyner
Hirwaen
Llanferres
Nercwys
Llanbedr Dyffryn Clwyd
Coed Talon
Pont-blyddyn
Rhewl
Forest
1214ft.
Pant-y-ffordd
Hope
Caergwrle
Rossett
Farndon
Ruthin
Eryrys
Llanfynydd
Trefalun
ntuchel
Llanfair Dyffryn Clwyd
Llanarmon yn Ial
Cefn-y-bedd
Llai
Gresford
Clutton
Efenechtyd
Rhydtalog 1239ft.
Frith
Holt
Llyn Gweryd
Moel Bwlch Gwyn
Brymbo
Hugmore
Pentre-celyn
Garegog
Ridley Wood
No Man's Heath
Cefn-coch
Llandegla
Pen-y-Stryt
Minera
Wrexham
Malpas
rwen
Llanelidan
Coed-poeth
Marchwiel
1083ft.
1330ft.
Esclusham Mountain
ERDDIG
Rhostyllen
World's End
Talwrn
Johnstown
Bangor-is-y-coed
Gwyddelwern
Bryneglwys
Rhosllannerchrugog
Stryt-yr-hwch
Bangor on Dee
Higher Wych
Ty-mawr
Rhos-llannerchrugog
1804ft.
PILLAR ELISEG'S
1648ft.
Pen-y-cae
VALLE CRUCIS ABBEY
Ruabon
Eyton
Haighton Mill
Tallarn Green
Carrog
Llantysilio Mountain
Rhewl
Morfudd
Acrefair
Overton
Eglwys Cross
Corwen
Glyndyfrdwy
Llantysilio
CASTELL DINAS BRAN
Garth
Cefn-mawr
Penley
The Chequer
VALE OF
AQUEDUCT
Froncysyllte
Erbistock
Hanmer
Whit
Llangollen

Map D
156

Miles 0 1 2 3 4 5
Kilometres 0 1 2 3 4 5 6 7 8
N

a b c d e

Goch
Maerdy
Tyn-y-cefn
Four Crosses
Dwyryd
Corwen A5
Glyndyfrdwy
Glan-yr-afon
Cynwyd
2071ft Moel Fferna
Mynydd Mynyllod
-ddwysarn
Llandrillo
Ceiriog Forest
Pen-plaenau 1775ft.
Cadair Fronwen 2572ft.
Clochnant
Cader Berwyn 2730ft.
Llanarmon D.C.
Mynydd Tarw 2230ft.
Nant-cwm-llawenog
Nant Rhyd Wilym
Tregeiriog
2713ft. Moel Sych
Blaen Glaswen
Garneddwen 1628ft.
Milltir Gerrig
Y Clogydd 1954ft.
PISTYLL RHAEADR FALLS
Pennant Melangell
Llanrhaeadr ym Mochnant
Llangynog
Penybontfawr
Pen-y-garnedd
Hirnant
Llangedwyn
Pentre'r felin
Bwlch-y-ddar
Pen-y-bont
Llansantffraid ym Mechain
Lake Vyrnwy
Llanfechain
Llanfyllin
Llanymynech
Llanwddyn
Abertridwr
Bwlch-y-Cibau
Four Crosses
Llandrinio
Crew Green
nt Forest
Llanfihangel -yng-Ngwynfa
Allt-y-main 1168ft.
Sarnau
Crigion 1202ft.
Breidden Hill
Cefn-y-castell
Pont Llogel
Geuffordd
Pool Quay
Middletown 1323ft.
Cardeston
Pont Robert
Meifod
Broniarth Hill
Guilsfield
Trewern
Dolanog
Llangadfan
Groes-lwyd
Maes-mawr
Westbury
Foel
Llanerfyl
Y Trallwng
Welshpool
Buttington
A458
WELSHPOOL AND LLANFAIR RAILWAY
Sylfaen
Melin-y-ddol
Banwy
Eira
Llyn Hir
Einion
POWIS CASTLE
Leighton
Minsterley
Pontesbury
Llanfair Caereinion
Castle Caereinion
Fron
Melyn
Mynydd y Gribin
Cefn Coch
Llanllugan
Manafon
Kingswood
Rhiw
Llanwyddelan
New Mills
Berriew
Forden
Rhyd
Adfa
Garthmyl
Chirbury
Y Glonc 1513ft.
Tregynon
Llyn Mawr
Llyn-y-tarw
Betws Cedewain
Montgomery
Corndon Hill 1683ft.
Clatter
Gregynog Hall
Highgate
Bwlch-y-ffridd
DOLFORWYN
Llandysul
Church Stoke
Hyssington
Aberhafesp
Cefn y Coed
Snead
Lydham
Caersws
Abermule
Sarn
Trefeglwys
Y Drenewydd Newtown
Mule
Llyn Ebyr
Kerry
A489
Bishop's Castle
Llandinam
Mochdre
Dolfor
Ceri Forest
Clun Forest
Lydbury North
Coed-y-gaer 1183ft.
Berth-ddu
Pentre
Kerry Hill
Anchor
Wist
Y Foel 1423ft.
Severn
Source of Ithon
Source of R.Teme
Black Mountain 1469ft.
Aston
Cra
Llyn-dwr Hill
1398ft. Chapel Hill
Rhydd Hywel 1920ft.
A483
Bryn Gydfa 1573ft.
Felindre
Clun
Beguildy
VALE OF EDEYRNION
VALE OF LLANGOLLEN
Llangollen
Foel 1713ft.
Glynceiriog
VALE OF CEIRIOG
BERWYN MOUNTAINS
Tanat
Vyrnwy
Severn
Long Mountain
LONG MYND
ELISEG'S PILLAR
VALLE CRUCIS ABBEY
1648ft.
Rhewl
Llantysilio Mountain 1804ft.
Morwynion
Morfudd
Llantysilio
Carrog
Llanysilio
Dee
Pentre
Chirk
Castell Dinas Bran
Froncysyllte
AQUEDUCT
Pen-y-cae
Acrefair
Cefn-mawr
Garth
Ruabon
Bangor-is-y-coed
Bangor on Dee
Haighton Mill
Tallarn Green
Overton
Erbistock
Penley
Ha
Trench
Park Lane
Gredington
Ellesmere
Whittington
Oswestry
Trefonen
Rhyd-y-croesau
Llansilin
Baschurch
Walford
Harr
Pandy
Teirw
Ceiriog
Llwynmawr
Rhyd-y-groesau
Eyton
Bangor on Dee
Pen-y-cae
157

Map F

N
Miles 0 1 2 3 4 5
Kilometres 0 1 2 3 4 5 6 7 8

a   b   c   d   e

Talbont
Borth
Dol-y-bont
Llandre
Wallog
Bow Street
Penrhy
Clarach
CLIFF RLY
Capel Dew
Aberystwyth
Waun-fawr
A44
Cap
Llanbadarn-fawr
Pen-parcau
VALE OF RHEIDOL RAILWAY
Rhyd-y-felin
NANTEOS 12
Llanfarian
Blaenplwyf
Llanilar
Llanddeiniol
Wyre
Traw
Llanrhystyd
Llangwyryfon
Mynydd Bach
Trefenter
Aeron
Llanon
Llyn Eiddwen
Bror
Nebo
Forest
Blaenpenal
Pennant
Cross Inn
Bethania
Aberarth
Penuwch
Aberaeron
Arth
Ffos-y-ffin
Cilcennin
Llangeitho
Cei Bach
Llanaeron
Bwlchllan
Llwyn-celyn
Llanina
Ciliau Aeron
Betws Leucu
New Quay
Cei Newydd
Gartheli
Cwm Tudu
Llanfihangel Ystrad
Tal-sarn
Llanllwchaearn
Llanarth
Dihewid
Felinfach
Langybi
Ynys Lochtyn
Llwyn Dafydd
Mydroilin
Temple Bar
Bettws Bledrws
Synod Inn
Llanfa Clydo
Llangrannog
Cribyn
Gors-goch
Traeth Penbryn FALLS
Penbryn
Talgarreg
Llanbedr Pont Steffan
Mwnt
Samau
Capel Cynon
1062 ft.
Lampeter
Aberporth
Tre-saith
Brynhoffnant
Cwrt-newydd
Verwig
Blaenannerch
Glyn Arthen
Llanwnnen
Ram
Penparc
Tre-main
Rhyd Lewis
Ffostrasol
Cwm-sychpant
Dre-fach
Aberteifi
Blaenporth
Ceri
Allt-y-blaca
Cardigan
Pont-sian
Pencarreg
Beulah
Penrhiw-pal
Tre-groes
Pen Tas-eithin
Llangoedmor
Brongest
Maes-llyn
Rhyd Owen
Llanwenog
136 ft.
Llechryd
Troed-yr-aur
Pren-gwyn
Llanybydder
Llandygwydd
Aber-banc
Horeb
Capel Dewi
Cilgerran
Cwm-cou
Llandyfriog
Penrhiw-llan
Llanllwni
Pumsa
Cenarth
Bangor
Llandysul
Maesycrugiau
Aber Cych
Castell Newydd Emlyn
Aberarad
Pont-tyweli
Llanfihangel-ar-arth
1256 ft.
Rhyd-cymerau
Newcastle Emlyn
Henllan
Pentre-cwrt
Mynydd Llanybydder
Crug
Newchapel
Felindre
Tre-fach
Banc-y-ffordd
Mynydd Llanllwni 1209 ft.
Boncath
Pentre-drefelin
New Inn
Llans
Blaenffos
Capel-Ifan
Penboyr
Llanfihangel Rhos-y-corn
Edwinsford
Bwlch-y-groes
Moelfre 1100 ft.
Rhos
Pencader
Gwyddgrug
ABBEY
Freni-Fawr 1297 ft.
Cwm Morgan 1070 ft.
Brechfa Forest
Abergorlech 1080 ft.
Star
Y Glog
Tegryn
Mynydd Cynros
Hermon
Allt Walis
Halfwa
Hermon 869 ft.
Cwm-duad 827 ft.
Brechfa
Mynydd Figyn
Drych 09 ft.
Llanfyrnach
Waun-deg
Llanllawddog
Trelech
Dinas
Llanfynydd
Glandwr
Cwm Morgan
Llanpumpsaint
Pont ar Sais
e-galar
Cynwyl Elfed
Salem
Hebron
Eglwys Fair a Churig
Trelech a'r Betws
Blaen-y-coed
Talog
Rhyd-ar-gaeau
Pen-y-banc
Llanglydwen
Cwm-bach
Felin-gwm-uchaf

N
Miles 0 1 2 3 4 5
Kilometres 0 1 2 3 4 5 6 7 8
a b c d e
Elerch
Penrhyn-coch
Disgwylfa Fawr 1661ft.
Drum Peithnant
PLYNLIMON
Tor Du 1659ft.
Y Foel 1791ft.
Pen-Bwlch-y-groes 1487ft.
Cwm-belan
Llanidloes
Clywedog
Coed-y-gaer 1183ft.
Berth-ddu
Y Foel 1423ft.
Llyn-dwr Hill
Severn
Source of R. Teme
Ithon
Dewi Capel Bangor
Goginan
Llywernog Silver Lead Mine
Dyffryn Castell
Ponterwyd
Ystwyth Forest
Llangurig
Dulas
Old Chapel Hill
1398ft.
Rhydd Hywel 1920ft.
Tylwch
Moel
Capel Bangor Power Station
Ysbyty Cynfyn
Cefn Cenarth 1508ft.
Coed
Llanbadarn Fynydd
Devil's Bridge
Llanfihangel-y-creuddyn
Bryn Garw 2003ft.
1870ft.
Yr Allt
Esgair Elan
Aber-gwngy
Dyrysgol
Pantydwr
St. Harmon
Ddyle
Llananno
ROOD SCREEN
Cnwch-coch
Cyrnau Bach 1271ft.
1183ft.
Sarnau
Llanb
Trawsgoed
Llanafan
Cwm Ystwyth
Elan
Wye
Moel Hywel 1658ft.
Wenallt 1546ft.
ABBEY CWMHIR
Pontrhydygroes
Ysbyty Ystwyth
Mynydd Bach
1873ft.
Geilas
Pant Llwyd 1798ft.
Craig-goch Resr.
Gwynllyn
Gamallt
Cemllo Hill
Maelie
Lledrod
Marchnant
Ffair-rhos
Trumau
Pen-y-garreg Resr.
Llansantffraid Cwmdeuddwr
Rhayader
Gaufron
Nantmel
Gwystr
Fron
Ystra
Ystrad Meurig
Swydd-y-ffynnon
Pontrhydfendigaid
Dibyn Du
Cefn Brwynog
Claerwen Resr.
Garreg-ddu Resr.
Elan
Corn Gafallt 1530ft.
Nant-glas
Llanfihangel Helygen
Cross Gates
Cors Goch Glanteifi
STRATA FLORIDA ABBEY
1738ft.
1649ft.
Pen-y-bwlch
1668ft.
Esgair Garthen
Pen Maen-wern 1784ft.
Llanwrthwl
Caban-coch Resr.
Rhiw Gwraidd
Llanyre
Llandrindod Wells
Carn Gron 1777ft.
Bryn Garw 1827ft.
1784ft.
Y Gamriw 1968ft.
Gorllwyn 2009ft.
Drum Ddu 1761ft.
Newbridge on Wye
Howey
Tregaron
Drum Ddu 1668ft.
Cefn Cnwc 1728ft
Drum yn Eira 1968ft.
Drygarn Fawr 2104ft.
Llanfihangel Bryn Pabuan
Disserth
Crossway
Bettws Disserth
Bryn Rhudd 1574ft.
Llyn Berwyn
Esgair Cerig
Tywi Forest
1732ft.
Llanerch-yrfa
Pen Carreg-dan 1620ft.
Llanafan Fawr
Pentre Llwyn-llwyd
Cymbach
Builth Road St
Llansaintfraed in Elfel
Llanddewi Brefi
Esgair Llethr 1543ft.
Cefn Coch 1642ft.
Abergwesyn
1516ft.
Llwyn Madoc
Cefn-y-bedd
Builth Wells
Llanfaredd
Llethr Llwyd 1524ft.
Maes-glas
Cefn Fynog
Cefn Crug 1476ft.
Irfon Forest
Beulah
Llanafan-fechan
Llanfair-ym-Muallt
Builth Wells
Llanbadarn Cwm
Bryn Rhyd 1588ft.
Bryn Brawd
Pen-y-gurnos 1498ft.
Soar-y-mynydd
Moelfre 1446ft.
Llanddewi'r Cwm
Aberedw
Llandeilo Hill
Carn Nant-yr-ast 1445ft.
Llyn Brianne
1695ft.
Mynydd Trawsnant
Gerth
Irfon
Alltmawr 1550ft.
Banc-y-celyn
Llandeilo-gra
Craig Twrch 1279ft.
Cefn Gwenffrwd
Llanwrtyd Wells
Llangammarch Wells
Cwm Owen
Gwenddwr
1471ft.
Mynydd Mallaen
Rhandirmwyn
Crychan
Drum Ddu 1554ft.
MYNYDD
EPYNT
Bryn Du 1554ft.
Crickadarn
Erwo
Caeo Forest
Llandre
Caio
Cefn Llwydlo 1175ft.
Llandulas
Forest
Cynghordy
Llanfair-ar-y-bryn
1485ft.
Gwrhyd
Cefn Clawdd 1261ft.
Upper Brycheiniog Forest
Ysgwydd Hwch
Llys
Crugybar
Porth-y-rhyd
Fforest Clydwen
Merthyr Cynog
Maerdy
Llandefalle Hill
Llandefalle
Llansawel
Noethgrug 1347ft.
Aber Crychan
Llandeilo'r Fan
Llanfihangel Nant Bran
Lower Chapel
Llanvddyfri
Llandovery
Halfway
Pentre-bach
Pont-faen
Talachddu
Talley
Llanwrda
Llywel
Pentre'r-felin
Trallong
Battle
Penoyre Llanddew
Tre-don
Llansadwrn
Myddfai
Mynydd Myddfai
Treecastle
Trecastle
Sennybridge
Penpont
GAER
Aberyscir
Aberhonddu Brecon
Groesffordd
Llangadog
Plas Glansevin
Mynydd Wysg Resr.
Llywel
Defynnog
Llansbyddid
Llanfaes
Felindre
Rhiwiau
Glasfynydd
Crai Resr.
MOUNTAIN CENTRE
Mynydd Illtyd
Libanus
Llanfrynach
Cantref
Pencelli
Manordeilo
Bethlehem
1361ft. Trichrug
Twynllannan
Llanddeusant
Moel Feity 1940ft.
Heol Senni
Allt Ddu 1845ft.
BRECON
Bryn
Llanfeugan
Talybont on Usk
Rhosmaen
Capel Gwynfe
Pont Aber
Llyn y Fan Fach
Fan Brycheiniog 2630ft.
Cefn Cul 1844ft.
Fan Frynych 1980ft.
Pen-y-fan 2907ft.
BEACONS
Gwaun-rhudd
1842ft.
Llandeilo
Ffair-fach
Cefn y Truman
MOUNTAIN
Fan Hir
238ft.
Fan Fawr 2409ft.
Storey Arms
Fan Llia
Neuadd Resrs.
Talybont
Maerdy
BRECON BEACONS
FFOREST FAWR
2176ft.

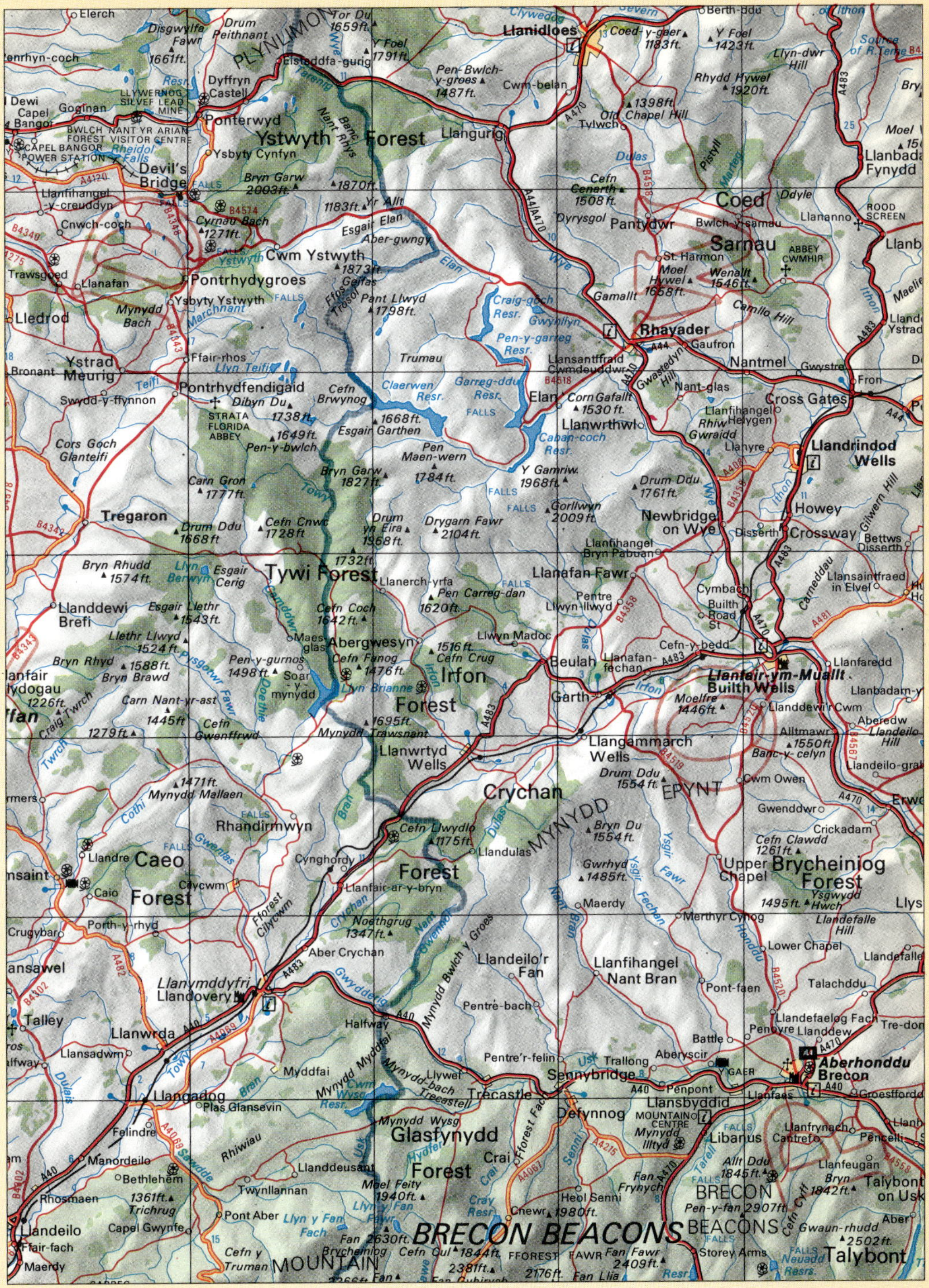

Map H

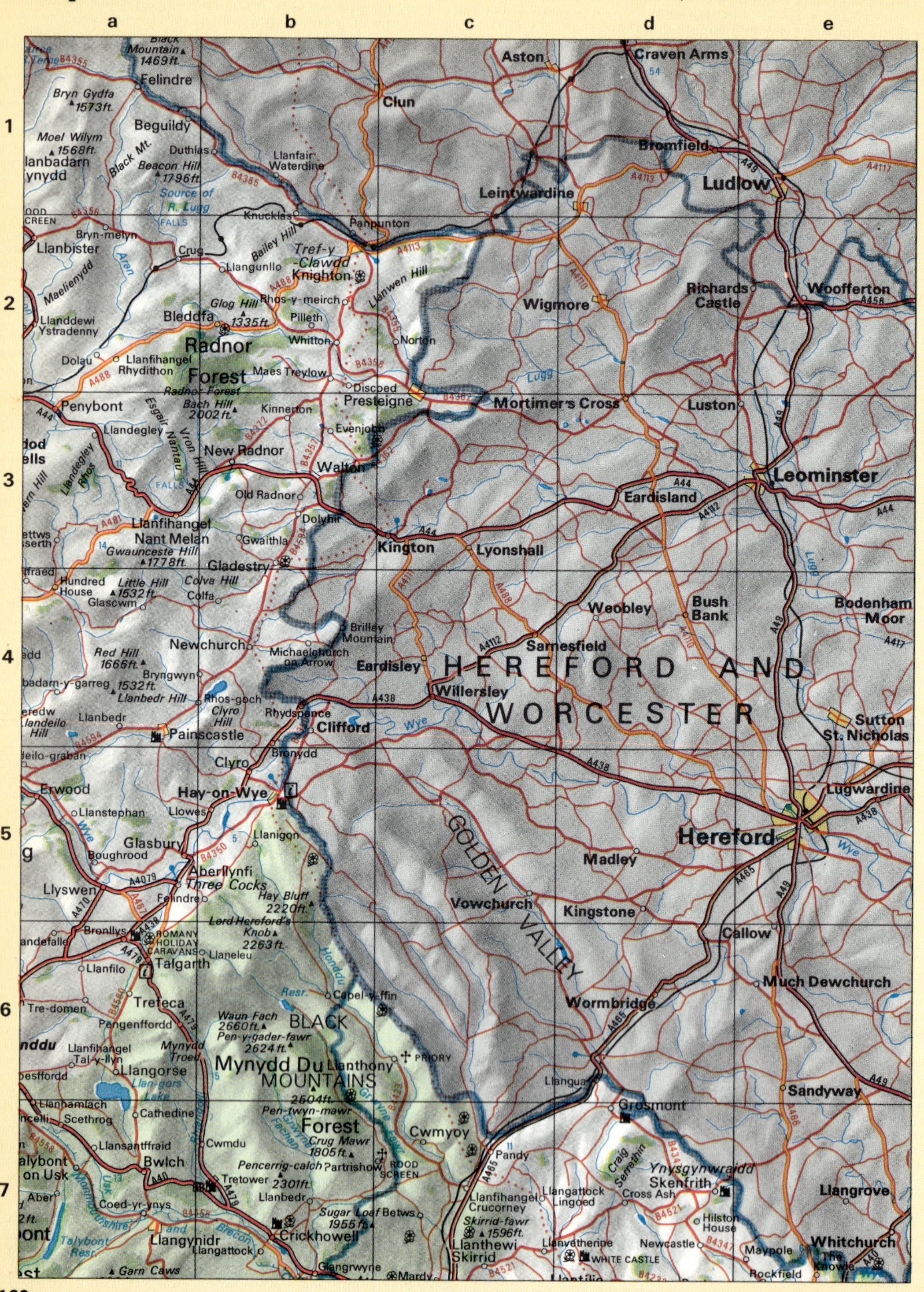

Miles 0 1 2 3 4 5
Kilometres 0 1 2 3 4 5 6 7 8
N
a b c d e
Black Mountain 1469ft.
Felindre
Bryn Gydfa 1573ft.
Beguildy
Moel Wilym 1568ft.
Black Mt.
Llanbadarn ynydd
Duthlas
Beacon Hill 1796ft.
Source of R. Lugg
FALLS
Aston
Craven Arms
Clun
Llanfair Waterdine
Leintwardine
Bromfield
Ludlow
Knucklas
Panpunton
Bryn-melyn
Bailey Hill
Tref-y-Clawdd
Knighton
Llanwen Hill
Wigmore
Richards Castle
Woofferton
Llanbister
Crug
Llangunllo
Rhos-y-meirch
Pilleth
Maelienydd
Bleddfa
Glog Hill 1335ft.
Whitton
Norton
Llanddewi Ystradenny
Radnor Forest
Dolau
Llanfihangel Rhydithon
Radnor Forest
Bach Hill 2002ft.
Discoed
Presteigne
Lugg
Mortimer's Cross
Luston
Leominster
Penybont
Llandegley
Espair Nantau
Vron Hill
Kinnerton
Evenjobb
Eardisland
Llandegley Rhos
FALLS
New Radnor
Walton
A44
Old Radnor
Dolyhir
Kington
Lyonshall
Eardisley
Llanfihangel Nant Melan
Gwaunceste Hill 1778ft.
Gladestry
Gwaithla
Weobley
Bush Bank
Bodenham Moor
Hundred House
Glascwm
Little Hill 1532ft.
Colva Hill
Colfa
HEREFORD AND WORCESTER
Newchurch
Red Hill 1666ft.
Bryngwyn
Llanbedr Hill 1532ft.
Michaelchurch on Arrow
Brilley Mountain
Sarnesfield
Willersley
Llandeilo Hill
Llanbedr
Rhos-goch
Clyro Hill
Rhydspence
Clifford
Wye
Sutton St. Nicholas
Painscastle
Bronydd
Clyro
Erwood
Llanstephan
Hay-on-Wye
Llowes
Llanigon
GOLDEN VALLEY
Hereford
Lugwardine
Glasbury
Boughrood
Aberllynfi
Three Cocks
Hay Bluff 2220ft.
Madley
Llyswen
Felindre
Lord Hereford's Knob 2263ft.
Vowchurch
Kingstone
Callow
Bronllys
ROMANY HOLIDAY CARAVANS
Llaneleu
Hoddni
Talgarth
Llanfilo
Capel-y-ffin
Wormbridge
Much Dewchurch
Tre-domen
Trefeca
Pengenffordd
BLACK
Waun Fach 2660ft.
Pen-y-gader-fawr 2624ft.
PRIORY
Sandyway
Llanfihangel Tal-y-llyn
Mynydd Troed
Llangorse
Llan-gors Lake
Mynydd Du
MOUNTAINS
Llanthony
Llangua
Grosmont
Scethrog
Cathedine
Pen-twyn-mawr 2504ft.
Forest
Cwmyoy
Craig Serrethin
Ynysgynwraidd Skenfrith
Llansantffraid
Cwmdu
Crug Mawr 1805ft.
Partrishow
ROOD SCREEN
Pandy
Cross Ash
Llangrove
Talybont on Usk
Bwlch
Pencerrig-calch 2301ft.
Tretower
Llanbedr
Sugar Loaf 1955ft.
Betws
Llanfihangel Crucorney
Skirrid-fawr 1596ft.
Hilston House
Maypole
Whitchurch
The Knowle
Aber
Coed-yr-ynys
Llangynidr
Llangattock
Crickhowell
Llanthewi Skirrid
Llanvetherine
Newcastle
WHITE CASTLE
Rockfield
Garn Caws
Glangrwyne
Mardy

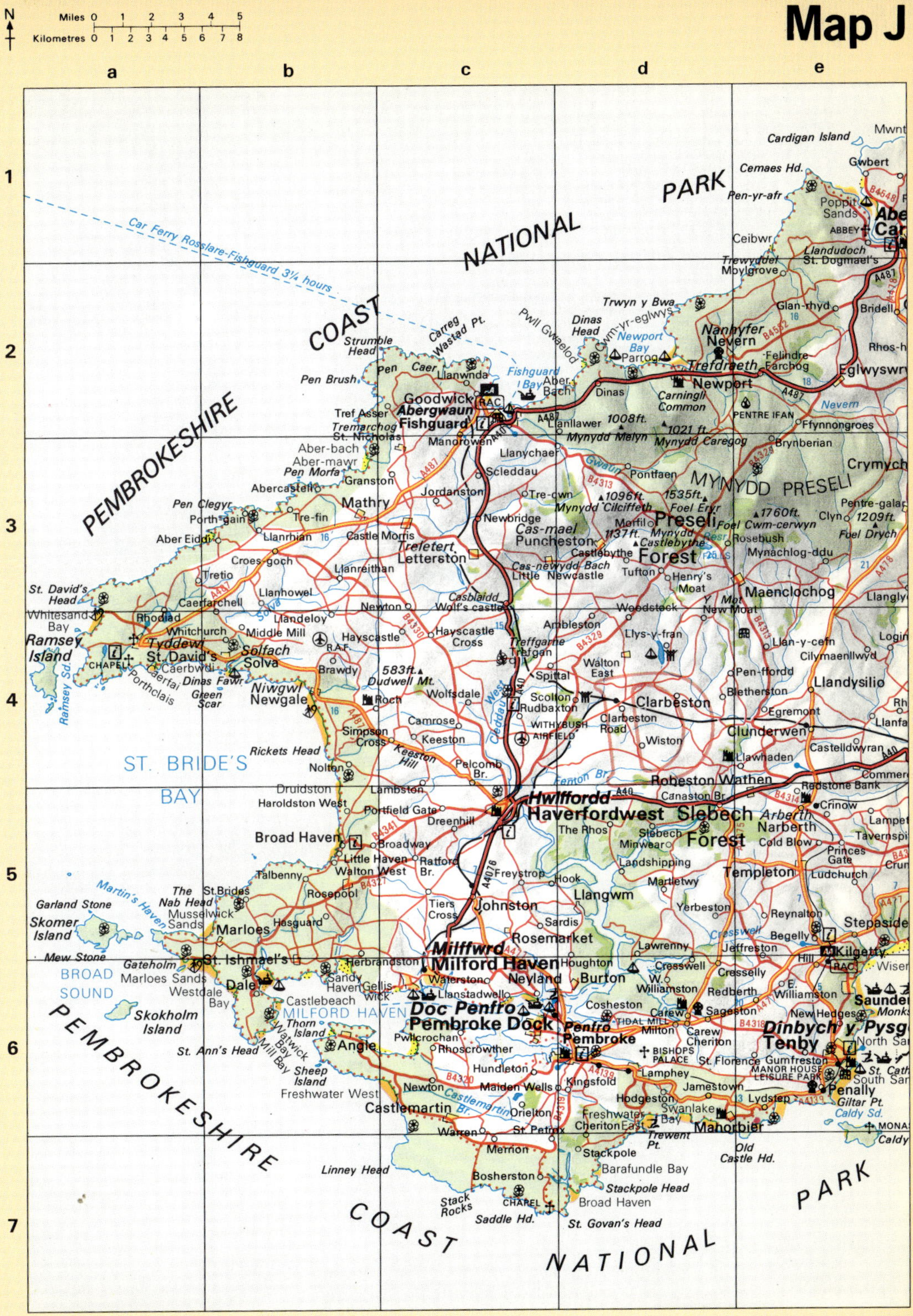

N
Miles 0 1 2 3 4 5
Kilometres 0 1 2 3 4 5 6 7 8

a
b
c
d
e

1
2
3
4
5
6
7

Cardigan Island
Cemaes Hd.
Mwnt
Gwbert
Pen-yr-afr
Poppit Sands
ABBEY
Aber Car
Ceibwr
Llandudoch
St. Dogmael's
Trewyddel
Moylgrove
Glan-rhyd
Bridell
Rhos-h
Car Ferry Rosslare-Fishguard 3¼ hours
NATIONAL PARK
COAST
Trwyn y Bwa
Cwm-yr-eglwys
Dinas Head
Newport Bay
Parrog
Nanhyfer
Nevern
Felindre
Farchog
Eglwyswr
Strumble Head
Carreg Wastad Pt.
Pwll Gwaelod
Newport
Nevern
PEMBROKESHIRE
Pen Caer
Llanwnda
Fishguard I Bay
Aber Bach
Dinas
Trefdraeth
Pen Brush
Goodwick
Abergwaun
Fishguard
RAC
Carningli Common
PENTRE IFAN
Ffynnongroes
Tref Asser
Tremarchog
St. Nicholas
Mandrowen
Llanllawer
1008ft.
Mynydd Melyn
1021 ft.
Mynydd Caregog
Brynberian
Crymych
Aber-bach
Aber-mawr
Pen Morfa
Granston
Llanychaer
Scleddau
Tre-cwn
Pontfaen
Gwaun
1096ft.
Mynydd Cilcifleth
1535ft.
Foel Eryr
1760ft.
Foel Cwm-cerwyn
Clyn
1209ft.
Foel Drych
Pentre-galar
Abercastell
Mathry
Jordanston
Newbridge
Cas-mael
Puncheston
MYNYDD PRESELI
Aber Eiddi
Pen Clegyr
Porth-gain
Tre-fin
Llanrhian
Castle Morris
Trefgarn
Letterston
1137ft.
Mynydd
Castlebythe
PRESELI
Forest
Rosebush
Mynachlog-ddu
A478
St. David's Head
Tretio
Croes-goch
Llanhowel
Llanreithan
Newton
Casblaidd
Wolf's Castle
Cas-newydd-Bach
Little Newcastle
Tufton
Henry's Moat
Maenclochog
Llangly
Whitesand Bay
Ramsey Island
Rhodiad
Whitchurch
Middle Mill
Hayscastle
Hayscastle Cross
Treffgarne
Ambleston
Weedstock
New Moat
Llan-y-cefn
Cilymaenllwyd
Login
CHAPEL
Tyddewi
St. David's
Caerbwdi
Solfach
Solva
R.A.F.
Brawdy
Spittal
Walton East
Llys-y-fran
Pen-ffordd
Bletherston
Llandysilio
Caerfarchell
583ft.
Dudwell Mt.
Scollon
A40
Clarbeston
Egremont
Llanfa
Ramsey Sd.
Caerfai
Porthclais
Dinas Fawr
Green Scar
Niwgwl
Newgale
Roch
Wolfsdale
Rudbaxton
WITHYBUSH AIRFIELD
Clarbeston Road
Wiston
Clunderwen
Castelldwyran
Commer
Simpson Cross
Camrose
Keeston
Llawhaden
Rh
Llanfa
Rickets Head
Keeston Hill
Pelcomb Br.
Fenton Br.
Robeston Wathen
Redstone Bank
ST. BRIDE'S BAY
Nolton
Lambston
Hwlffordd
Haverfordwest
A40
Cnaston Br.
Slebech Forest
Narberth
Arberth
Crinow
Lampet
Druidston
Haroldston West
Portfield Gate
Dreenhill
The Rhos
Slebech
Minwear
Cold Blow
Princes Gate
Tavernspi
Cru
Broad Haven
Broadway
Ratford Br.
Landshipping
Templeton
Ludchurch
Martin's Haven
Little Haven
Walton West
Freystrop
Hook
Martletwy
Reynalton
Stepaside
Garland Stone
The Nab Head
St. Brides
Talbenny
Rosepool
Tiers Cross
Johnston
Llangwm
Yerbeston
Begelly
Jeffreston
Kilgetty
Skomer Island
Musselwick Sands
Sardis
Rosemarket
Lawrenny
Cresswell
Hill
RAC
Mew Stone
Marloes
Hosguard
Milffwrd
Houghton
Cresswell
Cresselly
Redberth
New Hedges
Wiser
BROAD SOUND
Gateholm
St. Ishmael's
Herbrandston
Milford Haven
Waterston
Neyland
Burton
Williamston
Sageston
Saunders
Marloes Sands
Dale
Sandy Haven
Gellis wick
Llanstadwell
Cosheston
Carew
B4318
Dinbych y Pysg
Monks
Westdale Bay
Castlebeach
MILFORD HAVEN
Doc Penfro
Pembroke Dock
Pentro
Milton
Carew Cheriton
Tenby
Gumfreston
North Sa
Skokholm Island
Watwick Bay
Thorn Island
Mill Bay
Pwllcrochan
Pembroke
TIDAL MILL
St. Florence
MANOR HOUSE LEISURE PARK
St. Cath
South San
St. Ann's Head
Sheep Island
Angle
Rhoscrowther
Hundleton
BISHOPS PALACE
Lamphey
Jamestown
Penally
MONA
Freshwater West
Newton
Castlemartin Br.
Maiden Wells
Kingsfold
Hodgeston
Lydstep
Gitar Pt.
Caldy Sd.
Castlemartin
Orielton
Freshwater
Cheriton East
Swanlake
Manorbier
Caldy
Warren
St. Petrox
Trewent Pt.
Old Castle Hd.
Merrion
Stackpole
Barafundle Bay
Linney Head
Bosherston
Stackpole Head
PARK
Stack Rocks
CHAPEL
Broad Haven
Saddle Hd.
St. Govan's Head
COAST
NATIONAL

Map K

Miles 0 1 2 3 4 5
Kilometres 0 1 2 3 4 5 6 7 8
N
a
b
c
d
e
Y Glog
Hermon
869ft
Hermon
09ft.
Orych
Glandwr
Llanfyrnach
Dinas
Trelech
Waun-deg
Cwm-duad
827 ft.
Allt Walis
Llanpumpsaint
Llanllwddog
Pont ar Sais
Brechfa
Mynydd Figyn
Halfwa
Hebron
Eglwys
Fair a Churig
Trelech a'r Betws
Blaen-y-coed
Cynwyl Elfed
Rhyd-ar-gaeau
Llanfynydd
Salem
Llanglydwen
Cwm-bach
Talog
Newchurch
Bronwydd Arms
Felin-gwm-uchaf
Pen-y-banc
Login
Cwmfelinmynach
Gelliwen
Abernant
Ffynnon-ddrain
Broadoak
DINEFWR
Llanboidy
Castell-gorfod
Meidrim
Merthyr
AMPHITHEATRE
Caerfyrddin
Carmarthen
Abergwili
Nantgaredig
Felindre
Llangathen
DRYSLWYN
Rhyd-y-wrach
Bron-y-Gaer
Sarnau
Llanllwch
Llangynnwr
Llangunnor
Capel Dewi
Llanarthney
Llanfihangel Aberbythych
Dryslwyn
Llanfallteg
Banc-y-felin
Nant-y-caws
Pen-rhiw-goch
Hendygwyn
ar Daf
San Clêr
Pwll-trap
St. Clear's
Ebenezer
Croes-y-ceiliog
Cwm-Ffrwd
Llanddarog
Porth
Heol-ddu
Carmel
Pentre Gw
Whitland
Brandy Hill
Llanddowror
Llandeilo Abercywyn
Llangyndeyrn
Gwendraeth Fachy-rhyd
Crwbin
Dre-fach
Gors-las
Pen-y-groes
Cross Hands
Ammanford
Lampeter Velfrey
Red Roses
Llandawke
Laugharne
Llanybri
Llanstephan
Llandyfaelog
Pontantwn
Meinciau
Tumble
Pontyberem
Capel Hendre
Ty-croe
Crunwear
Eglwysgymun
Eglwycummin
Llansadyrnin
Broadway
Ferryside
Broadway
Pen-rhos
Four Roads
Pont Henry
Mynydd Sylen
Llan-non
Craig Fawr
Llanteg
Pentywyn
Pendine
Broadway
Llansaint
Ginst Pt.
St. Ishmael
Kidwelly
Pont-iets
Cynheidre
Brondini
Five Roads
Horeb
Amroth
Marros
Wiseman's Bridge
Pendine Sands
Gwendraeth Fawr
Trim-saran
Hengv
Pontardd
undersoot
Monkstone Pt.
Pysgod
orth Sands
Pembrey Forest
Towyn Burrows
Pembrey
Burry Port
Felin-foel
Llangennech
Dafen
Bynea
St. Catherine's Island
outh Sands
CARMARTHEN BAY
Cefn Sidan
Pwll
Bryn
Llwynhendy
Groves End
Gorseinon
MONASTERY
Caldy Island
BURRY INLET
Whiteford Pt.
Llanrhidian Sands
Llanelli
Salthouse Pt.
Penclawdd
Gowerton
Loughor
Fforest-fach
Broughton Bay
Whiteford Burrows
Llanmadoc
Landimore
Llanmorlais
Three Crosses
Waunarlw
Cockett
Dunvant
Burry Holms
Cheriton
Oldwalls
Llanrhidian
PARC LE BREOS
SWANSEA AIRPORT
Upper Killay
Killay
Rhosili Bay
Llangennith
Cefn Bryn
609ft.
Parkmill
Clyne Common
Reynoldston
Llanddewi
Rhosilli
Worms Hd.
Knelston
Penrice
Nicholaston
Southgate
Bishopston
Newton
We
Mewslade Bay
Port-Eynon
Horton
Oxwich
Pobbles Bay
Three Cliffs Bay
Pwll-du Hd.
Caswell Bay
Langla
Oxwich Pt.
Slade
Cork-Swansea 9½ hours

N

Miles 0 1 2 3 4 5
Kilometres 0 1 2 3 4 5 6 7 8

a b c d e

1

Salem · Manordeilo · Bethlehem · Rhosmaen · Trichrug 1361ft. · Llanddeusant · Twynllannan · Pont Aber · Moel Feity 1940ft. · Llyn y Fan Fawr · Cray Resr. · Cnewr · Heol Senni · Crai · Forest · Fan Frynych · Brecon · Pen-y-fan 2907ft. · Brecon Beacons · Allt Ddu 1845ft. · Llanfeugan · Bryn · 1842ft. · Talybont · Gwaun-rhudd 2502ft.

Llandeilo · ffair-fach · Maerdy · Capel Gwynfe · Cefn y Truman · Fan 2630ft. · Brychemiog · Cefn Cul 1844ft. · Fan Gyhirych · Fan Nedd · Fan Llia 2071ft. · Storey Arms · Resr. · Talybont · Forest

Trapp · CARREG CENNEN · Foel Fraith 1982ft. · 2366ft. · Fan Hir · Garreg-goch · 1832ft. · FFOREST FAWR · Fan Fawr 2409ft. · Neuadd Resrs.

BLACK · MOUNTAIN · Garreg-lwyd 2028ft. · 1506ft. · DAN-YR-OGOF SHOW CAVES · NATIONAL PARK · Nant-ddu · Pen-twyn Resr.

2

Llandybie · Glyn-hir · Glanaman · Brynaman · Craig-y-nos · Bryn Bugeiliaid 1254ft. · Ystradfellte · Coed Taf · Twyn Cross · Taf-fechan Resr.

Pantyman · Garnant · Gwauncaegurwen · Cwmllynfell · Cwm-gieda · Abercraf · HENRHYD FALLS · Coed y Rhaiadr · Cader Fawr 1592ft. · GARWNANT FOREST VISITOR CENTRE · Pontsticill

Betws · Mynydd Betws · Ystradgynlais · Pen-rhos · Coelbren · Onllwyn · Penderyn · Scwd-yr-eira · Pant Sychbant · Vaynor · Bute to Dowlais

Ty-croes · Cwmgorse · Cefn Gwrhyd 968ft. · Gurnos · Mynydd-y · Seven Sisters · Pont Nedd Fechan · Mynydd-y-glog · Fawr · Merthyr Tydfil

3

Craig Fawr · Godre'r-graig · Crynant Forest · Glyn Neath · Aber Pergwm · Walby · Rhigos · Hirwaun · Mynydd Aberdare · Aber-canaid · Cefn Pennar 1616ft. · Troed-y-rhiw

700ft. · Rhyd-y-fro · Cilybebyll · Mynydd Marchywel 1371ft. · Crynant · Rheola · Pentre-clwydau · Blaen-gwrach · Hirwaun Common · Trecynon · Cwmdare · Cwm-bach

ntarddulais · Pontardawe · Allt'wen · Rhos · Resolfen · Mynydd Resolfen 1257ft. · Cefn Grug · Cefn Tyle Brych · Rhondda · Aberdare · Aberdar · Mynydd Merthyr · Mountain Ash

Felindre · Clydach · Craig-cefn-parc · Ynysmeudwy · VALLEY OF NEATH · Moel-y-hyrddod 1560ft. · Cefn Mawr · Blaen-Rhondda · Forest · St. Gwynno · Penrhiw-ceiber

Pont Lliw · Bwllfa · Glais · Mynydd Drumau · WILDLIFE PARK · Ponscynor · Glyncorrwg · Tynewydd · Treherbert · Forest · Cwmaman · Maerdy · Ash · Miskin

4

Morriston · Heol-las · Cadoxton · Birchgrove · Tonna · Cefn Morfudd · Cymmer Forest · Duffryn · Abergwynfi · Treorchy · Cefn y Rhondda · Pentre · Tylorstown · Femdale · Ynys-boeth · Abercynon

Penllergaer · Llansamlet · ABBEY · Skewen · Neath · Cymmer · Mynydd Caerau · Cwm-parc · Llanwonno · Ynyshir

Fforest-fach · Landore · Bonymaen · Pont rhydyfen · Moel Trawsnant 1218ft. · Caerau 1828ft. · Nantymoel · Clydach Vale · Tonypandy · Ystrad Rhondda · Porth · Cilfynydd

Vaunarlwydd · Cockett · Pentre-chwyth · Kilvey Hill 633ft. · Briton Ferry · Foel Mynyddau 1218ft. · Dyffryn · Nant-y-ffyllon · Blaengarw · Ogmore Vale · Pen-y-graig · RHONDDA VALLEY

Sketty · Killay · Baglan · Michaelston · 846ft. · Mynydd Dinas · Cwmavon · Margam Forest · Maesteg · Garth · Gilfach Goch · Aber · Pontypridd · Treforest

5

Abertawe Swansea · Aberavon Beach · Port Talbot · Taibach · Margam · Mynydd Margam · Llangynwyd · Bettws · Llangeinor · Llandyfodwg · Pen-y-coedcae · Church Village

Black Pill · West Cross · The Mumbles · Moel Ton-mawr · Margam 1048ft. · Mynydd Baidan · Tondu · Abergarw · Blackmill 984ft. · Mynydd-y-gaer · Mynydd Maendy · Beddau · Llantrisant

Bracelet Bay · Mumbles Hd. · B.S.C. Resr. · Kenfig Hill · Melin Ciwc · Llanharan · Talbot Green · Groes

Limeslade Bay · Langland Bay · Caswell Bay · Margam Sands · Margam Burrows · Pyle · Abercynffig · M4 · Pen-coed · Coed Tre castell · Pontyclun · Llanilid Llanharri · Miskin

Kenfig Pool · Mawdlam · North Cornelly · Newcastle · Bridgend · Bryn-teg · Coychurch · St. Mary Hill · Llansannor · Tair Onen Forest

6

Kenfig · South Cornelly · Newton Down · Merthyr Mawr · Corntown · Treoes · Llan-gan · Maendy · Pendoylan

Nottage · Porthcawl · Rest Bay · Newton · Nottage · Ogmore · CANDLESTON · PRIORY · Ewenny · St. Brides Major · Colwinston · Welsh St. Donats · Bonvilston

Tusker Rocks · Ogmore-by-Sea · Pitcot · Llysworney · Cowbridge · St. Hilary

Southerndown · Nash · Sigingstone · Flemingston · Llancarfan

Broughton · Wick · Llandough · St. Mary Church · Llantrithyd

Monknash · Llanmaes · Llanbethery · Penmark

Marcross · St. Donat's · Llantwit Major · Boverton · St. Athan · CARDIFF WALES AIRPORT · Rhoose

Nash Pt. · Gileston · Aberthaw · Fontygary

Col-huw Beach · The Leys

P & A Campbell's Cruises

7

Map M

Arranging your holiday

Die Vorbereitung Ihrer Ferien

Dispositions à prendre pour vos vacances

Prices

The prices and other information quoted in this Guide were supplied during the period April and May 1982 to the Wales Tourist Board for publication, by the various establishments listed in the Guide. They are the prices which at that time the various establishments envisaged would be charged and the facilities offered during 1983 and must therefore be accepted as indications rather than firm quotations. The prices should include elements in respect of British breakfast, Value Added Tax (VAT), and the percentage Service Charge, where it applies, but different establishments may have different arrangements for dealing with these matters. The amount included in respect of VAT is 15%. The Wales Tourist Board therefore accepts no liability whatsoever in connection with the prices, facilities and other information mentioned in this Guide. It is essential that the prices and rates quoted and the facilities offered are confirmed with the establishment at the time of enquiry or booking. A stamped and self-addressed envelope should always be included with enquiries for prices and accommodation.

Preise

Die in dieser Broschüre enthaltenen Preis – und sonstigen Angaben wurden dem Wales Tourist Board im April/Mai 1982 von den einzelnen hier aufgeführten Unternehmen zur Veröffentlichung vorgelegt. Es handelt sich dabei um Preise und Leistungen, die nach Ansicht dieser Unternehmen für das Jahr 1983 zu erwarten waren; sie sind daher als Richt- und nicht als Festpreise zu verstehen. Die Preise beinhalten normalerweise englisches Frühstück, Mehrwertsteuer (MWSt.) und ggf. Bedienungszuschlag; es ist jedoch möglich dass einzelne Unternehmen diese Details unterschiedlich handhaben. Der für MWSt. angesetzte Betrag beläuft sich auf 15%. Das Wales Tourist Board übernimmt daher keinerlei Verantwortung in Verbindung mit den in dieser Broschüre genannten Preisen, Leistungen und sonstigen Informationen. Es ist unbedingt erforderlich, sich die angegebenen Preise und angebotenen Leistungen zum Zeitpunkt einer Anfrage oder Buchung von dem betreffenden Unternehmen bestätigen zu lassen. Bei schriftlichen Preis- und Unterkunftsanfragen stets einen vorad-ressierten und frankierten Umschlag beifügen.

Les Prix

Les prix et autres renseignements cités dans ce Guide ont été fournis entre avril et mai 1982 à l'Office Gallois du Tourisme en vue de leur publication, par les divers établissements dont la liste est fournie dans le Guide. Ce sont les prix que ces divers établissements envisageaient alors de faire payer pour les facilités qui seraient offertes en 1983 et l'on doit donc les considérer comme des indications plutôt que comme des cotations fermes. Les tarifs doivent comprendre divers éléments en ce qui concerne le petit déjeuner à l'anglaise, la taxe à la valeur ajoutée (T.V.A.) et le pourcentage pour le service, le cas échéant, mais il est possible que tous les établissements ne traitent pas ces questions de la même manière. Le montant inclus en ce qui concerne la T.V.A. est de 15%.
L'Office Gallois du Tourisme ne saurait donc accepter aucune responsabilité quelle qu'elle soit eu égard aux prix, aux facilités ou autres renseignements mentionneés dans ce Guide. Il est indispensable d'obtenir confirmation de l'établissement en question concernant les prix et tarifs cotés et les facilités offertes au moment de la demande de renseignements initiale ou de la réservation. Il faut toujours inclure une enveloppe portant son adresse et un timbre (ou un coupon-réponse international) avec les demandes de renseignements concernant les prix et les logements.

Accommodation enquiries and booking

When making a written enquiry please always enclose a stamped addressed envelope to ensure a speedy reply to your enquiry. In your enquiry you should always state:

1. The dates for which you wish to book as well as any alternatives.
2. The number of people in your party.
3. Any special requirements that you may need, i.e. terms for children, special diets, facilities for pets.

If the establishment can supply you with the accommodation required you should always confirm your definite requirement in writing as soon as possible to the establishment, enclosing any booking deposit that may be required.

Anfragen und Unterkunftsreservierung

Fügen Sie schriftlichen Anfragen bitte stets einen voradressierten Umschlag und einen internationalen Antwortschein für das Rückporto bei, damit Sie eine umgehende Antwort erhalten. Ihre Anfrage sollte folgende Angaben enthalten:

1. Den Zeitraum, für den Sie Zimmer reservieren möchten, sowie eventuelle Alternativtermine.
2. Die Zahl der zu Ihrer Gruppe gehörenden Personen.
3. Eventuelle Sonderwünsche, z.B. Bedingungen und Preise für Kinder, besondere Diät, Einrichtungen für Haustiere.

Wenn das angeschriebene Hotel o. ä. die von Ihnen benötigte Unterkunft bieten kann, sollten Sie dem Hotel Ihre endgültigen Anforderungen stets möglichst umgehend unter Beifügung einer eventuell verlangten Reservierungsanzahlung schriftlich bestätigen.

Correspondance et réservations

Dans toute correspondance, veuillez joindre à toute demande de renseignements une enveloppe à votre adresse et un coupon-réponse international afin d'être assuré d'une prompte réponse. Précisez:

1. Les dates auxquelles vous désirez réserver, et les autres dates possible le cas échéant.
2. Le nombre de personnes.
3. Vos désidérata particuliers: conditions spéciales pour enfants, régimes, animaux, etc.

Si l'établissement peut vous offrir le logement souhaité, veuillez confirmer dés que possible votre réservation par écrit en joignant les arrhes éventuellement demandées.

Late arrivals

Guests who have made prior bookings at establishments and who intend arriving late can help by phoning the establishment well in advance and advising the establishment of the intended time of their arrival.

Späte Ankunft

Gäste, die Zimmer im voraus reserviert haben und beabsichtigen, am späten Abend einzutreffen, können dadurch helfen, daß sie ddas betreffende Hotel telefonisch vom voraussichtlichen Zeitpunkt ihrer Ankunft unterrichten.

Arrivée tardive

Les personnes qui ont retenu un logement et qui comptent arriver tard dans la soirée sont priées d'en avertir l'établissement à l'avance par téléphone en indiquant l'heure à laquelle ils comptent arriver.

Complaints procedure

We naturally hope that you will not have any cause for complaint but problems do occur from time to time. If you are dissatisfied, make your complaint to the management or owner, immediately at the time of the incident. This gives an opportunity for action to be taken at once to investigate your complaint and rectify it without delay.

Beschwerden

Wir hoffen natürlich, daß Sie keine Ursache zur Beschwerde haben werden, aber manchmal treten doch Probleme auf. Wenn sie nicht zufrieden sind, beschweren sie sich sofort nach dem betreffenden Vorfall bei der Geschaftsleitung oder dem Besitzer. Dies ermöglicht unverzügliche Untersuchung Ihrer Beschwerde und sofortige Abhilfe.

En cas de réclamation

Nous expérons que vous n'aurez aucun motif de vous plaindre durant votre séjour; néanmoins il peut toujours surgir quelque difficulté. Si vous étes mécontent, faites-en part au directeur ou au propriétaire dès que survient l'incident. Il aura alors la possibilité de se rendre compte lui-même de la situation et d'y porter reméde sur-le-champ.

Cancellation of bookings

When you make a booking and accept the conditions of that booking, bear in mind you may be entering into a legally binding contract with the proprietor of the establishment which might entitle the proprietor of accommodation to compensation if you fail to take up the accommodation.
Accordingly, if you have to change your travel plans and cancel a booking, remember that it is in your interest to advise the management or owner immediately.

Abbestellung von Reservierungen

Wenn Sie eine Buchung machen und die damit verbundenen Bedingungen annehmen, müssen Sie sich darüber klar sein, daß dies einen gesetzlich bindenden Vertrag mit dem Inhaber des betreffenden Unternehmens bedeuten kann, der ihn zu Schadernersatz berechtigt, falls Sie keinen Gebrauch von der Unterkunft machen sollten.
Es liegt daher in Ihrem eigenen Interesse, die Geschäftsführung oder den Besitzer unverzüglich zu benachrichtigen, wenn Sie Ihre Reisepläne ändern und eine Reservierung abbestellen müssen.

Annulation de réservations

Lorsque vous faites une réservation et acceptez les conditions de cette réservation, il est possible que vous soyez engagé contractuellement avec le propriétaire de l'établissement, auquel cas celui-ci peut prétendre à une indemnisation au cas où vous ne donneriez pas suite.
Si donc les circonstances vous amènent à changer vos plans et à annuler votre réservation, il est de votre intérét d'en aviser immédiatement le directeur ou le propriétaire.

Deposits

It should be noted that some establishments may request payment in advance from clients. This may occur at hotels or motels, particularly when there is no written and confirmed reservation or cases where guests arrive with little or no luggage.
Most establishments will ask for deposits when a written reservation is being made.

Anzahlung

Einige Unterkunftseinrichtungen verlangen von ihren Gästen eine Vorauszahlung. Eine solche Vorauszahlung wird in Hotels und Motels besonders dann gefordert, wenn keine bestätigte schriftliche Buchung vorliegt oder Gäste mit wenig oder keinem Gepäck eintreffen.
Die meisten Unterkunftseinrichtungen verlangen bereits zum Zeitpunkt der schriftlichen Zimmerreservierung eine Anzahlung.

Paiement d'avance

On notera que certains établissements exigent des clients qu'ils acquittent d'avance le prix de leur logement. Il en est ainsi dans certains hôtels ou motels, notamment lorsqu'il n'y pas eu réservation écrite et confirmée, ou lorsque les visiteurs arrivent sans bagage ou avec peu de bagage.
La plupart des établissements demandent un versement d'arrhes à la réservation.

Bed booking service

For those who cannot book accommodation in advance or who are content to tour Wales without prior booking, Tourist Information Centres operate a bed booking service. It is designed to give tourists information on the type, location and price of suitable accommodation still available in the area in which they require it.
The Bed Booking Service operates only through Information Centres operated for the Wales Tourist Board by Regional Tourism Councils but not through Centres operated solely by National Parks and certain local authorities.

Reservierung

Besuchern, die ihre Unterkunft nicht im voraus buchen können oder bereit sind. Wales ohne vorherige Zimmerreservierung zu bereisen, steht der Unterkunftsreservierungsdienst des Wales Tourist Board zur Verfügung. Dieser Dienst hat den Zweck, Touristen Informationen über Art, Lage und Preis noch vorhandener geeigneter Unterkunftsmöglichkeiten in dem die Unterkunft benötigt wird. Der Reservierungsdienst kann nur über die Auskunftsbüros des Wales Tourist Board (siehe Rückseite der Broschüre), nicht aber über ausschließlich von den National Parks und bestimmten Gemeinden unterhaltene Auskunftsstellen in Anspruch genommen werden.

Réservations

Pour les personnes qui ne peuvent pas réserver à l'avance ou qui désirent visiter le Pays de Galles sans réservations préalables, le Wales Tourist Board offre un service de réservation. C'est un service destiné à donner aux touristes des renseignements concernant le type, l'emplacement et le prix logements adaptées à leurs besoins et encore disponibles dans la région de leur choix. Le service de réservation fonctionne seulement par l'intermédiaire des centres d'information du Board (voir adresses au dos de la couverture), et non par l'intermédiaire de centres ne dépendant que des Parcs nationaux ou de certaines administrations locales.

Classification Scheme of Standards for Serviced Accommodation

Maybe you are looking for accommodation with a wide range of facilities or you want a simple place to stay but with a reassurance that you will be able to obtain an evening meal. The official classification system helps you to spot quickly the establishments which are most likely to meet your needs. Each entry has three category numbers. The first number describes the bedrooms, toilets and bathrooms, the second covers public rooms and service, the third tells you what meals are served. The classification is on a scale from 1 to 6. The numbers are based on objective facts supplied by the proprietor and do not constitute a value-for-money assessment or quality grading.

The system is very easy to use. Just remember – the bigger the number, the greater the range of facilities and services.

As part of the Classification Scheme each establishment agrees to comply with the Code of Conduct (see below).

Bedrooms

Category 1

Bedrooms. Reasonable free space for movement and for easy access to beds, doors and drawers. Minimum floor areas, excluding private bath or shower areas: single bedrooms 60sq ft (5.60sq metres); double bedrooms 90sq ft (8.40sq metres); twin bedded rooms 110sq ft (10.20sq metres); family rooms 30sq ft (2.80sq metres) plus 60sq ft (5.60sq metres) for each double bed, and/or 40sq ft (3.70sq metres) for each single adult bed, and/or 20sq ft (1.85sq metres) for each cot. Minimum bed sizes (except children's beds): single beds 6ft x 2ft 6ins (183 x 76cm); double beds 6ft x 4ft (183 x 122cm) spring interior, foam or similar quality mattresses in sound condition; bedding clean and in sufficient quality.

Beds made daily. Linen changed at least weekly and for every new guest. Soap and clean towel for every new guest, replenished or changed as required. All bedrooms to have: one drinking vessel per person (minimum of two in family rooms); dressing table or equivalent and mirror; wardrobe or clothes hanging space with four hangers per person; adequate drawer space; bedside table or equivalent; one chair or equivalent; wastepaper container; ahstray; bedside rugs or mats where no carpet; at least one window and adequate ventilation; opaque curtains or blinds on all windows; adequate heating according to season.

Minimum lighting levels: single bedrooms 100 watts or equivalent; double bedrooms 150 watts or equivalent.

Bathrooms. At least one bathroom, adequately ventilated, with bath or shower, available for guests at all reasonable times. Hot water at all reasonable times. No extra charge for baths or showers.

WCs. At least one WC, adequately ventilated, equipped with toilet paper and disposal bin for guests' use.

General. Establishment clean throughout; all decorations, furnishings, floor coverings and fittings in good condition.

Category 2

All the above facilities, plus–
Bedrooms. Washbasin, with hot and cold running water, at all times, either in the bedroom or in a private bathroom. Mirror above, or adjacent to, washbasin. One chair, or equivalent, per person (minimum of two in family rooms). All bedrooms must be fitted with a lock that will ensure privacy for guests and security for their property. Guests must be provided with a key to their bedrooms, duplicate or master keys being kept by the management. Resident guests permitted access to their bedrooms at all times.
Bathrooms. At least one bathroom, equipped with a bath or shower, for every 15 resident guests (other than guests in bedrooms with private bathrooms). The bathroom/s must be for the sole use of guests.
WCs. At least one WC for every 10 resident guests (other than guests in bedrooms with private bathrooms). Where there is only one WC, it must not be in a bathroom. The WC/s must be for the sole use of guests.

Category 3

All the above facilities, plus–
All bedrooms have: heating without extra charge; electric shaver point; bedside light or equivalent, as well as light controlled from the door.

Category 4

All the above facilities, plus–
At least 90% of bedrooms have: single beds minimum size 6ft 3ins x 3ft (190 x 90cm); double beds minimum size 6ft 3ins x 4ft 6ins (190 x 137cm) – neither side of a double bed should be against a wall; full length mirror; easy chair; luggage stand(s); central heating. At least 35% of bedrooms have private bath/shower and WC en suite.

Category 5

All the above facilities, plus–
At least 90% of bedrooms have: Post Office telephone connection; radio or TV, if TV reception is available; easy chair per person; heated towel rail or other adequate heating in private bathroom. At least 75% of bedrooms have private bath/shower and WC en suite.

Category 6

All the above facilities, plus–
All bedrooms to have all the facilities listed in Categories 1–5 above and writing table or equivalent. Colour TV, if TV reception is available. All bedrooms with private bath, shower attachment and WC en suite. Some suites available.

Services

Category 1

Bed-making and room cleaning service.
Breakfast room (unless served in bedrooms).
Public areas adequately lit for safety and comfort.
Guests informed when booking if

access to establishment restricted during day. Adequate heating according to season.

Category 2
All the above facilities, plus–
Lounge area, with adequate seating. Use of the telephone.

Category 3
All the above facilities, plus–
Early morning call and tea (or tea making facilities in bedroom or nearby). Assistance with luggage on request. Reception facilities. Dining/breakfast room separate from lounge.

Category 4
All the above facilities, plus—
Porterage. Shoe cleaning facilities. A separate TV lounge (if no TV in bedrooms and reception available). Central heating. Public telephone.

Category 5
All the above facilities, plus–
Night porter on duty. Shoe cleaning service on request. Lounge service until 2300. Writing tables if no facilities in bedrooms.

Category 6
All the facilities, plus–
Valet service, 24 hour laundry service, except at weekends. All night lounge service. Two or more lounges (including bar lounge). Bookstall. Personal hairdressing arrangements for guests.

Meals
Category 1
Breakfast.

Category 2
Breakfast and evening meal (high tea or dinner).

Category 3
Breakfast, lunch (bar meals acceptable) and evening meal (high tea or dinner).

Category 4
Breakfast, lunch and dinner. Choice of main dishes at all meals.

Category 5
All the above facilities, plus–
Choice of full or Continental breakfast. Continental breakfast available in rooms on request. A la carte menu. Meal can be ordered until at least 2130 (Sunday or off season 2030).

Category 6
All the above facilities, plus–
Coffee shop/buttery/grill room or a second restaurant. Meal can be ordered until at least 2230 (Sunday or off season 2130). All meals served in bedrooms on request.

Code of Conduct
In addition to fulfilling its statutory obligations, including having applied for a certificate under the Fire Precautions Act 1971 (if applicable), the management undertakes to observe the following Code of Conduct:
1. To ensure high standards of courtesy and cleanliness; catering and service appropriate to the type of establishment.
2. To describe fairly to all visitors and prospective visitors the amenities, facilities and services provided by the establishment, whether by advertisement, brochure, word of mouth, or any other means. To allow visitors to see accommodation, if requested, before booking.
3. To make clear to visitors exactly what is included in all prices quoted for accommodation, meals and refreshments, including service charge, taxes and other surcharges. Details of charges for additional services or facilities available should also be made clear. If applicable the establishment should comply with the provisions of the Hotel Industry's Voluntary Code of Booking Practice.
4. To adhere to, and not to exceed, prices current at time of occupation for accommodation or other services.
5. To advise visitors at the time of booking, and subsequently of any change, if the accommodation offered is in an unconnected annexe, or similar, or by boarding out, and to indicate the location of such accommodation and any difference in comfort and amenities from accommodation in the main establishment.
6. To give each visitor, on request, details of payments due and a receipt, if required.
7. To deal promptly and courteously with all enquiries, requests, reservations, correspondence and complaints from visitors.

Disabled Guests
Your establishment may be able to accommodate severely disabled guests (eg those in wheelchairs). If you can accommodate disabled guests, and wish to be so designated in our publications, your establishment must conform to the following minimum requirements.
1. At least one entrance must either have no steps or be equipped with a ramp whose gradient does not exceed 1 in 12.
2. All doors (including those of WCs, private bathrooms etc) at least $29\frac{1}{2}$ins (75cm) wide, with a head-on approach.
3. All essential accommodation, if not on the ground floor, served by an adequately sized lift.
4. All lifts must have gate opening of at least $31\frac{1}{2}$ins (80cm): lifts must be at least 48ins (122cm) deep and 36ins (91cm) wide.
5. At least one bedroom and one public WC must be suitable for disabled guests.
6. In bedrooms, private or public bathrooms and WCs used by the disabled, the clearance around beds, and to reach washbasins, WCs etc, must be at least $29\frac{1}{2}$ins (75cm) and there must be turning space of 48ins (122cm) by 48ins (122cm).

Tourist Information Centres

Fremdenverkehrsämter

Centres de renseignements touristiques

SYMBOLS

⬓	**Bed booking reservation services**
⊙	**Regional Head Office**
1–12	**Open all the year round**
S	**Open during summer season only**
BABA	**Book-a-bed ahead scheme operates**

Office opening hours are generally from 10.00 – 18.00 daily but there are a few local variations.

London

Wales Tourist Board
Central London Office Information and Sales.
2–4 Maddox Street (Off Regent Street), London W1.
Tel: (01) 409 0969 Telex:
⬓ 1–12   BABA

Wales Tourist Information Services also available at:
Euston Station, Travel Centre,
London NW1. (Personal callers only).
⬓ 1–12   BABA

North Wales

Bangor, Gwynedd
Wales Tourist Information Centre,
Garth Road.
Tel. (0248) 52786.
⬓ 1–12   BABA

Betws-y-Coed, Gwynedd
Wales Tourist Information Centre.
Tel. (06902) 426.
⬓ S   BABA

Betws-y-Coed, Gwynedd
Snowdonia National Park Interpretive Centre.
S

Blaenau Ffestiniog, Gwynedd
Snowdonia National Park and Wales Tourist Centre, High Street.
Tel. (076 681) 360.
⬓ S   BABA

Caernarfon, Gwynedd
Wales Tourist Information Centre,
The Square.
Tel. (0286) 2232.
⬓ 1–12   BABA

Colwyn Bay, Clwyd
North Wales Tourism Council,
Glan-y-Don Hall, Civic Centre.
Tel. (0492) 56881.
(Written enquiries and bed bookings only).
⬓ 1–12   BABA

Colwyn Bay, Clwyd
Information Office, Prince of Wales Theatre.
Tel. (0492) 30478.
1–12 ⊙

Colwyn Bay, Clwyd
Colwyn Bay Hotels and Guest Houses Association.
Tel. (0492) 55719.
⬓ S

Conwy, Gwynedd
Wales Tourist & Snowdonia National Park Visitor Centre, Castle Street.
Tel. (049263) 2248.
⬓ S   BABA

Holyhead, Gwynedd
Wales Tourist Information Centre,
Marine Square, Salt Island Approach.
Tel. (0407) 2622.
⬓ S   BABA

Holywell, Clwyd
Wales Tourist Information Centre,
Little Chef Services, A55, Near Holywell.
Tel. (0352) 780144.
⬓ S   BABA

Llanberis, Gwynedd
Wales Tourist Information,
Snowdonia National Park & C.E.G.B. Centre.
Tel. (0286) 870765
⬓ 1–12   BABA

Llandudno, Gwynedd
Information Centre, Chapel Street.
Tel. (0492) 76413.
1–12

Llandudno, Gwynedd
Information Kiosk, North Promenade.
Tel. (0492) 76572.
S

Llandudno, Gwynedd
Information Office, Arcadia Theatre.
Tel. (0492) 76413 Ext. 264.
S

Llangollen, Clwyd
Wales Tourist Information Centre,
Town Hall.
Tel. (0978) 860828.
⬓ 1–12   BABA

Menai Bridge, Isle of Anglesey
Isle of Anglesey Tourist Association,
Information Centre, Coed Cyrnol.
Tel. (0248) 712626.
⬓ 1–12

Mold, Clwyd
Wales Tourist Information Centre,
Town Hall, Earl Street.
Tel. (0352) 59331.
⬓ S   BABA

Porthmadog, Gwynedd
Wales Tourist Information Centre,
High Street.
Tel. (0766) 2981.
⬓ 1–12   BABA

Prestatyn, Clwyd
Publicity Office, c/o Council Offices,
Nant Hall Road.
Tel. (07456) 2484.
S

Pwllheli, Gwynedd
Wales Tourist Information Centre,
Y Maes.
Tel. (0758) 3000.
S   BABA

Rhyl, Clwyd
Wales Tourist Information Centre,
Information Bureau, Promenade.
Tel. (0745) 55068.
S   BABA

Rhyl, Clwyd
Town Hall Information Bureau.
Tel. (0745) 31515.
1–12

Ruthin, Clwyd
Wales Tourist Information Centre,
Ruthin Craft Centre.
Tel. (08242) 3992
S   BABA

Whittington, Salop
Tourist Information Centre,
Babbinswood, Near Oswestry.
Tel. (0691) 62488.
S

Wrexham, Clwyd
Wales Tourist Information Centre,
Guildhall Car Park, Town Centre.
Tel. (0978) 578459.
S   BABA

Mid Wales

Aberaeron, Dyfed
Wales Tourist Information Centre,
The Harbour.
Tel. (0545) 570602.
S   BABA

Aberdovey, Gwynedd
Snowdonia National Park Centre,
The Wharf.
Tel. (065472) 321.
S   BABA

Aberystwyth, Dyfed
Wales Tourist & Ceredigion District
Council Information Centre, Eastgate.
Tel. (0970) 612125 & 617911.
1–12   BABA

Bala, Gwynedd
Snowdonia National Park Visitor
Centre, High Street.
Tel. (0678) 520367.
S   BABA

Barmouth, Gwynedd
Tourist Information Centre,
The Promenade.
Tel. (0341) 280787.

Builth Wells, Powys
Wales Tourist Information Centre,
Groe Car Park.
Tel. (0982) 553307.
S   BABA

Cardigan, Dyfed
Wales Tourist Information Centre,
3 Heathfield, Pendre.
Tel. (0239) 613230.
S   BABA

Dinas Mawddwy, Gwynedd
Local Information from Meirion Mill.
Tel. (06504) 311.
S

Dolgellau, Gwynedd
Snowdonia National Park Visitor
Centre, The Bridge.
Tel. (0341) 422888.
S   BABA

Harlech, Gwynedd
Snowdonia National Park Visitor
Centre, High Street.
Tel. (0766) 780658.
S   BABA

Knighton, Powys
Offa's Dyke Association Information
Centre, The Old School.
Tel. (0547) 528573.
1–12

Lampeter, Dyfed
Ceredigion District Council Offices,
Town Hall.
Tel. (0570) 422426.
1–12

Llandrindod Wells, Powys
Wales Tourist & Radnor District
Council Information Centre, Town
Hall Gardens.
Tel. (0597) 2600.
1–12   BABA

Llanidloes, Powys
Wales Tourist Information Centre,
Great Oak Street.
Tel. (05512) 2606.
S   BABA

Machynlleth, Powys
Wales Tourist Information Centre,
Canolfan Owain Glyndwr.
Tel. (0654) 2401.
1–12   BABA ☺

Newtown, Powys
Wales Tourist Information Centre,
Central Car Park.
Tel. (0686) 25580.
S   BABA

Ponterwyd, Dyfed
Local Information from Llywernog
Silver Lead Mine.
Tel. (097085) 620.
S

Rhayader, Powys
Wales Tourist Information Centre,
The Old Swan, West Street.
Tel. (0597) 810591.
S   BABA

Tregaron, Dyfed
Ceredigion District Council,
Information Centre, The Square.
Tel. (08744) 415.
S

Tywyn, Gwynedd
Tywyn and District Publicity Bureau,
Information Centre.
Tel. (0654) 710070.
S

Welshpool, Powys
Wales Tourist Information Centre,
Vicarage Garden Car Park.
Tel. (0938) 2043.
1–12   BABA

South Wales

Aberavon, West Glamorgan
Afan District Council Offices.
Tel. Port Talbot (06396) 3141.
1–12

Abercraf, Powys
Tourist Information Centre,
Dan-yr-Ogof Caves.
Tel. (063977) 284.
S

Abergavenny, Gwent
Wales Tourist Information Centre &
Brecon Beacons National Park
Information Centre, 2 Lower Monk St.
Tel. (0873) 3254.
S   BABA

Barry, South Glamorgan
Vale of Glamorgan Borough Council,
Town Hall, King Square.
Tel. (0446) 730311.
1–12
Tourist Information Centre,
Barry Island.
Tel. (0466) 747171.
S

Brecon, Powys
Wales Tourist Information Centre,
Market Car Park.
Tel. (0874) 2485.
🛏 S   BABA

Brecon, Powys
Brecon Beacons National Park,
7 Glamorgan Street.
Tel. (0874) 4437.
S

Brecon, Powys
Brecon Beacons Mountain Centre,
near Libanus, Brecon LD3 8ER.
Tel. (0874) 3366.
1–12

Broad Haven, Dyfed
Pembrokeshire Coast National Park,
Countryside Unit, Car Park.
Tel. (043783) 412.
S

Caerphilly, Mid Glamorgan
Tourist Information Centre,
Tywyn Car Park.
Tel. (0222) 863378.
🛏 S

Cardiff, South Glamorgan
Wales Tourist Information Centre,
3 Castle Street.
Tel. (0222) 27281.
🛏 1–12   BABA

Carmarthen, Dyfed
Wales Tourist Information Centre,
Lammas Street.
Tel. (0267) 31557.
🛏 S   BABA

Chepstow, Gwent
Wales Tourist Information Centre,
The Gatehouse, High Street.
Tel. (02912) 3772.
🛏 S   BABA

Cwmbran, Gwent
Torfaen District Council,
42 Gwent Square.
Tel. (0633) 67411.
1–12

Fishguard, Dyfed
Wales Tourist Information Centre,
Town Hall.
Tel. (0348) 873484.
🛏 S   BABA

Haverfordwest, Dyfed
Wales Tourist Information Centre &
Pembrokeshire Coast National Park
Information Centre, 40 High Street.
Tel. (0437) 3110.
🛏 S   BABA

Kilgetty, Dyfed
Wales Tourist Information Centre &
Pembrokeshire Coast National
Park Information Centre, Kingsmoor
Common.
Tel. (0834) 813672./3.
🛏 S   BABA

Llandovery, Dyfed
Wales Tourist Board and Brecon
Beacons National Park Information
Centre, Central Car Park, Broad St.
Tel. (0550) 20693.
🛏 S   BABA

Merthyr Tydfil, Mid Glamorgan
Tourist Information Centre,
Cyfarthfa Park.
(Written enquiries to Town Hall,
Merthyr).
S

Monmouth, Gwent
Wales Tourist Information Centre,
c/o Nelson Museum.
Tel. (0600) 3899.
🛏 S   BABA

Newport, Dyfed
Pembrokeshire Coast National Park,
Information Centre, Carn Ingli
Centre, East Street.
Tel. (0239) 820912.
S

Newport, Gwent
Wales Tourist Information Centre,
John Frost Square.
Tel. (0633) 842962.
🛏 S   BABA

Pembroke, Dyfed
Pembrokeshire Coast National Park,
Drill Hall, Main Street.
Tel. (06463) 2148.
S

Penarth, South Glamorgan
Information Office, West House.
Tel. (0222) 707201.
1–12
Tourist Information Centre,
Piermaster's Office, The Pier.
Tel. (0222) 706555.
🛏 S

Porthcawl, Mid Glamorgan
Wales Tourist Information Centre,
Old Police Station, John Street.
Tel. (065671) 6639.
🛏 S   BABA

Raglan, Gwent
Wales Tourist Information Centre,
Pen-y-Clawdd Service Area.
Tel. Dingestow (060083) 694.
🛏 S   BABA

St. David's, Dyfed
Wales Tourist Information Centre,
Grove Car Park.
Tel. (0437) 720747.
🛏 S   BABA

St. David's, Dyfed
Pembrokeshire Coast National Park
Information Centre, City Hall.
Tel. (0437) 720392
S

Swansea, West Glamorgan
South Wales Tourism Council,
Tŷ Croeso,
Gloucester Place,
Swansea S4 1TY.
Tel. (0792) 465204.
🛏 1–12

Swansea, West Glamorgan
Civic Information Centre,
Singleton St., Guildhall.
Tel. (0792) 50821. Ansafone (0792)
468321.
1–12

Swansea, West Glamorgan
Wales Tourist Information Centre,
Crymlyn Burrows, Jersey Marine.
Tel. (0792) 462403.
🛏 S   BABA

Swansea, West Glamorgan
Tourist Information Centre,
Oystermouth Square, The Mumbles.
Tel. (0792) 61302.
🛏 S

Tenby, Dyfed
South Pembrokeshire District
Council & Pembrokeshire Coast
National Park, Guildhall, The Norton.
Tel. (0834) 2402 (South Pembs.) or
Tel. (0834) 3510 (Nat. Park).
1–12

Tintern, Gwent
Wales Tourist Information Centre,
Tintern Abbey.
Tel. (02918) 431.
🛏 S   BABA

**Treffgarne, Haverfordwest,
Dyfed**
Tourist Information Centre,
Nant-y-Coy Mill.
Tel. (043787) 671 or 686
🛏 S

British Tourist Authority Offices

If you live outside the British Isles, write to the British Tourist Authority:

Australia
British Tourist Authority
171 Clarence St.
Sydney N.S.W. 2000
Tel. 29–8627

Austria
British Tourist Authority
Wiedner Hauptstrasse 5/8
1040 Wien
Tel. (0222) 65 03 76

Belgium
British Tourist Authority
Rue de la Montagne
52 Bergstraat, B2
1000 Brussels
Tel. 02/511.43.90

Brazil
British Tourist Authority
Avenida Ipiranga 318-A, 12° Andar,
conj 1201
01046 Saõ Paulo = SP
Tel. 257–1834

Canada
British Tourist Authority
94 Cumberland Street, Suite 600
Toronto, Ontario M5R 3N3
Tel. (416) 925–6326

Denmark
Det Britiske Turistkontor
Møntergade 3
DK-1116 København
Tel. (01) 12 07 93

France
British Tourist Authority
6 Place Vendôme
75001 Paris
Tel. 296 47 60

Germany
British Tourist Authority
Nueu Mainzer Str. 22
6000 Frankfurt a.M.
Tel. (0611) 23 64 28/29

Italy
British Tourist Authority
Via S. Eufemia 5
00187 Rome
Tel. 678.4998 or 678.5548

Japan
British Tourist Authority
Tokyo Club Building
3–2–6 Kasumigaseki, Chiyoda-ku
Tokyo 100
Tel. (03) 581–3603

Mexico
British Tourist Authority
Río Tiber 103– 6 piso
México 5 D.F.
Tel. 511.39.27 or 514.93.56

Netherlands
British Tourist Authority
(Written enquiries only)
Leidseplein 5
1017 PR Amsterdam
Tel. (020) 23.46.67

Netherlands
British Tourist Authority
(Personal callers only)
Leidseplein 5,
Amsterdam 1017 PR

Netherlands
British Travel Centre
(Personal callers only)
Leidseplein 23
Amsterdam

New Zealand
British Tourist Authority
Box 3655
Wellington

Norway
British Tourist Authority
Mariboes gt 11
Oslo 1
Tel. (02) 41.18.49

Singapore
British Tourist Authority
Room 403 Singapore Rubber House
14 Collyer Quay
Singapore 0104
Tel. Singapore 2242966/7

South Africa
British Tourist Authority
7th Floor, JBS Building
107 Commissioner Street
PO Box 6256
Johannesburg 2001
Tel. (010 27 11) 29 6770

Spain
British Tourist Authority
Torre de Madrid 6/4
Plaza de España
Madrid 13 España
Tel. 241 13 96

Sweden
British Tourist Authority
For visitors: Malmskillnadsg 42 1st
Floor
For Mail: Box 7293
S– 103 90 Stockholm
Tel. 08–21 24 44

Switzerland
British Tourist Authority
Limmatquai 78
8001 Zurich
Tel. 01/47 42 77 or 47 42 97

USA Chicago
British Tourist Authority
John Hancock Center (Suite 3320)
875 N. Michigan Avenue
Chicago, Illinois 60611

USA Dallas
British Tourist Authority
Plaza of the Americas
750 North Tower LB 346
Dallas, Texas 75201
Tel. (214) 748-2279

USA Los Angeles
British Tourist Authority
612 South Flower Street
Los Angeles CA 90017
Tel. (213) 623–8196

USA New York
British Tourist Authority
680 Fifth Avenue
New York N.Y. 10019
Tel. (212) 581–4700

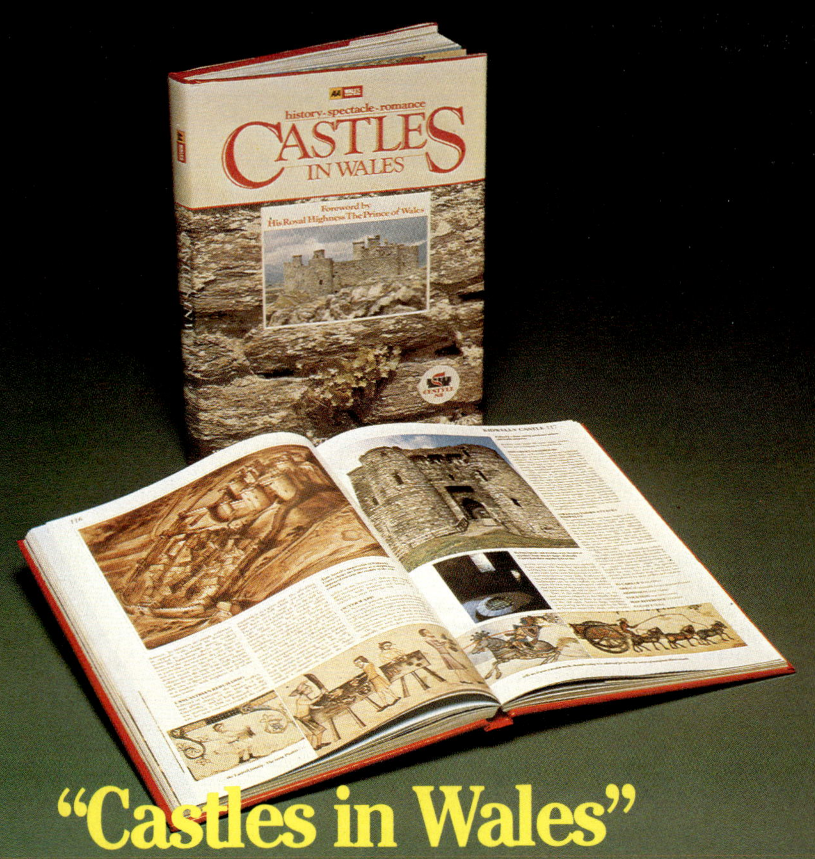

"Castles in Wales"

is a new book, produced jointly by the Wales Tourist Board and the Automobile Association. The only book of its kind, it provides for the first time a comprehensive guide to Wales's most precious legacy – its wealth of castles. It is designed to appeal to all ages, especially to those interested in the story and spectacle of the past. Over 80 castles are featured in this 192 page publication, ranging from mighty medieval fortresses to atmospheric, beautifully-located ruins. Colour photographs and detailed descriptions are used throughout, giving a unique insight into the power and politics, warfare and the way of life in the Wales of the Middle Ages. The book also contains layout plans of many of the castles and artists' impressions of how they looked at the height of their splendour. In addition, an introductory section brings Wales's exciting history to life, covering the past, from prehistoric to industrial times, with particular reference to the medieval period.

The book is a memorable armchair guide – and also invaluable to those out and about within Wales. A full-colour atlas, on which all the castles are located, is supported by a 16 page section describing 18 newly compiled motor tours. These routes include many of the castles featured in the book as well as some of Wales's most famous beauty spots, tourist attractions and other places of interest.

Send for your copy now, enclosing a cheque or postal order to the value of £10.90, to Automobile Association Publications, Dept. WTB, PO Box 50, Mail Order, Basingstoke, Hants RG21 2EA.

Accommodation Booking Form

Note to Applicants and establishments using this form.

Please note that this form is supplied by the Wales Tourist Board to facilitate the making of bookings direct between Applicants (acting either as Principals or through their Agents) and Establishments. It must be clearly understood, therefore, that the Wales Tourist Board is in no way connected with the booking and accepts no liability whatsoever in any way connected with, arising out of the booking, or the use of this form. Establishments should note that Applicants (or their Agents, as the case may be) should be informed direct as to any terms of booking.

This form should be sent directly to this address:
(Hotel/Guest House etc.)

____

____

____

Tel: _______________

Arrival date _________________________ No. of people _________________________

Departure date _________________________ Is this confirmation of telephone booking? _______

No. of nights _________________________ Details of party: _________________________

Mr./Mrs.	Initials	Surname	Age if under 16	Address to which correspondence should be sent

ACCOMMODATION Section 1: Hotel, Guest House, etc.

Single room(s)
With bath/shower ☐ Without bath ☐

Double-bedded room(s)
With bath/shower ☐ Without bath ☐

Twin-bedded room(s)
With bath/shower ☐ Without bath ☐

Family room(s)
With bath/shower ☐ Without bath ☐

Please complete the appropriate box(es)

Additional requirements or supplements:
e.g. special diets, extra bed in parent's room.

____

____

____

____

Activity/Special Interest Breaks (Use with Section 1). Please give details of activity/ special interest break required:

____

____

____

____

Total cost of holiday
(inc. supplements where applicable) £__________

Deposit payable
(where applicable)   £__________

Balance payable   £__________

By (date) ___________________________

I agree to the terms of booking as notified to me by the establishment concerned.

I enclose a deposit of   £__________

Signed _______________________________

Date _________________________________

Any other remarks

____

____

____

____

____

____

____

____

____

____

TRAVEL AGENT'S STAMP
(where appropriate)

Accommodation Booking Form

Note to Applicants and establishments using this form.

Please note that this form is supplied by the Wales Tourist Board to facilitate the making of bookings direct between Applicants (acting either as Principals or through their Agents) and Establishments. It must be clearly understood, therefore, that the Wales Tourist Board is in no way connected with the booking and accepts no liability whatsoever in any way connected with, arising out of the booking, or the use of this form. Establishments should note that Applicants (or their Agents, as the case may be) should be informed direct as to any terms of booking.

This form should be sent directly to this address:
(Hotel/Guest House etc.)

____

____

____

Tel: _______________

Arrival date _________________   No. of people _________________

Departure date _______________   Is this confirmation of telephone booking? ______

No. of nights _________________   Details of party: _________________

Mr./Mrs.	Initials	Surname	Age if under 16	Address to which correspondence should be sent

ACCOMMODATION Section 1: Hotel, Guest House, etc.

Single room(s) ☐ Without ☐ **Double-bedded room(s)** ☐ Without ☐
With bath/shower bath With bath/shower bath

Twin-bedded room(s) ☐ Without ☐ **Family room(s)** ☐ Without ☐
With bath/shower bath With bath/shower bath

Please complete the appropriate box(es)

Additional requirements or supplements:
e.g. special diets, extra bed in parent's room.

____

____

____

____

Activity/Special Interest Breaks (Use with Section 1). Please give details of activity/ special interest break required:

____

____

____

____

Total cost of holiday
(inc. supplements where applicable) £_________

Deposit payable
(where applicable) £_________

Balance payable £_________

By (date) _____________________________

I agree to the terms of booking as notified to me by the establishment concerned.

I enclose a deposit of £_________

Signed _______________________________

Date _________________________________

Any other remarks

____

____

____

____

____

____

____

____

____

____

TRAVEL AGENT'S STAMP
(where appropriate)